RAY BRADBURY'S
THE MARTIAN CHRONICLES

THE AUTHORIZED ADAPTATION

DENNIS CALERO

INTRODUCTION BY RAY BRADBURY

A NOVEL GRAPHIC FROM HILL AND WANG

A DIVISION OF FARRAR, STRAUS AND GIROUX
NEW YORK

To the ladies in my life,
Kris and Paloma
–Dennis Calero

HILL AND WANG
A DIVISION OF FARRAR, STRAUS AND GIROUX
18 WEST 18TH STREET, NEW YORK 10011

THIS IS A Z FILE, INC. BOOK

DISTRIBUTED IN CANADA BY D&M PUBLISHERS, INC.
PRINTED IN THE UNITED STATES OF AMERICA
PUBLISHED SIMULTANEOUSLY IN HARDCOVER AND PAPERBACK
FIRST EDITION, 2011

LIBRARY OF CONGRESS CATALOGING-IN-PUBLICATION DATA
CALERO, DENNIS
RAY BRADBURY'S THE MARTIAN CHRONICLES : THE AUTHORIZED ADAPTATION/
DENNIS CALERO ; INTRODUCTION BY RAY BRADBURY. — 1ST ED.
P. CM.
ISBN 978-0-8090-6793-0 (HARDCOVER : ALK. PAPER) — ISBN 978-0-8090-8045-8
(PBK : ALK PAPER).
1. GRAPHIC NOVELS I. BRADBURY, RAY, 1920- MARTIAN CHRONICLES. II. TITLE.
III. TITLE: MARTIAN CHRONICLES
PN6727.C26R39 2011
741.5'973—DC22
2011005169

ART BY DENNIS CALERO
EDITED BY HOWARD ZIMMERMAN
DESIGNED BY DEAN MOTTER

CONTRIBUTING ARTISTS:
"THE OFF SEASON": JOE ST. PIERRE
"THE MILLION-YEAR PICNIC": JOSH ADAMS
"THE EARTH MEN": JAMES SMITH

DIAGRAMATICS BASED ON OBSERVATIONS BY GIOVANNI SCHIAPARELLI, CIRCA 1877

WWW.FSGBOOKS.COM

1 3 5 7 9 10 8 6 4 2

MARE AUSTRALE
MARE AUSTRALE

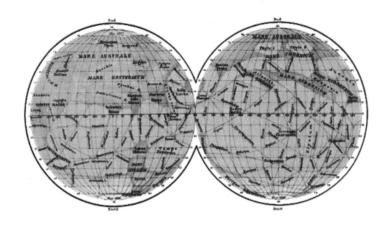

CONTENTS

INTRODUCTION

BY RAY BRADBURY

WHEN I WAS SIX YEARS OLD I LIVED ON A STREET IN TUCSON, ARIZONA: LOWELL AVENUE. WHEN I'D BEEN THERE FOR A FEW MONTHS I DISCOVERED THAT IT HAD BEEN NAMED FOR PERCIVAL LOWELL, WHO WAS THE PHOTOGRAPHER OF MARS. I SAW PHOTOGRAPHS THAT HE MADE OF THE PLANET AND WAS INTRIGUED BY THE FACT THAT I LIVED ON THE STREET NAMED FOR HIM.

WHEN I WAS TEN YEARS OLD I BEGAN TO READ THE BOOKS OF EDGAR RICE BURROUGHS. I FELL IN LOVE WITH *JOHN CARTER, WARLORD OF MARS* AND *THUVIA, MAID OF MARS* AND EVERYTHING ELSE THAT HAD TO DO WITH THE PLANET MARS. I TOOK THE ADVICE OF JOHN CARTER WHEN I WAS TWELVE YEARS OLD. HE SAID, "GO OUT ON THE LAWN AT NIGHT AND LOOK UP AT THE RED PLANET IN THE SKY AND SAY, MARS, TAKE ME HOME."

THAT AUTUMN IN 1932 I THOUGHT THAT I'D TRY JUST THAT AND WENT OUT ON THE LAWN AND SHOUTED, "MARS, TAKE ME HOME!" IT TOOK ME HOME AND I STAYED THERE FOREVER.

THAT SAME WEEK I HAD AN ENCOUNTER WITH MR. ELECTRICO, WHO TOLD ME TO LIVE FOREVER.

I TOOK HIS ADVICE, AS WELL AS JOHN CARTER'S, AND THAT VERY WEEK I DID MY FIRST WRITING ON A TYPEWRITER.

JOHN CARTER CHANGED MY LIFE AND HERE IS THE PROOF. HERE IS THE PLANET MARS, LAID OUT FOR YOU TO READ.

IN MY TWENTIES I WROTE A SERIES OF SHORT STORIES, WHICH I SOLD FOR FANTASTIC SUMS ($20–30!) TO MAGAZINES CALLED *WONDER STORIES* AND *PLANET STORIES*.

I WROTE ALMOST DAILY ABOUT THE PLANET MARS AND DURING THAT TIME I MET A PRODUCER/DIRECTOR OF RADIO PROGRAMS, NORMAN CORWIN. ONE EVENING AT DINNER I TOLD HIM A STORY THAT I HAD WRITTEN ABOUT A WOMAN NAMED YLLA, MY MARTIAN MAIDEN, WHO HAD DREAMS ABOUT EARTHMEN COMING TO MARS.

NORMAN THOUGHT IT WAS A WONDERFUL STORY AND SUGGESTED THAT I WRITE MORE OF THESE, SO OVER THE NEXT FEW YEARS I WROTE OVER A DOZEN MARTIAN STORIES, LITTLE REALIZING I WAS WRITING A NOVEL.

AT THE SAME TIME, I READ *THE GRAPES OF WRATH*, BY JOHN STEINBECK. STEINBECK WAS TEACHING ME HOW TO WRITE NOT ONLY ORDINARY CHAPTERS BUT PROSE POEMS.

DURING THAT SAME PERIOD MY WIFE, MAGGIE, GOT PREGNANT. HAVING LITTLE MONEY, I DECIDED TO TRY AND GET TO NEW YORK TO SEE IF I COULD SELL MY STORIES.

I MET MANY EDITORS ON THAT TRIP, BUT NONE OF THEM WANTED ANYTHING TO DO WITH ME BECAUSE I WAS A SHORT STORY WRITER AND NOT A NOVELIST.

ON MY LAST NIGHT IN NEW YORK I HAD DINNER WITH WALTER BRADBURY--NO RELATION--OF DOUBLEDAY, AND HE SAID TO ME, "RAY, I THINK YOU'VE WRITTEN A NOVEL BUT YOU DON'T KNOW IT."

I SAID, "WHAT HAVE I DONE?"

HE SAID, "ALL THOSE MARTIAN STORIES THAT YOU'VE PUBLISHED, WHAT IF YOU PUT THEM TOGETHER AND MADE A TAPESTRY OF THEM AND WE'D CALL IT *THE MARTIAN CHRONICLES.*"

I SAID, "THAT'S A GOOD TITLE, CAN I BORROW THAT?"

HE SAID, "YES, IT'S YOURS."

HE THEN TOLD ME, "GO BACK TO THE YMCA AND TYPE AN OUTLINE OF THIS TAPESTRY OF STORIES YOU'VE WRITTEN AND BRING IT TO ME TOMORROW. IF IT'S ANY GOOD I'LL GIVE YOU AN ADVANCE OF $700."

I WENT BACK TO THE YMCA--THE ONLY PLACE I COULD AFFORD--STAYED UP ALL NIGHT AND TYPED AN OUTLINE FOR THIS BOOK. I BROUGHT IT TO WALTER BRADBURY THE NEXT DAY AND HE SAID:

"MY GOD, THAT'S IT! YOU'VE WRITTEN A BOOK ABOUT MARS. EVERYTHING IS INTUITION WITH YOU AND THIS IS PURE POETRY. NOW GO HOME AND FINISH THE BOOK."

I WENT BACK TO MY PREGNANT WIFE IN VENICE, CALIFORNIA, AND OVER THE NEXT SEVERAL MONTHS I FILLED IN ALL THE CORNERS AND CREVICES OF THIS BOOK ABOUT MARS AND FINALLY SENT IT TO DOUBLEDAY, WHO PUBLISHED IT IN THE SPRING OF 1950.

THERE WERE NO REVIEWS OF THAT BOOK; NOBODY REALLY CARED THAT I WROTE BOOKS, ESPECIALLY ABOUT MARS. BUT ONE DAY I WENT INTO A BOOKSTORE AND BUMPED INTO CHRISTOPHER ISHERWOOD, THE ENGLISH AUTHOR, AND GAVE HIM A COPY OF MY BOOK.

HIS FACE FELL AND I COULD SEE THAT HE DIDN'T WANT TO READ THE DARNED THING, BUT THREE DAYS LATER HE CALLED ME AND SAID, "RAY, DO YOU KNOW WHAT YOU'VE DONE?"

I SAID, "WHAT?"

HE SAID, "YOU'VE WRITTEN AN EXTRAORDINARY BOOK ABOUT MARS AND I'M GOING TO REVIEW IT FOR *TOMORROW MAGAZINE.*"

HE DID THAT REVIEW, WHICH WAS WONDERFUL, AND THEN CALLED AND SAID, "ALDOUS HUXLEY WANTS TO MEET YOU FOR TEA."

I TOLD HIM, "I'LL GO TO SEE MR. HUXLEY. I WON'T HAVE TEA, BUT I'LL TALK WITH HIM."

WHEN I GOT TO MR. HUXLEY'S HOUSE HE SAID TO ME, "MR. BRADBURY, DO YOU KNOW WHAT YOU ARE?"

I SAID, "WHAT AM I?"

"YOU ARE A POET," HE SAID. "YOU ARE A POET. YOU HAVE WRITTEN A BOOK OF POETRY ABOUT MARS. IT'S MORE THAN JUST FICTION, IT'S MORE THAN JUST WORDS, IT'S MAGICAL WORDS. YOU'VE MADE MARS A REAL PLACE AND WE'RE ALL GOING TO TRAVEL THERE AND WE'RE NOT GOING TO COME BACK, ALL BECAUSE OF YOU. YOU GOT THERE FIRST, WERE THE FIRST MARTIAN. THANK YOU FOR THAT BOOK."

SO HERE IT ALL IS: MY LIVING ON LOWELL AVENUE WHEN I WAS SIX, MY FALLING IN LOVE WITH JOHN CARTER AND MARS WHEN I WAS TWELVE, AND MEETING ALL THESE OTHER WONDERFUL PEOPLE IN MY TWENTIES AND WRITING THESE STORIES. HERE THEY ALL ARE, IN WHAT APPEARS TO BE A NOVEL. I INVITE YOU TO COME TO MARS WITH ME AND STAY FOREVER.

RAY BRADBURY
JUNE 2011

RAY BRADBURY'S

THE MARTIAN CHRONICLES

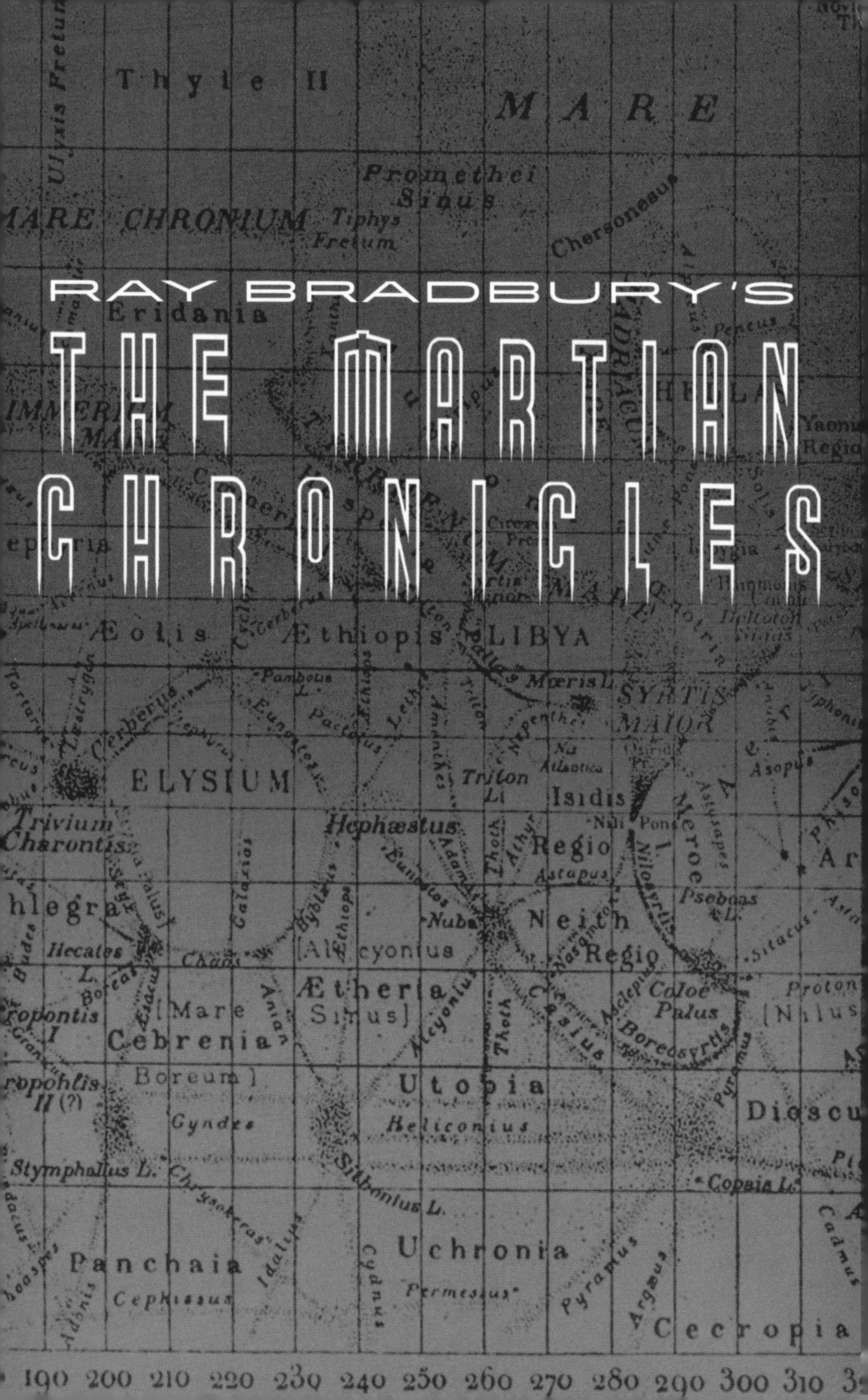

Thyle II
MARE
Ulyxis Fretum
Promethei Sinus
MARE CHRONIUM
Tiphys Fretum
Chersonesus
Eridania
Æolis
Æthiopis
LIBYA
Mœris L.
SYRTIS MAIOR
ELYSIUM
Triton L.
Isidis Regio
Trivium Charontis
Hephæstus
Nili Pons
Meroe
Neith Regio
Hecates L.
Chaos
[Alcyonius
Ætheria Sinus]
[Mare Cebrenia Boreum]
Coloe Palus
Boreosyrtis
Utopia
Heliconius
Gyndes
Stymphalus L.
Sithonius L.
Uchronia
Panchaia
Cephissus
Permessus
Cecropia
Copais L.
Cadmus
190 200 210 220 230 240 250 260 270 280 290 300 310

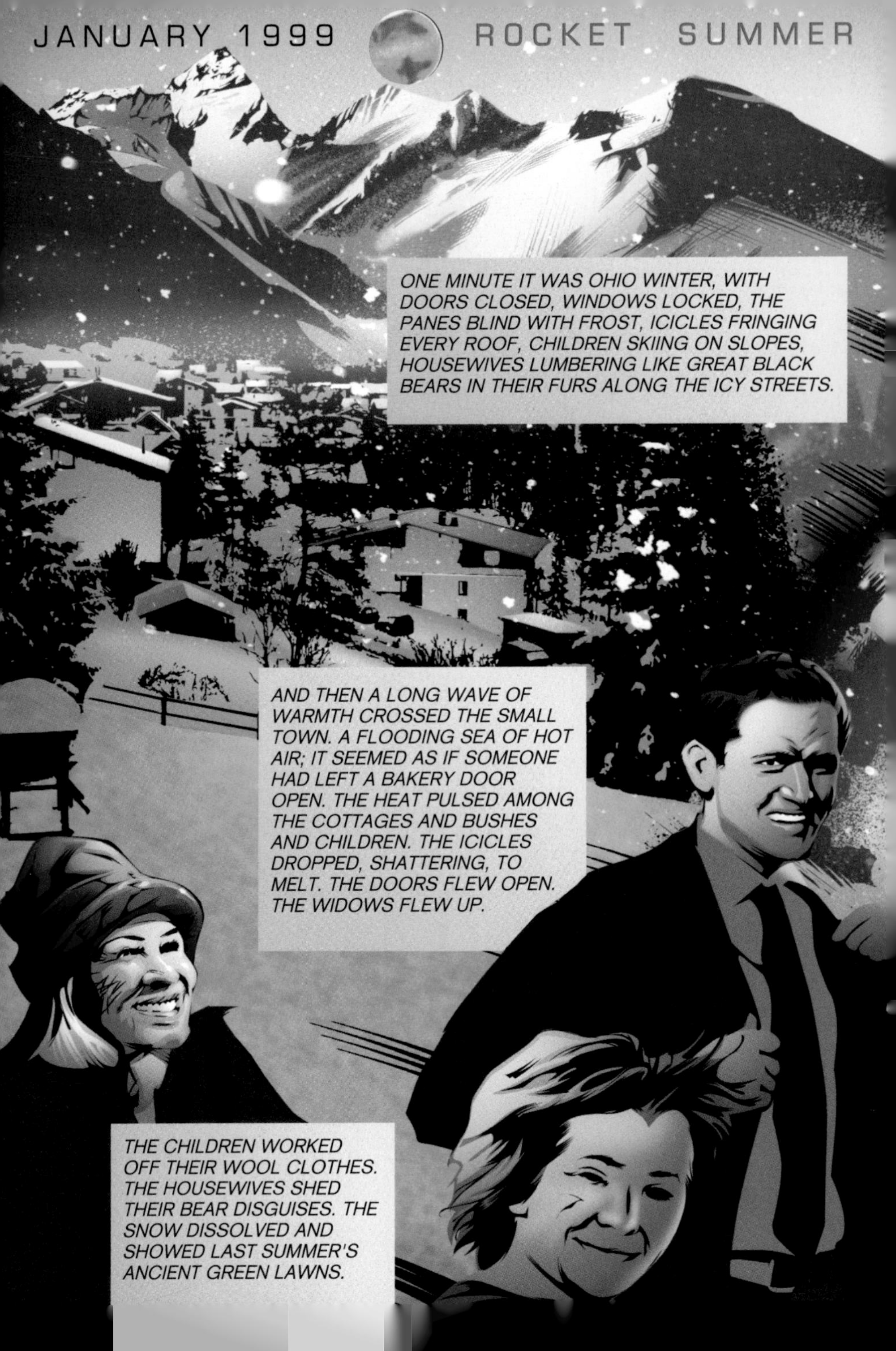
JANUARY 1999 ROCKET SUMMER
ONE MINUTE IT WAS OHIO WINTER, WITH DOORS CLOSED, WINDOWS LOCKED, THE PANES BLIND WITH FROST, ICICLES FRINGING EVERY ROOF, CHILDREN SKIING ON SLOPES, HOUSEWIVES LUMBERING LIKE GREAT BLACK BEARS IN THEIR FURS ALONG THE ICY STREETS.
AND THEN A LONG WAVE OF WARMTH CROSSED THE SMALL TOWN. A FLOODING SEA OF HOT AIR; IT SEEMED AS IF SOMEONE HAD LEFT A BAKERY DOOR OPEN. THE HEAT PULSED AMONG THE COTTAGES AND BUSHES AND CHILDREN. THE ICICLES DROPPED, SHATTERING, TO MELT. THE DOORS FLEW OPEN. THE WIDOWS FLEW UP.
THE CHILDREN WORKED OFF THEIR WOOL CLOTHES. THE HOUSEWIVES SHED THEIR BEAR DISGUISES. THE SNOW DISSOLVED AND SHOWED LAST SUMMER'S ANCIENT GREEN LAWNS.

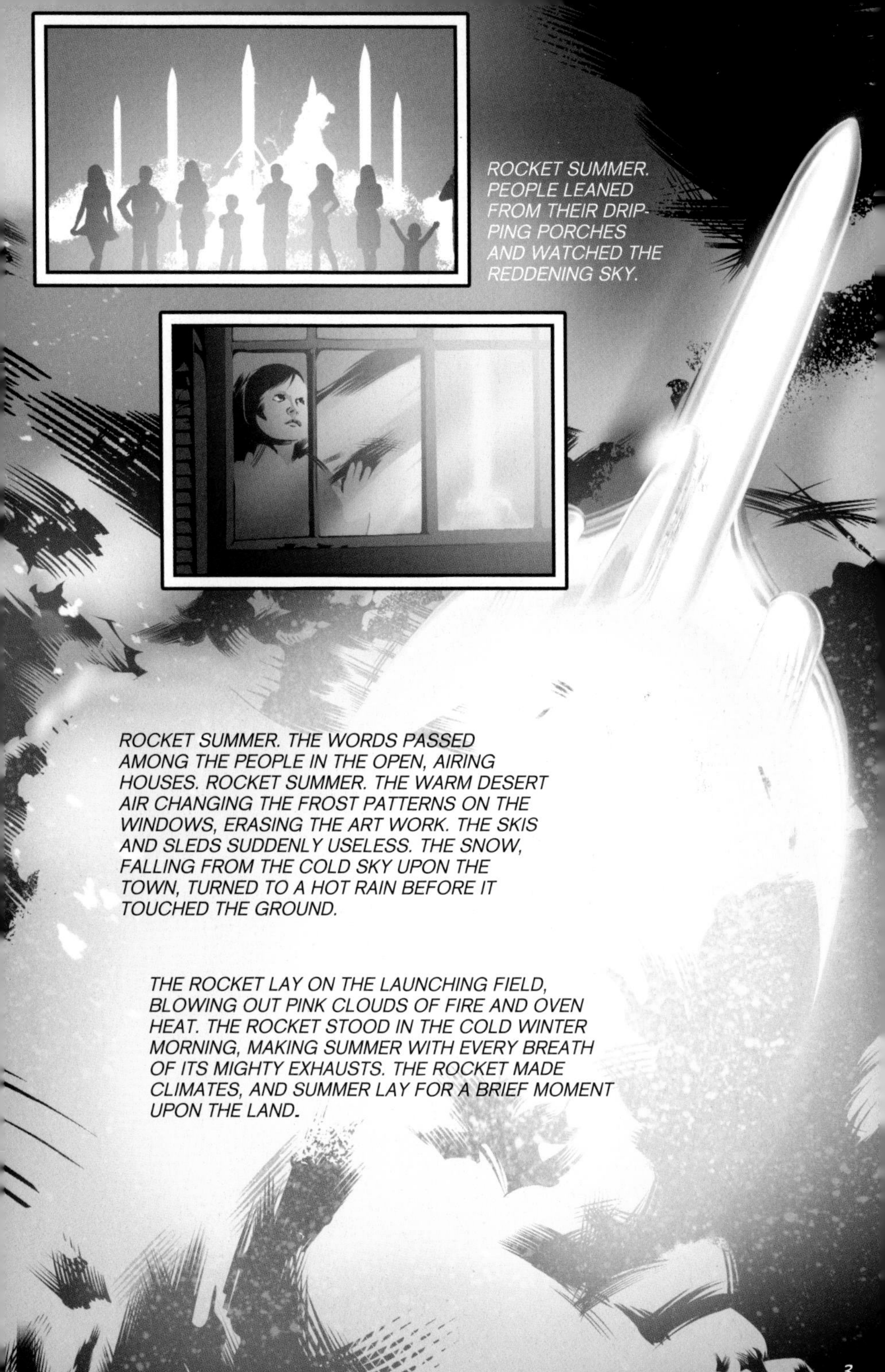
ROCKET SUMMER. PEOPLE LEANED FROM THEIR DRIP-PING PORCHES AND WATCHED THE REDDENING SKY.
ROCKET SUMMER. THE WORDS PASSED AMONG THE PEOPLE IN THE OPEN, AIRING HOUSES. ROCKET SUMMER. THE WARM DESERT AIR CHANGING THE FROST PATTERNS ON THE WINDOWS, ERASING THE ART WORK. THE SKIS AND SLEDS SUDDENLY USELESS. THE SNOW, FALLING FROM THE COLD SKY UPON THE TOWN, TURNED TO A HOT RAIN BEFORE IT TOUCHED THE GROUND.
THE ROCKET LAY ON THE LAUNCHING FIELD, BLOWING OUT PINK CLOUDS OF FIRE AND OVEN HEAT. THE ROCKET STOOD IN THE COLD WINTER MORNING, MAKING SUMMER WITH EVERY BREATH OF ITS MIGHTY EXHAUSTS. THE ROCKET MADE CLIMATES, AND SUMMER LAY FOR A BRIEF MOMENT UPON THE LAND.

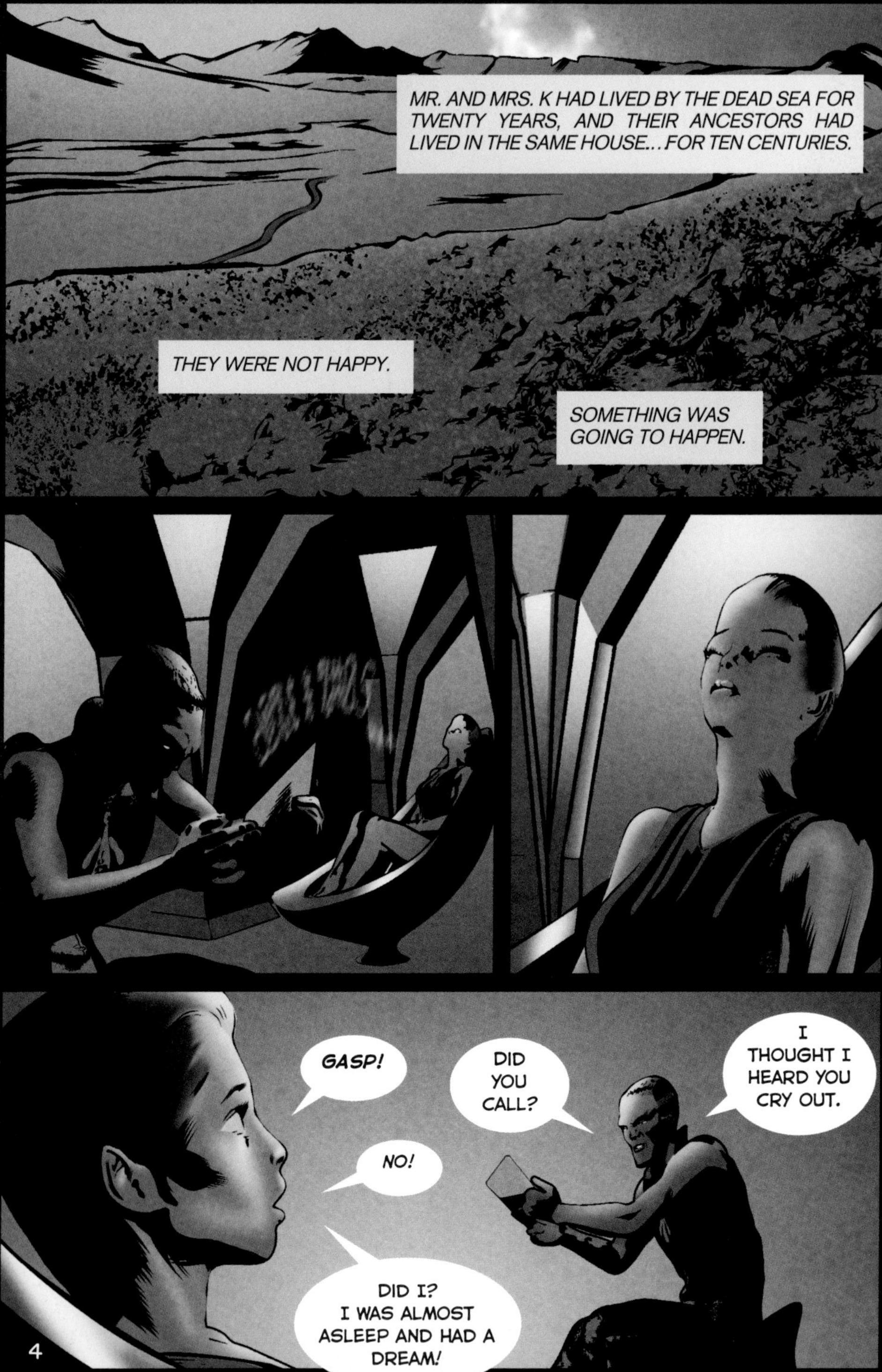
MR. AND MRS. K HAD LIVED BY THE DEAD SEA FOR TWENTY YEARS, AND THEIR ANCESTORS HAD LIVED IN THE SAME HOUSE... FOR TEN CENTURIES.
THEY WERE NOT HAPPY.
SOMETHING WAS GOING TO HAPPEN.
GASP!
DID YOU CALL?
I THOUGHT I HEARD YOU CRY OUT.
NO!
DID I? I WAS ALMOST ASLEEP AND HAD A DREAM!

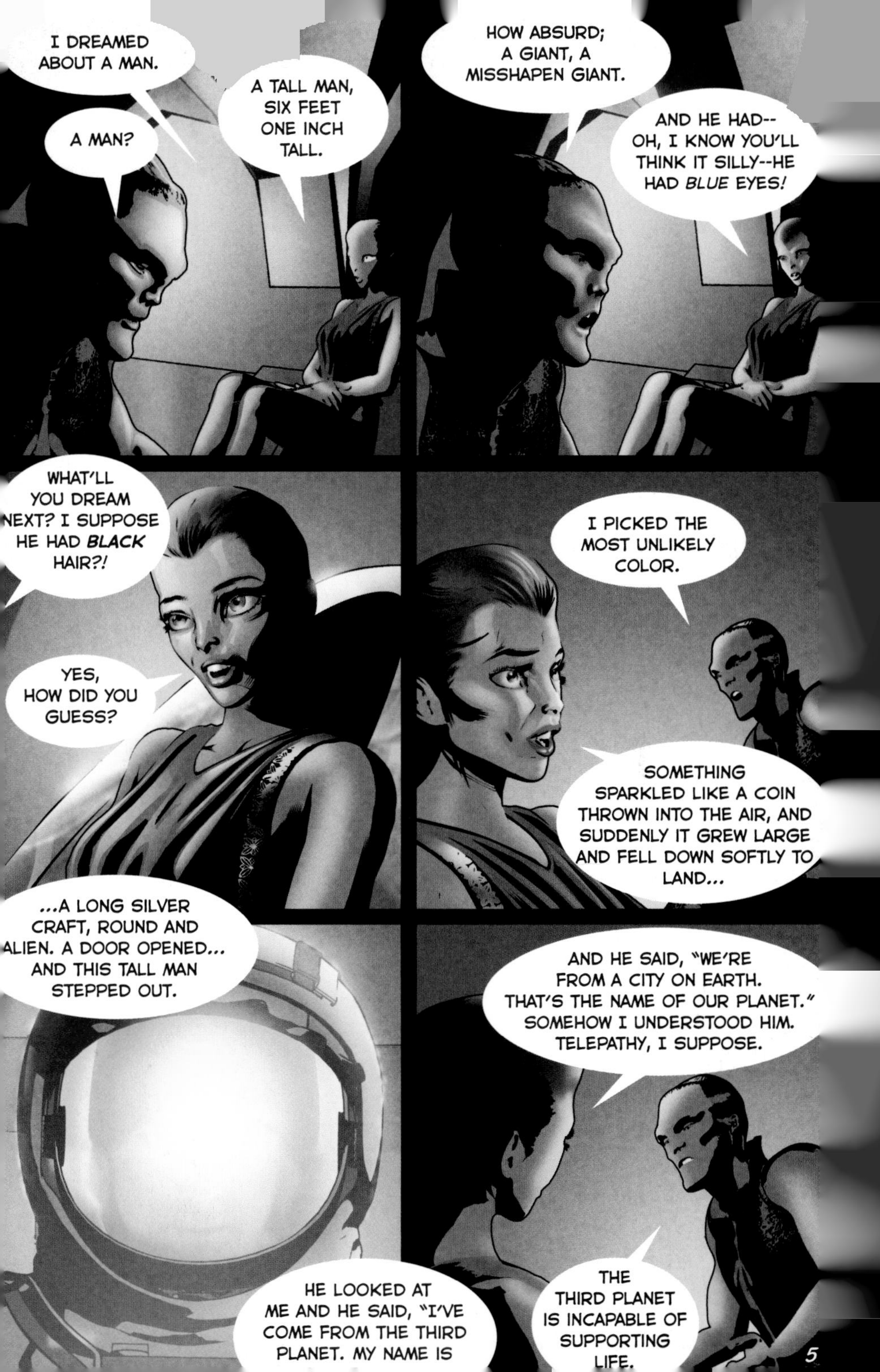

I DREAMED ABOUT A MAN.
A MAN?
A TALL MAN, SIX FEET ONE INCH TALL.
HOW ABSURD; A GIANT, A MISSHAPEN GIANT.
AND HE HAD-- OH, I KNOW YOU'LL THINK IT SILLY--HE HAD *BLUE* EYES!
WHAT'LL YOU DREAM NEXT? I SUPPOSE HE HAD *BLACK* HAIR?!
YES, HOW DID YOU GUESS?
I PICKED THE MOST UNLIKELY COLOR.
SOMETHING SPARKLED LIKE A COIN THROWN INTO THE AIR, AND SUDDENLY IT GREW LARGE AND FELL DOWN SOFTLY TO LAND...
...A LONG SILVER CRAFT, ROUND AND ALIEN. A DOOR OPENED... AND THIS TALL MAN STEPPED OUT.
HE LOOKED AT ME AND HE SAID, "I'VE COME FROM THE THIRD PLANET. MY NAME IS
AND HE SAID, "WE'RE FROM A CITY ON EARTH. THAT'S THE NAME OF OUR PLANET." SOMEHOW I UNDERSTOOD HIM. TELEPATHY, I SUPPOSE.
THE THIRD PLANET IS INCAPABLE OF SUPPORTING LIFE.

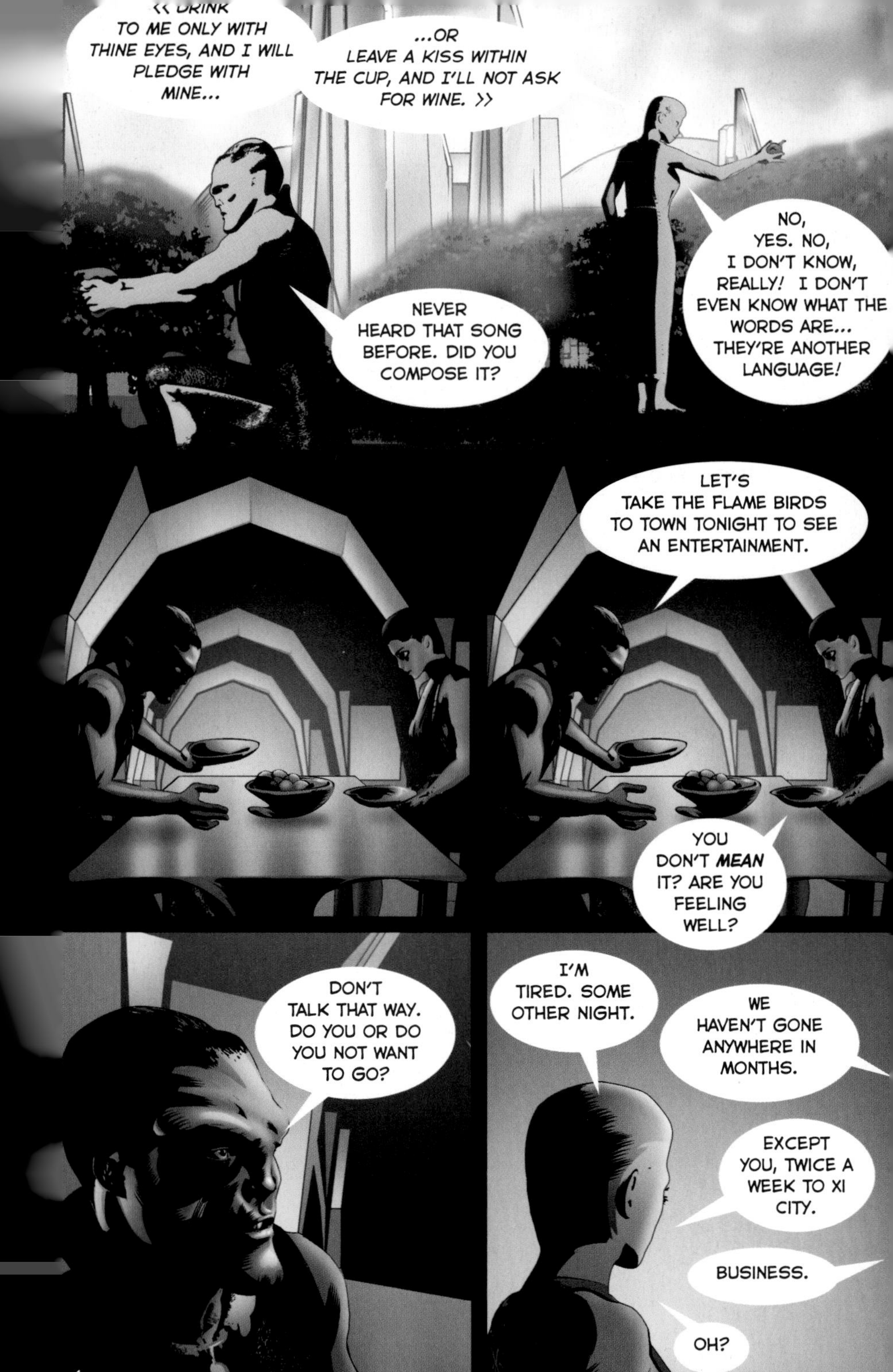
<< DRINK TO ME ONLY WITH THINE EYES, AND I WILL PLEDGE WITH MINE...
...OR LEAVE A KISS WITHIN THE CUP, AND I'LL NOT ASK FOR WINE. >>
NEVER HEARD THAT SONG BEFORE. DID YOU COMPOSE IT?
NO, YES. NO, I DON'T KNOW, REALLY! I DON'T EVEN KNOW WHAT THE WORDS ARE... THEY'RE ANOTHER LANGUAGE!
LET'S TAKE THE FLAME BIRDS TO TOWN TONIGHT TO SEE AN ENTERTAINMENT.
YOU DON'T *MEAN* IT? ARE YOU FEELING WELL?
DON'T TALK THAT WAY. DO YOU OR DO YOU NOT WANT TO GO?
I'M TIRED. SOME OTHER NIGHT.
WE HAVEN'T GONE ANYWHERE IN MONTHS.
EXCEPT YOU, TWICE A WEEK TO XI CITY.
BUSINESS.
OH?

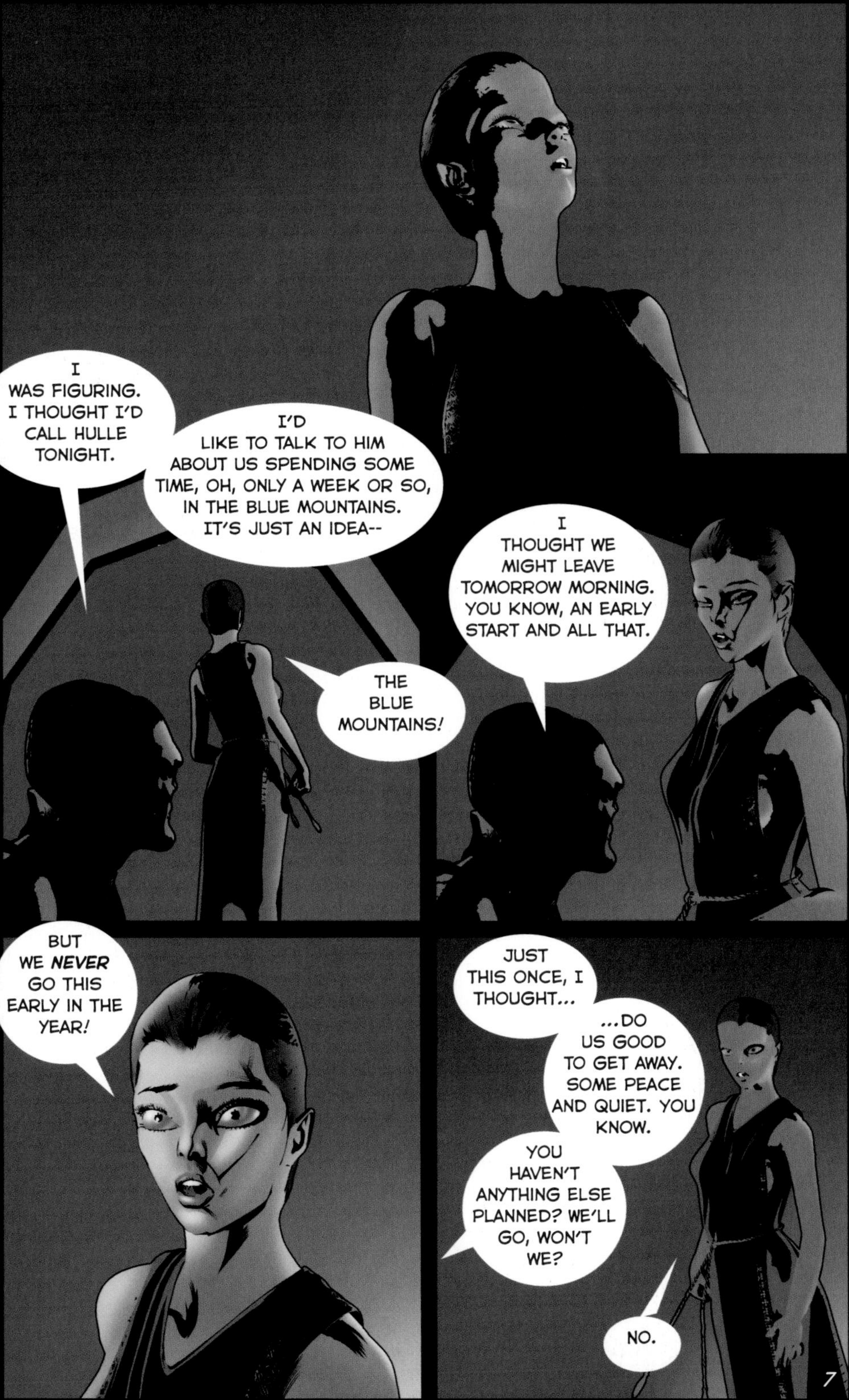
I WAS FIGURING. I THOUGHT I'D CALL HULLE TONIGHT.
I'D LIKE TO TALK TO HIM ABOUT US SPENDING SOME TIME, OH, ONLY A WEEK OR SO, IN THE BLUE MOUNTAINS. IT'S JUST AN IDEA--
THE BLUE MOUNTAINS!
I THOUGHT WE MIGHT LEAVE TOMORROW MORNING. YOU KNOW, AN EARLY START AND ALL THAT.
BUT WE *NEVER* GO THIS EARLY IN THE YEAR!
JUST THIS ONCE, I THOUGHT...
...DO US GOOD TO GET AWAY. SOME PEACE AND QUIET. YOU KNOW.
YOU HAVEN'T ANYTHING ELSE PLANNED? WE'LL GO, WON'T WE?
NO.

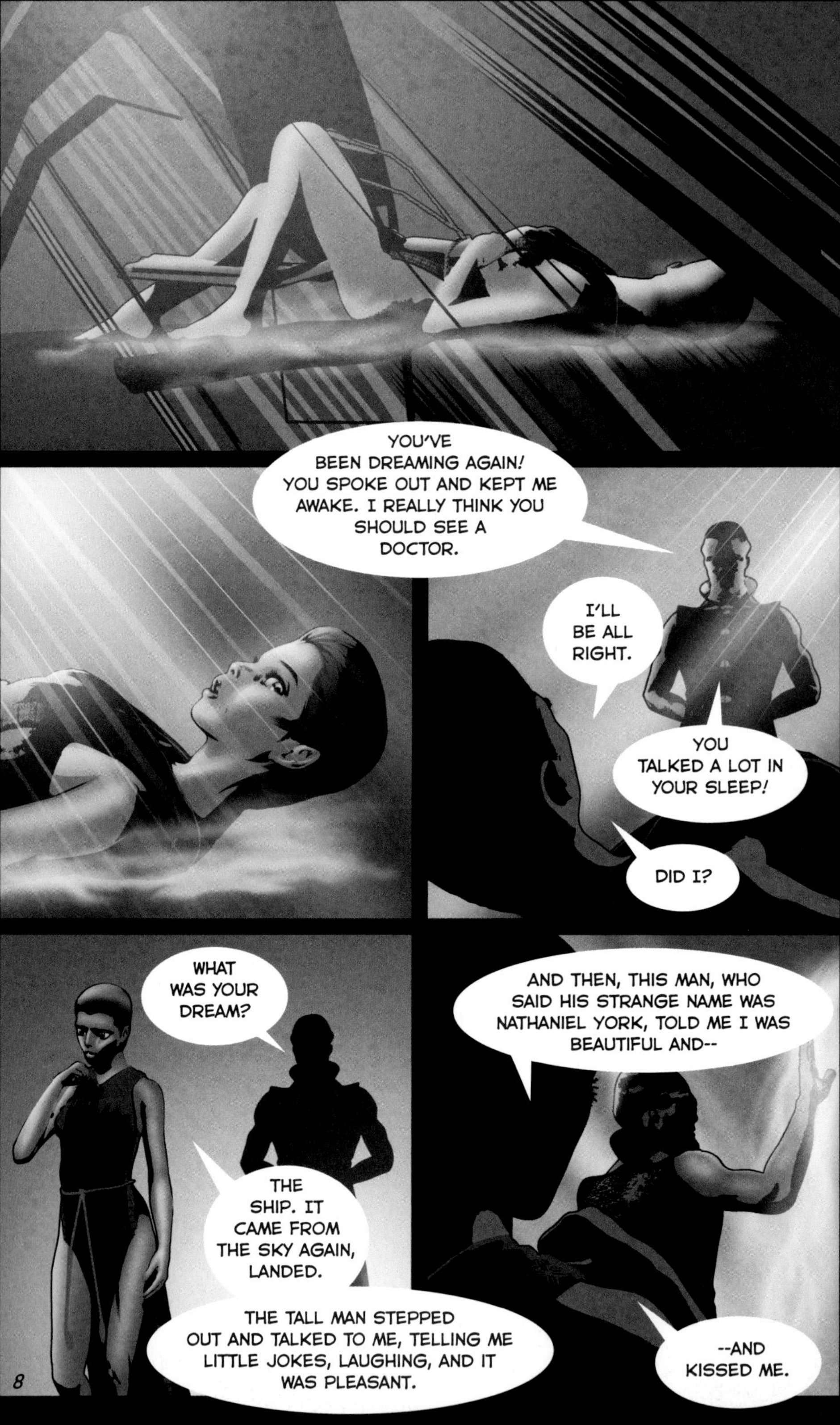
YOU'VE BEEN DREAMING AGAIN! YOU SPOKE OUT AND KEPT ME AWAKE. I REALLY THINK YOU SHOULD SEE A DOCTOR.
I'LL BE ALL RIGHT.
YOU TALKED A LOT IN YOUR SLEEP!
DID I?
WHAT WAS YOUR DREAM?
THE SHIP. IT CAME FROM THE SKY AGAIN, LANDED.
THE TALL MAN STEPPED OUT AND TALKED TO ME, TELLING ME LITTLE JOKES, LAUGHING, AND IT WAS PLEASANT.
AND THEN, THIS MAN, WHO SAID HIS STRANGE NAME WAS NATHANIEL YORK, TOLD ME I WAS BEAUTIFUL AND--
--AND KISSED ME.

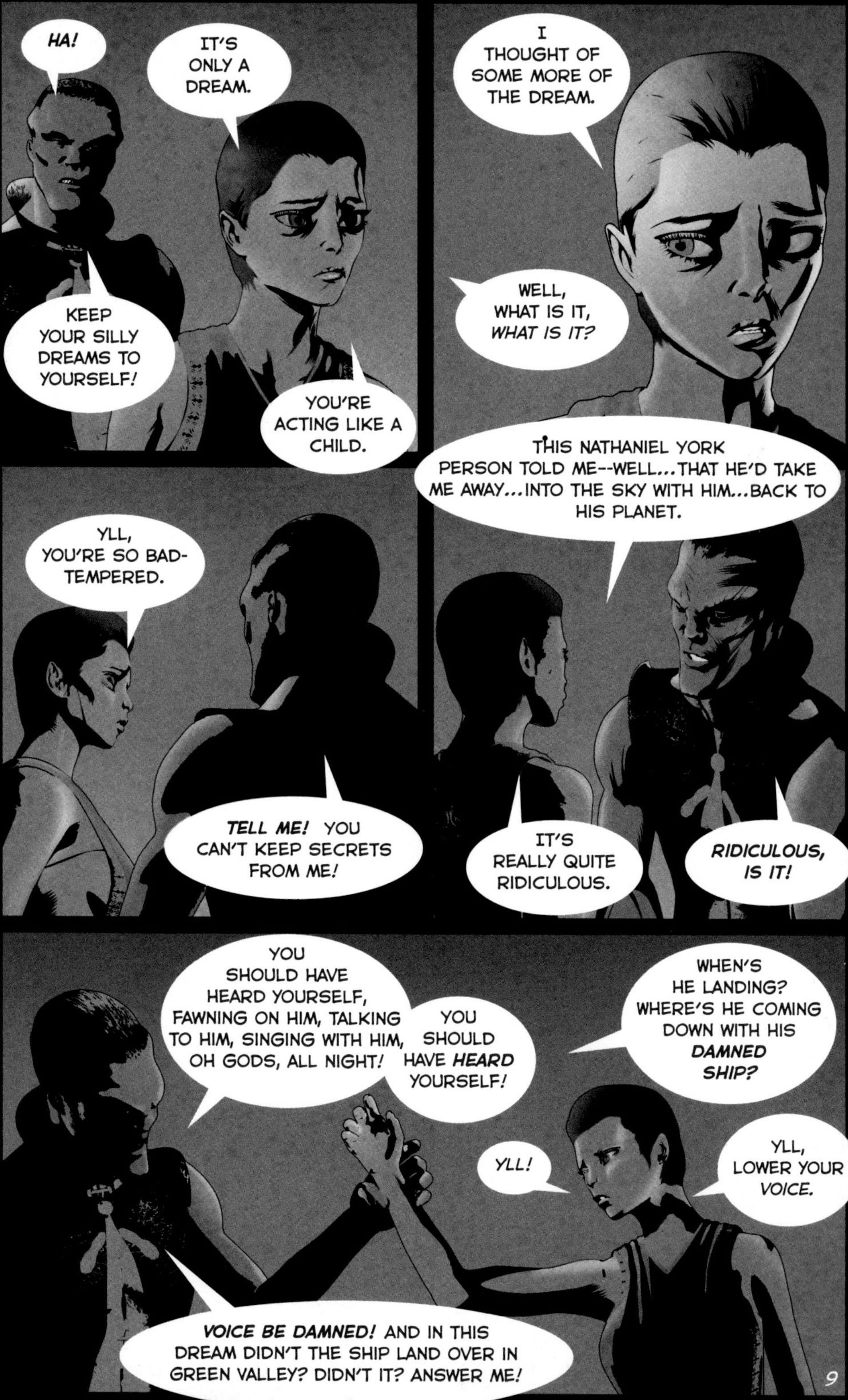
HA!
IT'S ONLY A DREAM.
KEEP YOUR SILLY DREAMS TO YOURSELF!
YOU'RE ACTING LIKE A CHILD.
I THOUGHT OF SOME MORE OF THE DREAM.
WELL, WHAT IS IT, *WHAT IS IT?*
YLL, YOU'RE SO BAD-TEMPERED.
TELL ME! YOU CAN'T KEEP SECRETS FROM ME!
THIS NATHANIEL YORK PERSON TOLD ME--WELL...THAT HE'D TAKE ME AWAY...INTO THE SKY WITH HIM...BACK TO HIS PLANET.
IT'S REALLY QUITE RIDICULOUS.
RIDICULOUS, IS IT!
YOU SHOULD HAVE HEARD YOURSELF, FAWNING ON HIM, TALKING TO HIM, SINGING WITH HIM, OH GODS, ALL NIGHT!
YOU SHOULD HAVE ***HEARD*** YOURSELF!
WHEN'S HE LANDING? WHERE'S HE COMING DOWN WITH HIS ***DAMNED SHIP?***
YLL!
YLL, LOWER YOUR *VOICE.*
VOICE BE DAMNED! AND IN THIS DREAM DIDN'T THE SHIP LAND OVER IN GREEN VALLEY? DIDN'T IT? ANSWER ME!

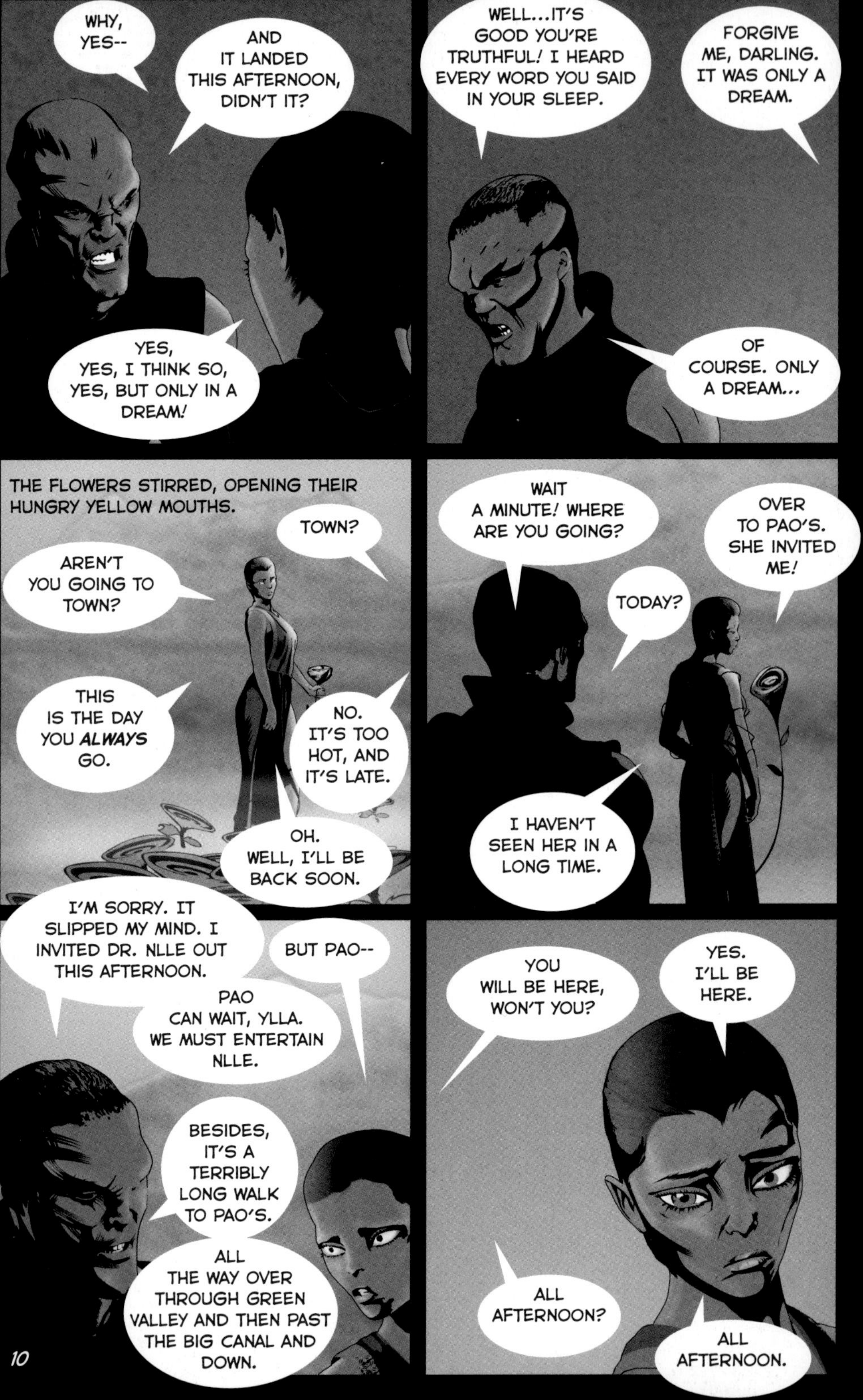
WHY, YES--
AND IT LANDED THIS AFTERNOON, DIDN'T IT?
YES, YES, I THINK SO, YES, BUT ONLY IN A DREAM!
WELL...IT'S GOOD YOU'RE TRUTHFUL! I HEARD EVERY WORD YOU SAID IN YOUR SLEEP.
FORGIVE ME, DARLING. IT WAS ONLY A DREAM.
OF COURSE. ONLY A DREAM...
THE FLOWERS STIRRED, OPENING THEIR HUNGRY YELLOW MOUTHS.
TOWN?
AREN'T YOU GOING TO TOWN?
THIS IS THE DAY YOU ALWAYS GO.
NO. IT'S TOO HOT, AND IT'S LATE.
OH. WELL, I'LL BE BACK SOON.
WAIT A MINUTE! WHERE ARE YOU GOING?
OVER TO PAO'S. SHE INVITED ME!
TODAY?
I HAVEN'T SEEN HER IN A LONG TIME.
I'M SORRY. IT SLIPPED MY MIND. I INVITED DR. NLLE OUT THIS AFTERNOON.
BUT PAO--
PAO CAN WAIT, YLLA. WE MUST ENTERTAIN NLLE.
BESIDES, IT'S A TERRIBLY LONG WALK TO PAO'S.
ALL THE WAY OVER THROUGH GREEN VALLEY AND THEN PAST THE BIG CANAL AND DOWN.
YOU WILL BE HERE, WON'T YOU?
YES. I'LL BE HERE.
ALL AFTERNOON?
ALL AFTERNOON.

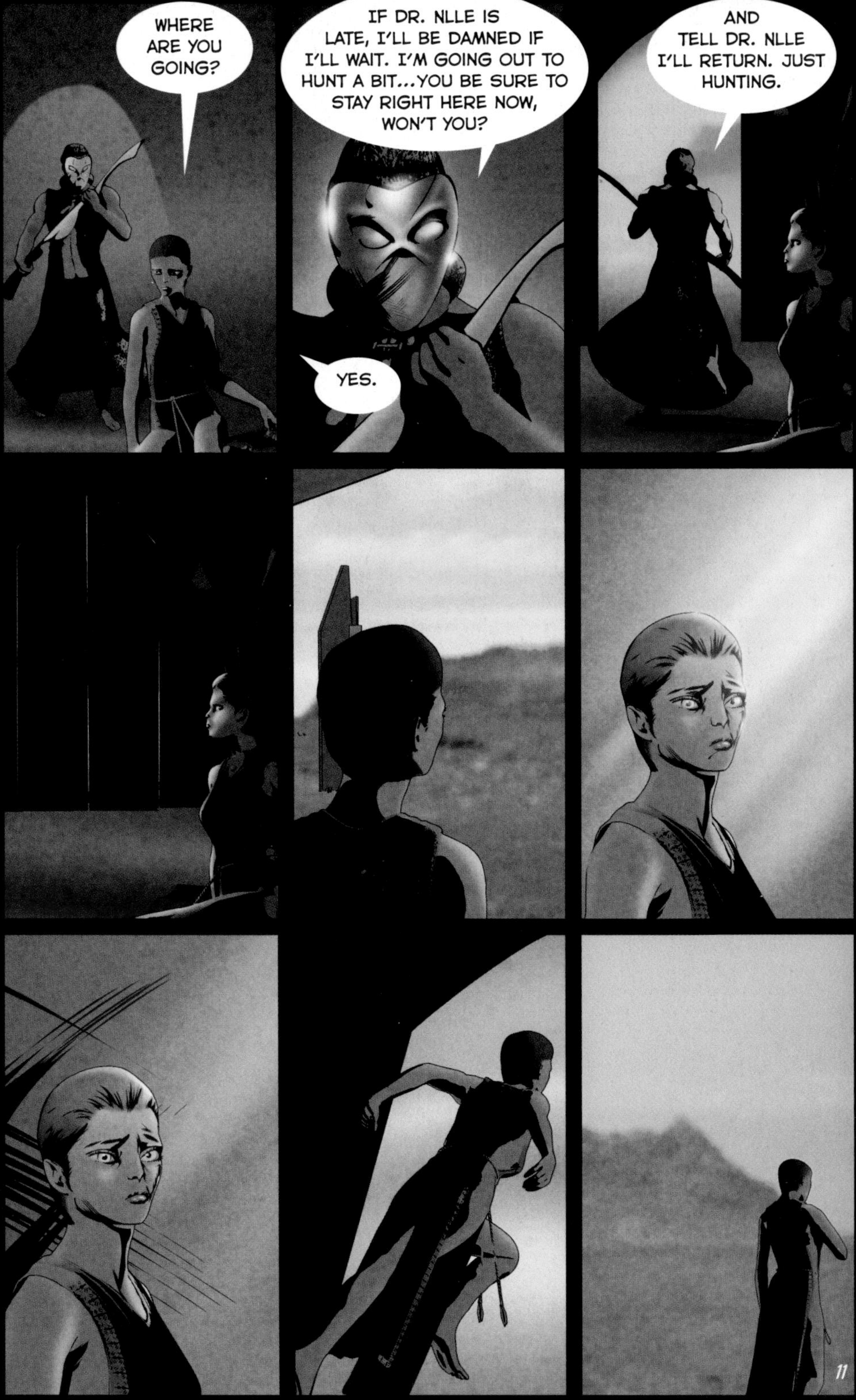

WHERE ARE YOU GOING?
IF DR. NLLE IS LATE, I'LL BE DAMNED IF I'LL WAIT. I'M GOING OUT TO HUNT A BIT...YOU BE SURE TO STAY RIGHT HERE NOW, WON'T YOU?
YES.
AND TELL DR. NLLE I'LL RETURN. JUST HUNTING.

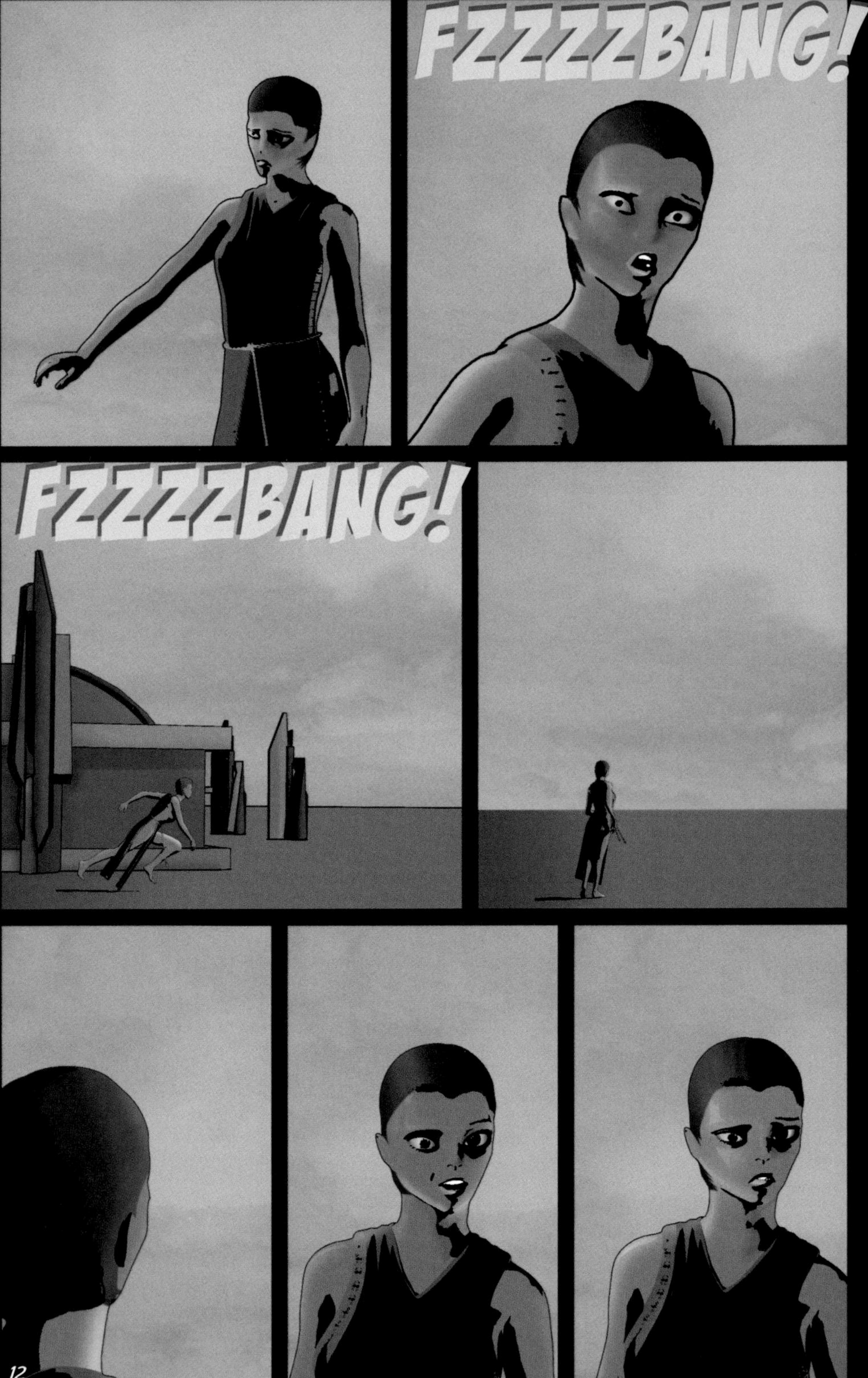
FZZZZBANG!
FZZZZBANG!

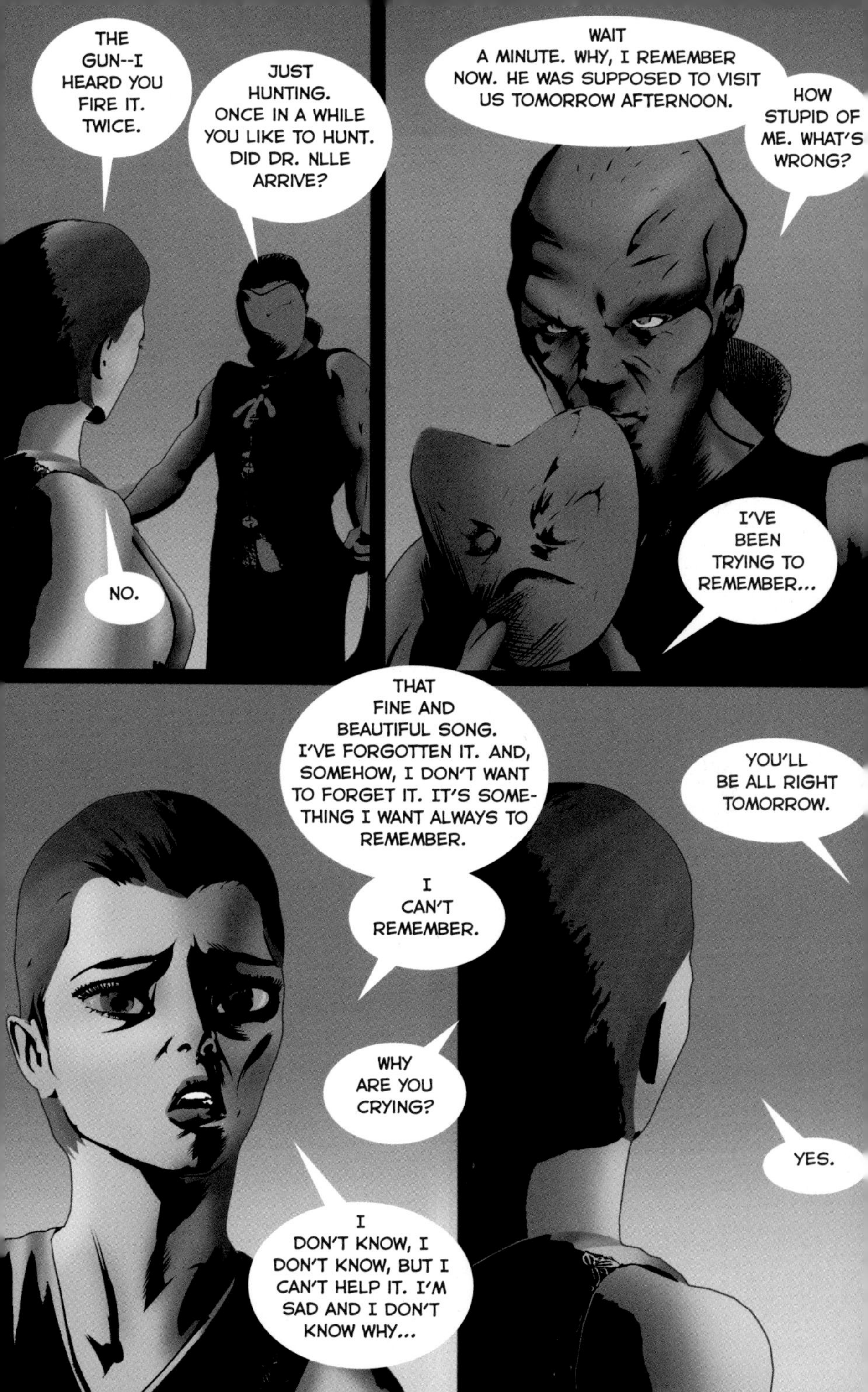
THE GUN--I HEARD YOU FIRE IT. TWICE.
JUST HUNTING. ONCE IN A WHILE YOU LIKE TO HUNT. DID DR. NLLE ARRIVE?
NO.
WAIT A MINUTE. WHY, I REMEMBER NOW. HE WAS SUPPOSED TO VISIT US TOMORROW AFTERNOON.
HOW STUPID OF ME. WHAT'S WRONG?
I'VE BEEN TRYING TO REMEMBER...
THAT FINE AND BEAUTIFUL SONG. I'VE FORGOTTEN IT. AND, SOMEHOW, I DON'T WANT TO FORGET IT. IT'S SOME-THING I WANT ALWAYS TO REMEMBER.
I CAN'T REMEMBER.
YOU'LL BE ALL RIGHT TOMORROW.
WHY ARE YOU CRYING?
I DON'T KNOW, I DON'T KNOW, BUT I CAN'T HELP IT. I'M SAD AND I DON'T KNOW WHY...
YES.

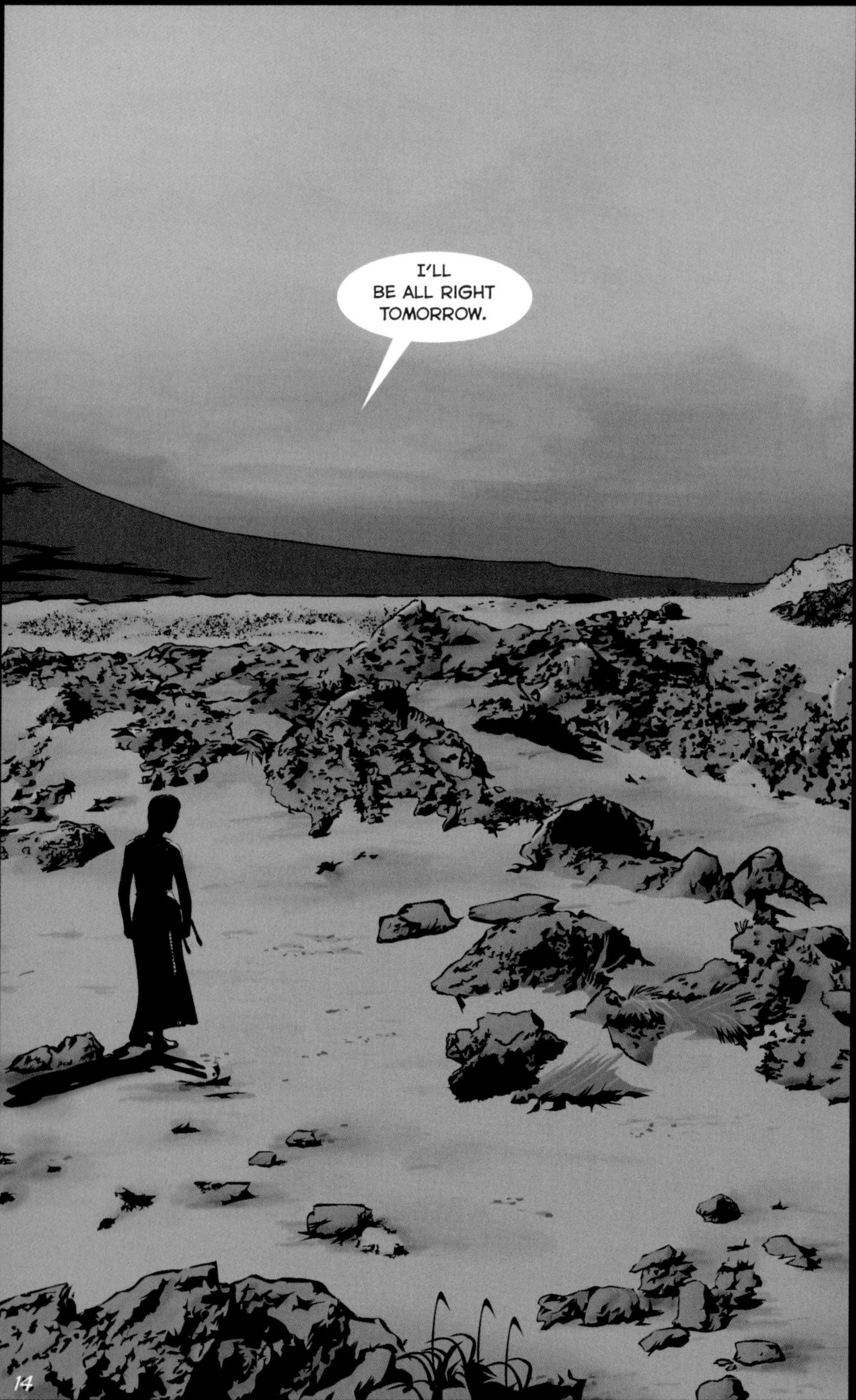
I'LL BE ALL RIGHT TOMORROW.

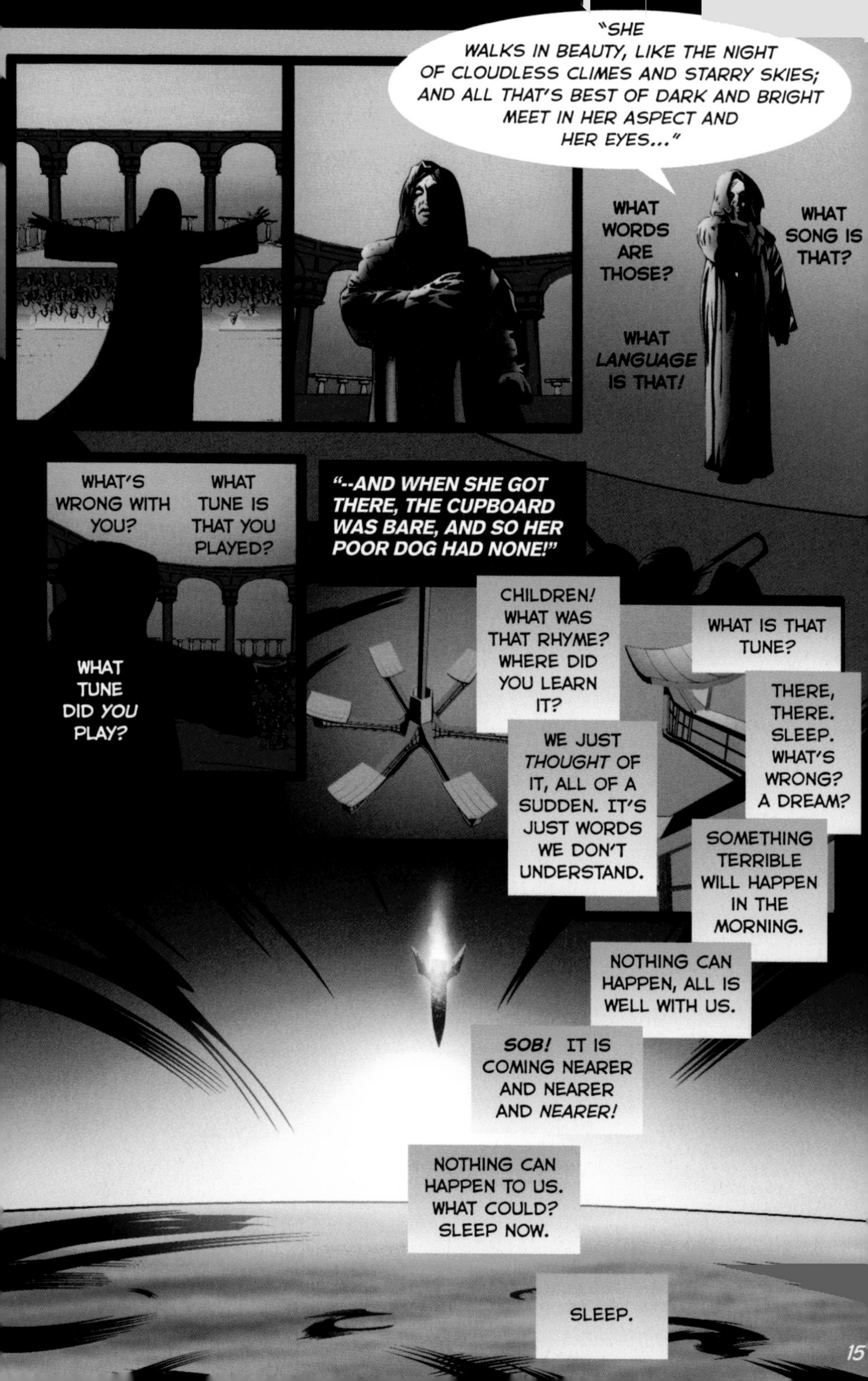
"SHE WALKS IN BEAUTY, LIKE THE NIGHT OF CLOUDLESS CLIMES AND STARRY SKIES; AND ALL THAT'S BEST OF DARK AND BRIGHT MEET IN HER ASPECT AND HER EYES..."
WHAT WORDS ARE THOSE?
WHAT SONG IS THAT?
WHAT *LANGUAGE* IS THAT!
WHAT'S WRONG WITH YOU?
WHAT TUNE IS THAT YOU PLAYED?
WHAT TUNE DID *YOU* PLAY?
"--AND WHEN SHE GOT THERE, THE CUPBOARD WAS BARE, AND SO HER POOR DOG HAD NONE!"
CHILDREN! WHAT WAS THAT RHYME? WHERE DID YOU LEARN IT?
WHAT IS THAT TUNE?
WE JUST *THOUGHT* OF IT, ALL OF A SUDDEN. IT'S JUST WORDS WE DON'T UNDERSTAND.
THERE, THERE. SLEEP. WHAT'S WRONG? A DREAM?
SOMETHING TERRIBLE WILL HAPPEN IN THE MORNING.
NOTHING CAN HAPPEN, ALL IS WELL WITH US.
SOB! IT IS COMING NEARER AND NEARER AND *NEARER!*
NOTHING CAN HAPPEN TO US. WHAT COULD? SLEEP NOW.
SLEEP.

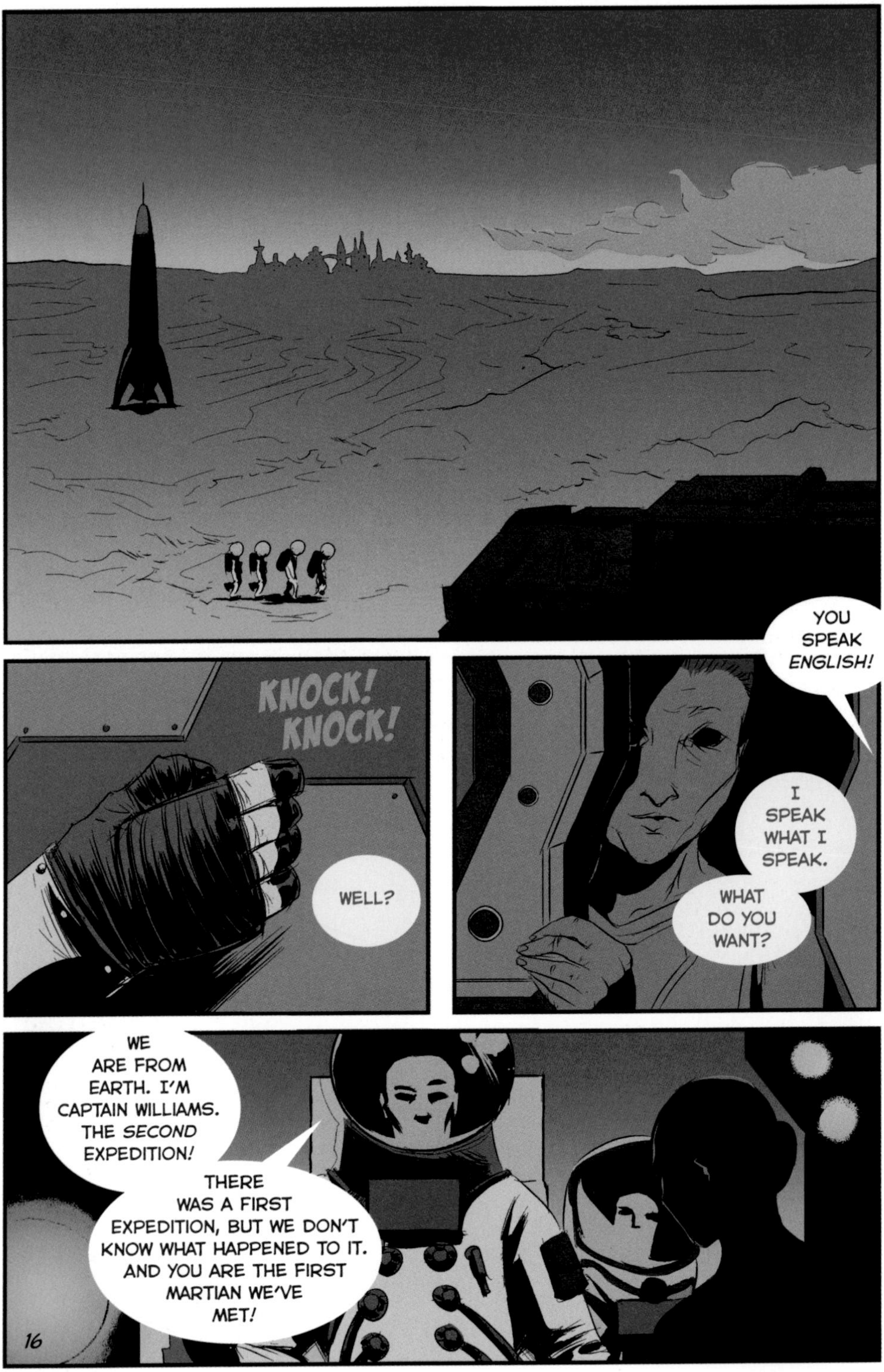
KNOCK! KNOCK!
WELL?
YOU SPEAK *ENGLISH!*
I SPEAK WHAT I SPEAK.
WHAT DO YOU WANT?
WE ARE FROM EARTH. I'M CAPTAIN WILLIAMS. THE *SECOND* EXPEDITION!
THERE WAS A FIRST EXPEDITION, BUT WE DON'T KNOW WHAT HAPPENED TO IT. AND YOU ARE THE FIRST MARTIAN WE'VE MET!

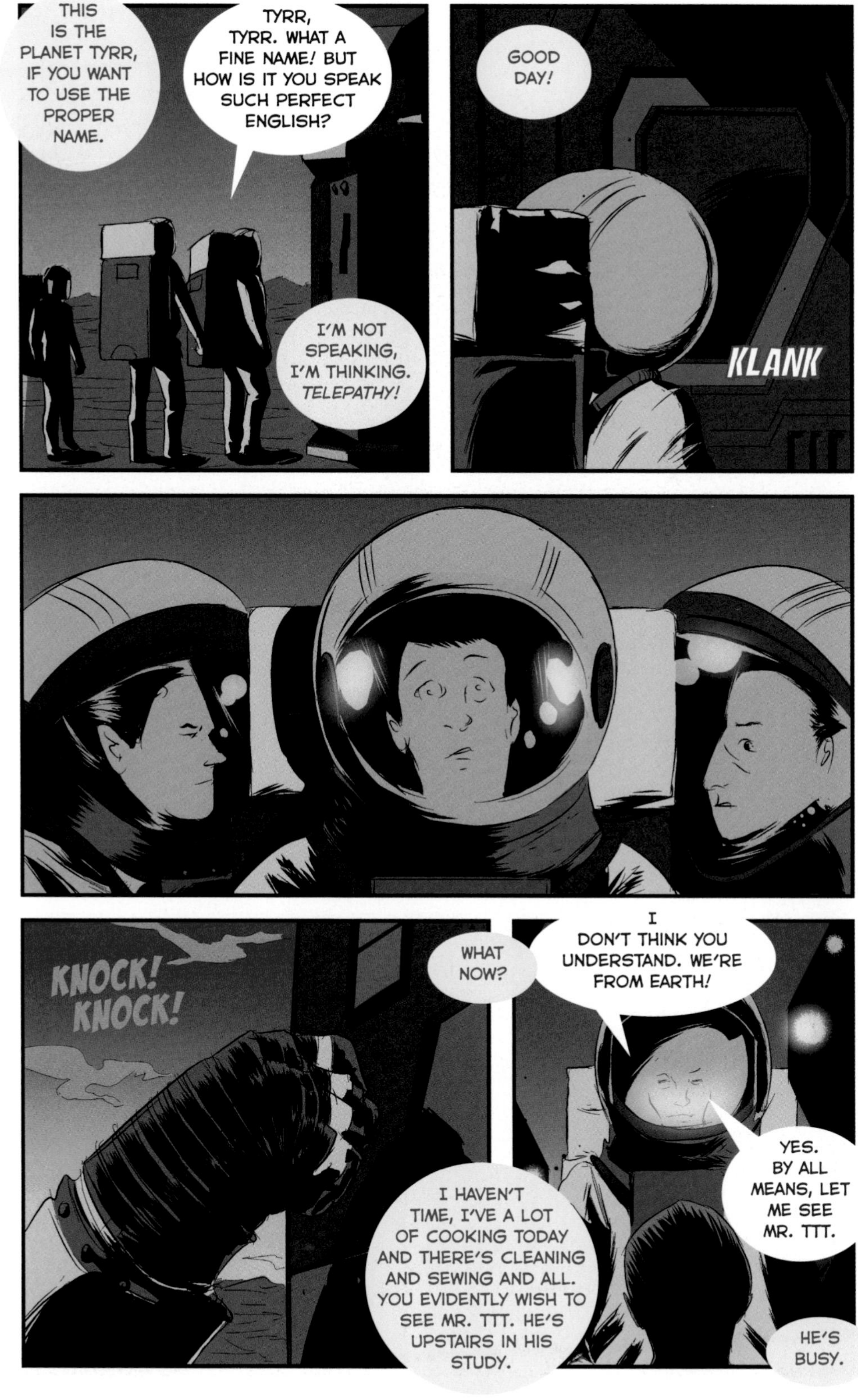
THIS IS THE PLANET TYRR, IF YOU WANT TO USE THE PROPER NAME.
TYRR, TYRR. WHAT A FINE NAME! BUT HOW IS IT YOU SPEAK SUCH PERFECT ENGLISH?
I'M NOT SPEAKING, I'M THINKING. *TELEPATHY!*
GOOD DAY!
KLANK
KNOCK! KNOCK!
WHAT NOW?
I DON'T THINK YOU UNDERSTAND. WE'RE FROM EARTH!
I HAVEN'T TIME, I'VE A LOT OF COOKING TODAY AND THERE'S CLEANING AND SEWING AND ALL. YOU EVIDENTLY WISH TO SEE MR. TTT. HE'S UPSTAIRS IN HIS STUDY.
YES. BY ALL MEANS, LET ME SEE MR. TTT.
HE'S BUSY.

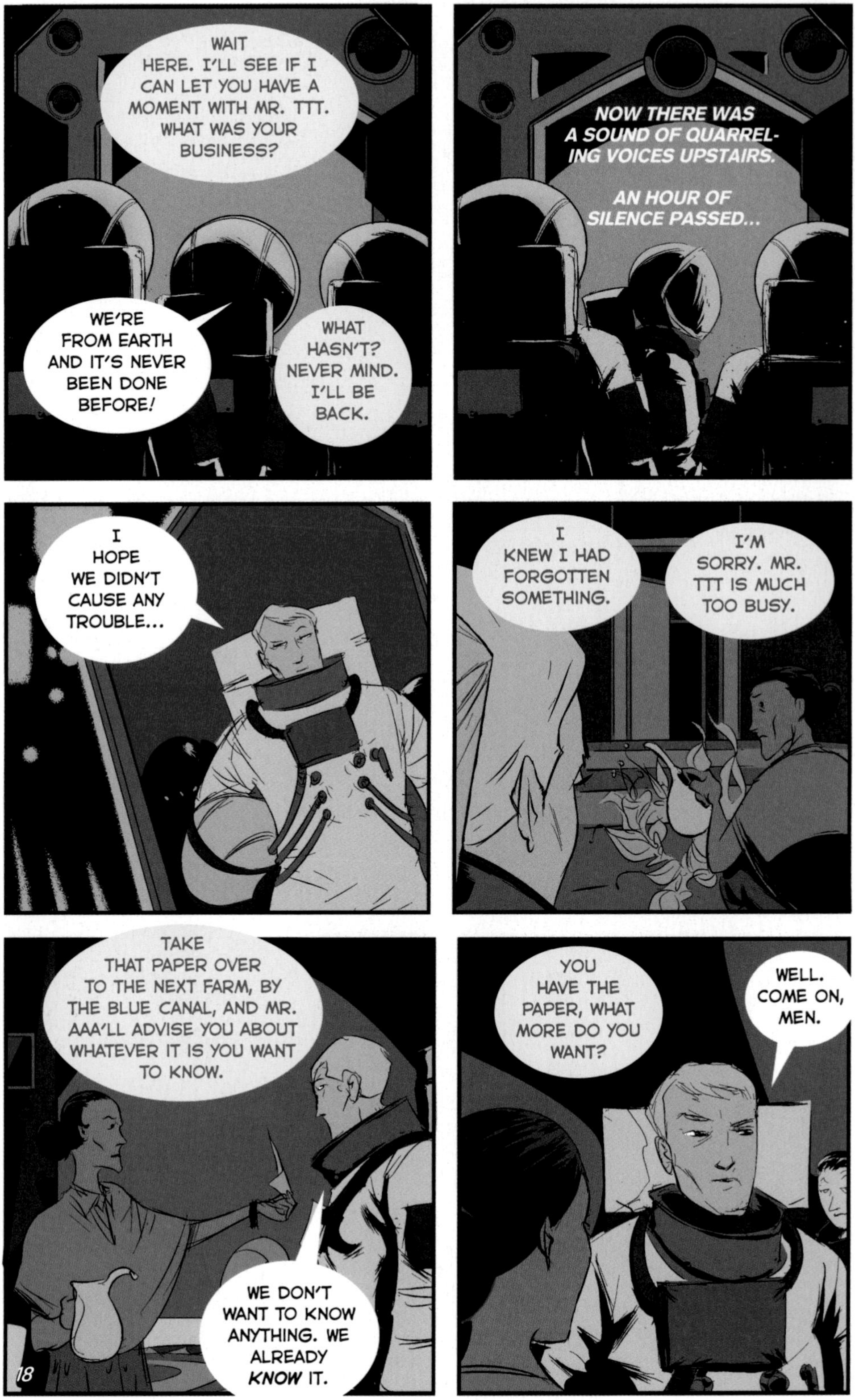
WAIT HERE. I'LL SEE IF I CAN LET YOU HAVE A MOMENT WITH MR. TTT. WHAT WAS YOUR BUSINESS?
WE'RE FROM EARTH AND IT'S NEVER BEEN DONE BEFORE!
WHAT HASN'T? NEVER MIND. I'LL BE BACK.
NOW THERE WAS A SOUND OF QUARREL-ING VOICES UPSTAIRS.
AN HOUR OF SILENCE PASSED...
I HOPE WE DIDN'T CAUSE ANY TROUBLE...
I KNEW I HAD FORGOTTEN SOMETHING.
I'M SORRY. MR. TTT IS MUCH TOO BUSY.
TAKE THAT PAPER OVER TO THE NEXT FARM, BY THE BLUE CANAL, AND MR. AAA'LL ADVISE YOU ABOUT WHATEVER IT IS YOU WANT TO KNOW.
WE DON'T WANT TO KNOW ANYTHING. WE ALREADY *KNOW* IT.
YOU HAVE THE PAPER, WHAT MORE DO YOU WANT?
WELL. COME ON, MEN.

HALF AN HOUR LATER, MR. AAA, SEATED IN HIS LIBRARY SIPPING A BIT OF ELECTRIC FIRE FROM A METAL CUP, HEARD THE VOICES OUTSIDE IN THE STONE CAUSEWAY.

ARE YOU MR. AAA?

I AM.

MR. TTT SENT US TO SEE YOU!

WHY DID HE DO THAT?

HE WAS BUSY!

DOES HE THINK I HAVE NOTHING ELSE TO DO BUT ENTERTAIN PEOPLE HE'S TOO BUSY TO BOTHER WITH?

THAT'S NOT THE IMPORTANT THING, SIR!

WELL, IT IS TO ME. I HAVE MUCH READING TO DO.

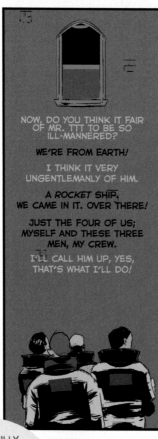

NOW, DO YOU THINK IT FAIR OF MR. TTT TO BE SO ILL-MANNERED?

WE'RE FROM EARTH!

I THINK IT VERY UNGENTLEMANLY OF HIM.

A ROCKET SHIP, WE CAME IN IT. OVER THERE!

JUST THE FOUR OF US; MYSELF AND THESE THREE MEN, MY CREW.

I'LL CALL HIM UP, YES, THAT'S WHAT I'LL DO!

CHALLENGED HIM TO A DUEL, BY THE GODS! A DUEL!

MR. AAA--

I'LL SHOOT HIM DEAD, DO YOU HEAR!

MR. AAA...WE CAME SIXTY MILLION MILES.

WHERE'D YOU SAY YOU WERE FROM?

FROM EARTH!

THAT'S ONLY FIFTY MILLION MILES THIS TIME OF YEAR.

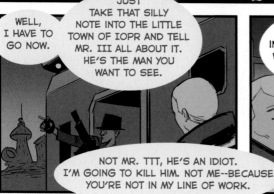

WELL, I HAVE TO GO NOW.

JUST TAKE THAT SILLY NOTE INTO THE LITTLE TOWN OF IOPR AND TELL MR. III ALL ABOUT IT. HE'S THE MAN YOU WANT TO SEE.

NOT MR. TTT, HE'S AN IDIOT. I'M GOING TO KILL HIM. NOT ME--BECAUSE YOU'RE NOT IN MY LINE OF WORK.

DO YOU HAVE TO BE IN A CERTAIN LINE OF WORK TO WELCOME EARTH MEN!

DON'T BE SILLY, EVERYONE KNOWS THAT! GOOD-BY!

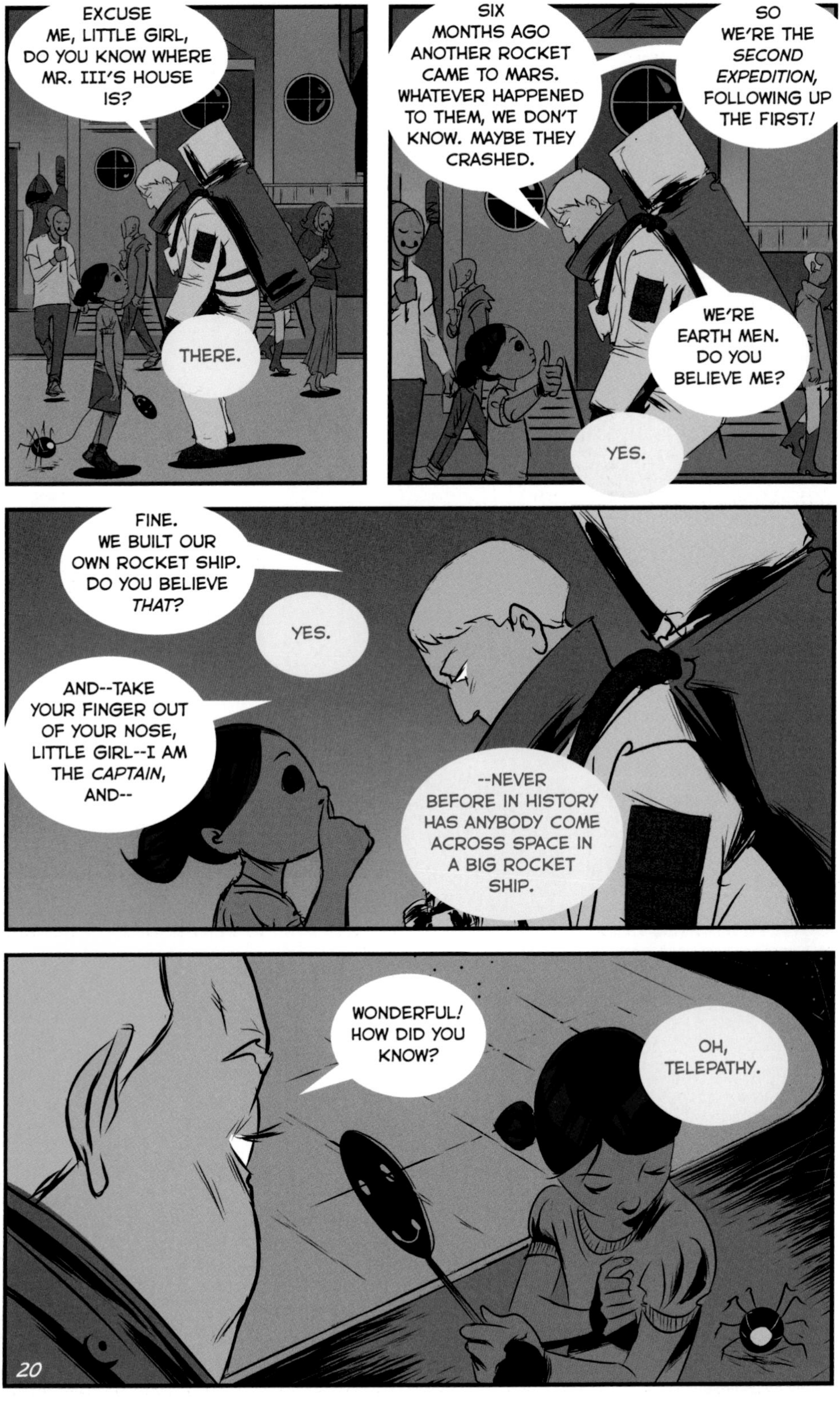
EXCUSE ME, LITTLE GIRL, DO YOU KNOW WHERE MR. III'S HOUSE IS?
THERE.
SIX MONTHS AGO ANOTHER ROCKET CAME TO MARS. WHATEVER HAPPENED TO THEM, WE DON'T KNOW. MAYBE THEY CRASHED.
SO WE'RE THE *SECOND EXPEDITION*, FOLLOWING UP THE FIRST!
WE'RE EARTH MEN. DO YOU BELIEVE ME?
YES.
FINE. WE BUILT OUR OWN ROCKET SHIP. DO YOU BELIEVE *THAT*?
YES.
AND--TAKE YOUR FINGER OUT OF YOUR NOSE, LITTLE GIRL--I AM THE *CAPTAIN*, AND--
--NEVER BEFORE IN HISTORY HAS ANYBODY COME ACROSS SPACE IN A BIG ROCKET SHIP.
WONDERFUL! HOW DID YOU KNOW?
OH, TELEPATHY.

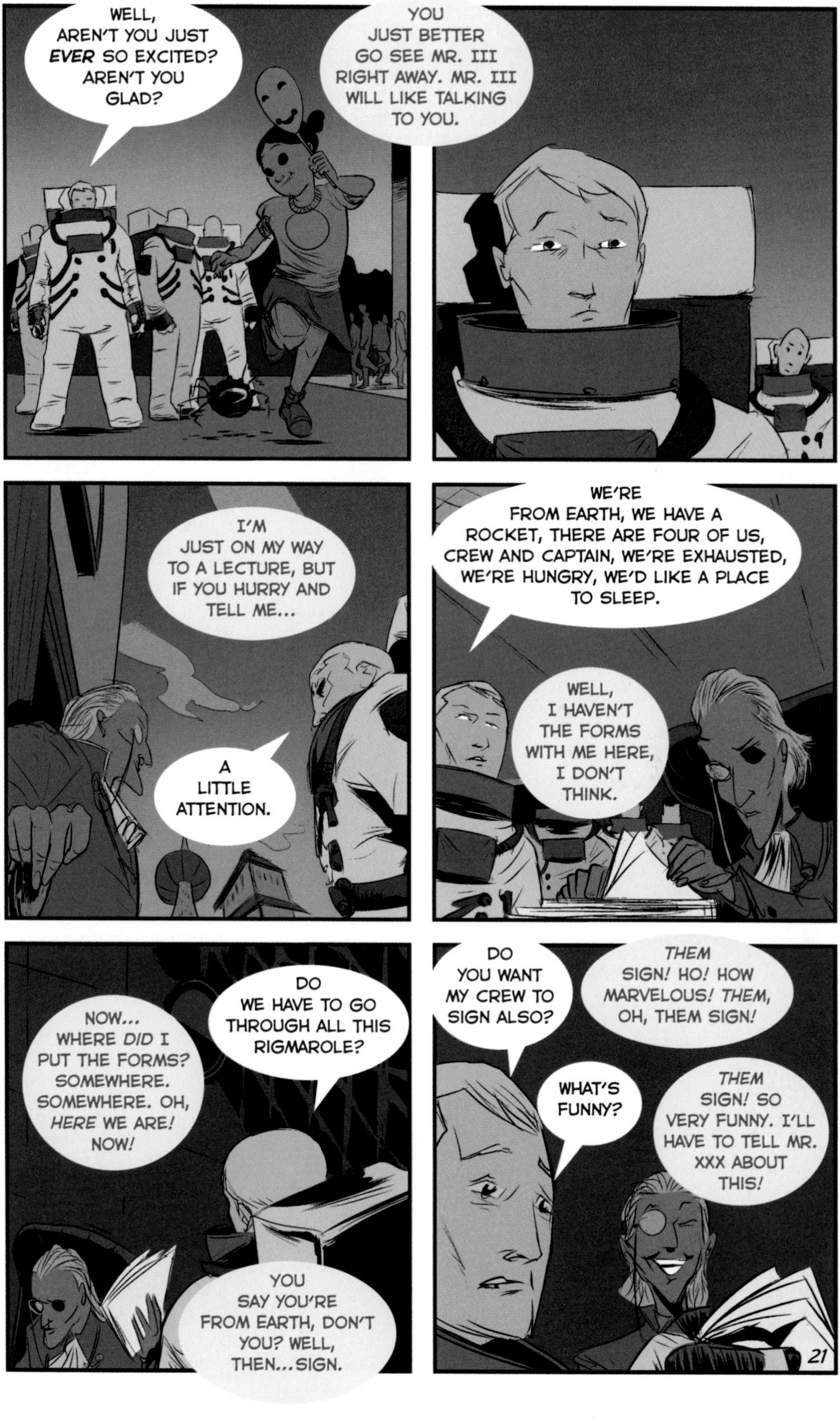
WELL, AREN'T YOU JUST *EVER* SO EXCITED? AREN'T YOU GLAD?
YOU JUST BETTER GO SEE MR. III RIGHT AWAY. MR. III WILL LIKE TALKING TO YOU.
I'M JUST ON MY WAY TO A LECTURE, BUT IF YOU HURRY AND TELL ME...
A LITTLE ATTENTION.
WE'RE FROM EARTH, WE HAVE A ROCKET, THERE ARE FOUR OF US, CREW AND CAPTAIN, WE'RE EXHAUSTED, WE'RE HUNGRY, WE'D LIKE A PLACE TO SLEEP.
WELL, I HAVEN'T THE FORMS WITH ME HERE, I DON'T THINK.
DO WE HAVE TO GO THROUGH ALL THIS RIGMAROLE?
NOW... WHERE *DID* I PUT THE FORMS? SOMEWHERE. SOMEWHERE. OH, *HERE* WE ARE! NOW!
YOU SAY YOU'RE FROM EARTH, DON'T YOU? WELL, THEN...SIGN.
DO YOU WANT MY CREW TO SIGN ALSO?
THEM SIGN! HO! HOW MARVELOUS! *THEM*, OH, THEM SIGN!
WHAT'S FUNNY?
THEM SIGN! SO VERY FUNNY. I'LL HAVE TO TELL MR. XXX ABOUT THIS!

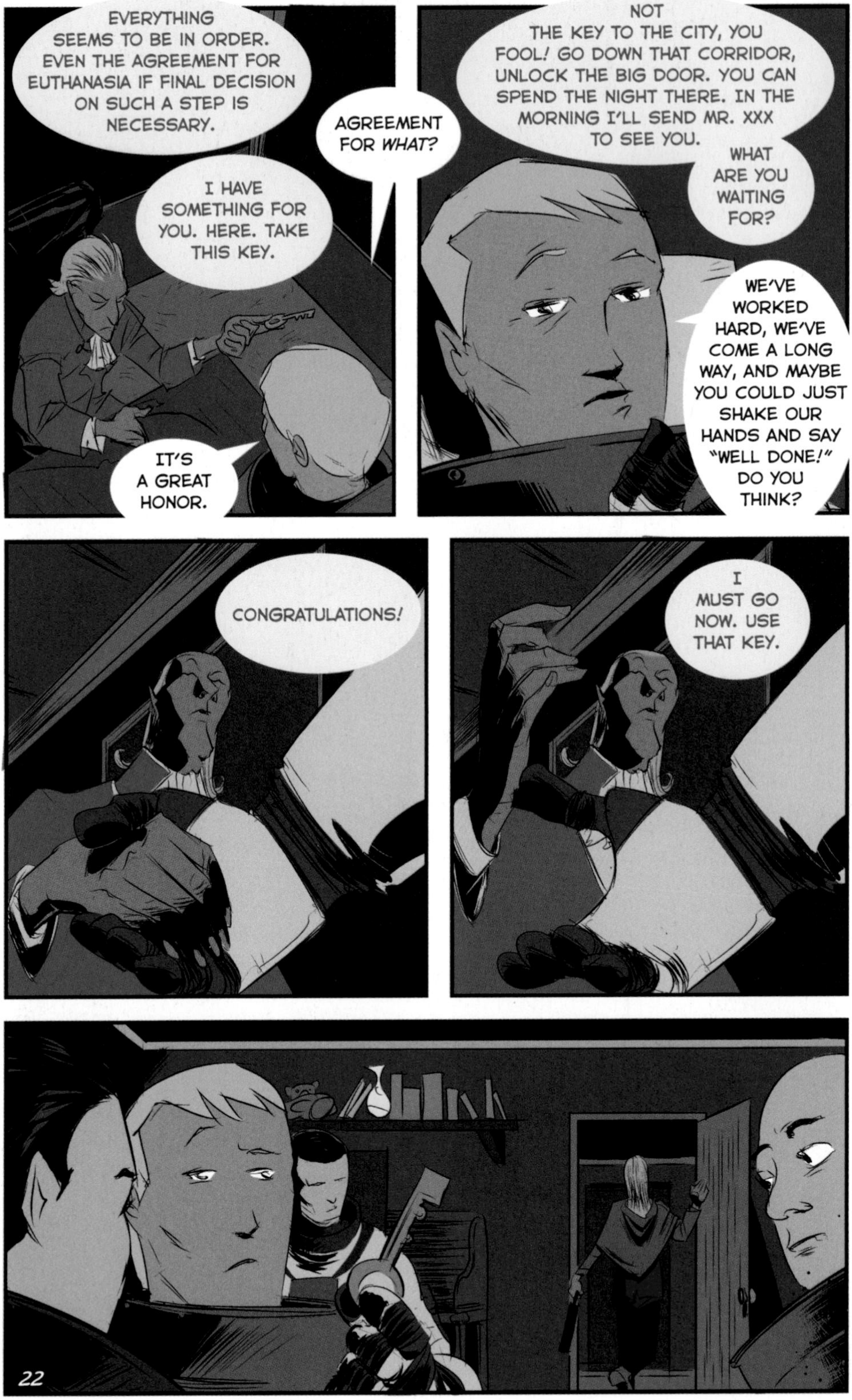
EVERYTHING SEEMS TO BE IN ORDER. EVEN THE AGREEMENT FOR EUTHANASIA IF FINAL DECISION ON SUCH A STEP IS NECESSARY.
AGREEMENT FOR WHAT?
I HAVE SOMETHING FOR YOU. HERE. TAKE THIS KEY.
IT'S A GREAT HONOR.
NOT THE KEY TO THE CITY, YOU FOOL! GO DOWN THAT CORRIDOR, UNLOCK THE BIG DOOR. YOU CAN SPEND THE NIGHT THERE. IN THE MORNING I'LL SEND MR. XXX TO SEE YOU.
WHAT ARE YOU WAITING FOR?
WE'VE WORKED HARD, WE'VE COME A LONG WAY, AND MAYBE YOU COULD JUST SHAKE OUR HANDS AND SAY "WELL DONE!" DO YOU THINK?
CONGRATULATIONS!
I MUST GO NOW. USE THAT KEY.

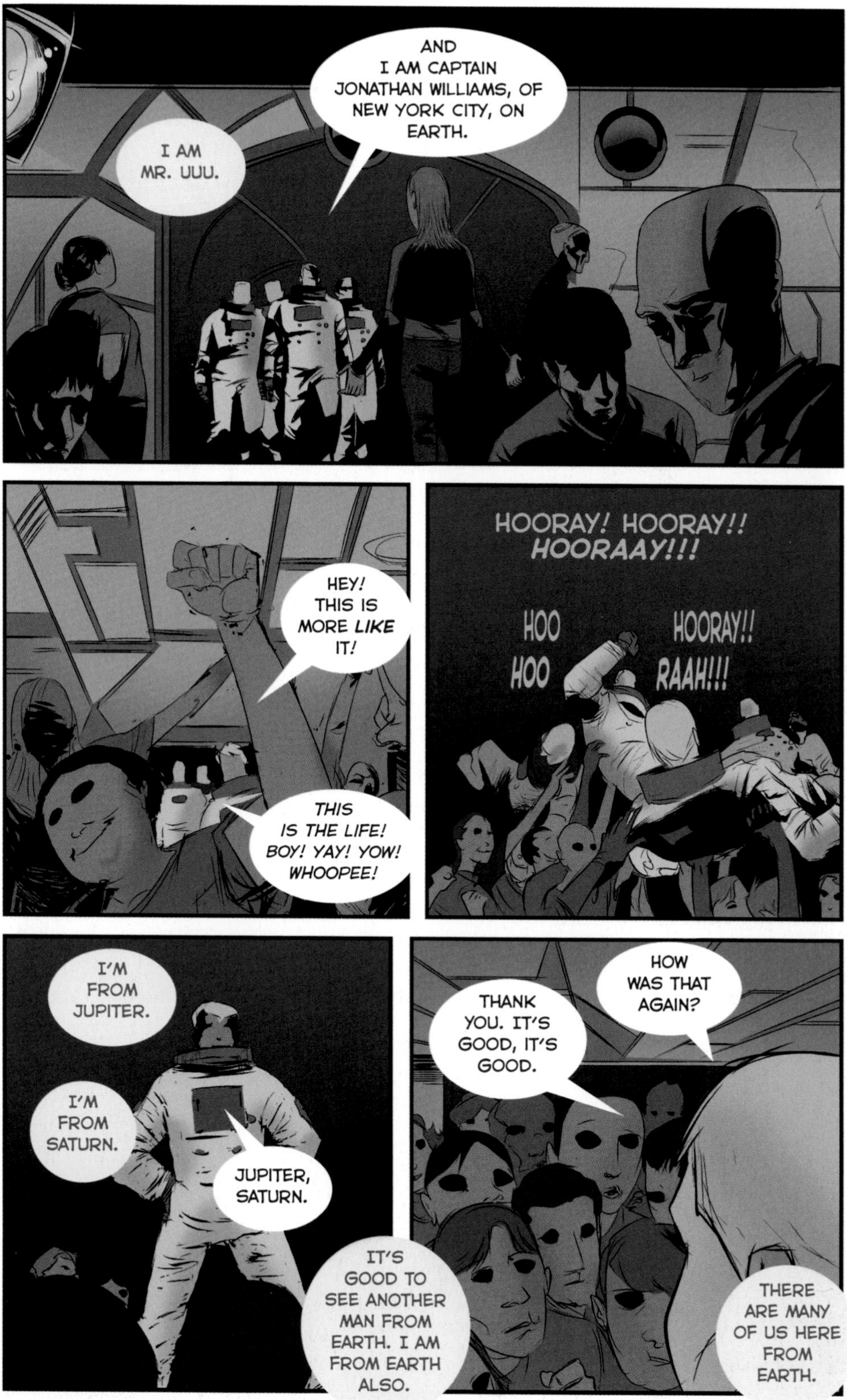
I AM MR. UUU.
AND I AM CAPTAIN JONATHAN WILLIAMS, OF NEW YORK CITY, ON EARTH.
HEY! THIS IS MORE *LIKE* IT!
THIS IS THE LIFE! BOY! YAY! YOW! WHOOPEE!
HOORAY! HOORAY!! *HOORAAY!!!*
HOO HOO
HOORAY!! RAAH!!!
I'M FROM JUPITER.
I'M FROM SATURN.
JUPITER, SATURN.
IT'S GOOD TO SEE ANOTHER MAN FROM EARTH. I AM FROM EARTH ALSO.
HOW WAS THAT AGAIN?
THANK YOU. IT'S GOOD, IT'S GOOD.
THERE ARE MANY OF US HERE FROM EARTH.

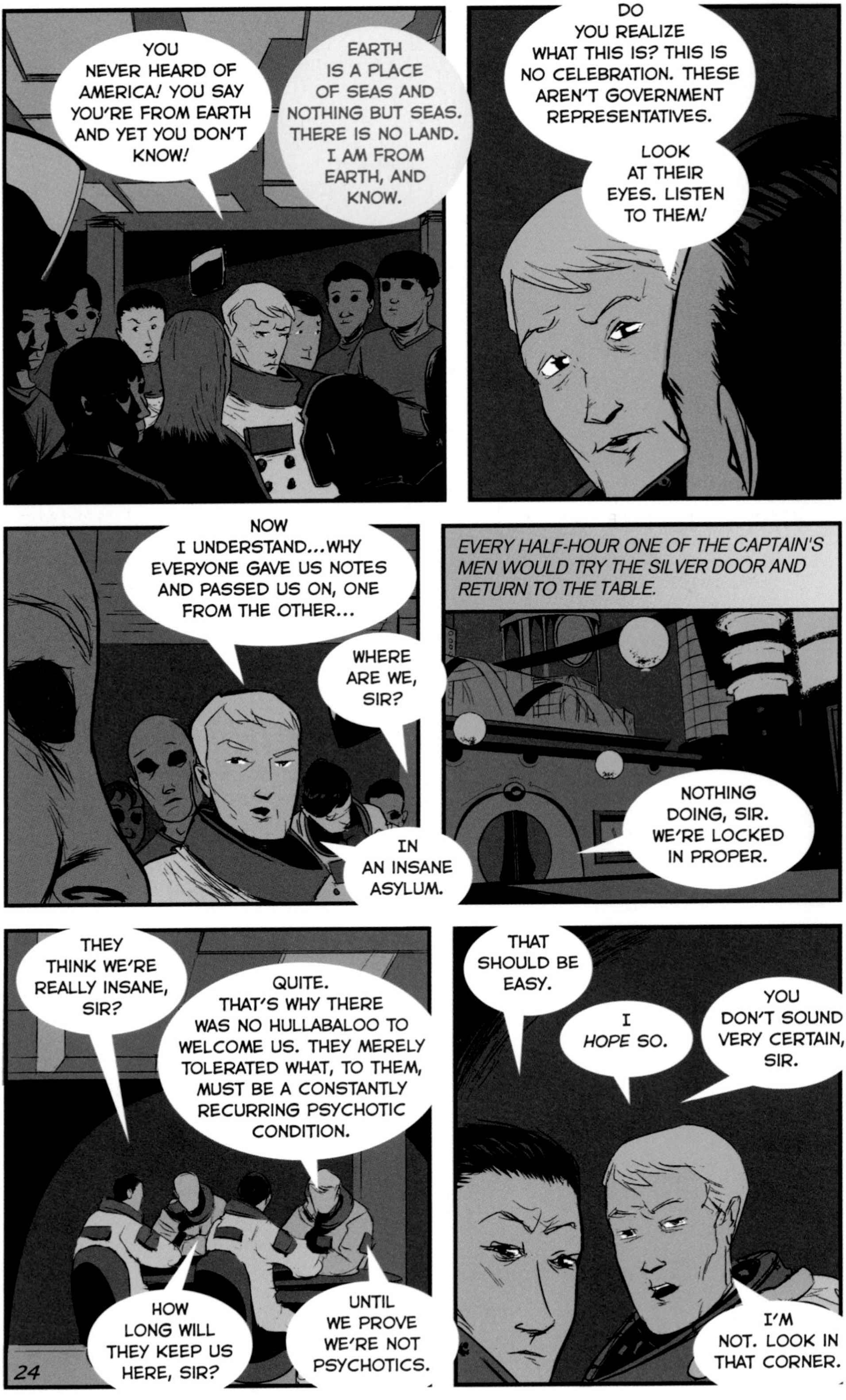
YOU NEVER HEARD OF AMERICA! YOU SAY YOU'RE FROM EARTH AND YET YOU DON'T KNOW!
EARTH IS A PLACE OF SEAS AND NOTHING BUT SEAS. THERE IS NO LAND. I AM FROM EARTH, AND KNOW.
DO YOU REALIZE WHAT THIS IS? THIS IS NO CELEBRATION. THESE AREN'T GOVERNMENT REPRESENTATIVES.
LOOK AT THEIR EYES. LISTEN TO THEM!
NOW I UNDERSTAND...WHY EVERYONE GAVE US NOTES AND PASSED US ON, ONE FROM THE OTHER...
WHERE ARE WE, SIR?
IN AN INSANE ASYLUM.
EVERY HALF-HOUR ONE OF THE CAPTAIN'S MEN WOULD TRY THE SILVER DOOR AND RETURN TO THE TABLE.
NOTHING DOING, SIR. WE'RE LOCKED IN PROPER.
THEY THINK WE'RE REALLY INSANE, SIR?
QUITE. THAT'S WHY THERE WAS NO HULLABALOO TO WELCOME US. THEY MERELY TOLERATED WHAT, TO THEM, MUST BE A CONSTANTLY RECURRING PSYCHOTIC CONDITION.
HOW LONG WILL THEY KEEP US HERE, SIR?
UNTIL WE PROVE WE'RE NOT PSYCHOTICS.
THAT SHOULD BE EASY.
I HOPE SO.
YOU DON'T SOUND VERY CERTAIN, SIR.
I'M NOT. LOOK IN THAT CORNER.

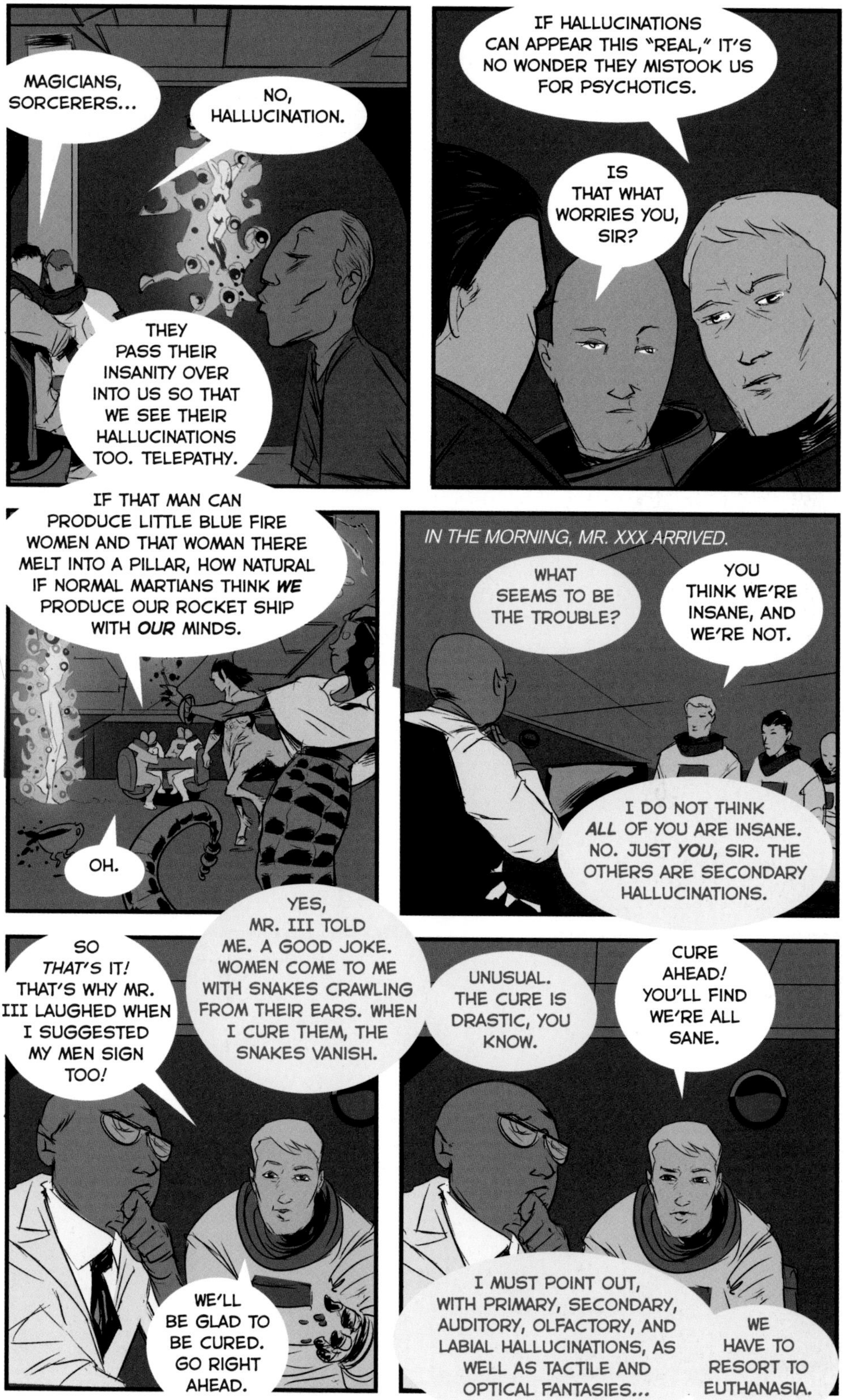
MAGICIANS, SORCERERS...
NO, HALLUCINATION.
THEY PASS THEIR INSANITY OVER INTO US SO THAT WE SEE THEIR HALLUCINATIONS TOO. TELEPATHY.
IF HALLUCINATIONS CAN APPEAR THIS "REAL," IT'S NO WONDER THEY MISTOOK US FOR PSYCHOTICS.
IS THAT WHAT WORRIES YOU, SIR?
IF THAT MAN CAN PRODUCE LITTLE BLUE FIRE WOMEN AND THAT WOMAN THERE MELT INTO A PILLAR, HOW NATURAL IF NORMAL MARTIANS THINK *WE* PRODUCE OUR ROCKET SHIP WITH *OUR* MINDS.
OH.
IN THE MORNING, MR. XXX ARRIVED.
WHAT SEEMS TO BE THE TROUBLE?
YOU THINK WE'RE INSANE, AND WE'RE NOT.
I DO NOT THINK *ALL* OF YOU ARE INSANE. NO. JUST *YOU*, SIR. THE OTHERS ARE SECONDARY HALLUCINATIONS.
SO *THAT'S* IT! THAT'S WHY MR. III LAUGHED WHEN I SUGGESTED MY MEN SIGN TOO!
YES, MR. III TOLD ME. A GOOD JOKE. WOMEN COME TO ME WITH SNAKES CRAWLING FROM THEIR EARS. WHEN I CURE THEM, THE SNAKES VANISH.
WE'LL BE GLAD TO BE CURED. GO RIGHT AHEAD.
UNUSUAL. THE CURE IS DRASTIC, YOU KNOW.
CURE AHEAD! YOU'LL FIND WE'RE ALL SANE.
I MUST POINT OUT, WITH PRIMARY, SECONDARY, AUDITORY, OLFACTORY, AND LABIAL HALLUCINATIONS, AS WELL AS TACTILE AND OPTICAL FANTASIES...
WE HAVE TO RESORT TO EUTHANASIA.

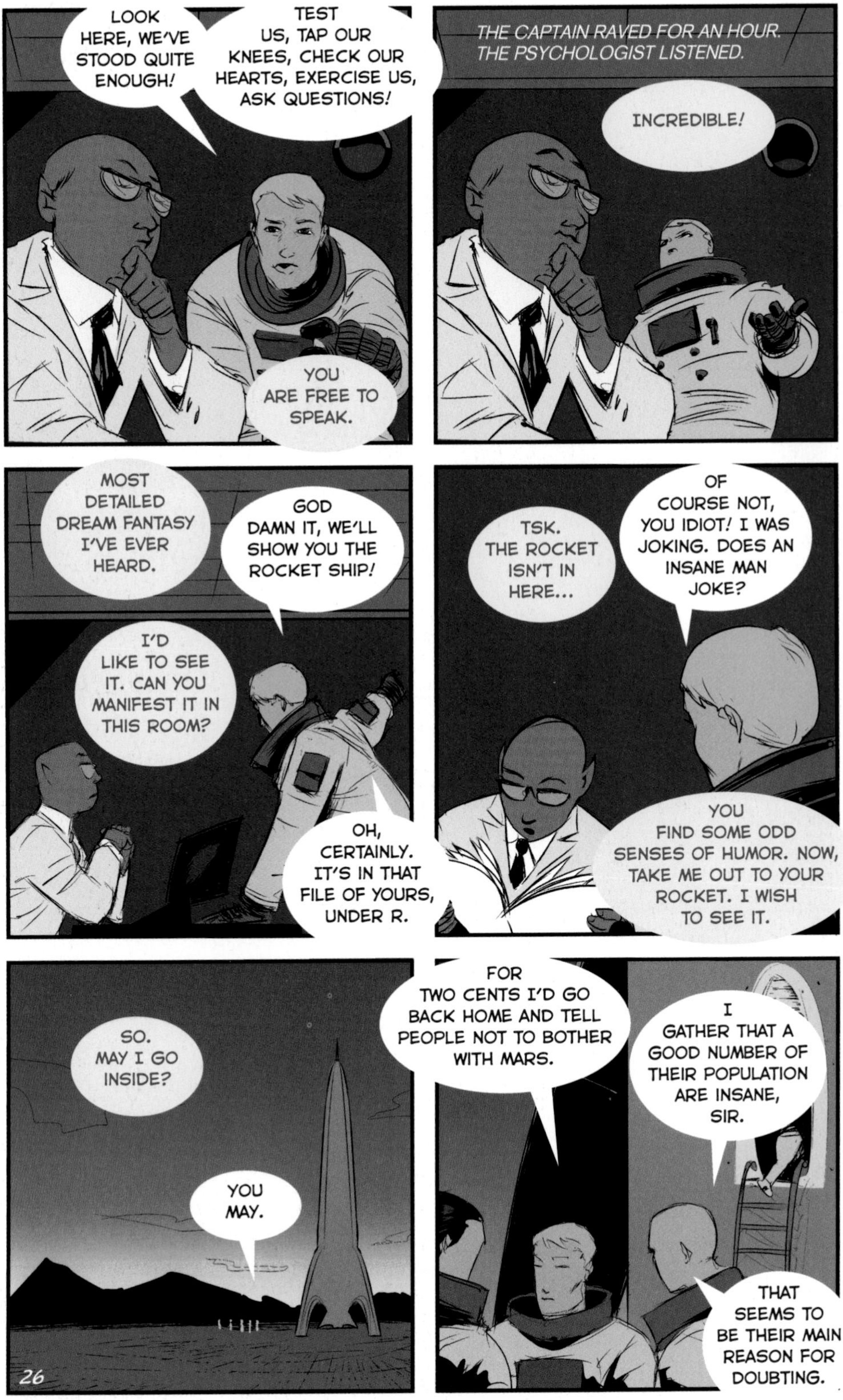
LOOK HERE, WE'VE STOOD QUITE ENOUGH!
TEST US, TAP OUR KNEES, CHECK OUR HEARTS, EXERCISE US, ASK QUESTIONS!
YOU ARE FREE TO SPEAK.
THE CAPTAIN RAVED FOR AN HOUR. THE PSYCHOLOGIST LISTENED.
INCREDIBLE!
MOST DETAILED DREAM FANTASY I'VE EVER HEARD.
GOD DAMN IT, WE'LL SHOW YOU THE ROCKET SHIP!
I'D LIKE TO SEE IT. CAN YOU MANIFEST IT IN THIS ROOM?
OH, CERTAINLY. IT'S IN THAT FILE OF YOURS, UNDER R.
TSK. THE ROCKET ISN'T IN HERE...
OF COURSE NOT, YOU IDIOT! I WAS JOKING. DOES AN INSANE MAN JOKE?
YOU FIND SOME ODD SENSES OF HUMOR. NOW, TAKE ME OUT TO YOUR ROCKET. I WISH TO SEE IT.
SO. MAY I GO INSIDE?
YOU MAY.
FOR TWO CENTS I'D GO BACK HOME AND TELL PEOPLE NOT TO BOTHER WITH MARS.
I GATHER THAT A GOOD NUMBER OF THEIR POPULATION ARE INSANE, SIR.
THAT SEEMS TO BE THEIR MAIN REASON FOR DOUBTING.

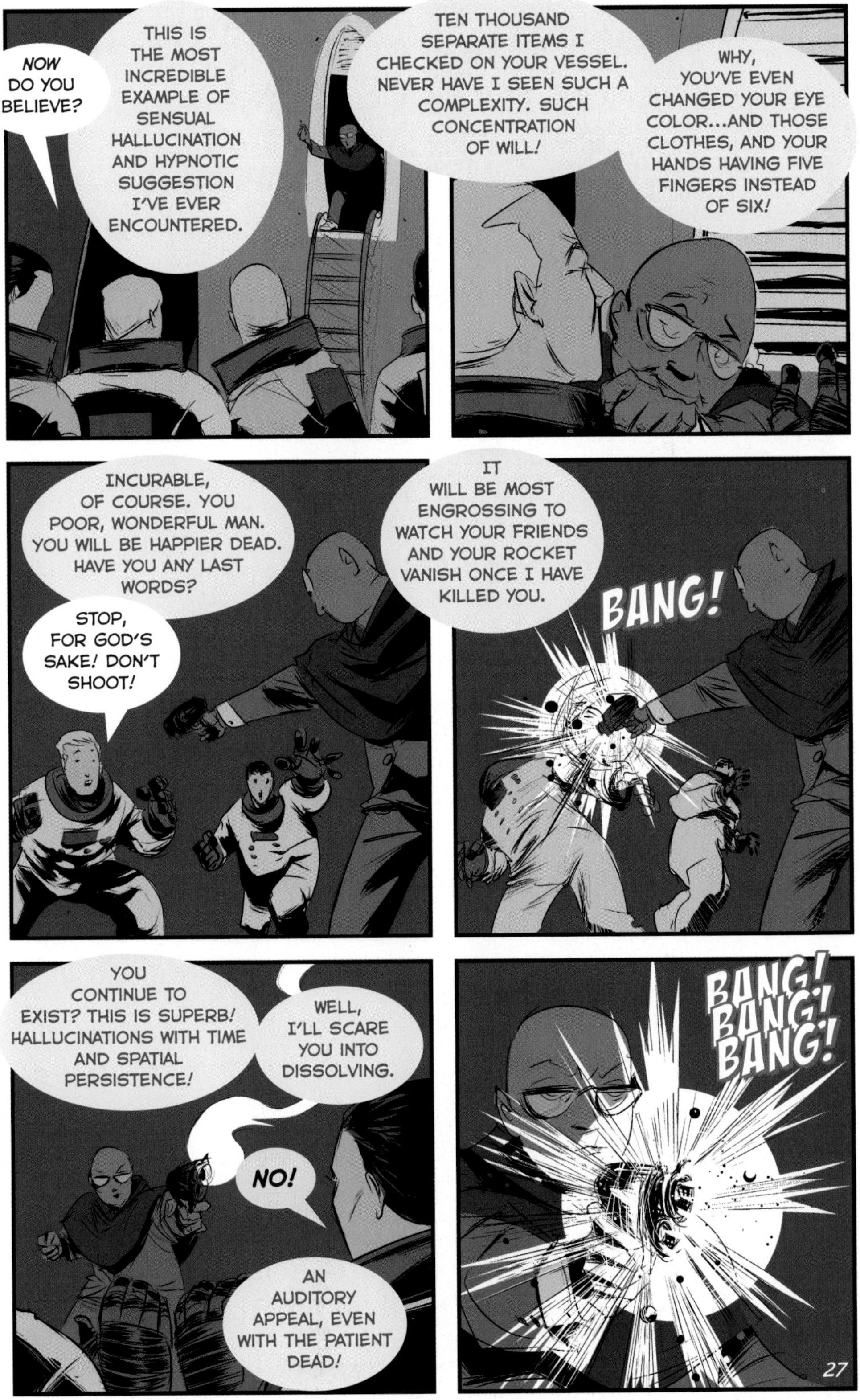
NOW DO YOU BELIEVE?
THIS IS THE MOST INCREDIBLE EXAMPLE OF SENSUAL HALLUCINATION AND HYPNOTIC SUGGESTION I'VE EVER ENCOUNTERED.
TEN THOUSAND SEPARATE ITEMS I CHECKED ON YOUR VESSEL. NEVER HAVE I SEEN SUCH A COMPLEXITY. SUCH CONCENTRATION OF WILL!
WHY, YOU'VE EVEN CHANGED YOUR EYE COLOR...AND THOSE CLOTHES, AND YOUR HANDS HAVING FIVE FINGERS INSTEAD OF SIX!
INCURABLE, OF COURSE. YOU POOR, WONDERFUL MAN. YOU WILL BE HAPPIER DEAD. HAVE YOU ANY LAST WORDS?
STOP, FOR GOD'S SAKE! DON'T SHOOT!
IT WILL BE MOST ENGROSSING TO WATCH YOUR FRIENDS AND YOUR ROCKET VANISH ONCE I HAVE KILLED YOU.
BANG!
YOU CONTINUE TO EXIST? THIS IS SUPERB! HALLUCINATIONS WITH TIME AND SPATIAL PERSISTENCE!
WELL, I'LL SCARE YOU INTO DISSOLVING.
NO!
AN AUDITORY APPEAL, EVEN WITH THE PATIENT DEAD!
BANG! BANG! BANG!

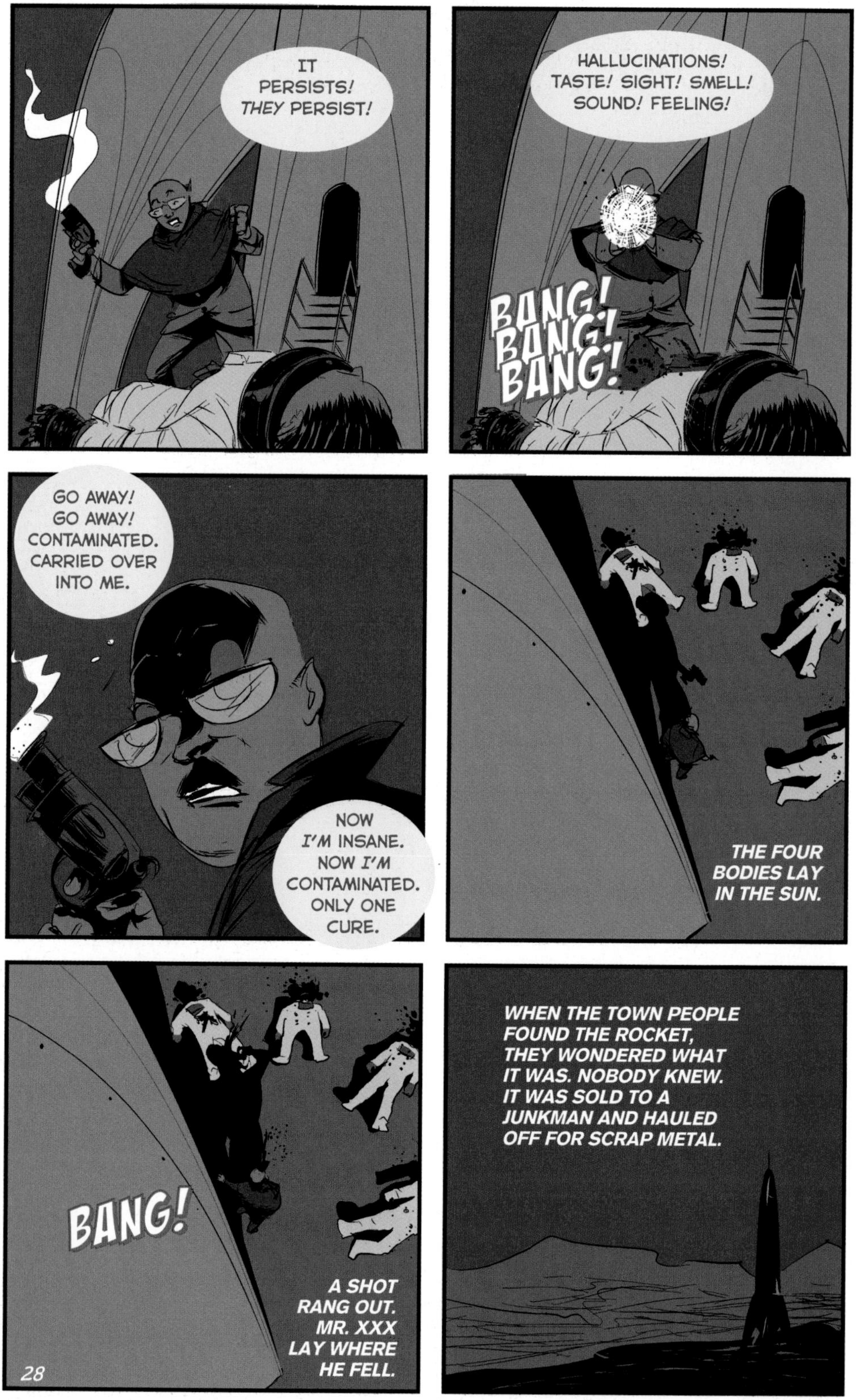
IT PERSISTS! THEY PERSIST!
HALLUCINATIONS! TASTE! SIGHT! SMELL! SOUND! FEELING!
BANG! BANG! BANG!
GO AWAY! GO AWAY! CONTAMINATED. CARRIED OVER INTO ME.
NOW I'M INSANE. NOW I'M CONTAMINATED. ONLY ONE CURE.
THE FOUR BODIES LAY IN THE SUN.
BANG!
A SHOT RANG OUT. MR. XXX LAY WHERE HE FELL.
WHEN THE TOWN PEOPLE FOUND THE ROCKET, THEY WONDERED WHAT IT WAS. NOBODY KNEW. IT WAS SOLD TO A JUNKMAN AND HAULED OFF FOR SCRAP METAL.

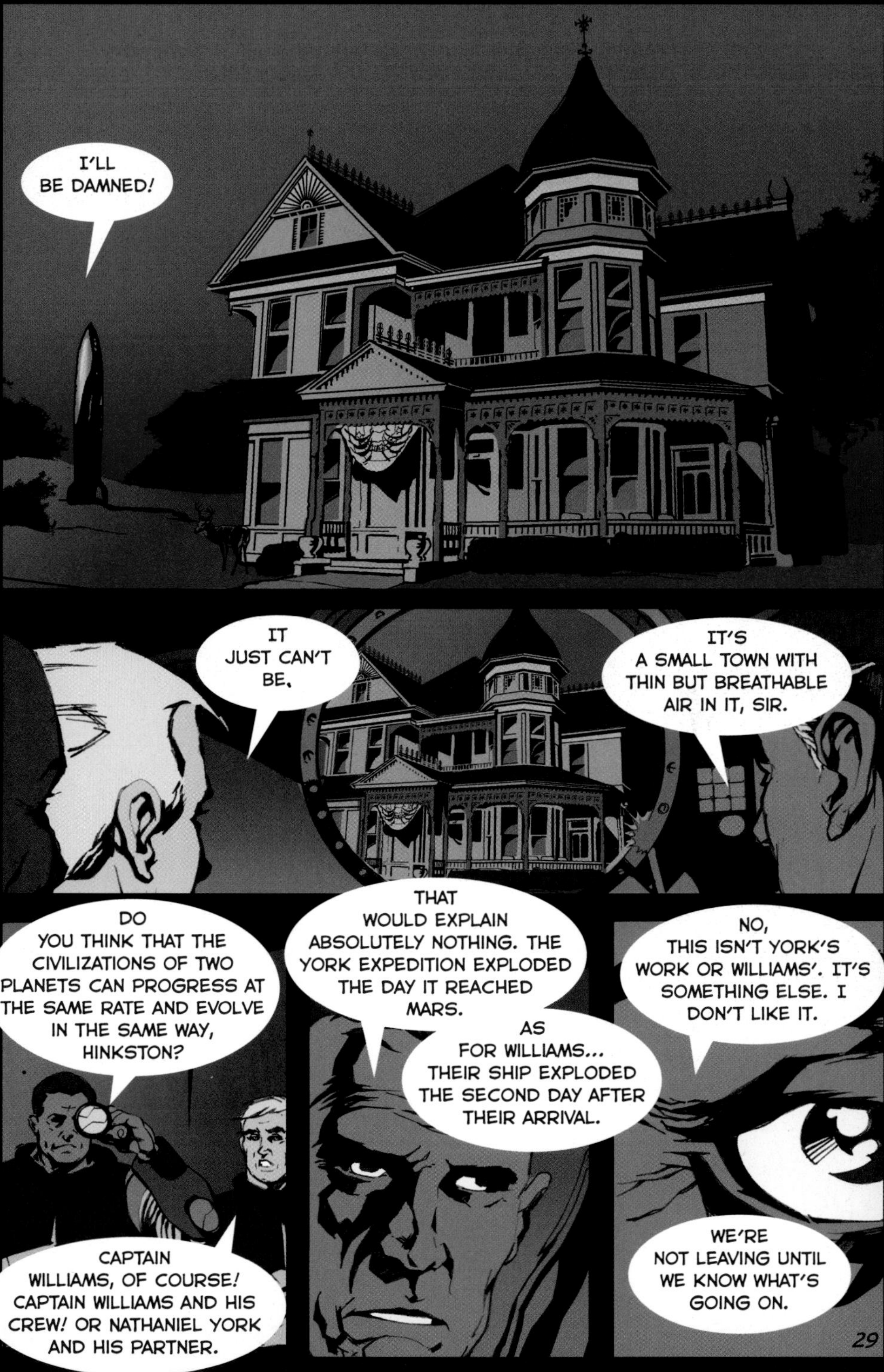
I'LL BE DAMNED!
IT JUST CAN'T BE.
IT'S A SMALL TOWN WITH THIN BUT BREATHABLE AIR IN IT, SIR.
DO YOU THINK THAT THE CIVILIZATIONS OF TWO PLANETS CAN PROGRESS AT THE SAME RATE AND EVOLVE IN THE SAME WAY, HINKSTON?
CAPTAIN WILLIAMS, OF COURSE! CAPTAIN WILLIAMS AND HIS CREW! OR NATHANIEL YORK AND HIS PARTNER.
THAT WOULD EXPLAIN ABSOLUTELY NOTHING. THE YORK EXPEDITION EXPLODED THE DAY IT REACHED MARS.
AS FOR WILLIAMS... THEIR SHIP EXPLODED THE SECOND DAY AFTER THEIR ARRIVAL.
NO, THIS ISN'T YORK'S WORK OR WILLIAMS'. IT'S SOMETHING ELSE. I DON'T LIKE IT.
WE'RE NOT LEAVING UNTIL WE KNOW WHAT'S GOING ON.

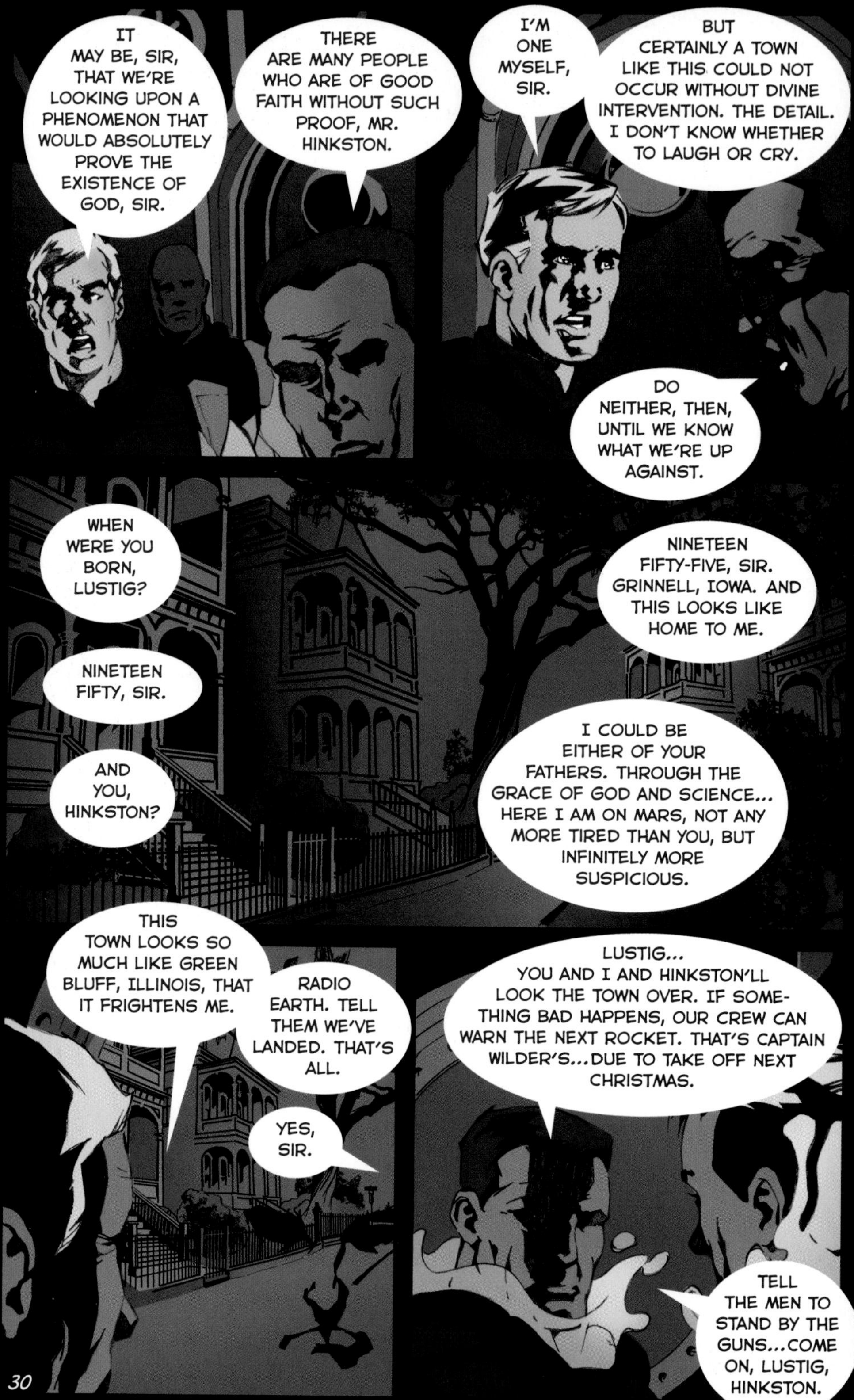
IT MAY BE, SIR, THAT WE'RE LOOKING UPON A PHENOMENON THAT WOULD ABSOLUTELY PROVE THE EXISTENCE OF GOD, SIR.
THERE ARE MANY PEOPLE WHO ARE OF GOOD FAITH WITHOUT SUCH PROOF, MR. HINKSTON.
I'M ONE MYSELF, SIR.
BUT CERTAINLY A TOWN LIKE THIS COULD NOT OCCUR WITHOUT DIVINE INTERVENTION. THE DETAIL. I DON'T KNOW WHETHER TO LAUGH OR CRY.
DO NEITHER, THEN, UNTIL WE KNOW WHAT WE'RE UP AGAINST.
WHEN WERE YOU BORN, LUSTIG?
NINETEEN FIFTY-FIVE, SIR. GRINNELL, IOWA. AND THIS LOOKS LIKE HOME TO ME.
NINETEEN FIFTY, SIR.
AND YOU, HINKSTON?
I COULD BE EITHER OF YOUR FATHERS. THROUGH THE GRACE OF GOD AND SCIENCE... HERE I AM ON MARS, NOT ANY MORE TIRED THAN YOU, BUT INFINITELY MORE SUSPICIOUS.
THIS TOWN LOOKS SO MUCH LIKE GREEN BLUFF, ILLINOIS, THAT IT FRIGHTENS ME.
RADIO EARTH. TELL THEM WE'VE LANDED. THAT'S ALL.
YES, SIR.
LUSTIG... YOU AND I AND HINKSTON'LL LOOK THE TOWN OVER. IF SOMETHING BAD HAPPENS, OUR CREW CAN WARN THE NEXT ROCKET. THAT'S CAPTAIN WILDER'S...DUE TO TAKE OFF NEXT CHRISTMAS.
TELL THE MEN TO STAND BY THE GUNS...COME ON, LUSTIG, HINKSTON.

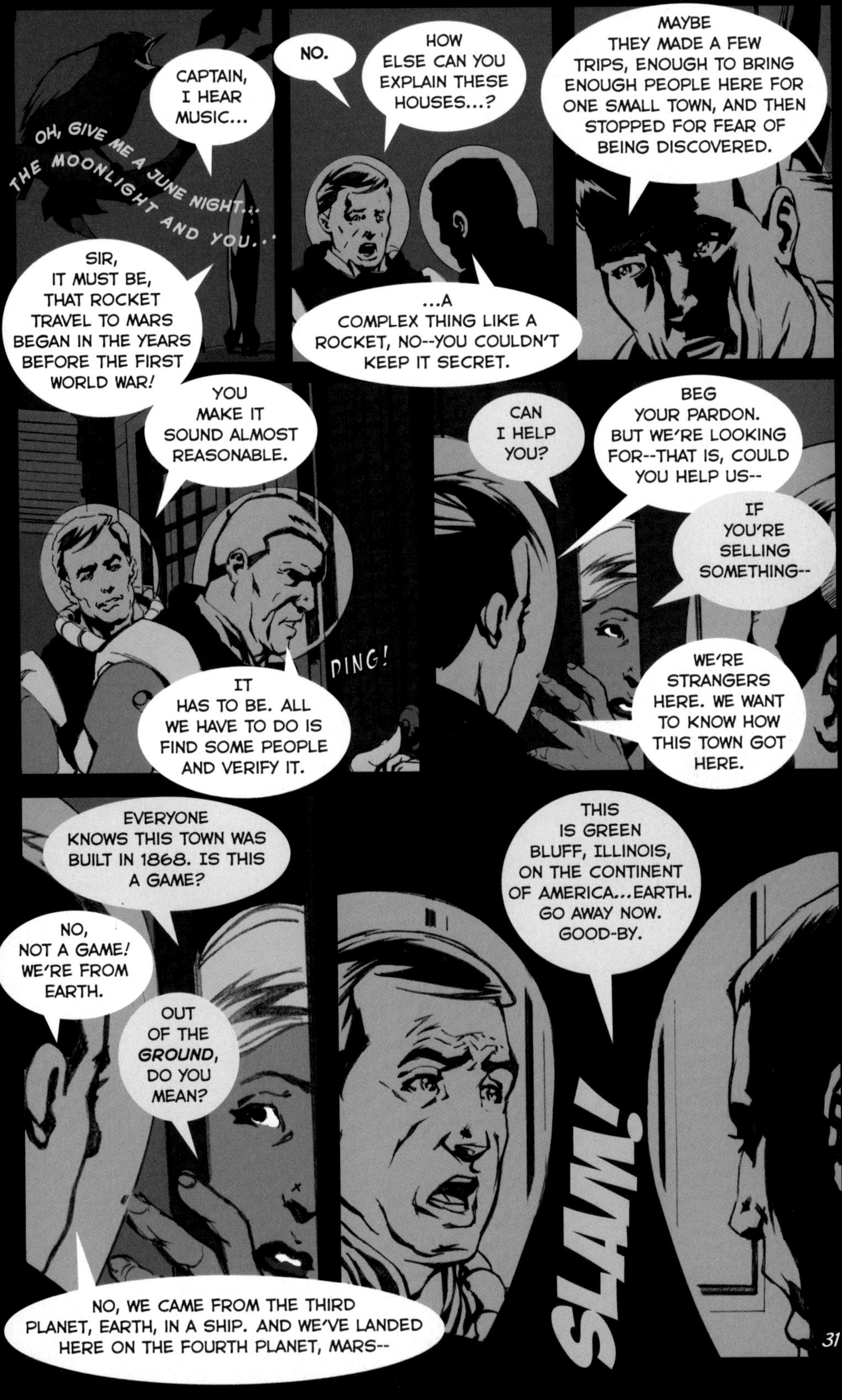
CAPTAIN, I HEAR MUSIC...
OH, GIVE ME A JUNE NIGHT... THE MOONLIGHT AND YOU...
SIR, IT MUST BE, THAT ROCKET TRAVEL TO MARS BEGAN IN THE YEARS BEFORE THE FIRST WORLD WAR!
NO.
HOW ELSE CAN YOU EXPLAIN THESE HOUSES...?
...A COMPLEX THING LIKE A ROCKET, NO--YOU COULDN'T KEEP IT SECRET.
MAYBE THEY MADE A FEW TRIPS, ENOUGH TO BRING ENOUGH PEOPLE HERE FOR ONE SMALL TOWN, AND THEN STOPPED FOR FEAR OF BEING DISCOVERED.
YOU MAKE IT SOUND ALMOST REASONABLE.
IT HAS TO BE. ALL WE HAVE TO DO IS FIND SOME PEOPLE AND VERIFY IT.
DING!
CAN I HELP YOU?
BEG YOUR PARDON. BUT WE'RE LOOKING FOR--THAT IS, COULD YOU HELP US--
IF YOU'RE SELLING SOMETHING--
WE'RE STRANGERS HERE. WE WANT TO KNOW HOW THIS TOWN GOT HERE.
EVERYONE KNOWS THIS TOWN WAS BUILT IN 1868. IS THIS A GAME?
NO, NOT A GAME! WE'RE FROM EARTH.
OUT OF THE GROUND, DO YOU MEAN?
NO, WE CAME FROM THE THIRD PLANET, EARTH, IN A SHIP. AND WE'VE LANDED HERE ON THE FOURTH PLANET, MARS--
THIS IS GREEN BLUFF, ILLINOIS, ON THE CONTINENT OF AMERICA...EARTH. GO AWAY NOW. GOOD-BY.
SLAM!

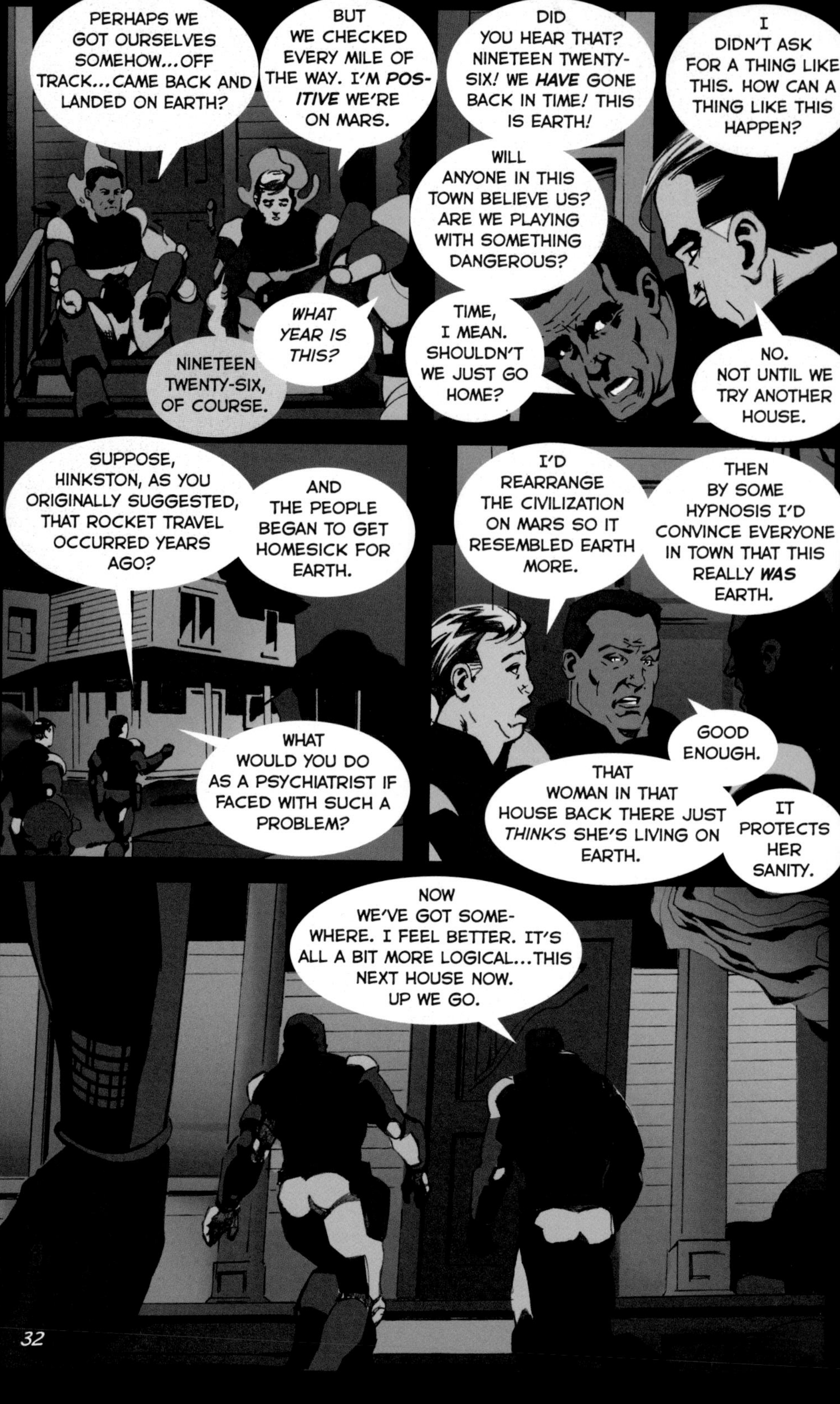
PERHAPS WE GOT OURSELVES SOMEHOW...OFF TRACK...CAME BACK AND LANDED ON EARTH?
BUT WE CHECKED EVERY MILE OF THE WAY. I'M *POSITIVE* WE'RE ON MARS.
WHAT YEAR IS THIS?
NINETEEN TWENTY-SIX, OF COURSE.
DID YOU HEAR THAT? NINETEEN TWENTY-SIX! WE *HAVE* GONE BACK IN TIME! THIS IS EARTH!
I DIDN'T ASK FOR A THING LIKE THIS. HOW CAN A THING LIKE THIS HAPPEN?
WILL ANYONE IN THIS TOWN BELIEVE US? ARE WE PLAYING WITH SOMETHING DANGEROUS?
TIME, I MEAN. SHOULDN'T WE JUST GO HOME?
NO. NOT UNTIL WE TRY ANOTHER HOUSE.
SUPPOSE, HINKSTON, AS YOU ORIGINALLY SUGGESTED, THAT ROCKET TRAVEL OCCURRED YEARS AGO?
AND THE PEOPLE BEGAN TO GET HOMESICK FOR EARTH.
WHAT WOULD YOU DO AS A PSYCHIATRIST IF FACED WITH SUCH A PROBLEM?
I'D REARRANGE THE CIVILIZATION ON MARS SO IT RESEMBLED EARTH MORE.
THEN BY SOME HYPNOSIS I'D CONVINCE EVERYONE IN TOWN THAT THIS REALLY **WAS** EARTH.
GOOD ENOUGH.
THAT WOMAN IN THAT HOUSE BACK THERE JUST *THINKS* SHE'S LIVING ON EARTH.
IT PROTECTS HER SANITY.
NOW WE'VE GOT SOMEWHERE. I FEEL BETTER. IT'S ALL A BIT MORE LOGICAL...THIS NEXT HOUSE NOW. UP WE GO.

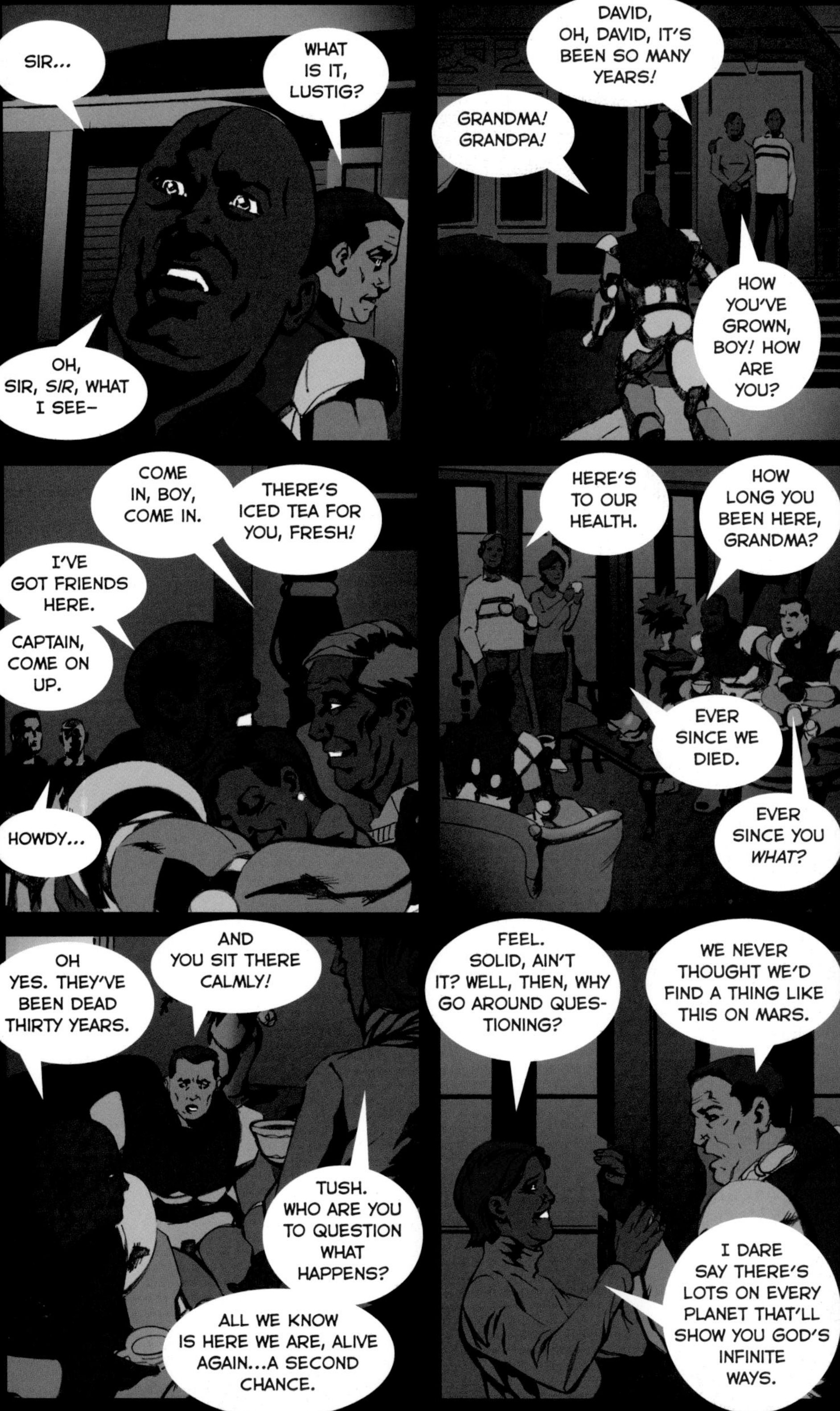
SIR...
WHAT IS IT, LUSTIG?
OH, SIR, *SIR*, WHAT I SEE–
DAVID, OH, DAVID, IT'S BEEN SO MANY YEARS!
GRANDMA! GRANDPA!
HOW YOU'VE GROWN, BOY! HOW ARE YOU?
COME IN, BOY, COME IN.
THERE'S ICED TEA FOR YOU, FRESH!
I'VE GOT FRIENDS HERE.
CAPTAIN, COME ON UP.
HOWDY...
HERE'S TO OUR HEALTH.
HOW LONG YOU BEEN HERE, GRANDMA?
EVER SINCE WE DIED.
EVER SINCE YOU *WHAT?*
OH YES. THEY'VE BEEN DEAD THIRTY YEARS.
AND YOU SIT THERE CALMLY!
TUSH. WHO ARE YOU TO QUESTION WHAT HAPPENS?
ALL WE KNOW IS HERE WE ARE, ALIVE AGAIN...A SECOND CHANCE.
FEEL. SOLID, AIN'T IT? WELL, THEN, WHY GO AROUND QUES-TIONING?
WE NEVER THOUGHT WE'D FIND A THING LIKE THIS ON MARS.
I DARE SAY THERE'S LOTS ON EVERY PLANET THAT'LL SHOW YOU GOD'S INFINITE WAYS.

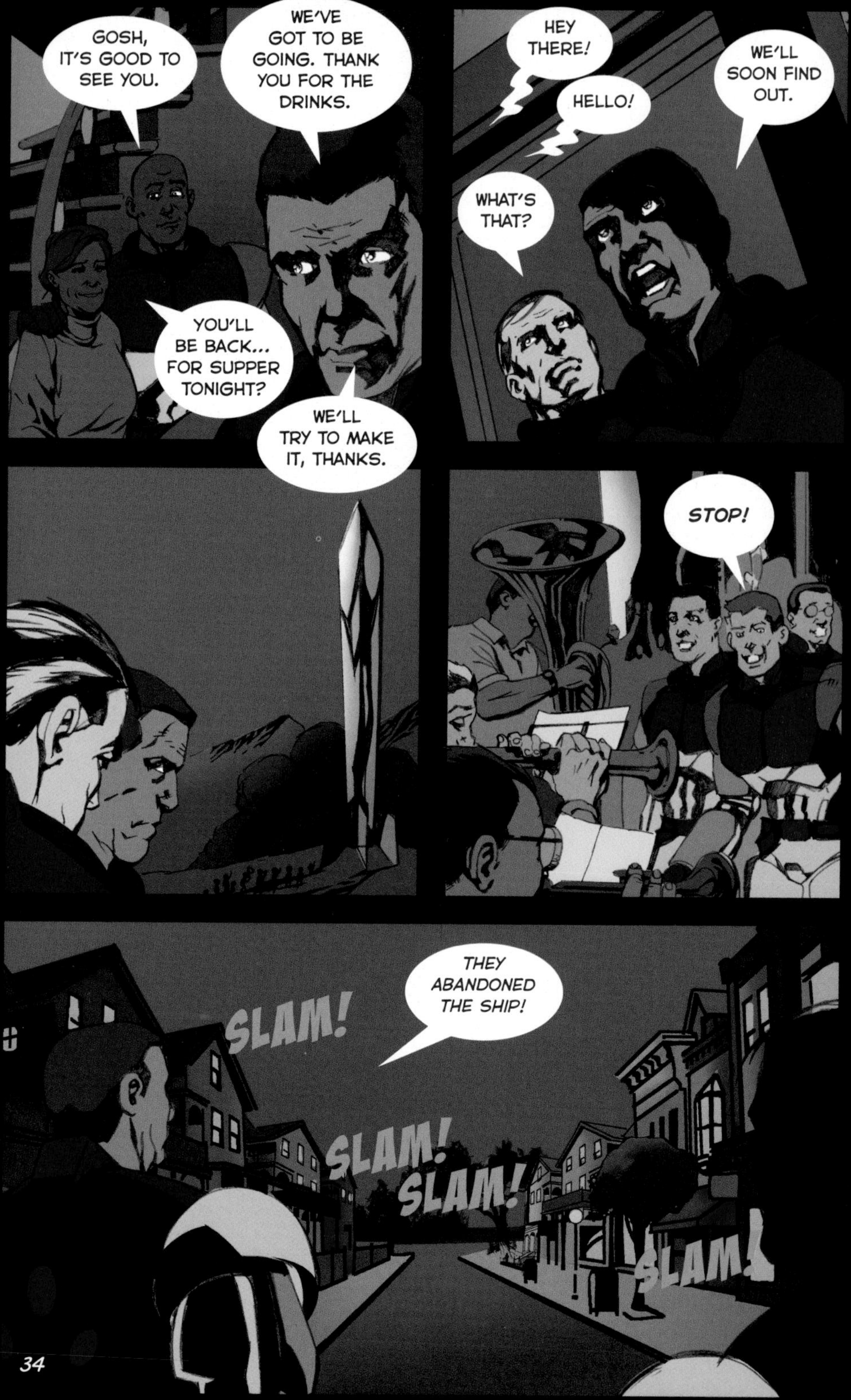
GOSH, IT'S GOOD TO SEE YOU.
WE'VE GOT TO BE GOING. THANK YOU FOR THE DRINKS.
YOU'LL BE BACK... FOR SUPPER TONIGHT?
WE'LL TRY TO MAKE IT, THANKS.
HEY THERE!
HELLO!
WHAT'S THAT?
WE'LL SOON FIND OUT.
STOP!
SLAM!
THEY ABANDONED THE SHIP!
SLAM!
SLAM!
SLAM!

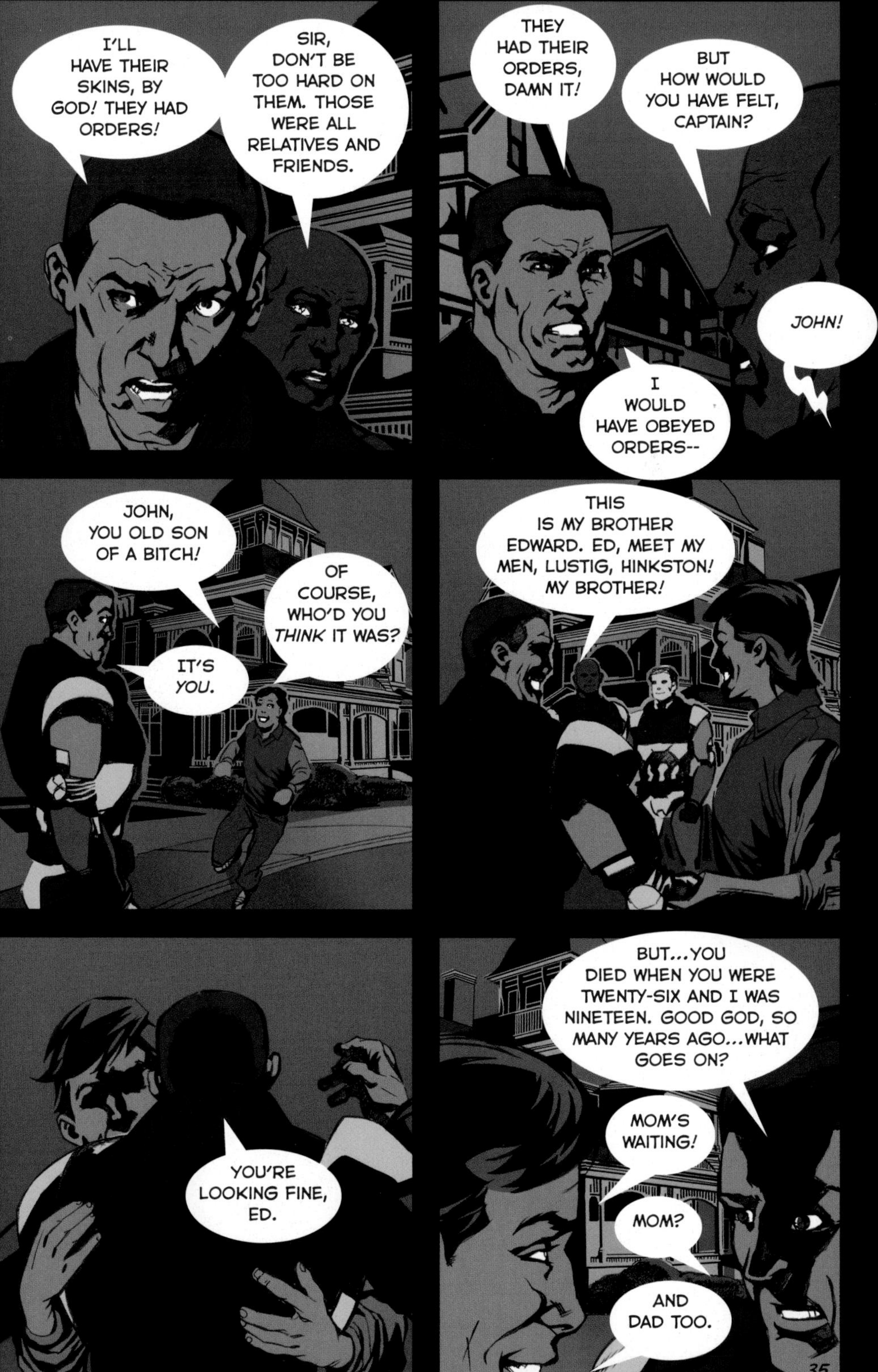
I'LL HAVE THEIR SKINS, BY GOD! THEY HAD ORDERS!
SIR, DON'T BE TOO HARD ON THEM. THOSE WERE ALL RELATIVES AND FRIENDS.
THEY HAD THEIR ORDERS, DAMN IT!
BUT HOW WOULD YOU HAVE FELT, CAPTAIN?
I WOULD HAVE OBEYED ORDERS--
JOHN!
JOHN, YOU OLD SON OF A BITCH!
IT'S *YOU*.
OF COURSE, WHO'D YOU *THINK* IT WAS?
THIS IS MY BROTHER EDWARD. ED, MEET MY MEN, LUSTIG, HINKSTON! MY BROTHER!
YOU'RE LOOKING FINE, ED.
BUT...YOU DIED WHEN YOU WERE TWENTY-SIX AND I WAS NINETEEN. GOOD GOD, SO MANY YEARS AGO...WHAT GOES ON?
MOM'S WAITING!
MOM?
AND DAD TOO.

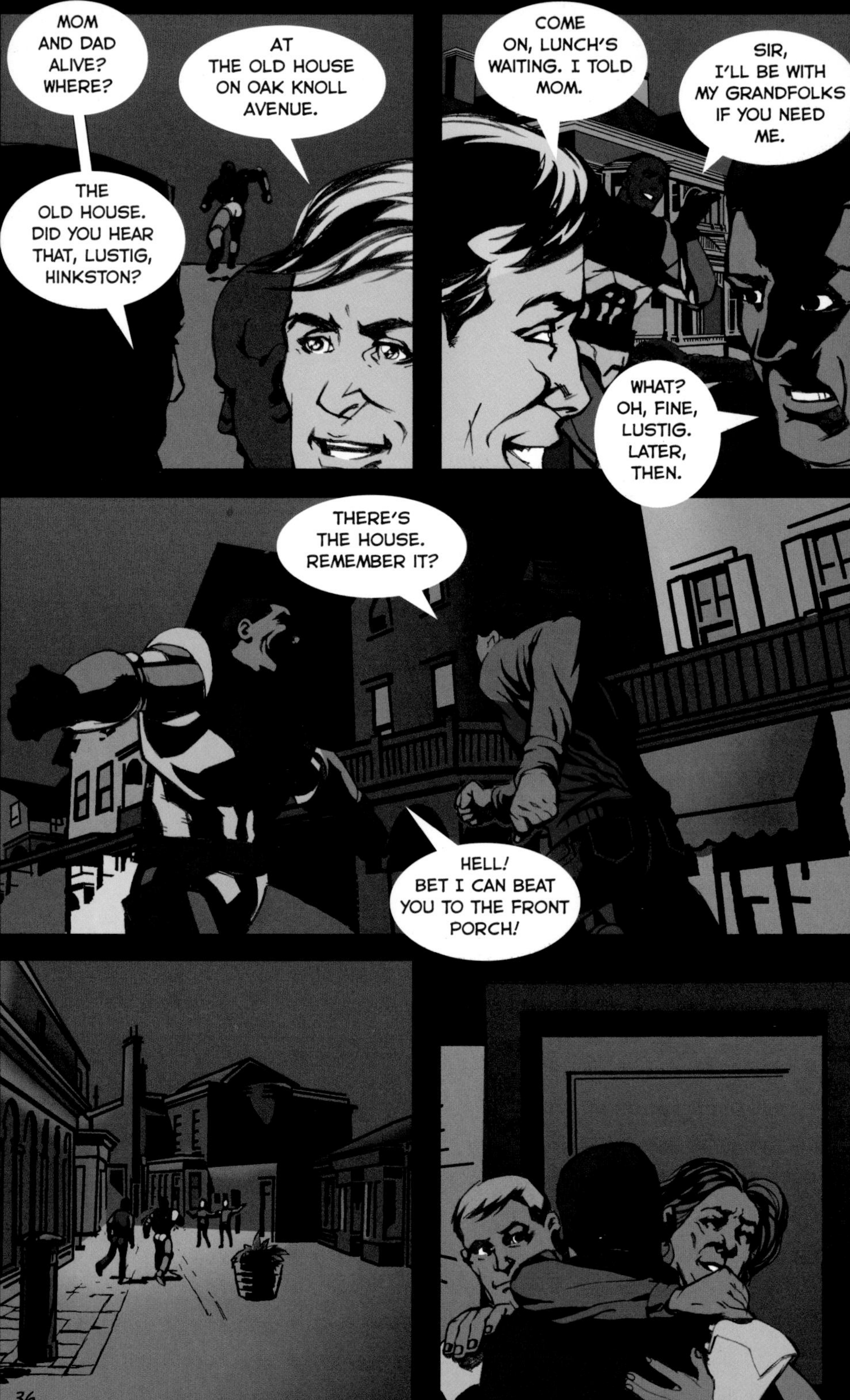
MOM AND DAD ALIVE? WHERE?
AT THE OLD HOUSE ON OAK KNOLL AVENUE.
THE OLD HOUSE. DID YOU HEAR THAT, LUSTIG, HINKSTON?
COME ON, LUNCH'S WAITING. I TOLD MOM.
SIR, I'LL BE WITH MY GRANDFOLKS IF YOU NEED ME.
WHAT? OH, FINE, LUSTIG. LATER, THEN.
THERE'S THE HOUSE. REMEMBER IT?
HELL! BET I CAN BEAT YOU TO THE FRONT PORCH!

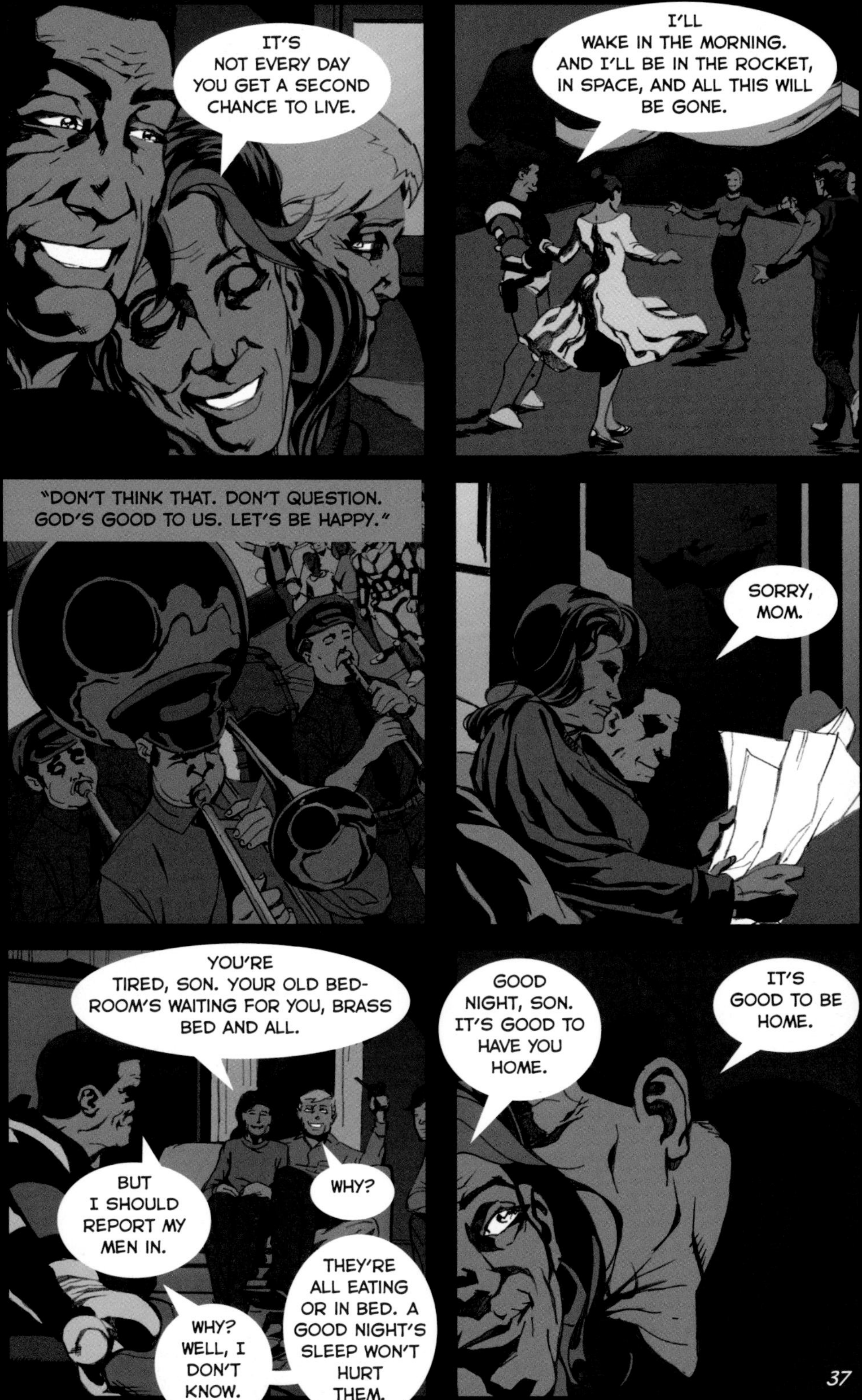
IT'S NOT EVERY DAY YOU GET A SECOND CHANCE TO LIVE.
I'LL WAKE IN THE MORNING. AND I'LL BE IN THE ROCKET, IN SPACE, AND ALL THIS WILL BE GONE.
"DON'T THINK THAT. DON'T QUESTION. GOD'S GOOD TO US. LET'S BE HAPPY."
SORRY, MOM.
YOU'RE TIRED, SON. YOUR OLD BED-ROOM'S WAITING FOR YOU, BRASS BED AND ALL.
BUT I SHOULD REPORT MY MEN IN.
WHY?
WHY? WELL, I DON'T KNOW.
THEY'RE ALL EATING OR IN BED. A GOOD NIGHT'S SLEEP WON'T HURT THEM.
GOOD NIGHT, SON. IT'S GOOD TO HAVE YOU HOME.
IT'S GOOD TO BE HOME.

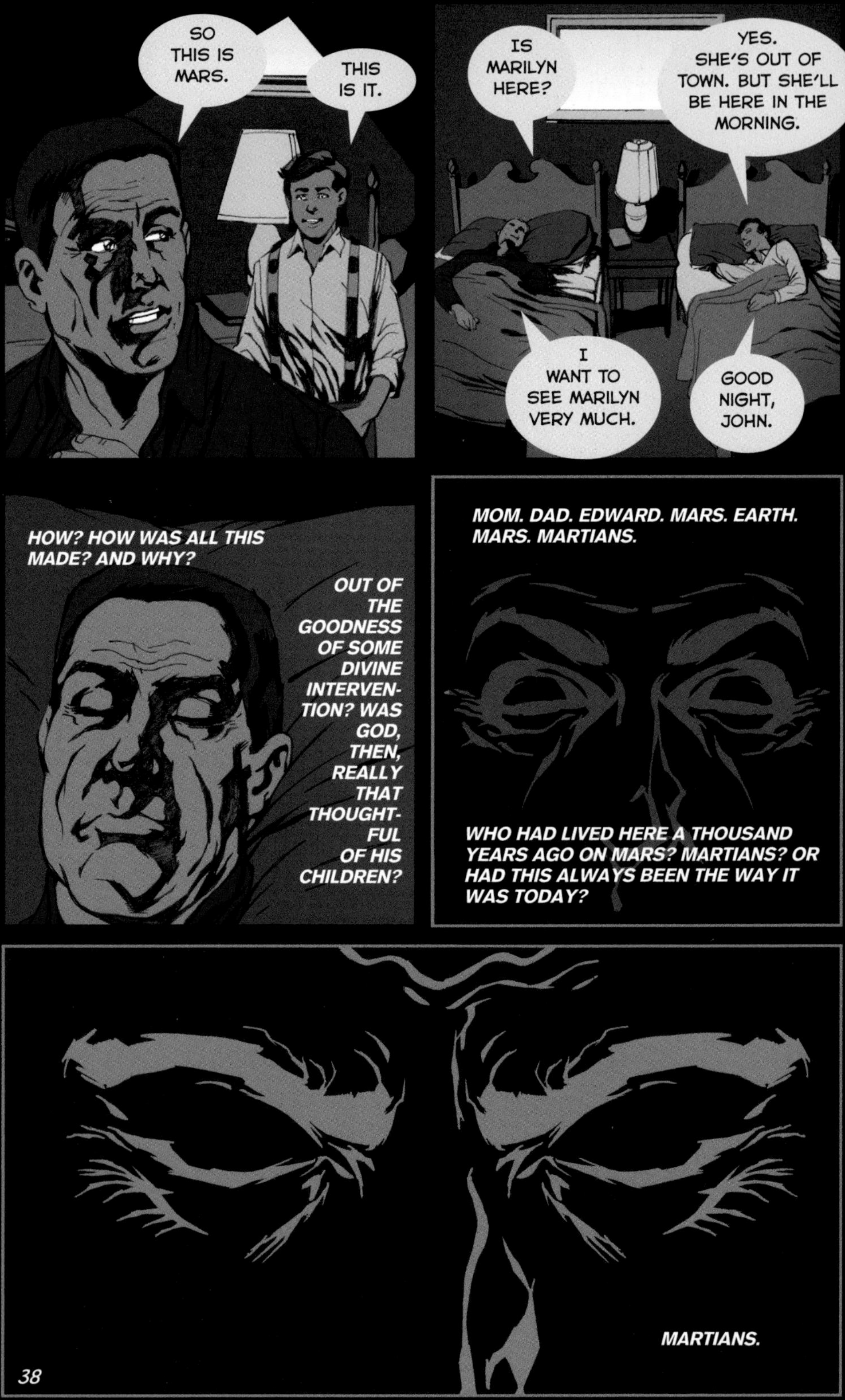
SO THIS IS MARS.
THIS IS IT.
IS MARILYN HERE?
YES. SHE'S OUT OF TOWN. BUT SHE'LL BE HERE IN THE MORNING.
I WANT TO SEE MARILYN VERY MUCH.
GOOD NIGHT, JOHN.
HOW? HOW WAS ALL THIS MADE? AND WHY?
OUT OF THE GOODNESS OF SOME DIVINE INTERVENTION? WAS GOD, THEN, REALLY THAT THOUGHTFUL OF HIS CHILDREN?
MOM. DAD. EDWARD. MARS. EARTH. MARS. MARTIANS.
WHO HAD LIVED HERE A THOUSAND YEARS AGO ON MARS? MARTIANS? OR HAD THIS ALWAYS BEEN THE WAY IT WAS TODAY?
MARTIANS.

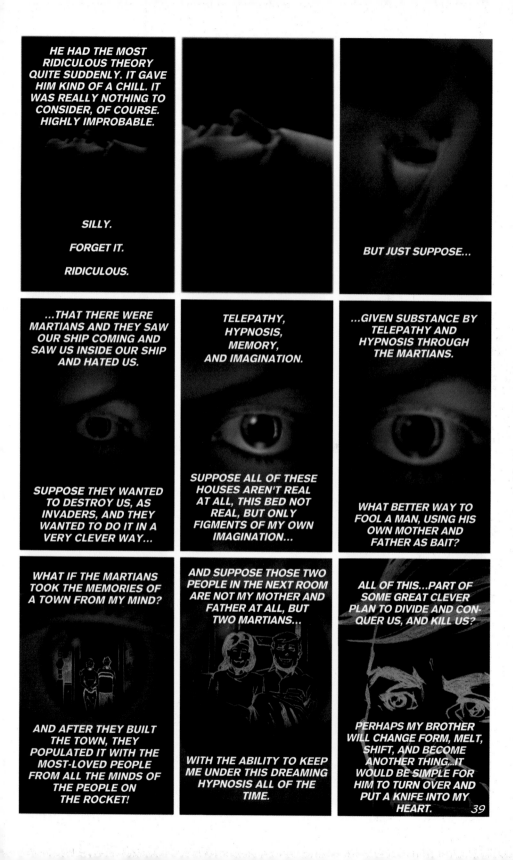

HE HAD THE MOST RIDICULOUS THEORY QUITE SUDDENLY. IT GAVE HIM KIND OF A CHILL. IT WAS REALLY NOTHING TO CONSIDER, OF COURSE. HIGHLY IMPROBABLE.

SILLY.

FORGET IT.

RIDICULOUS.

BUT JUST SUPPOSE...

...THAT THERE WERE MARTIANS AND THEY SAW OUR SHIP COMING AND SAW US INSIDE OUR SHIP AND HATED US.

SUPPOSE THEY WANTED TO DESTROY US, AS INVADERS, AND THEY WANTED TO DO IT IN A VERY CLEVER WAY...

TELEPATHY, HYPNOSIS, MEMORY, AND IMAGINATION.

SUPPOSE ALL OF THESE HOUSES AREN'T REAL AT ALL, THIS BED NOT REAL, BUT ONLY FIGMENTS OF MY OWN IMAGINATION...

...GIVEN SUBSTANCE BY TELEPATHY AND HYPNOSIS THROUGH THE MARTIANS.

WHAT BETTER WAY TO FOOL A MAN, USING HIS OWN MOTHER AND FATHER AS BAIT?

WHAT IF THE MARTIANS TOOK THE MEMORIES OF A TOWN FROM MY MIND?

AND AFTER THEY BUILT THE TOWN, THEY POPULATED IT WITH THE MOST-LOVED PEOPLE FROM ALL THE MINDS OF THE PEOPLE ON THE ROCKET!

AND SUPPOSE THOSE TWO PEOPLE IN THE NEXT ROOM ARE NOT MY MOTHER AND FATHER AT ALL, BUT TWO MARTIANS...

WITH THE ABILITY TO KEEP ME UNDER THIS DREAMING HYPNOSIS ALL OF THE TIME.

ALL OF THIS...PART OF SOME GREAT CLEVER PLAN TO DIVIDE AND CON-QUER US, AND KILL US?

PERHAPS MY BROTHER WILL CHANGE FORM, MELT, SHIFT, AND BECOME ANOTHER THING...IT WOULD BE SIMPLE FOR HIM TO TURN OVER AND PUT A KNIFE INTO MY HEART. 39

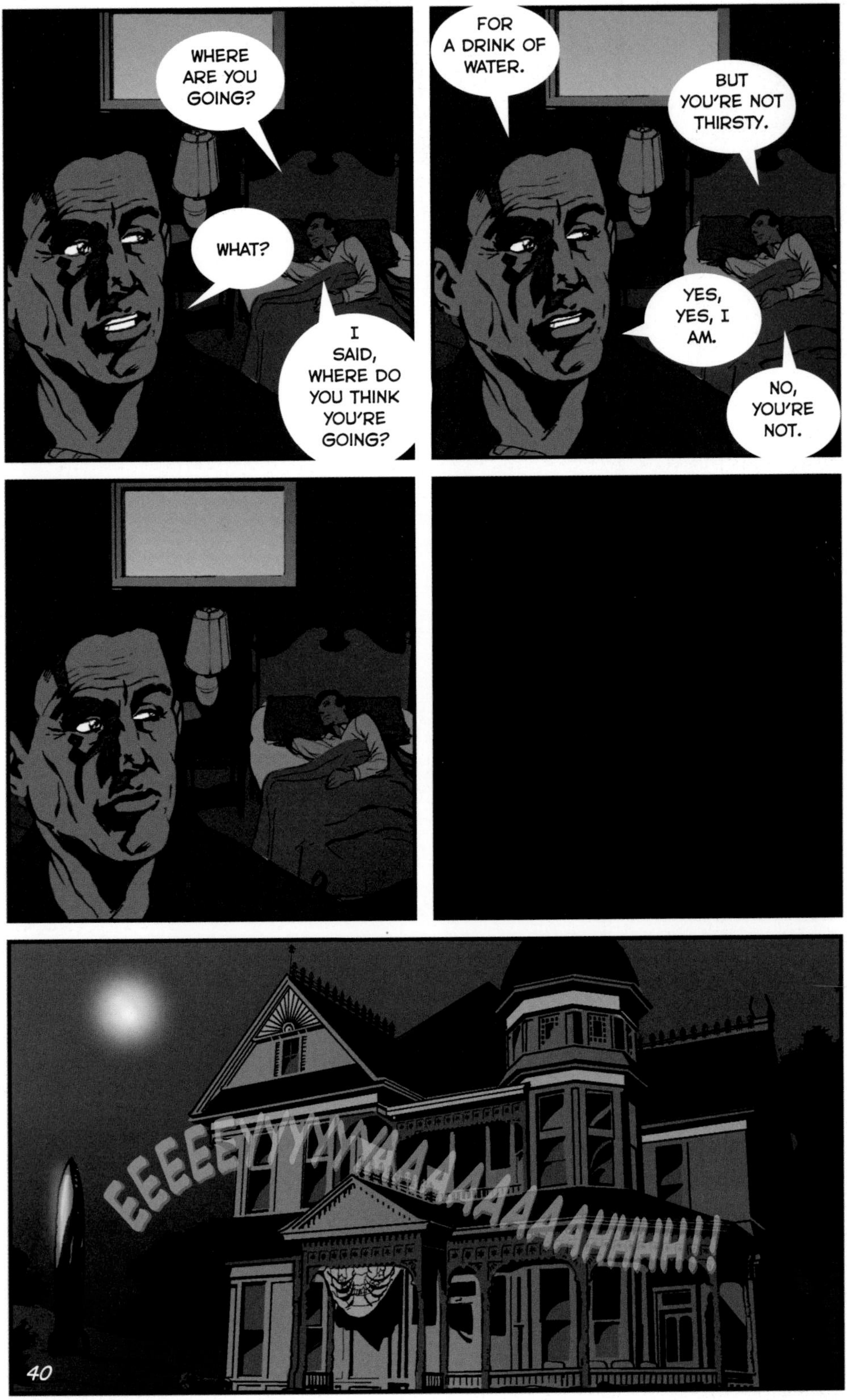

WHERE ARE YOU GOING?
WHAT?
I SAID, WHERE DO YOU THINK YOU'RE GOING?
FOR A DRINK OF WATER.
BUT YOU'RE NOT THIRSTY.
YES, YES, I AM.
NO, YOU'RE NOT.
EEEEEYYYYAAAAAAAAAAAAAHHHHH!!

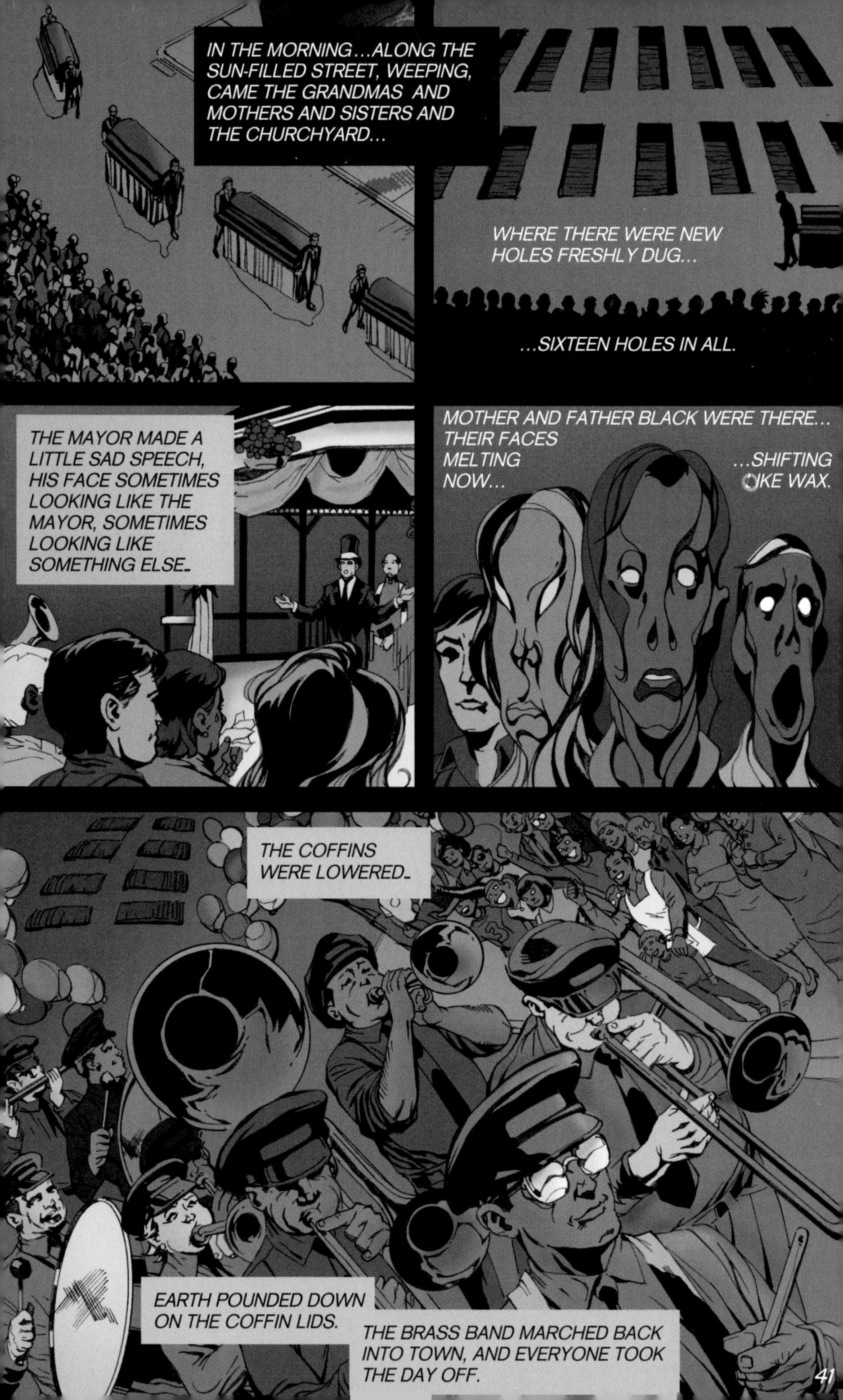
IN THE MORNING…ALONG THE SUN-FILLED STREET, WEEPING, CAME THE GRANDMAS AND MOTHERS AND SISTERS AND THE CHURCHYARD…
WHERE THERE WERE NEW HOLES FRESHLY DUG…
…SIXTEEN HOLES IN ALL.
THE MAYOR MADE A LITTLE SAD SPEECH, HIS FACE SOMETIMES LOOKING LIKE THE MAYOR, SOMETIMES LOOKING LIKE SOMETHING ELSE…
MOTHER AND FATHER BLACK WERE THERE… THEIR FACES MELTING NOW…
…SHIFTING LIKE WAX.
THE COFFINS WERE LOWERED…
EARTH POUNDED DOWN ON THE COFFIN LIDS.
THE BRASS BAND MARCHED BACK INTO TOWN, AND EVERYONE TOOK THE DAY OFF.

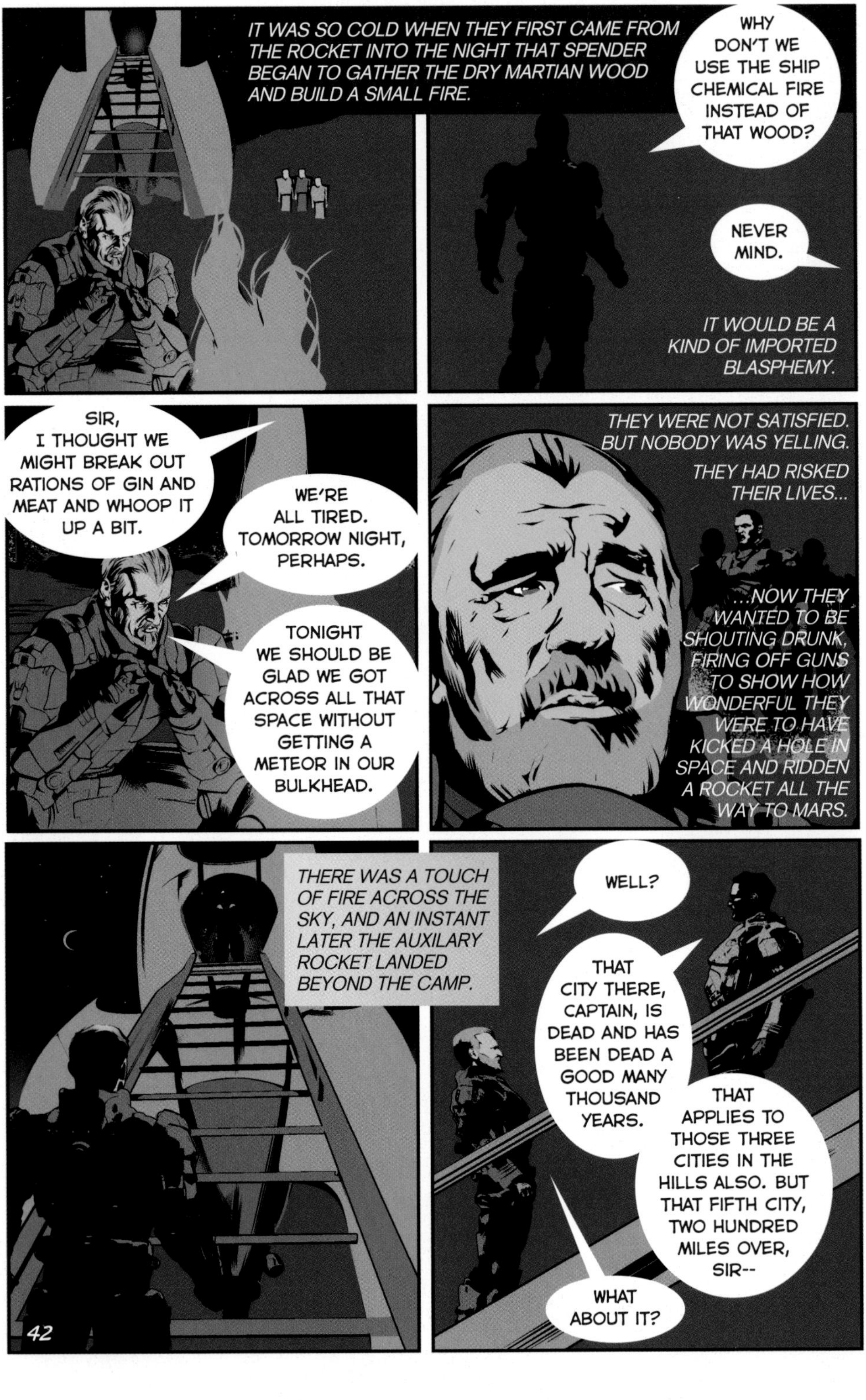
IT WAS SO COLD WHEN THEY FIRST CAME FROM THE ROCKET INTO THE NIGHT THAT SPENDER BEGAN TO GATHER THE DRY MARTIAN WOOD AND BUILD A SMALL FIRE.
WHY DON'T WE USE THE SHIP CHEMICAL FIRE INSTEAD OF THAT WOOD?
NEVER MIND.
IT WOULD BE A KIND OF IMPORTED BLASPHEMY.
SIR, I THOUGHT WE MIGHT BREAK OUT RATIONS OF GIN AND MEAT AND WHOOP IT UP A BIT.
WE'RE ALL TIRED. TOMORROW NIGHT, PERHAPS.
TONIGHT WE SHOULD BE GLAD WE GOT ACROSS ALL THAT SPACE WITHOUT GETTING A METEOR IN OUR BULKHEAD.
THEY WERE NOT SATISFIED. BUT NOBODY WAS YELLING.
THEY HAD RISKED THEIR LIVES...
...NOW THEY WANTED TO BE SHOUTING DRUNK, FIRING OFF GUNS TO SHOW HOW WONDERFUL THEY WERE TO HAVE KICKED A HOLE IN SPACE AND RIDDEN A ROCKET ALL THE WAY TO MARS.
THERE WAS A TOUCH OF FIRE ACROSS THE SKY, AND AN INSTANT LATER THE AUXILARY ROCKET LANDED BEYOND THE CAMP.
WELL?
THAT CITY THERE, CAPTAIN, IS DEAD AND HAS BEEN DEAD A GOOD MANY THOUSAND YEARS.
THAT APPLIES TO THOSE THREE CITIES IN THE HILLS ALSO. BUT THAT FIFTH CITY, TWO HUNDRED MILES OVER, SIR--
WHAT ABOUT IT?

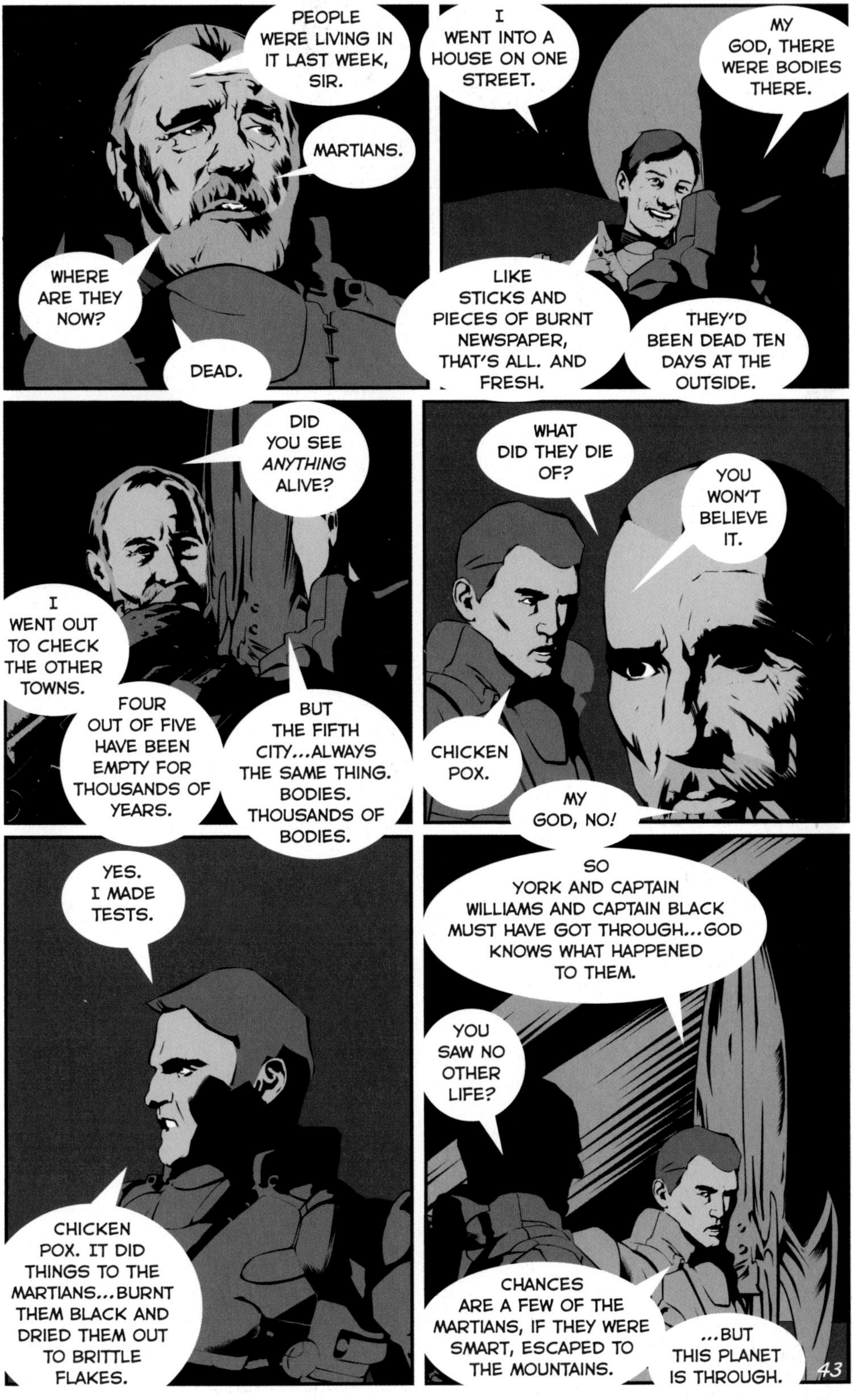
PEOPLE WERE LIVING IN IT LAST WEEK, SIR.
MARTIANS.
WHERE ARE THEY NOW?
DEAD.
I WENT INTO A HOUSE ON ONE STREET.
MY GOD, THERE WERE BODIES THERE.
LIKE STICKS AND PIECES OF BURNT NEWSPAPER, THAT'S ALL. AND FRESH.
THEY'D BEEN DEAD TEN DAYS AT THE OUTSIDE.
DID YOU SEE *ANYTHING* ALIVE?
I WENT OUT TO CHECK THE OTHER TOWNS.
FOUR OUT OF FIVE HAVE BEEN EMPTY FOR THOUSANDS OF YEARS.
BUT THE FIFTH CITY...ALWAYS THE SAME THING. BODIES. THOUSANDS OF BODIES.
WHAT DID THEY DIE OF?
YOU WON'T BELIEVE IT.
CHICKEN POX.
MY GOD, NO!
YES. I MADE TESTS.
CHICKEN POX. IT DID THINGS TO THE MARTIANS...BURNT THEM BLACK AND DRIED THEM OUT TO BRITTLE FLAKES.
SO YORK AND CAPTAIN WILLIAMS AND CAPTAIN BLACK MUST HAVE GOT THROUGH...GOD KNOWS WHAT HAPPENED TO THEM.
YOU SAW NO OTHER LIFE?
CHANCES ARE A FEW OF THE MARTIANS, IF THEY WERE SMART, ESCAPED TO THE MOUNTAINS.
...BUT THIS PLANET IS THROUGH.

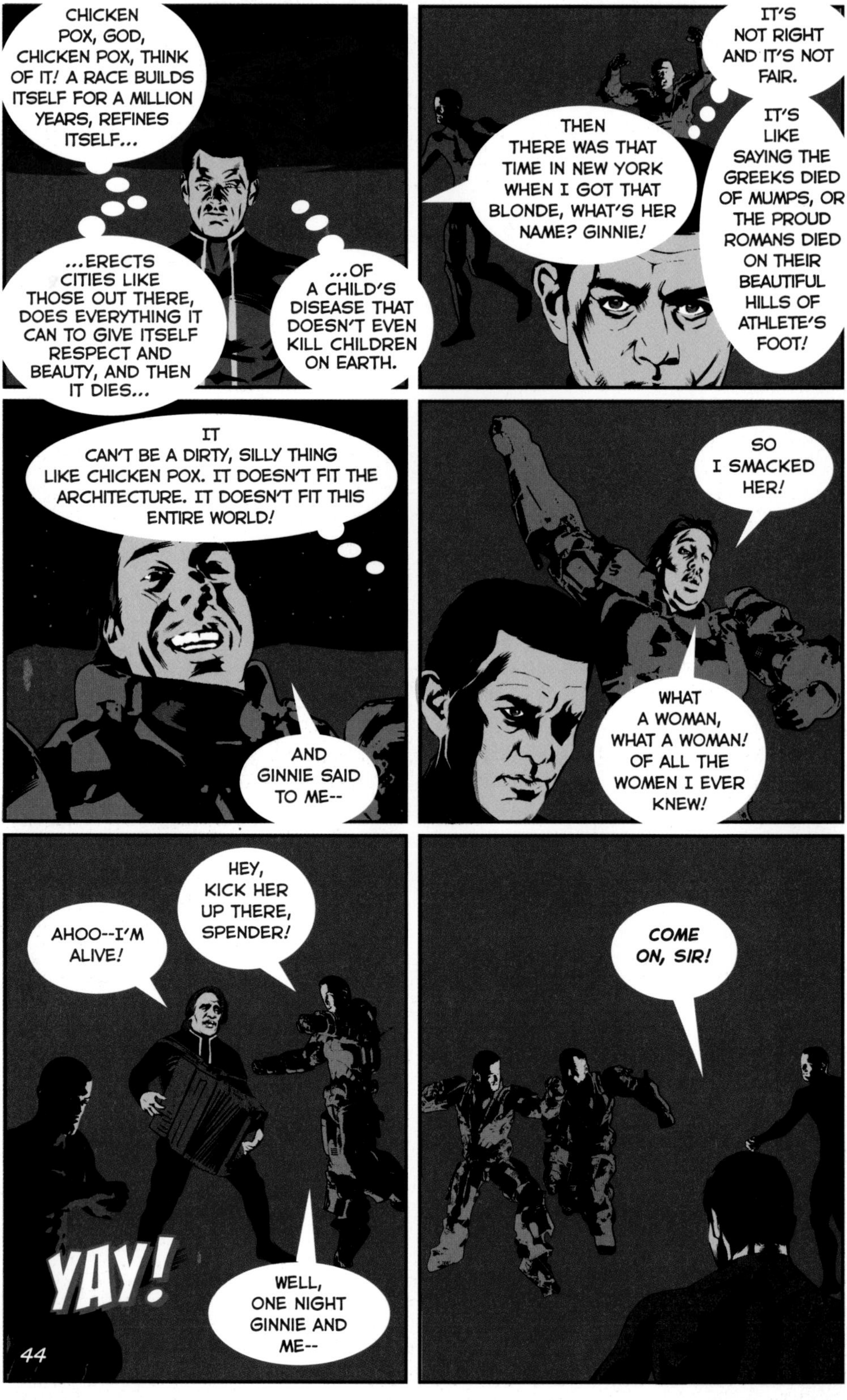
CHICKEN POX, GOD, CHICKEN POX, THINK OF IT! A RACE BUILDS ITSELF FOR A MILLION YEARS, REFINES ITSELF...
...ERECTS CITIES LIKE THOSE OUT THERE, DOES EVERYTHING IT CAN TO GIVE ITSELF RESPECT AND BEAUTY, AND THEN IT DIES...
...OF A CHILD'S DISEASE THAT DOESN'T EVEN KILL CHILDREN ON EARTH.
THEN THERE WAS THAT TIME IN NEW YORK WHEN I GOT THAT BLONDE, WHAT'S HER NAME? GINNIE!
IT'S NOT RIGHT AND IT'S NOT FAIR.
IT'S LIKE SAYING THE GREEKS DIED OF MUMPS, OR THE PROUD ROMANS DIED ON THEIR BEAUTIFUL HILLS OF ATHLETE'S FOOT!
IT CAN'T BE A DIRTY, SILLY THING LIKE CHICKEN POX. IT DOESN'T FIT THE ARCHITECTURE. IT DOESN'T FIT THIS ENTIRE WORLD!
AND GINNIE SAID TO ME--
SO I SMACKED HER!
WHAT A WOMAN, WHAT A WOMAN! OF ALL THE WOMEN I EVER KNEW!
AHOO--I'M ALIVE!
HEY, KICK HER UP THERE, SPENDER!
YAY!
WELL, ONE NIGHT GINNIE AND ME--
COME ON, SIR!

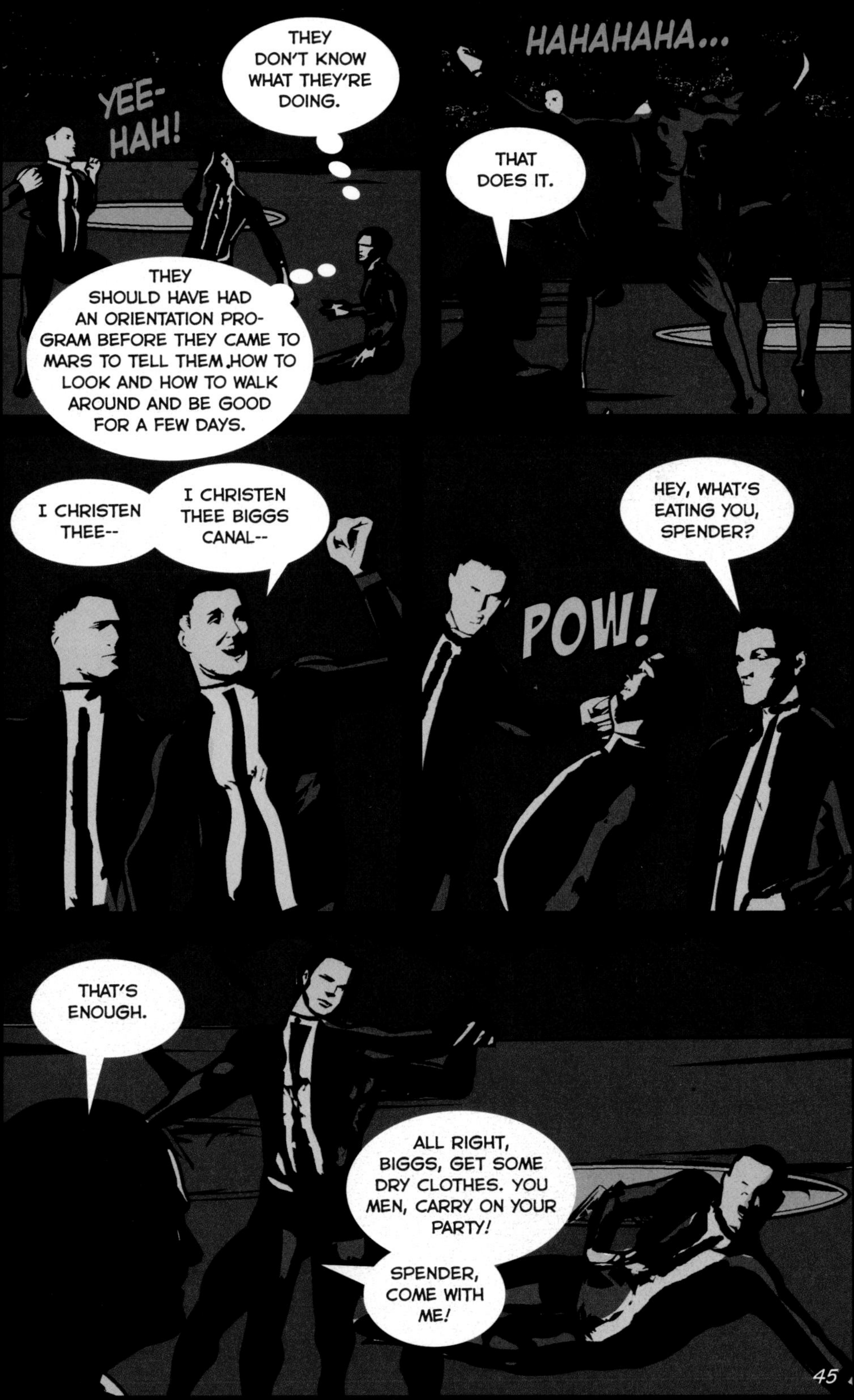
YEE-HAH!
THEY DON'T KNOW WHAT THEY'RE DOING.
THEY SHOULD HAVE HAD AN ORIENTATION PRO-GRAM BEFORE THEY CAME TO MARS TO TELL THEM HOW TO LOOK AND HOW TO WALK AROUND AND BE GOOD FOR A FEW DAYS.
HAHAHAHA...
THAT DOES IT.
I CHRISTEN THEE--
I CHRISTEN THEE BIGGS CANAL--
POW!
HEY, WHAT'S EATING YOU, SPENDER?
THAT'S ENOUGH.
ALL RIGHT, BIGGS, GET SOME DRY CLOTHES. YOU MEN, CARRY ON YOUR PARTY!
SPENDER, COME WITH ME!

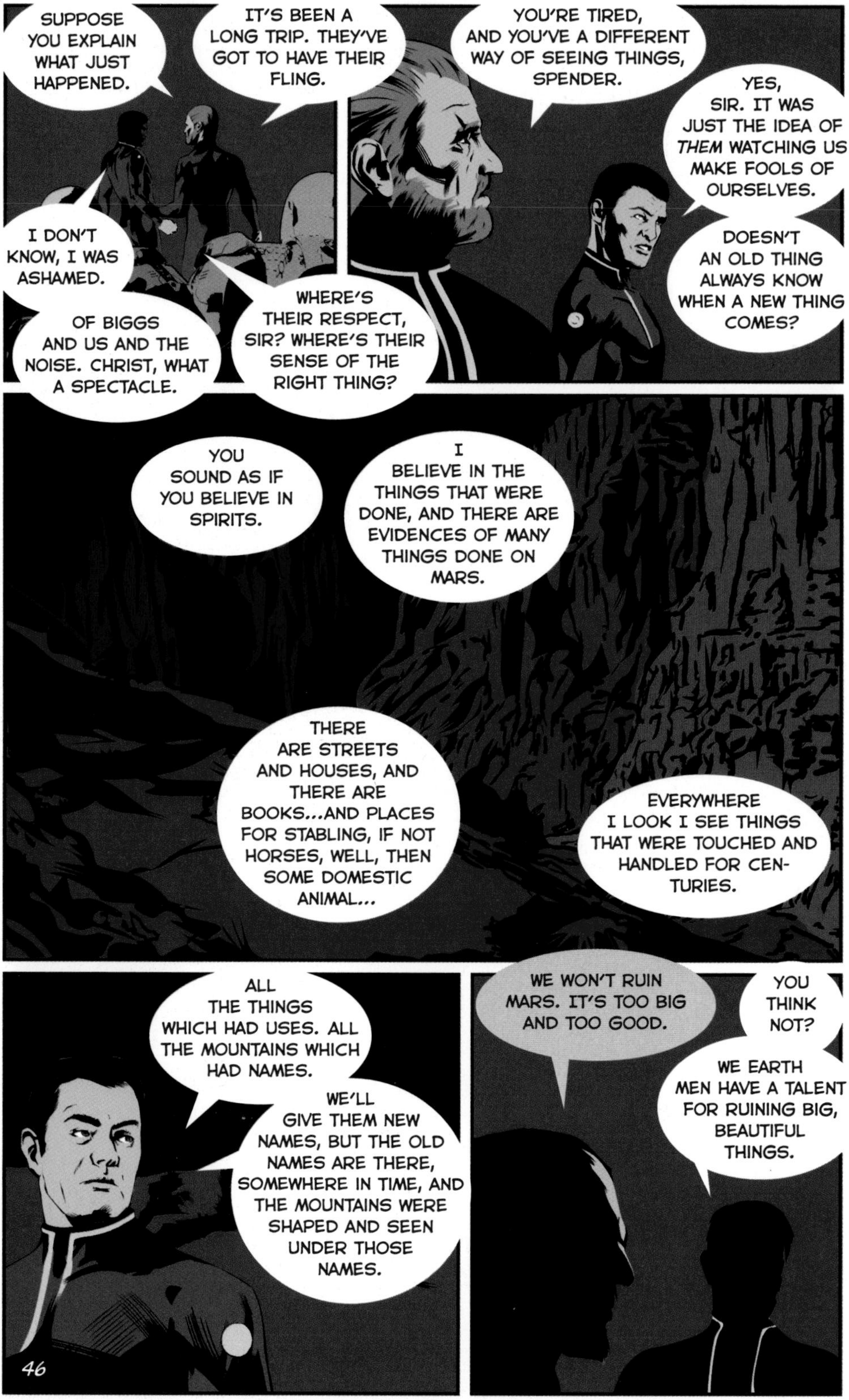
SUPPOSE YOU EXPLAIN WHAT JUST HAPPENED.
IT'S BEEN A LONG TRIP. THEY'VE GOT TO HAVE THEIR FLING.
I DON'T KNOW, I WAS ASHAMED.
OF BIGGS AND US AND THE NOISE. CHRIST, WHAT A SPECTACLE.
WHERE'S THEIR RESPECT, SIR? WHERE'S THEIR SENSE OF THE RIGHT THING?
YOU'RE TIRED, AND YOU'VE A DIFFERENT WAY OF SEEING THINGS, SPENDER.
YES, SIR. IT WAS JUST THE IDEA OF *THEM* WATCHING US MAKE FOOLS OF OURSELVES.
DOESN'T AN OLD THING ALWAYS KNOW WHEN A NEW THING COMES?
YOU SOUND AS IF YOU BELIEVE IN SPIRITS.
I BELIEVE IN THE THINGS THAT WERE DONE, AND THERE ARE EVIDENCES OF MANY THINGS DONE ON MARS.
THERE ARE STREETS AND HOUSES, AND THERE ARE BOOKS...AND PLACES FOR STABLING, IF NOT HORSES, WELL, THEN SOME DOMESTIC ANIMAL...
EVERYWHERE I LOOK I SEE THINGS THAT WERE TOUCHED AND HANDLED FOR CEN-TURIES.
ALL THE THINGS WHICH HAD USES. ALL THE MOUNTAINS WHICH HAD NAMES.
WE'LL GIVE THEM NEW NAMES, BUT THE OLD NAMES ARE THERE, SOMEWHERE IN TIME, AND THE MOUNTAINS WERE SHAPED AND SEEN UNDER THOSE NAMES.
WE WON'T RUIN MARS. IT'S TOO BIG AND TOO GOOD.
YOU THINK NOT?
WE EARTH MEN HAVE A TALENT FOR RUINING BIG, BEAUTIFUL THINGS.

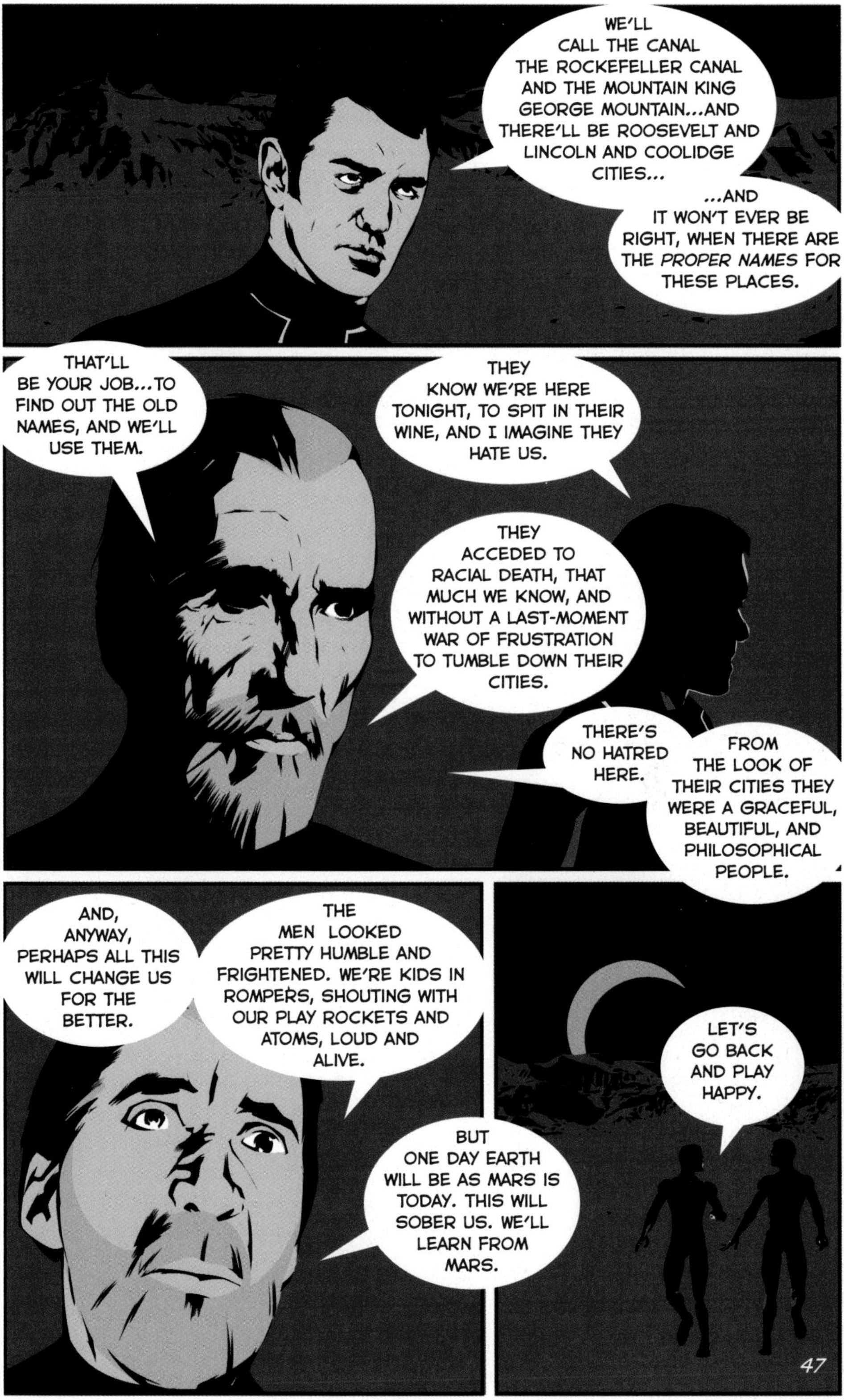
WE'LL CALL THE CANAL THE ROCKEFELLER CANAL AND THE MOUNTAIN KING GEORGE MOUNTAIN...AND THERE'LL BE ROOSEVELT AND LINCOLN AND COOLIDGE CITIES...
...AND IT WON'T EVER BE RIGHT, WHEN THERE ARE THE *PROPER NAMES* FOR THESE PLACES.
THAT'LL BE YOUR JOB...TO FIND OUT THE OLD NAMES, AND WE'LL USE THEM.
THEY KNOW WE'RE HERE TONIGHT, TO SPIT IN THEIR WINE, AND I IMAGINE THEY HATE US.
THEY ACCEDED TO RACIAL DEATH, THAT MUCH WE KNOW, AND WITHOUT A LAST-MOMENT WAR OF FRUSTRATION TO TUMBLE DOWN THEIR CITIES.
THERE'S NO HATRED HERE.
FROM THE LOOK OF THEIR CITIES THEY WERE A GRACEFUL, BEAUTIFUL, AND PHILOSOPHICAL PEOPLE.
AND, ANYWAY, PERHAPS ALL THIS WILL CHANGE US FOR THE BETTER.
THE MEN LOOKED PRETTY HUMBLE AND FRIGHTENED. WE'RE KIDS IN ROMPERS, SHOUTING WITH OUR PLAY ROCKETS AND ATOMS, LOUD AND ALIVE.
BUT ONE DAY EARTH WILL BE AS MARS IS TODAY. THIS WILL SOBER US. WE'LL LEARN FROM MARS.
LET'S GO BACK AND PLAY HAPPY.

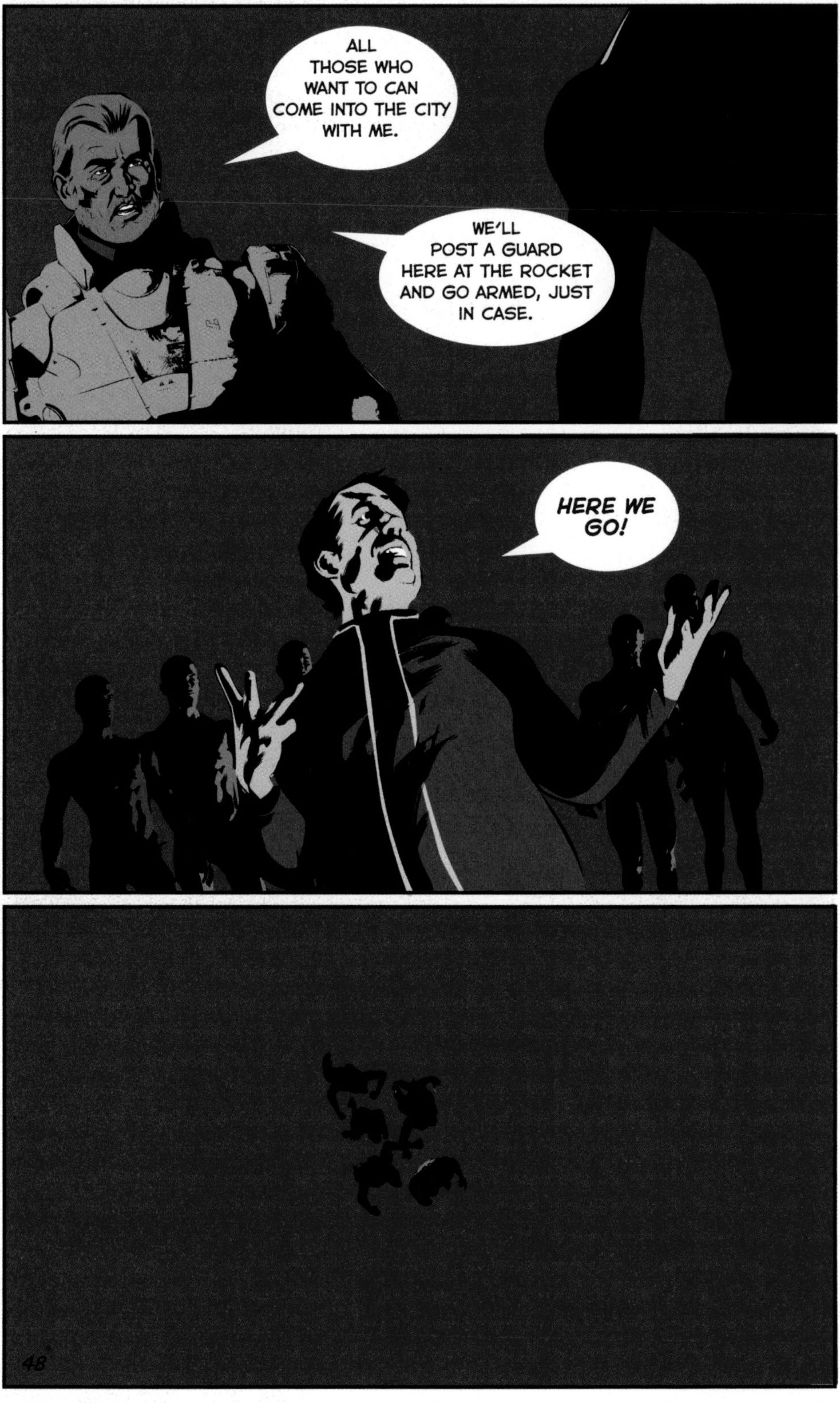
ALL THOSE WHO WANT TO CAN COME INTO THE CITY WITH ME.
WE'LL POST A GUARD HERE AT THE ROCKET AND GO ARMED, JUST IN CASE.
HERE WE GO!

THEY WERE ALL WHISPERING NOW, FOR IT WAS LIKE ENTERING A VAST OPEN LIBRARY OR A MAUSOLEUM IN WHICH THE WIND LIVED AND OVER WHICH THE STARS SHONE...

THE CAPTAIN WONDERED WHERE THE PEOPLE HAD GONE, AND WHAT THEY HAD BEEN, AND WHO THEIR KINGS WERE, AND HOW THEY HAD DIED.

AND HE WONDERED HOW THEY HAD BUILT THIS CITY TO LAST THE AGES THROUGH, AND HAD THEY EVER COME TO EARTH? WERE THEY ANCESTORS OF EARTH MEN TEN THOUSAND YEARS REMOVED?

LORD BYRON.

LORD WHO?

LORD BYRON, A NINETEENTH-CENTURY POET.

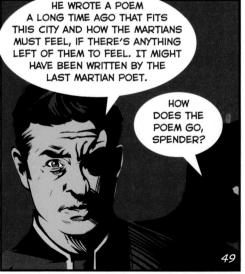

HE WROTE A POEM A LONG TIME AGO THAT FITS THIS CITY AND HOW THE MARTIANS MUST FEEL, IF THERE'S ANYTHING LEFT OF THEM TO FEEL. IT MIGHT HAVE BEEN WRITTEN BY THE LAST MARTIAN POET.

HOW DOES THE POEM GO, SPENDER?

49

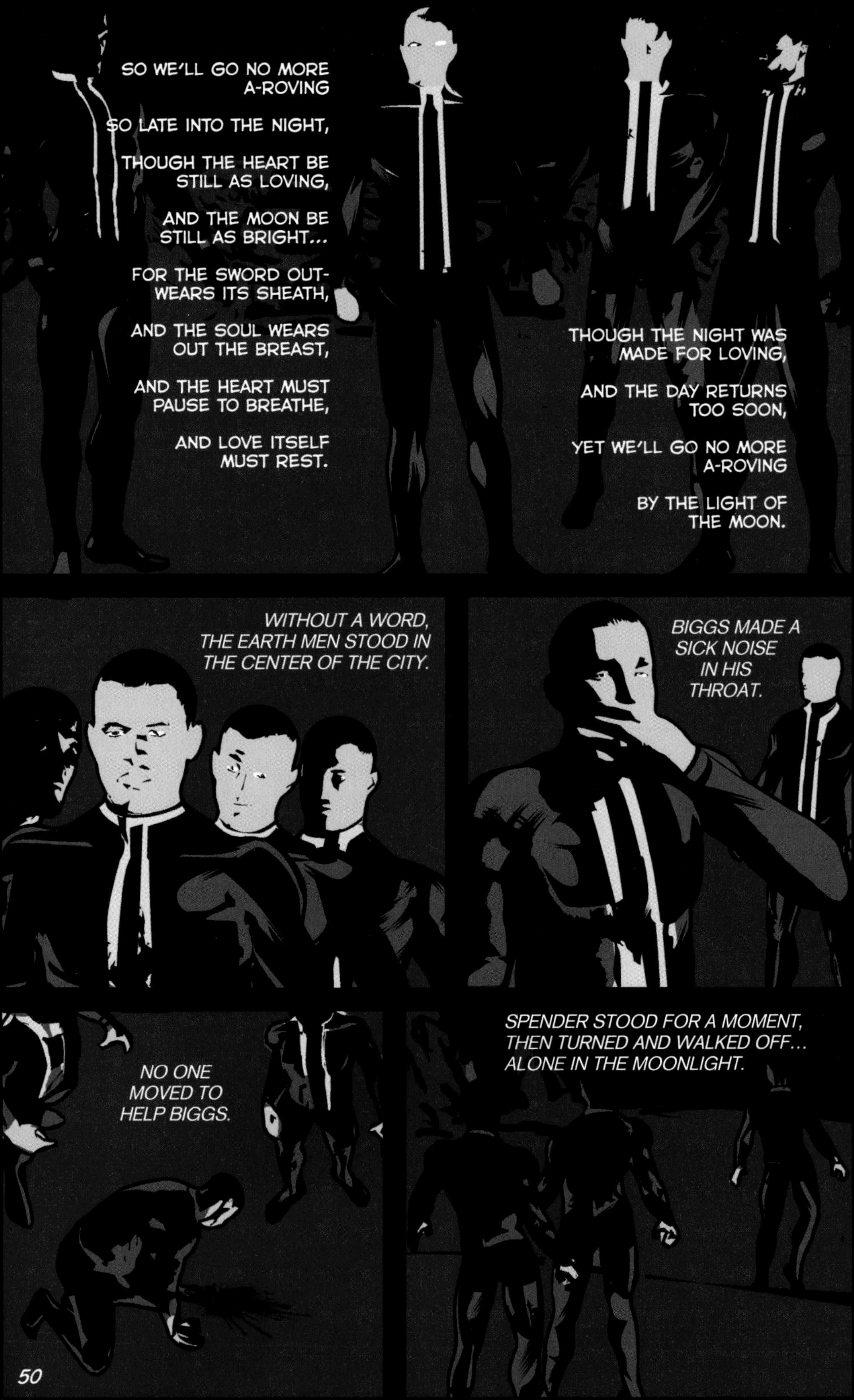
SO WE'LL GO NO MORE A-ROVING
SO LATE INTO THE NIGHT,
THOUGH THE HEART BE STILL AS LOVING,
AND THE MOON BE STILL AS BRIGHT...
FOR THE SWORD OUT-WEARS ITS SHEATH,
AND THE SOUL WEARS OUT THE BREAST,
AND THE HEART MUST PAUSE TO BREATHE,
AND LOVE ITSELF MUST REST.
THOUGH THE NIGHT WAS MADE FOR LOVING,
AND THE DAY RETURNS TOO SOON,
YET WE'LL GO NO MORE A-ROVING
BY THE LIGHT OF THE MOON.
WITHOUT A WORD, THE EARTH MEN STOOD IN THE CENTER OF THE CITY.
BIGGS MADE A SICK NOISE IN HIS THROAT.
NO ONE MOVED TO HELP BIGGS.
SPENDER STOOD FOR A MOMENT, THEN TURNED AND WALKED OFF... ALONE IN THE MOONLIGHT.

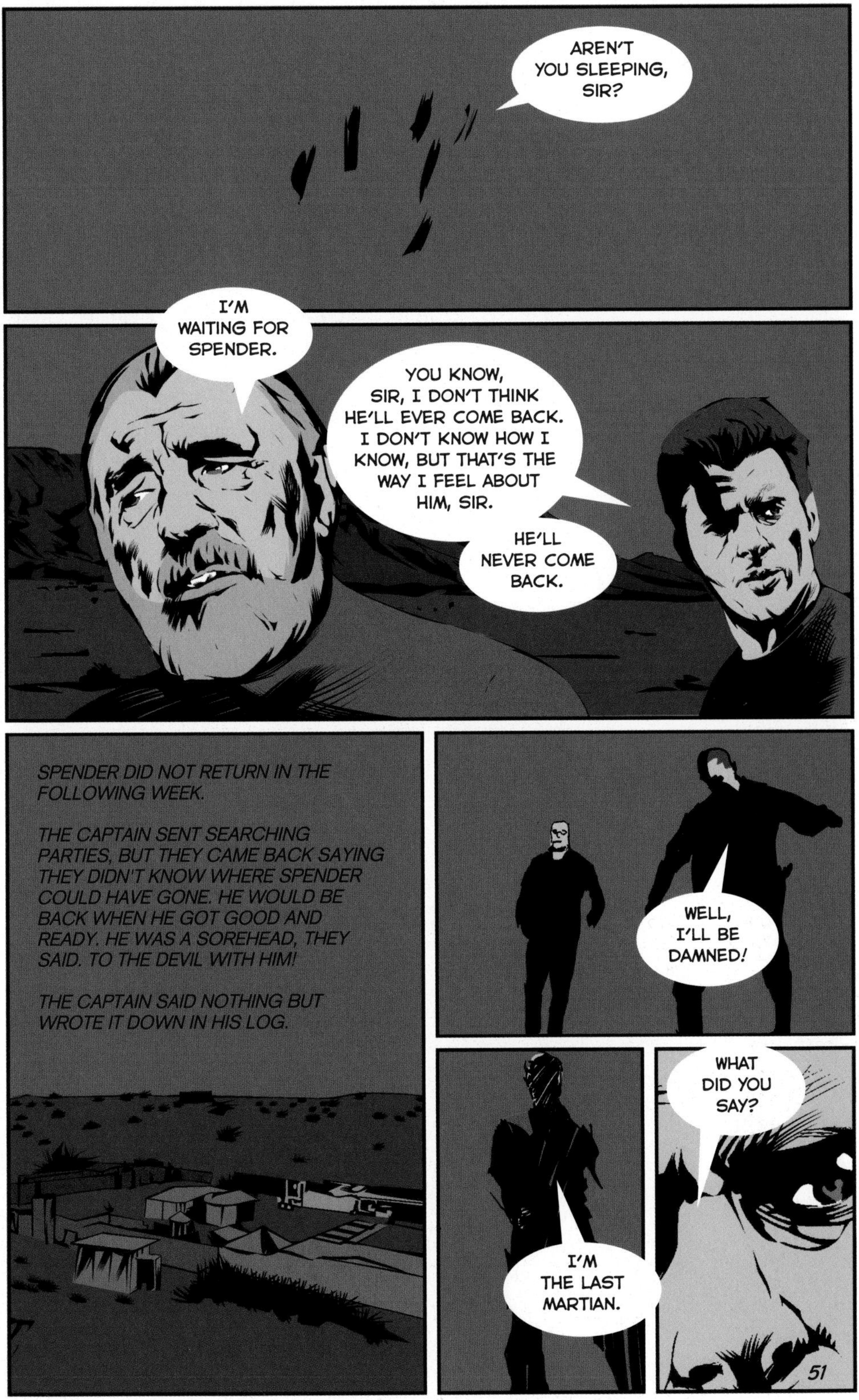
AREN'T YOU SLEEPING, SIR?
I'M WAITING FOR SPENDER.
YOU KNOW, SIR, I DON'T THINK HE'LL EVER COME BACK. I DON'T KNOW HOW I KNOW, BUT THAT'S THE WAY I FEEL ABOUT HIM, SIR.
HE'LL NEVER COME BACK.
SPENDER DID NOT RETURN IN THE FOLLOWING WEEK.
THE CAPTAIN SENT SEARCHING PARTIES, BUT THEY CAME BACK SAYING THEY DIDN'T KNOW WHERE SPENDER COULD HAVE GONE. HE WOULD BE BACK WHEN HE GOT GOOD AND READY. HE WAS A SOREHEAD, THEY SAID. TO THE DEVIL WITH HIM!
THE CAPTAIN SAID NOTHING BUT WROTE IT DOWN IN HIS LOG.
WELL, I'LL BE DAMNED!
I'M THE LAST MARTIAN.
WHAT DID YOU SAY?

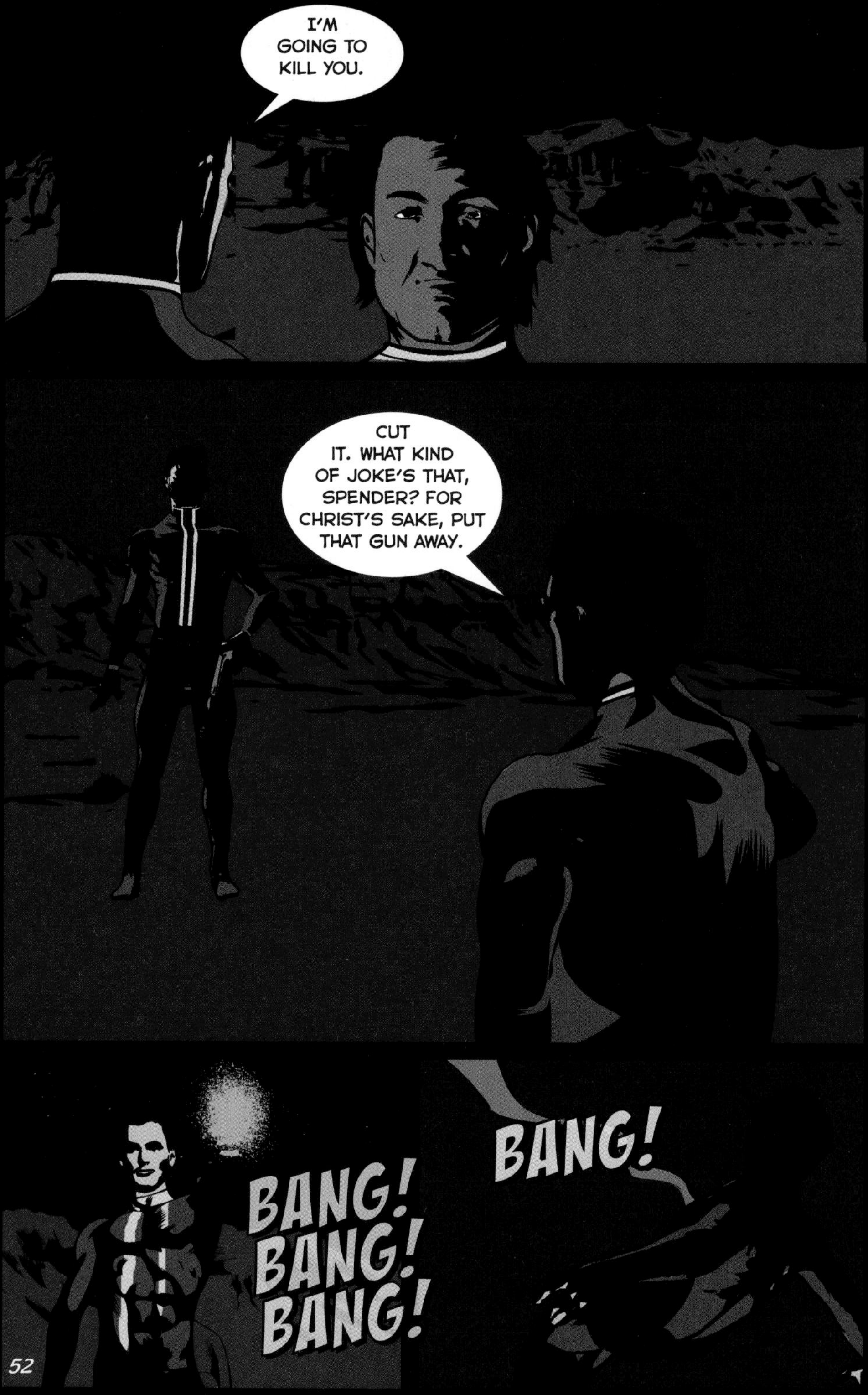
I'M GOING TO KILL YOU.
CUT IT. WHAT KIND OF JOKE'S THAT, SPENDER? FOR CHRIST'S SAKE, PUT THAT GUN AWAY.
BANG!
BANG! BANG! BANG!

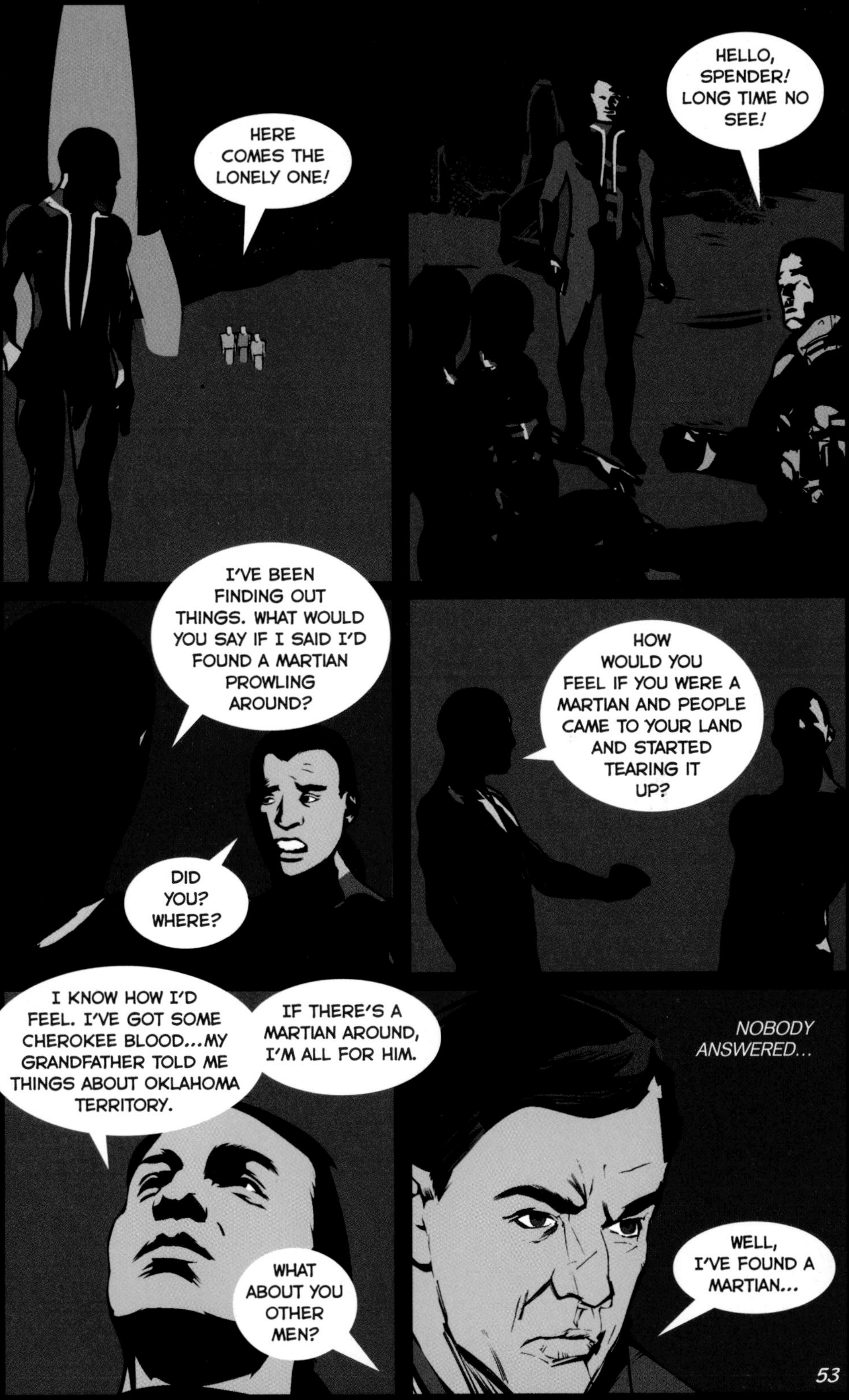
HERE COMES THE LONELY ONE!
HELLO, SPENDER! LONG TIME NO SEE!
I'VE BEEN FINDING OUT THINGS. WHAT WOULD YOU SAY IF I SAID I'D FOUND A MARTIAN PROWLING AROUND?
DID YOU? WHERE?
HOW WOULD YOU FEEL IF YOU WERE A MARTIAN AND PEOPLE CAME TO YOUR LAND AND STARTED TEARING IT UP?
I KNOW HOW I'D FEEL. I'VE GOT SOME CHEROKEE BLOOD...MY GRANDFATHER TOLD ME THINGS ABOUT OKLAHOMA TERRITORY.
IF THERE'S A MARTIAN AROUND, I'M ALL FOR HIM.
WHAT ABOUT YOU OTHER MEN?
NOBODY ANSWERED...
WELL, I'VE FOUND A MARTIAN...

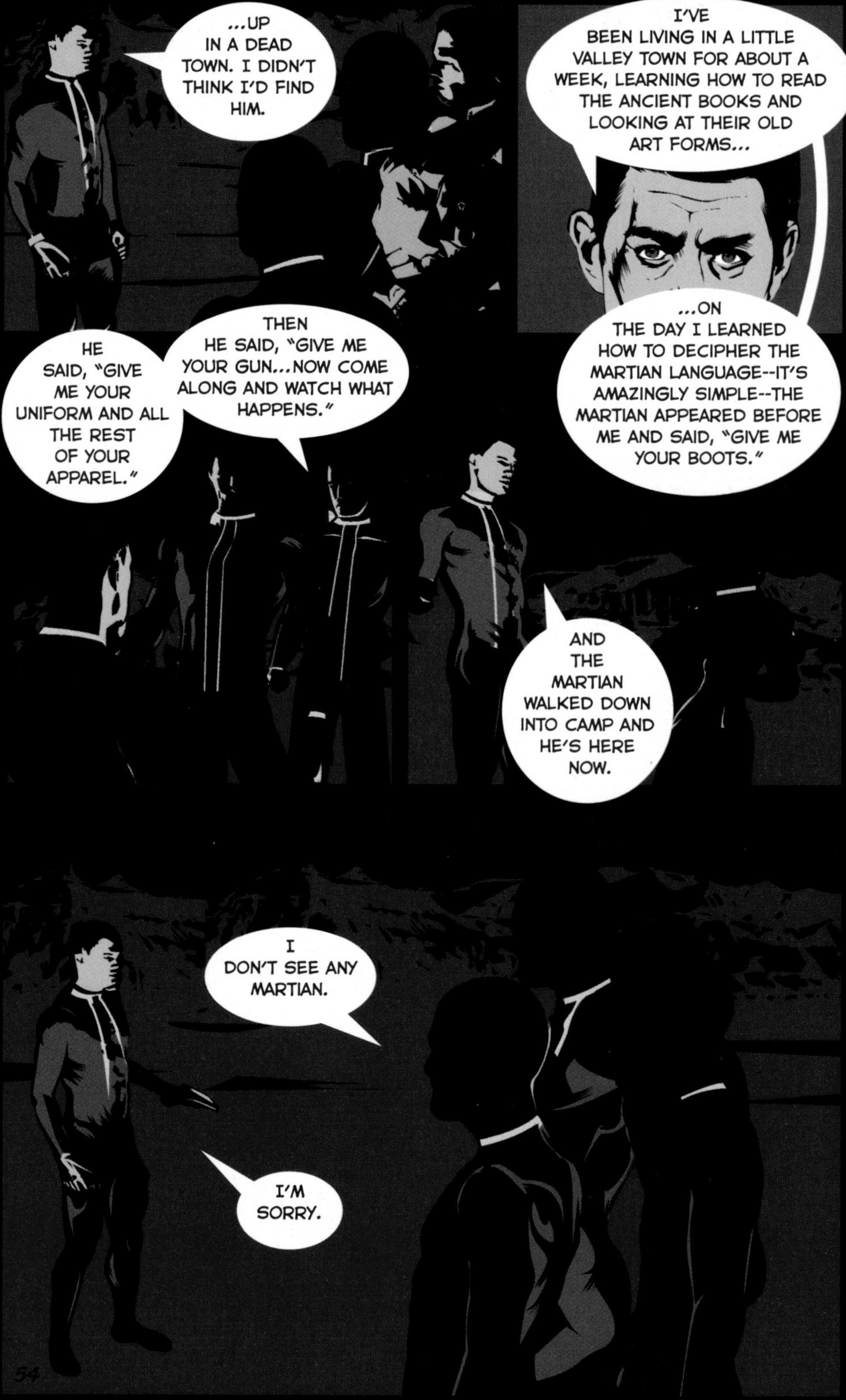
...UP IN A DEAD TOWN. I DIDN'T THINK I'D FIND HIM.
I'VE BEEN LIVING IN A LITTLE VALLEY TOWN FOR ABOUT A WEEK, LEARNING HOW TO READ THE ANCIENT BOOKS AND LOOKING AT THEIR OLD ART FORMS...
...ON THE DAY I LEARNED HOW TO DECIPHER THE MARTIAN LANGUAGE--IT'S AMAZINGLY SIMPLE--THE MARTIAN APPEARED BEFORE ME AND SAID, "GIVE ME YOUR BOOTS."
HE SAID, "GIVE ME YOUR UNIFORM AND ALL THE REST OF YOUR APPAREL."
THEN HE SAID, "GIVE ME YOUR GUN...NOW COME ALONG AND WATCH WHAT HAPPENS."
AND THE MARTIAN WALKED DOWN INTO CAMP AND HE'S HERE NOW.
I DON'T SEE ANY MARTIAN.
I'M SORRY.

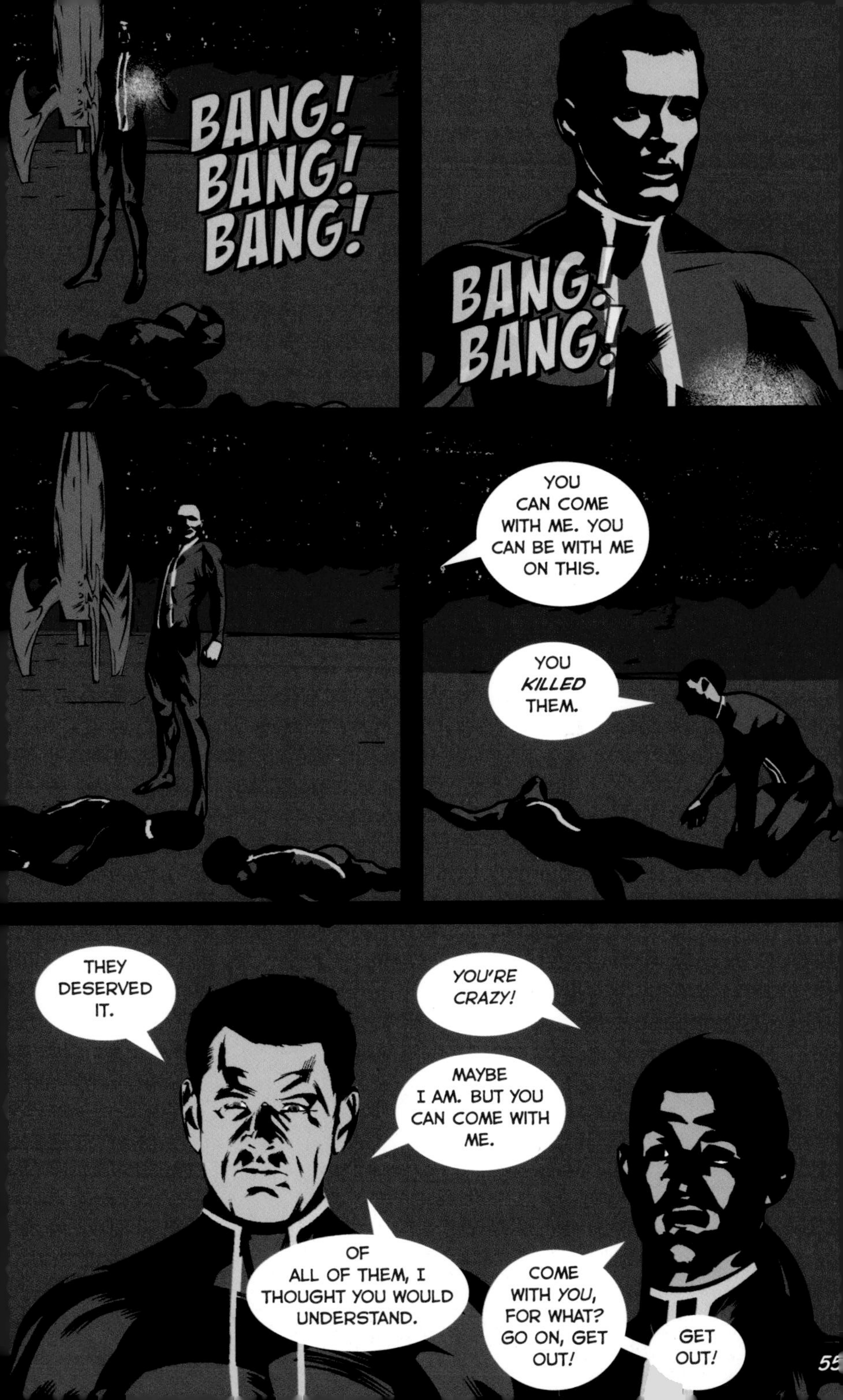
BANG! BANG! BANG!
BANG! BANG!
YOU CAN COME WITH ME. YOU CAN BE WITH ME ON THIS.
YOU *KILLED* THEM.
THEY DESERVED IT.
YOU'RE CRAZY!
MAYBE I AM. BUT YOU CAN COME WITH ME.
OF ALL OF THEM, I THOUGHT YOU WOULD UNDERSTAND.
COME WITH *YOU*, FOR WHAT? GO ON, GET OUT*!*
GET OUT*!*

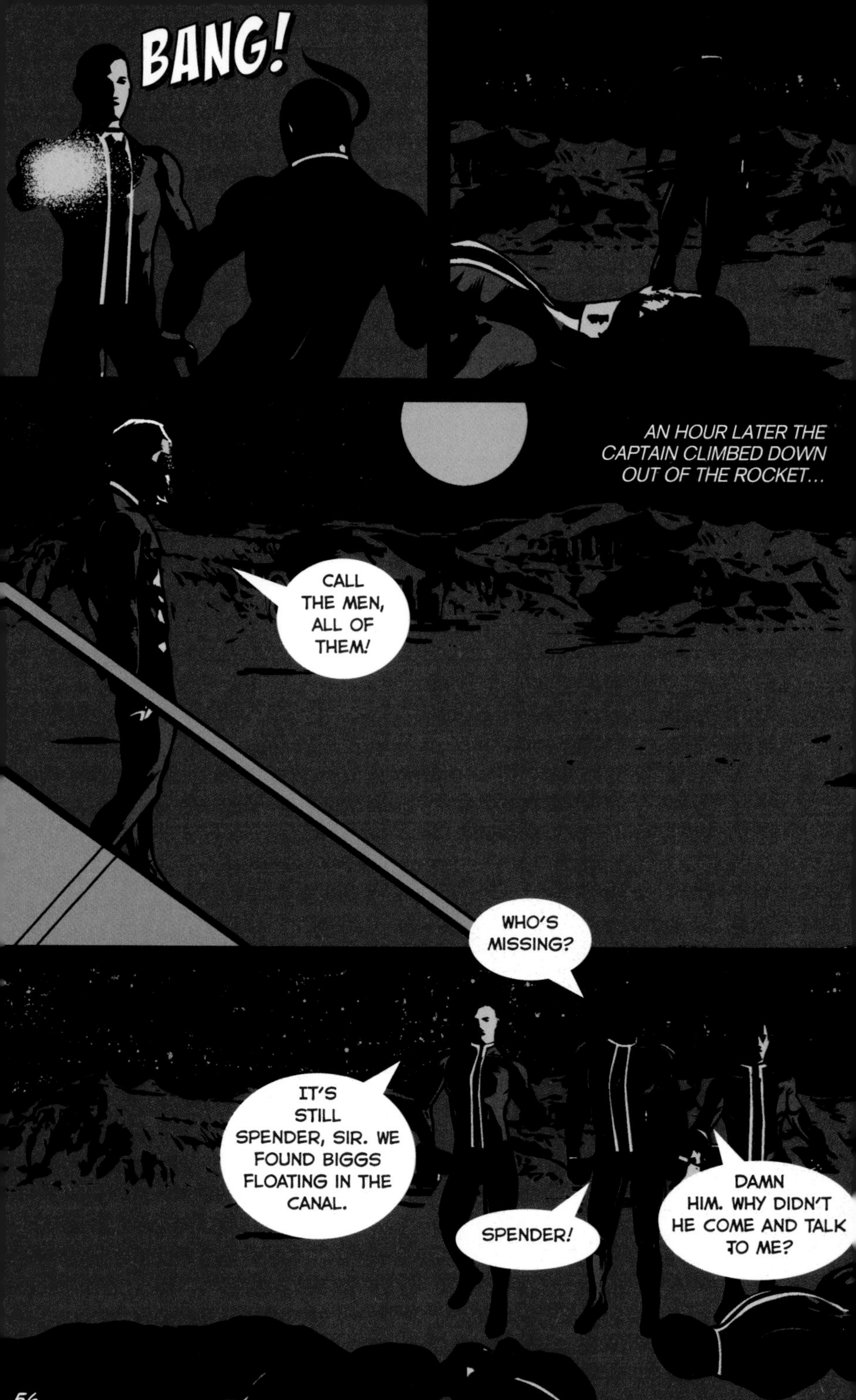
BANG!
AN HOUR LATER THE CAPTAIN CLIMBED DOWN OUT OF THE ROCKET...
CALL THE MEN, ALL OF THEM!
WHO'S MISSING?
IT'S STILL SPENDER, SIR. WE FOUND BIGGS FLOATING IN THE CANAL.
SPENDER!
DAMN HIM. WHY DIDN'T HE COME AND TALK TO ME?

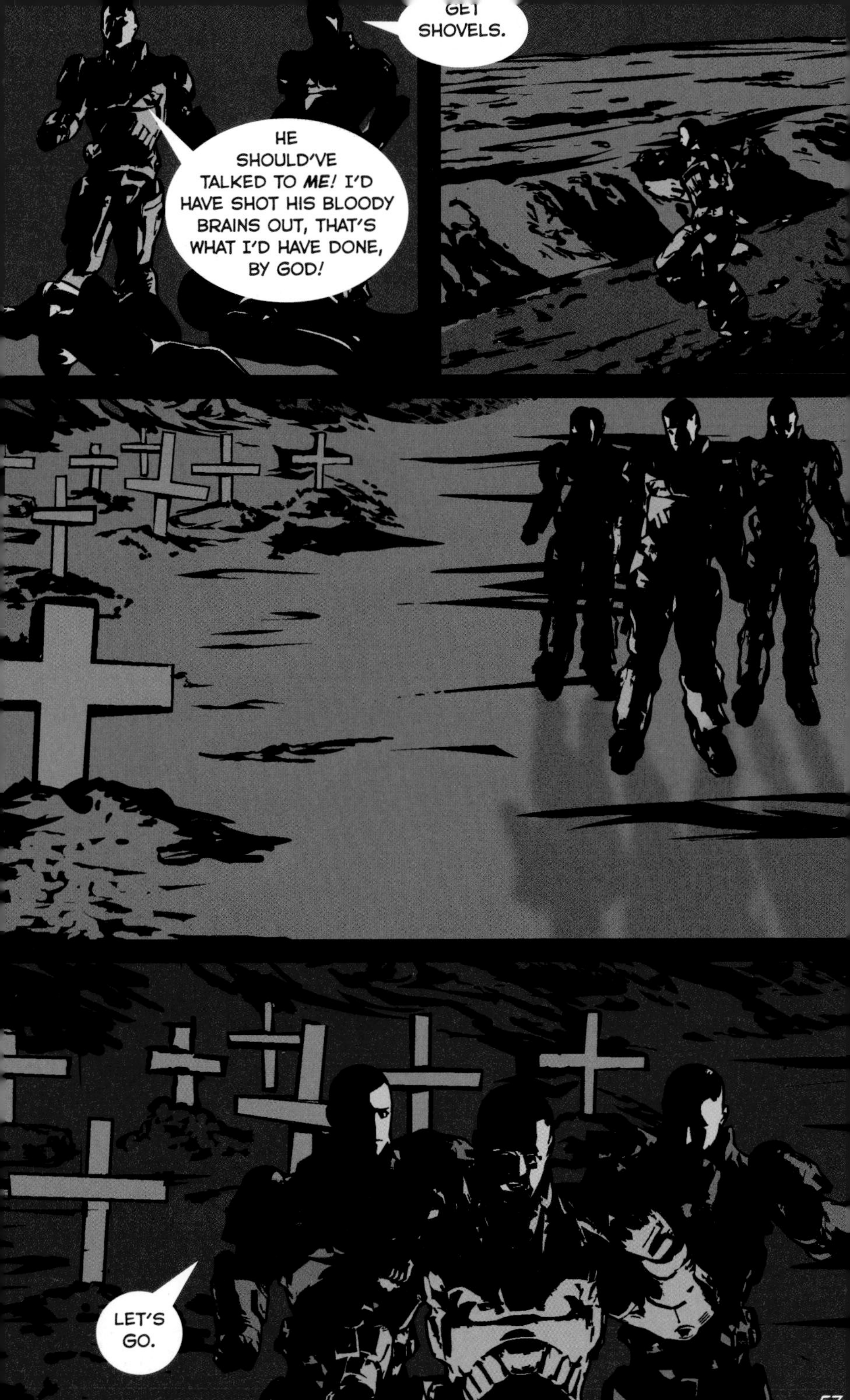
GET SHOVELS.
HE SHOULD'VE TALKED TO ME! I'D HAVE SHOT HIS BLOODY BRAINS OUT, THAT'S WHAT I'D HAVE DONE, BY GOD!
LET'S GO.

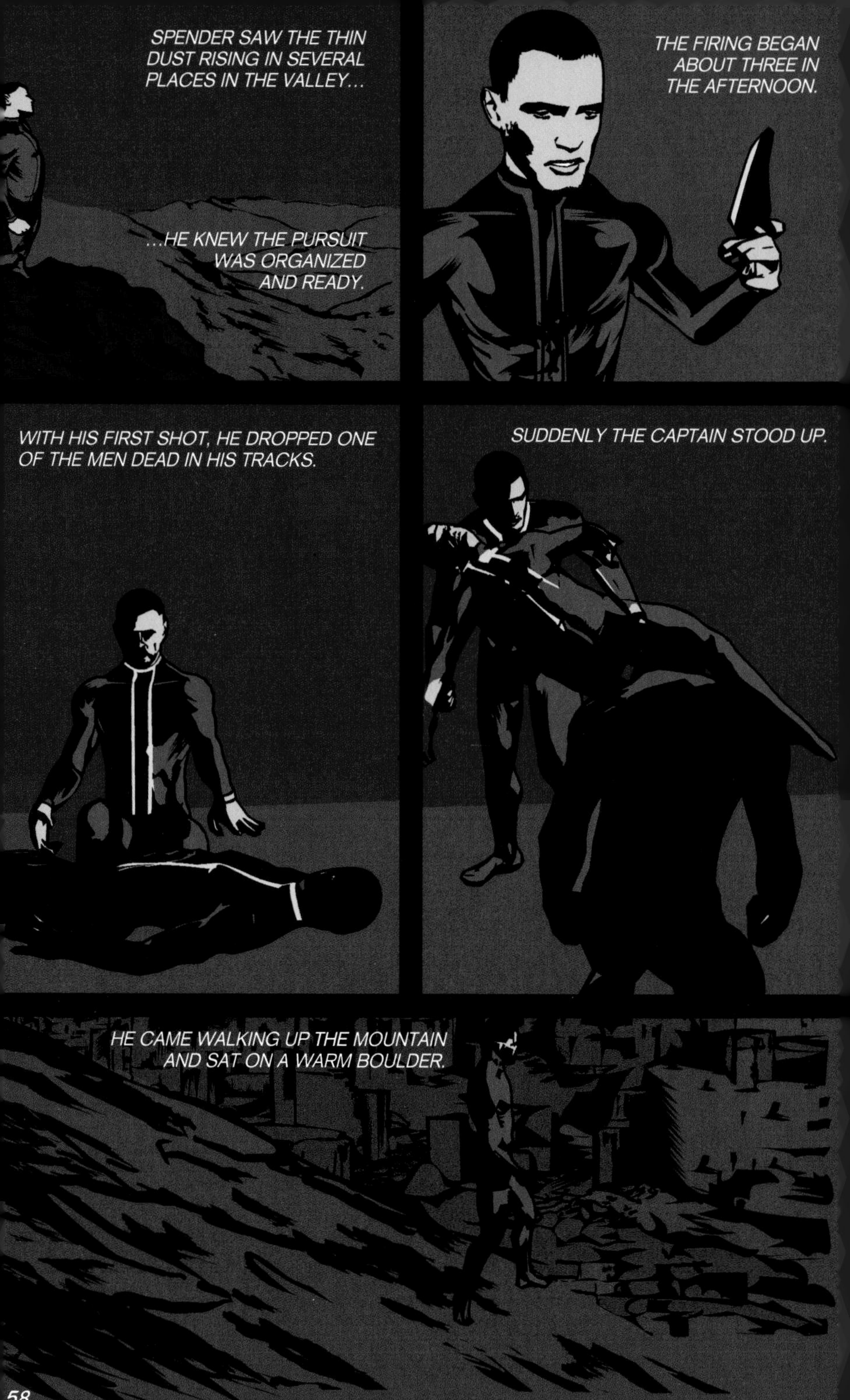
SPENDER SAW THE THIN DUST RISING IN SEVERAL PLACES IN THE VALLEY...
...HE KNEW THE PURSUIT WAS ORGANIZED AND READY.
THE FIRING BEGAN ABOUT THREE IN THE AFTERNOON.
WITH HIS FIRST SHOT, HE DROPPED ONE OF THE MEN DEAD IN HIS TRACKS.
SUDDENLY THE CAPTAIN STOOD UP.
HE CAME WALKING UP THE MOUNTAIN AND SAT ON A WARM BOULDER.

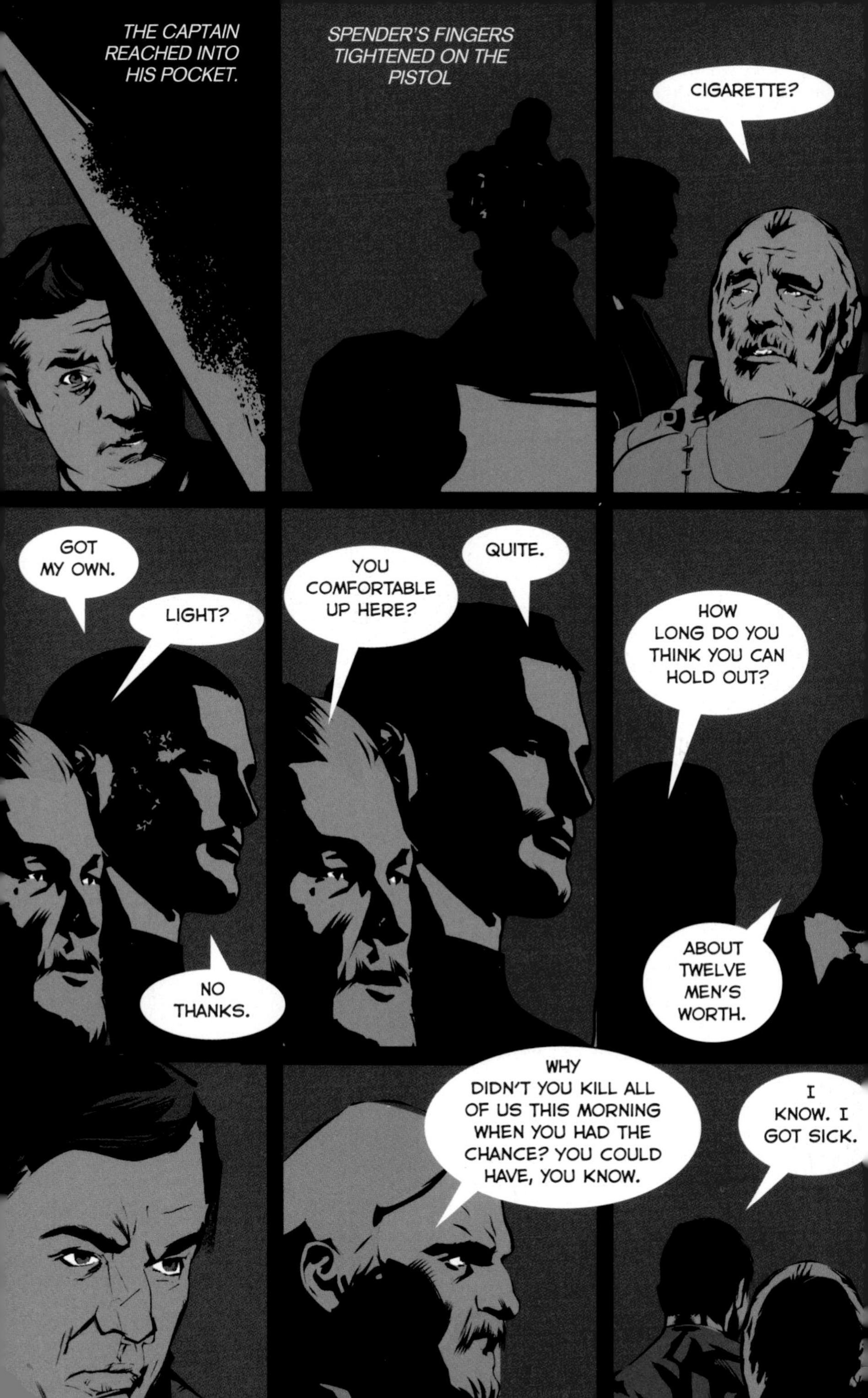

THE CAPTAIN REACHED INTO HIS POCKET.
SPENDER'S FINGERS TIGHTENED ON THE PISTOL
CIGARETTE?
GOT MY OWN.
LIGHT?
NO THANKS.
YOU COMFORTABLE UP HERE?
QUITE.
HOW LONG DO YOU THINK YOU CAN HOLD OUT?
ABOUT TWELVE MEN'S WORTH.
WHY DIDN'T YOU KILL ALL OF US THIS MORNING WHEN YOU HAD THE CHANCE? YOU COULD HAVE, YOU KNOW.
I KNOW. I GOT SICK.

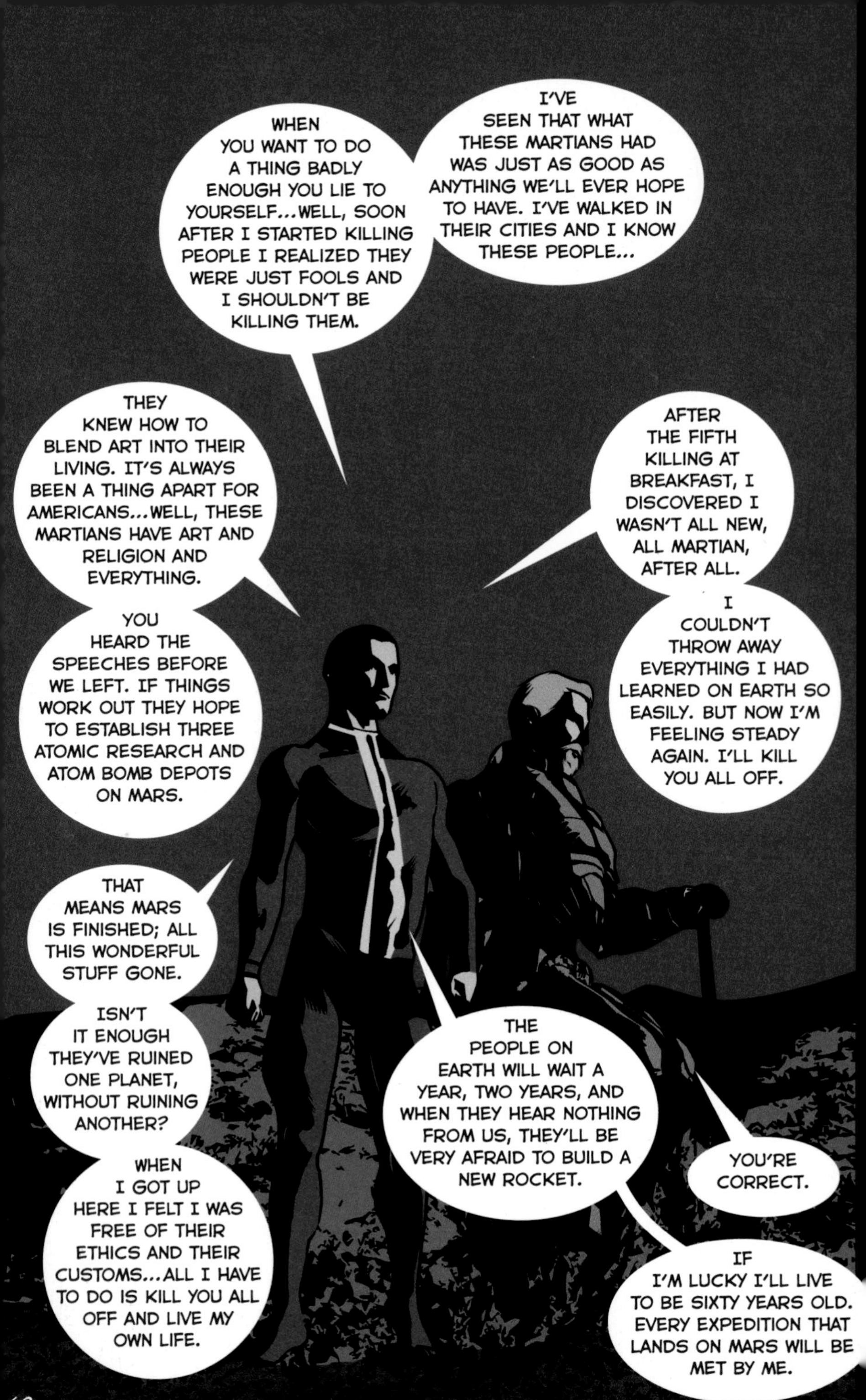
WHEN YOU WANT TO DO A THING BADLY ENOUGH YOU LIE TO YOURSELF...WELL, SOON AFTER I STARTED KILLING PEOPLE I REALIZED THEY WERE JUST FOOLS AND I SHOULDN'T BE KILLING THEM.
I'VE SEEN THAT WHAT THESE MARTIANS HAD WAS JUST AS GOOD AS ANYTHING WE'LL EVER HOPE TO HAVE. I'VE WALKED IN THEIR CITIES AND I KNOW THESE PEOPLE...
THEY KNEW HOW TO BLEND ART INTO THEIR LIVING. IT'S ALWAYS BEEN A THING APART FOR AMERICANS...WELL, THESE MARTIANS HAVE ART AND RELIGION AND EVERYTHING.
YOU HEARD THE SPEECHES BEFORE WE LEFT. IF THINGS WORK OUT THEY HOPE TO ESTABLISH THREE ATOMIC RESEARCH AND ATOM BOMB DEPOTS ON MARS.
AFTER THE FIFTH KILLING AT BREAKFAST, I DISCOVERED I WASN'T ALL NEW, ALL MARTIAN, AFTER ALL.
I COULDN'T THROW AWAY EVERYTHING I HAD LEARNED ON EARTH SO EASILY. BUT NOW I'M FEELING STEADY AGAIN. I'LL KILL YOU ALL OFF.
THAT MEANS MARS IS FINISHED; ALL THIS WONDERFUL STUFF GONE.
ISN'T IT ENOUGH THEY'VE RUINED ONE PLANET, WITHOUT RUINING ANOTHER?
WHEN I GOT UP HERE I FELT I WAS FREE OF THEIR ETHICS AND THEIR CUSTOMS...ALL I HAVE TO DO IS KILL YOU ALL OFF AND LIVE MY OWN LIFE.
THE PEOPLE ON EARTH WILL WAIT A YEAR, TWO YEARS, AND WHEN THEY HEAR NOTHING FROM US, THEY'LL BE VERY AFRAID TO BUILD A NEW ROCKET.
YOU'RE CORRECT.
IF I'M LUCKY I'LL LIVE TO BE SIXTY YEARS OLD. EVERY EXPEDITION THAT LANDS ON MARS WILL BE MET BY ME.

YOU'VE GOT IT ALL PLANNED. YET YOU'RE OUTNUMBERED. IN AN HOUR WE'LL HAVE YOU SURROUNDED. IN AN HOUR YOU'LL BE DEAD.

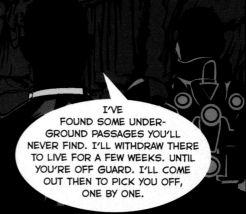

I'VE FOUND SOME UNDER-GROUND PASSAGES YOU'LL NEVER FIND. I'LL WITHDRAW THERE TO LIVE FOR A FEW WEEKS. UNTIL YOU'RE OFF GUARD. I'LL COME OUT THEN TO PICK YOU OFF, ONE BY ONE.

TELL ME ABOUT YOUR CIVILIZATION HERE.

THEY KNEW HOW TO LIVE WITH NATURE AND GET ALONG WITH NATURE. THEY DIDN'T TRY TOO HARD TO BE ALL MEN AND NO ANIMAL.

THEY KNEW HOW TO COMBINE SCIENCE AND RELIGION SO THE TWO WORKED SIDE BY SIDE, NEITHER DENYING THE OTHER, EACH ENRICHING THE OTHER.

THAT SOUNDS IDEAL.

IT WAS. I'D LIKE TO SHOW YOU HOW THE MARTIANS DID IT.

MY MEN ARE WAITING.

WE'LL BE GONE HALF AN HOUR. TELL THEM THAT, SIR.

THERE'S YOUR ANSWER, CAPTAIN.

I DON'T SEE.

61

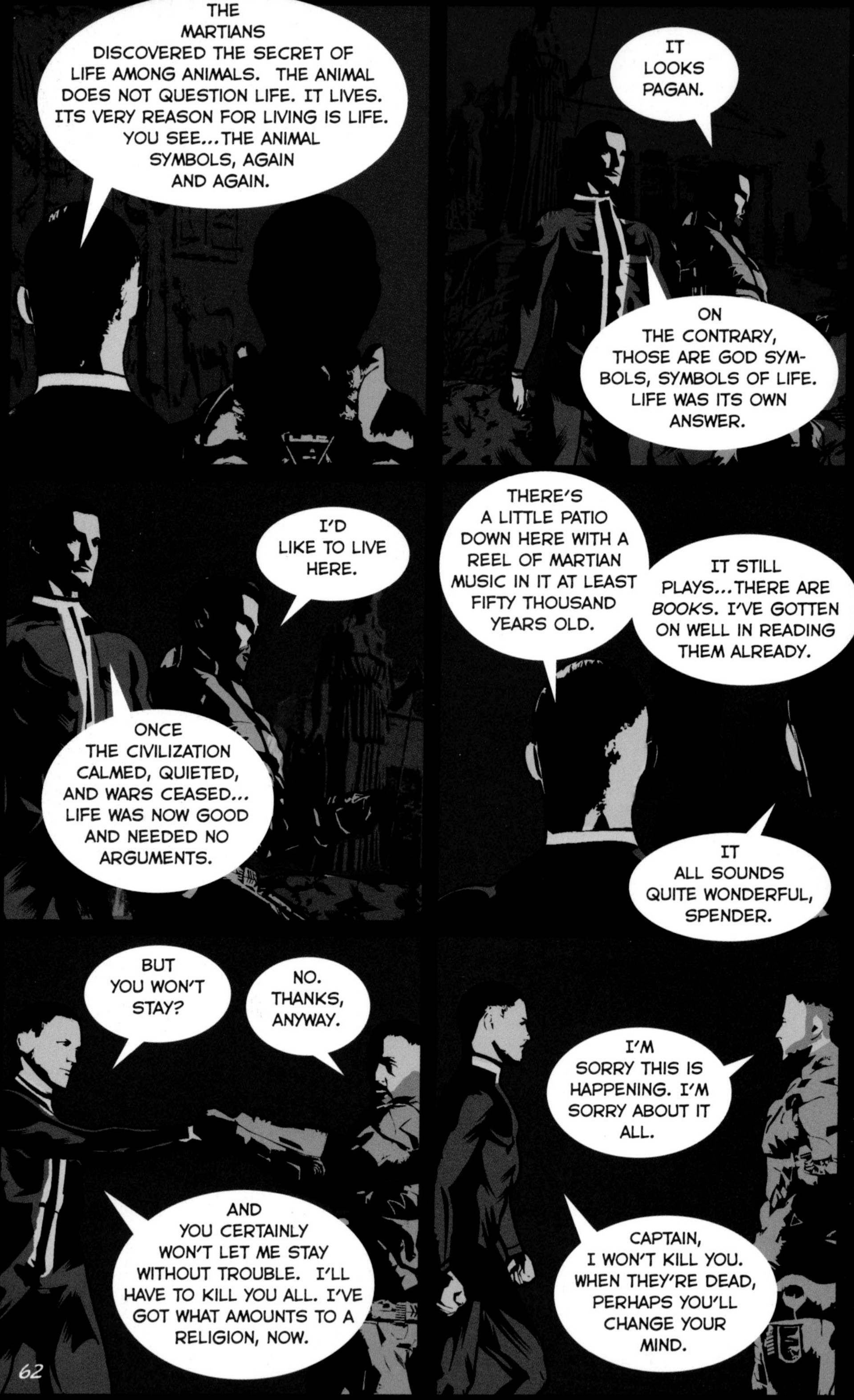
THE MARTIANS DISCOVERED THE SECRET OF LIFE AMONG ANIMALS. THE ANIMAL DOES NOT QUESTION LIFE. IT LIVES. ITS VERY REASON FOR LIVING IS LIFE. YOU SEE...THE ANIMAL SYMBOLS, AGAIN AND AGAIN.
IT LOOKS PAGAN.
ON THE CONTRARY, THOSE ARE GOD SYMBOLS, SYMBOLS OF LIFE. LIFE WAS ITS OWN ANSWER.
I'D LIKE TO LIVE HERE.
ONCE THE CIVILIZATION CALMED, QUIETED, AND WARS CEASED... LIFE WAS NOW GOOD AND NEEDED NO ARGUMENTS.
THERE'S A LITTLE PATIO DOWN HERE WITH A REEL OF MARTIAN MUSIC IN IT AT LEAST FIFTY THOUSAND YEARS OLD.
IT STILL PLAYS...THERE ARE *BOOKS*. I'VE GOTTEN ON WELL IN READING THEM ALREADY.
IT ALL SOUNDS QUITE WONDERFUL, SPENDER.
BUT YOU WON'T STAY?
NO. THANKS, ANYWAY.
AND YOU CERTAINLY WON'T LET ME STAY WITHOUT TROUBLE. I'LL HAVE TO KILL YOU ALL. I'VE GOT WHAT AMOUNTS TO A RELIGION, NOW.
I'M SORRY THIS IS HAPPENING. I'M SORRY ABOUT IT ALL.
CAPTAIN, I WON'T KILL YOU. WHEN THEY'RE DEAD, PERHAPS YOU'LL CHANGE YOUR MIND.

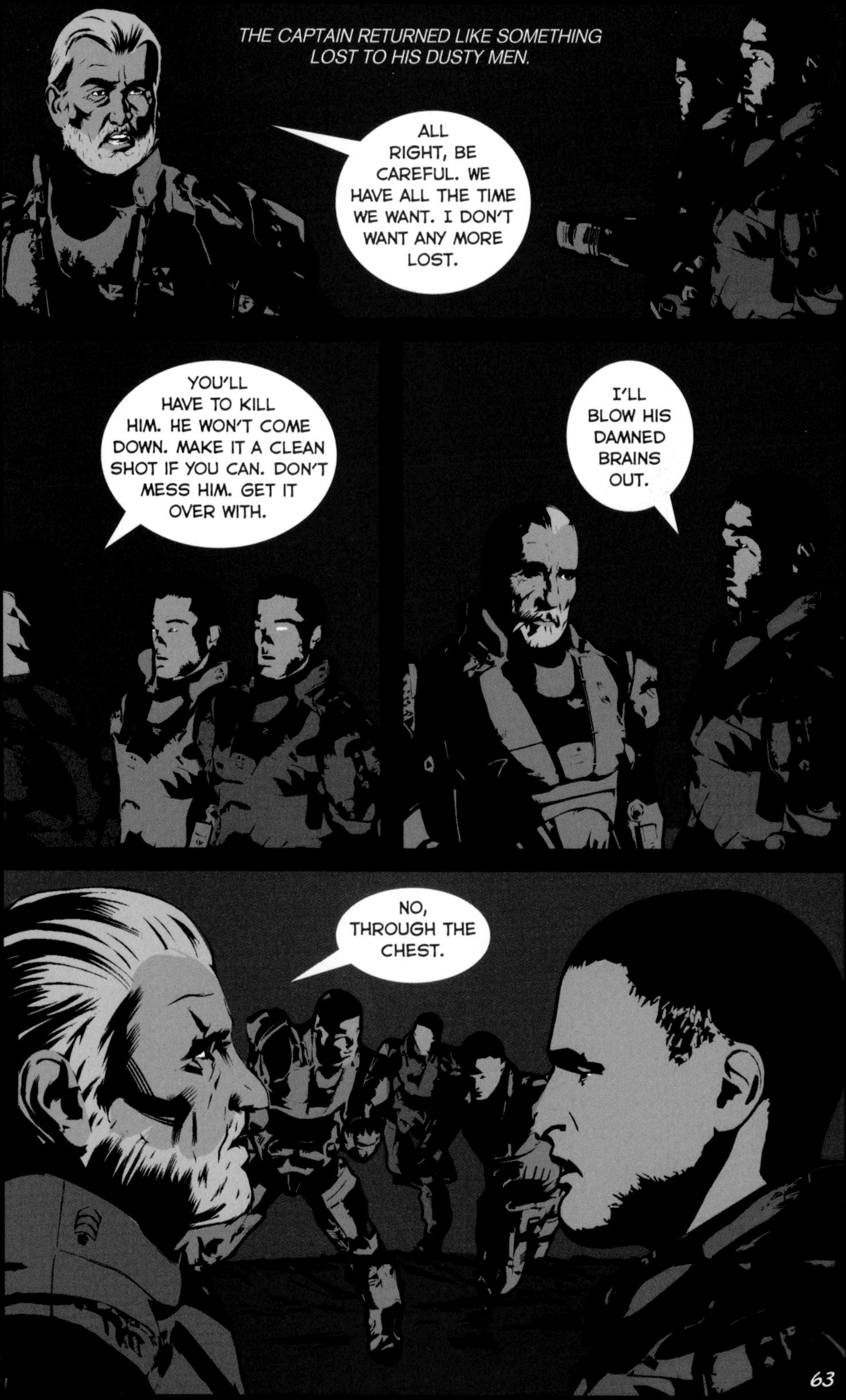
THE CAPTAIN RETURNED LIKE SOMETHING LOST TO HIS DUSTY MEN.
ALL RIGHT, BE CAREFUL. WE HAVE ALL THE TIME WE WANT. I DON'T WANT ANY MORE LOST.
YOU'LL HAVE TO KILL HIM. HE WON'T COME DOWN. MAKE IT A CLEAN SHOT IF YOU CAN. DON'T MESS HIM. GET IT OVER WITH.
I'LL BLOW HIS DAMNED BRAINS OUT.
NO, THROUGH THE CHEST.

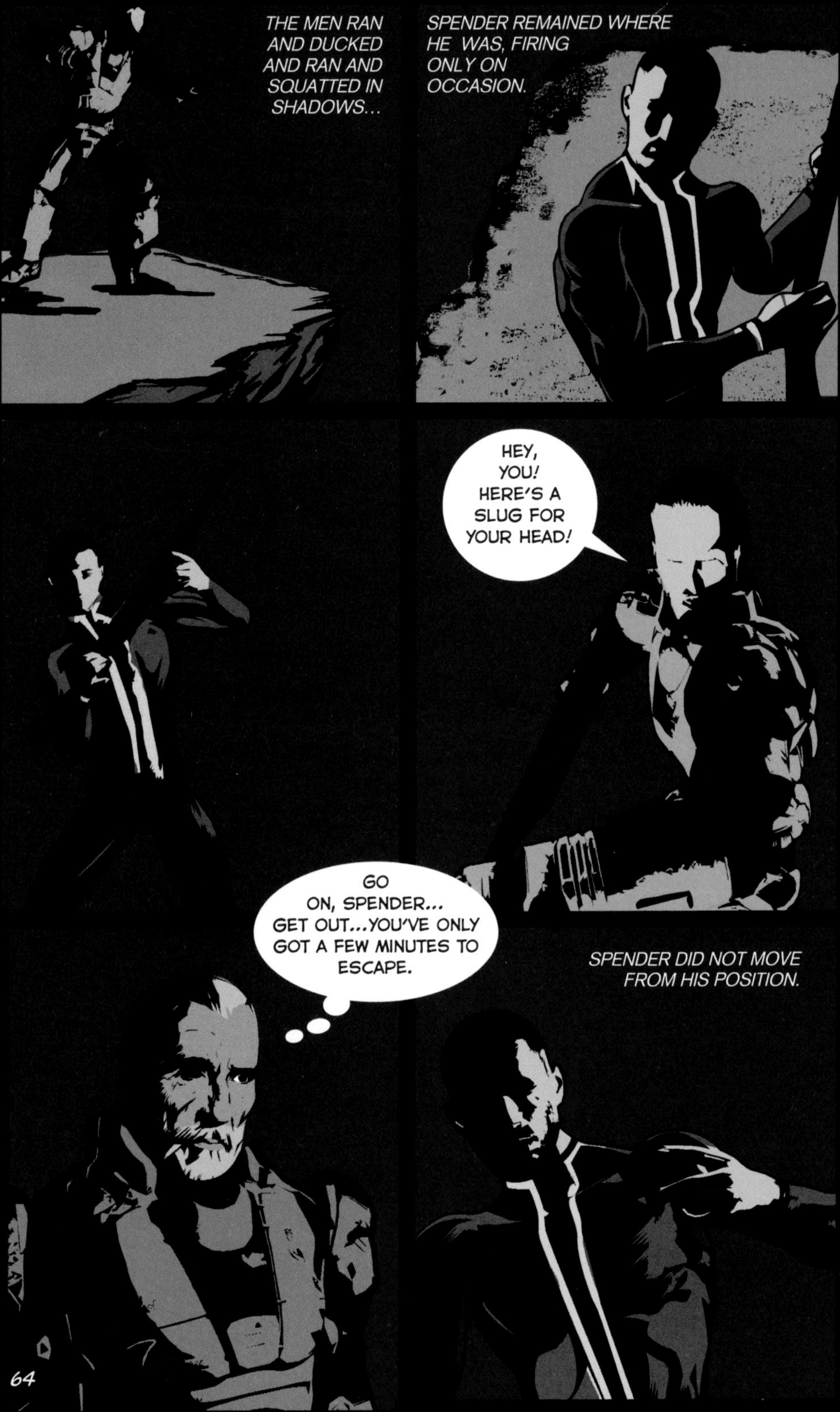
THE MEN RAN AND DUCKED AND RAN AND SQUATTED IN SHADOWS...
SPENDER REMAINED WHERE HE WAS, FIRING ONLY ON OCCASION.
HEY, YOU! HERE'S A SLUG FOR YOUR HEAD!
GO ON, SPENDER... GET OUT...YOU'VE ONLY GOT A FEW MINUTES TO ESCAPE.
SPENDER DID NOT MOVE FROM HIS POSITION.

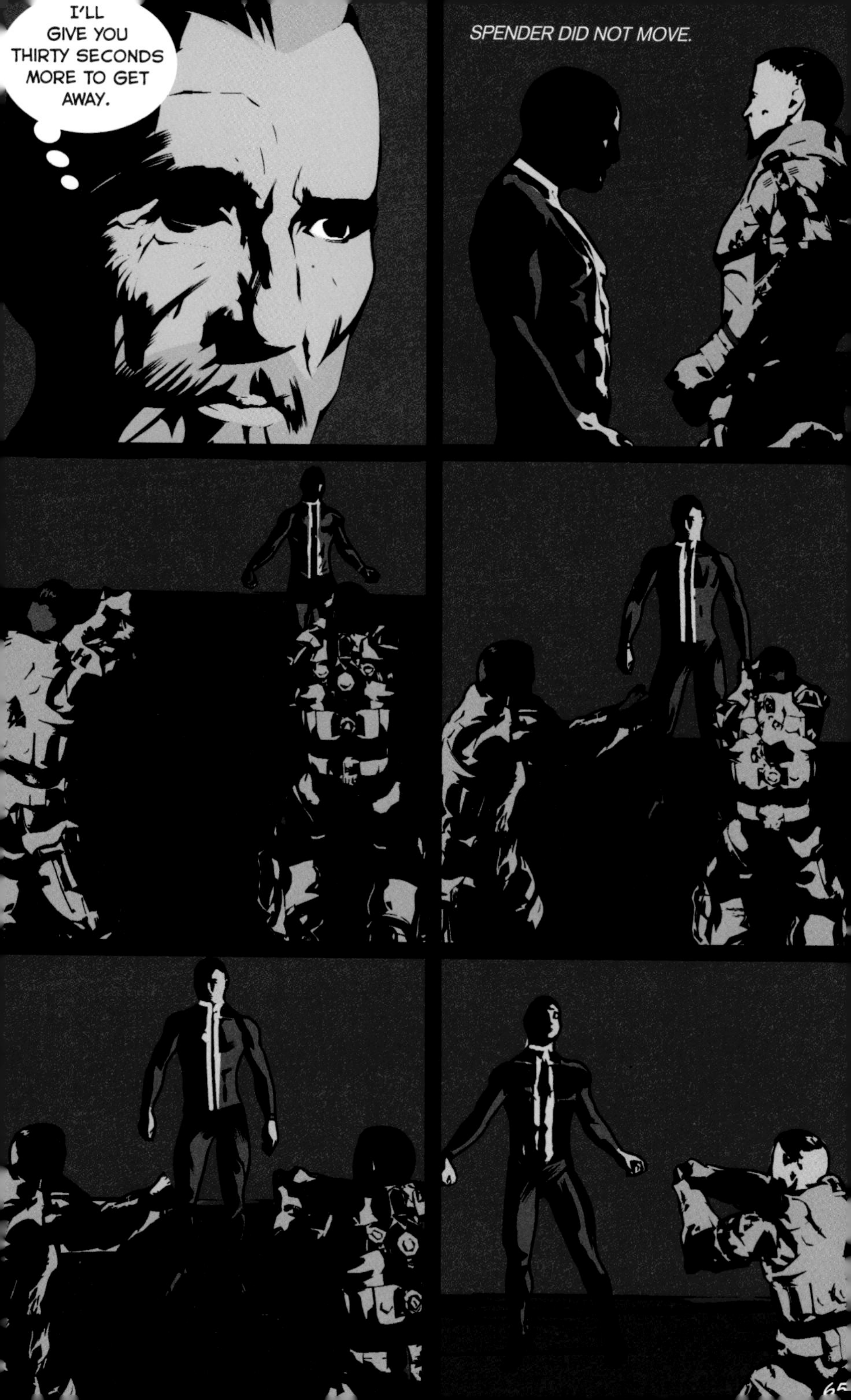
I'LL GIVE YOU THIRTY SECONDS MORE TO GET AWAY.
SPENDER DID NOT MOVE.

NO, PARKHILL. I CAN'T LET YOU DO IT. NOR THE OTHERS. NO, NONE OF YOU. ONLY ME.

WILL I BE CLEAN AFTER THIS?

IS IT RIGHT THAT IT'S ME WHO DOES IT? YES...I KNOW WHAT I'M DOING FOR WHAT REASON AND IT'S RIGHT...

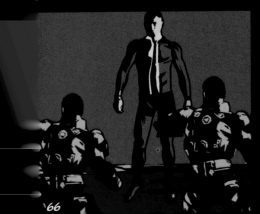

BANG!

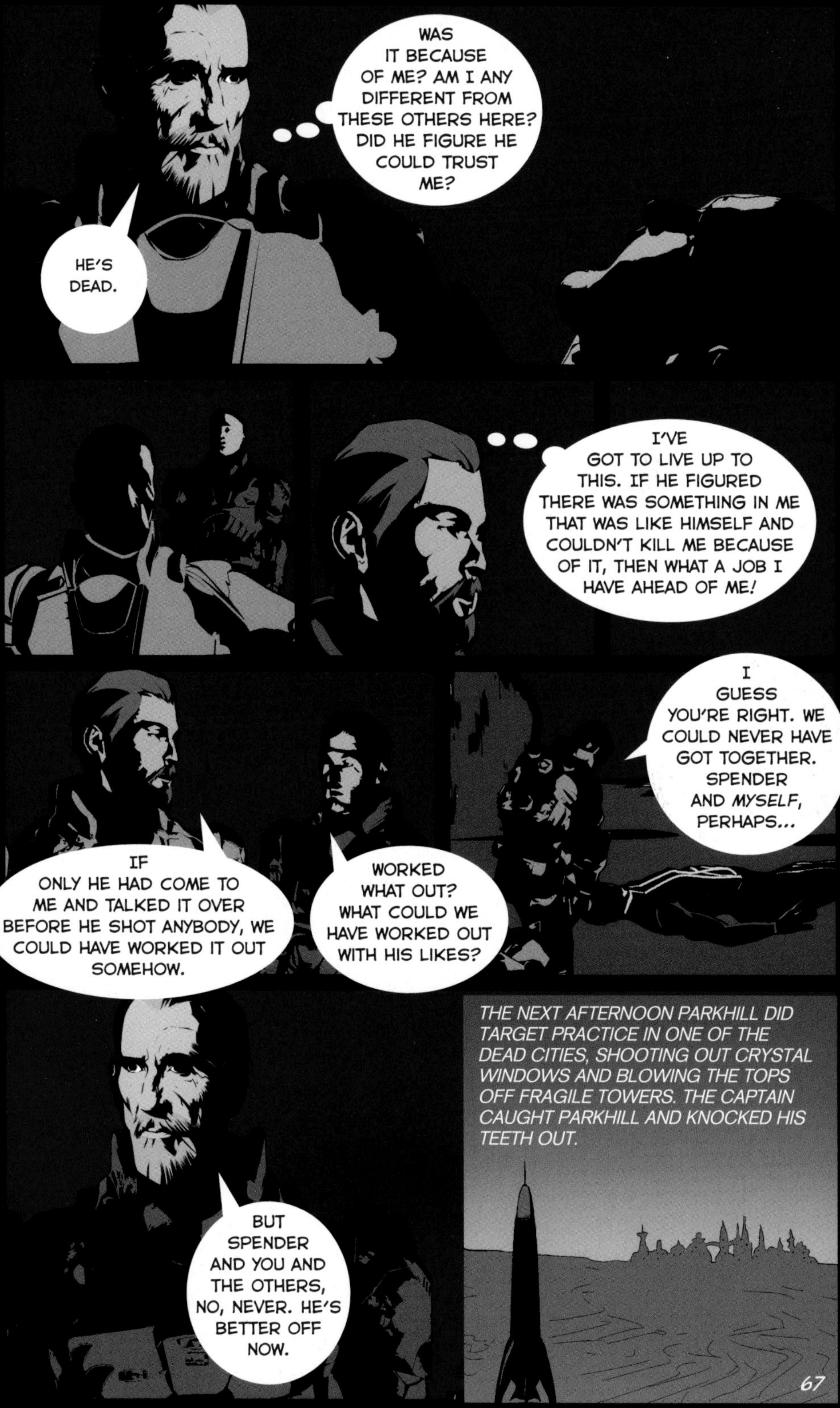
WAS IT BECAUSE OF ME? AM I ANY DIFFERENT FROM THESE OTHERS HERE? DID HE FIGURE HE COULD TRUST ME?
HE'S DEAD.
I'VE GOT TO LIVE UP TO THIS. IF HE FIGURED THERE WAS SOMETHING IN ME THAT WAS LIKE HIMSELF AND COULDN'T KILL ME BECAUSE OF IT, THEN WHAT A JOB I HAVE AHEAD OF ME!
IF ONLY HE HAD COME TO ME AND TALKED IT OVER BEFORE HE SHOT ANYBODY, WE COULD HAVE WORKED IT OUT SOMEHOW.
WORKED WHAT OUT? WHAT COULD WE HAVE WORKED OUT WITH HIS LIKES?
I GUESS YOU'RE RIGHT. WE COULD NEVER HAVE GOT TOGETHER. SPENDER AND *MYSELF*, PERHAPS...
BUT SPENDER AND YOU AND THE OTHERS, NO, NEVER. HE'S BETTER OFF NOW.
THE NEXT AFTERNOON PARKHILL DID TARGET PRACTICE IN ONE OF THE DEAD CITIES, SHOOTING OUT CRYSTAL WINDOWS AND BLOWING THE TOPS OFF FRAGILE TOWERS. THE CAPTAIN CAUGHT PARKHILL AND KNOCKED HIS TEETH OUT.

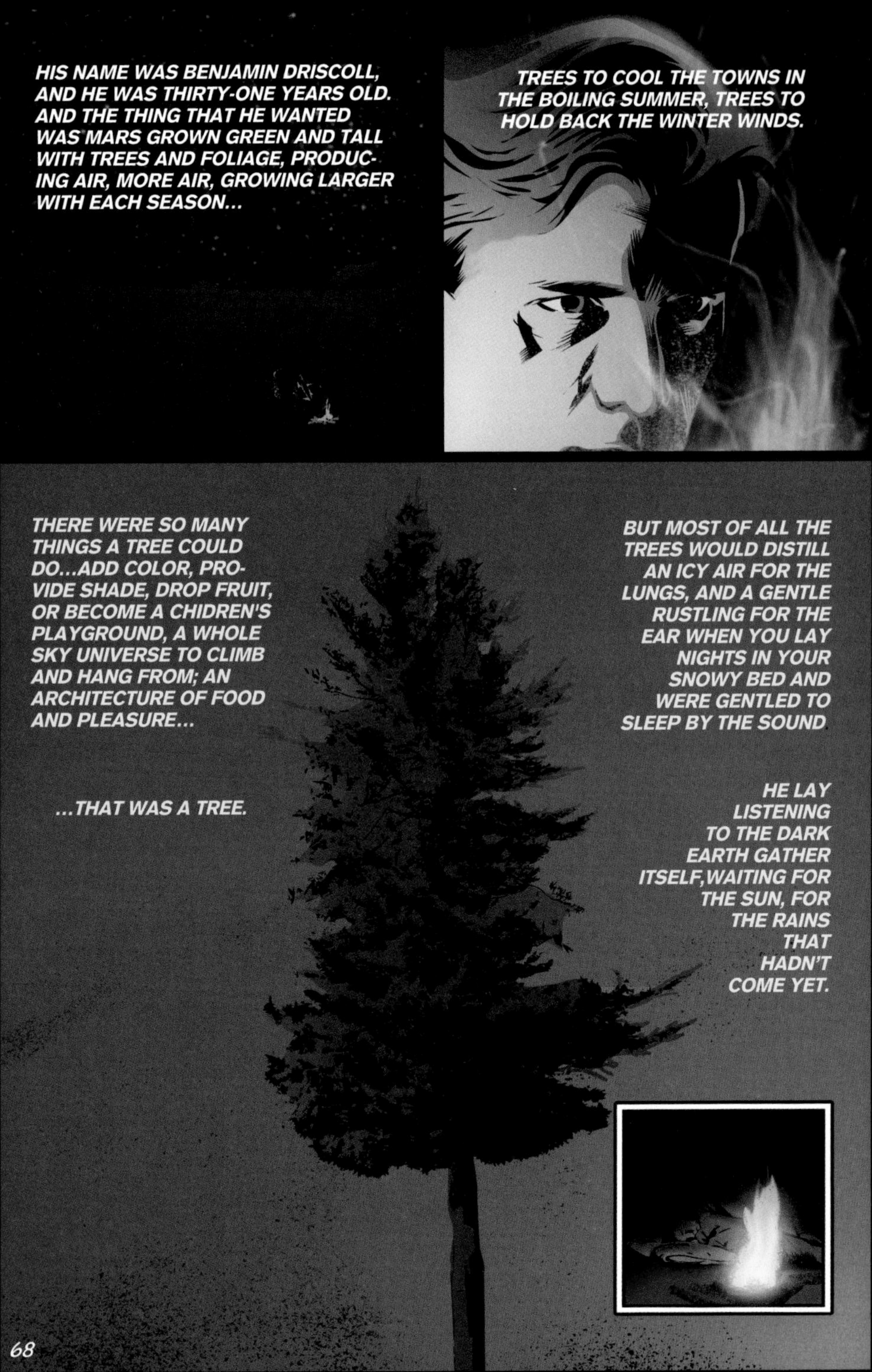
HIS NAME WAS BENJAMIN DRISCOLL, AND HE WAS THIRTY-ONE YEARS OLD. AND THE THING THAT HE WANTED WAS MARS GROWN GREEN AND TALL WITH TREES AND FOLIAGE, PRODUCING AIR, MORE AIR, GROWING LARGER WITH EACH SEASON...
TREES TO COOL THE TOWNS IN THE BOILING SUMMER, TREES TO HOLD BACK THE WINTER WINDS.
THERE WERE SO MANY THINGS A TREE COULD DO...ADD COLOR, PROVIDE SHADE, DROP FRUIT, OR BECOME A CHIDREN'S PLAYGROUND, A WHOLE SKY UNIVERSE TO CLIMB AND HANG FROM; AN ARCHITECTURE OF FOOD AND PLEASURE...
...THAT WAS A TREE.
BUT MOST OF ALL THE TREES WOULD DISTILL AN ICY AIR FOR THE LUNGS, AND A GENTLE RUSTLING FOR THE EAR WHEN YOU LAY NIGHTS IN YOUR SNOWY BED AND WERE GENTLED TO SLEEP BY THE SOUND.
HE LAY LISTENING TO THE DARK EARTH GATHER ITSELF,WAITING FOR THE SUN, FOR THE RAINS THAT HADN'T COME YET.

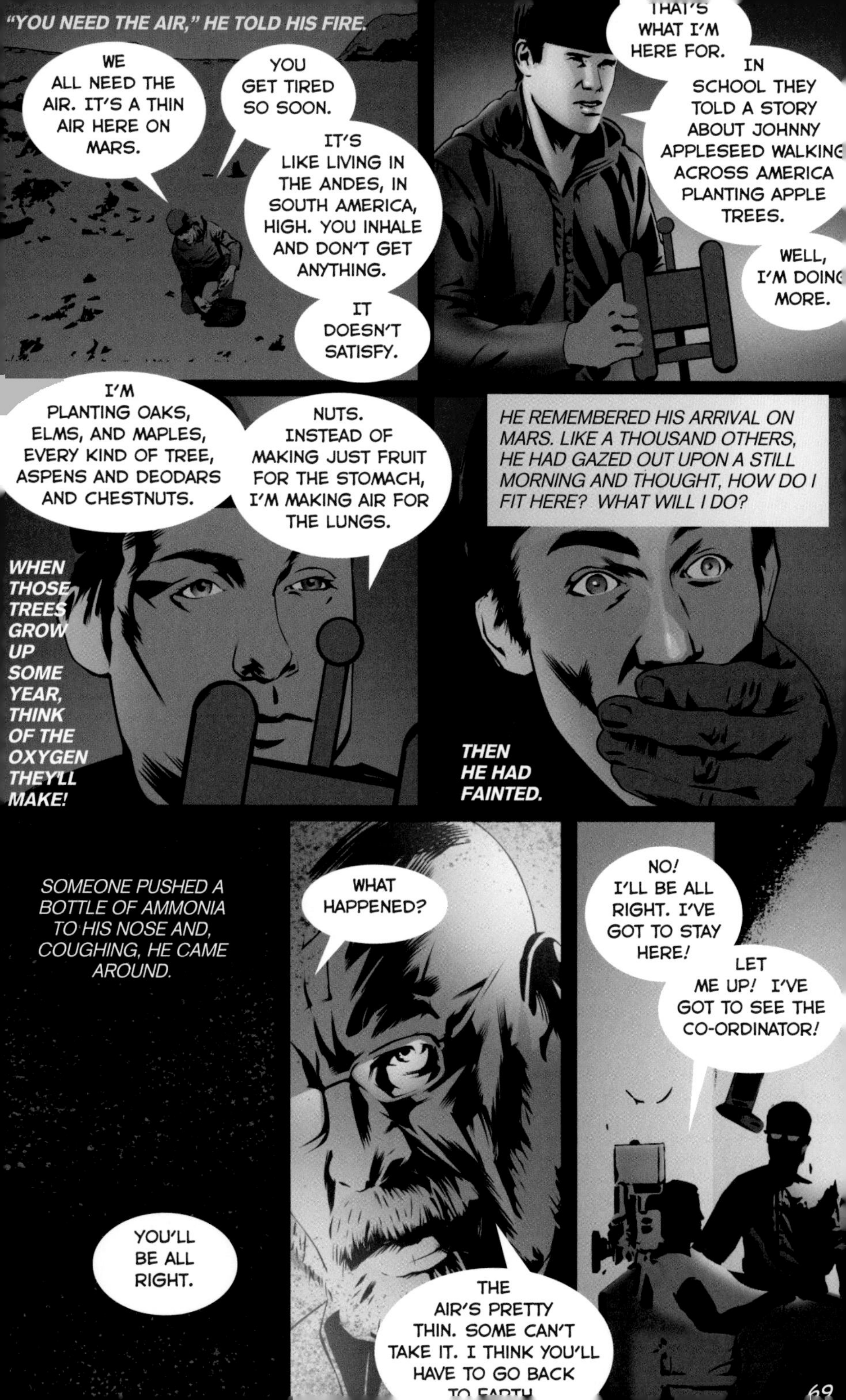
"YOU NEED THE AIR," HE TOLD HIS FIRE.
WE ALL NEED THE AIR. IT'S A THIN AIR HERE ON MARS.
YOU GET TIRED SO SOON.
IT'S LIKE LIVING IN THE ANDES, IN SOUTH AMERICA, HIGH. YOU INHALE AND DON'T GET ANYTHING.
IT DOESN'T SATISFY.
THAT'S WHAT I'M HERE FOR.
IN SCHOOL THEY TOLD A STORY ABOUT JOHNNY APPLESEED WALKING ACROSS AMERICA PLANTING APPLE TREES.
WELL, I'M DOING MORE.
I'M PLANTING OAKS, ELMS, AND MAPLES, EVERY KIND OF TREE, ASPENS AND DEODARS AND CHESTNUTS.
NUTS. INSTEAD OF MAKING JUST FRUIT FOR THE STOMACH, I'M MAKING AIR FOR THE LUNGS.
WHEN THOSE TREES GROW UP SOME YEAR, THINK OF THE OXYGEN THEY'LL MAKE!
HE REMEMBERED HIS ARRIVAL ON MARS. LIKE A THOUSAND OTHERS, HE HAD GAZED OUT UPON A STILL MORNING AND THOUGHT, HOW DO I FIT HERE? WHAT WILL I DO?
THEN HE HAD FAINTED.
SOMEONE PUSHED A BOTTLE OF AMMONIA TO HIS NOSE AND, COUGHING, HE CAME AROUND.
WHAT HAPPENED?
YOU'LL BE ALL RIGHT.
THE AIR'S PRETTY THIN. SOME CAN'T TAKE IT. I THINK YOU'LL HAVE TO GO BACK
NO! I'LL BE ALL RIGHT. I'VE GOT TO STAY HERE!
LET ME UP! I'VE GOT TO SEE THE CO-ORDINATOR!

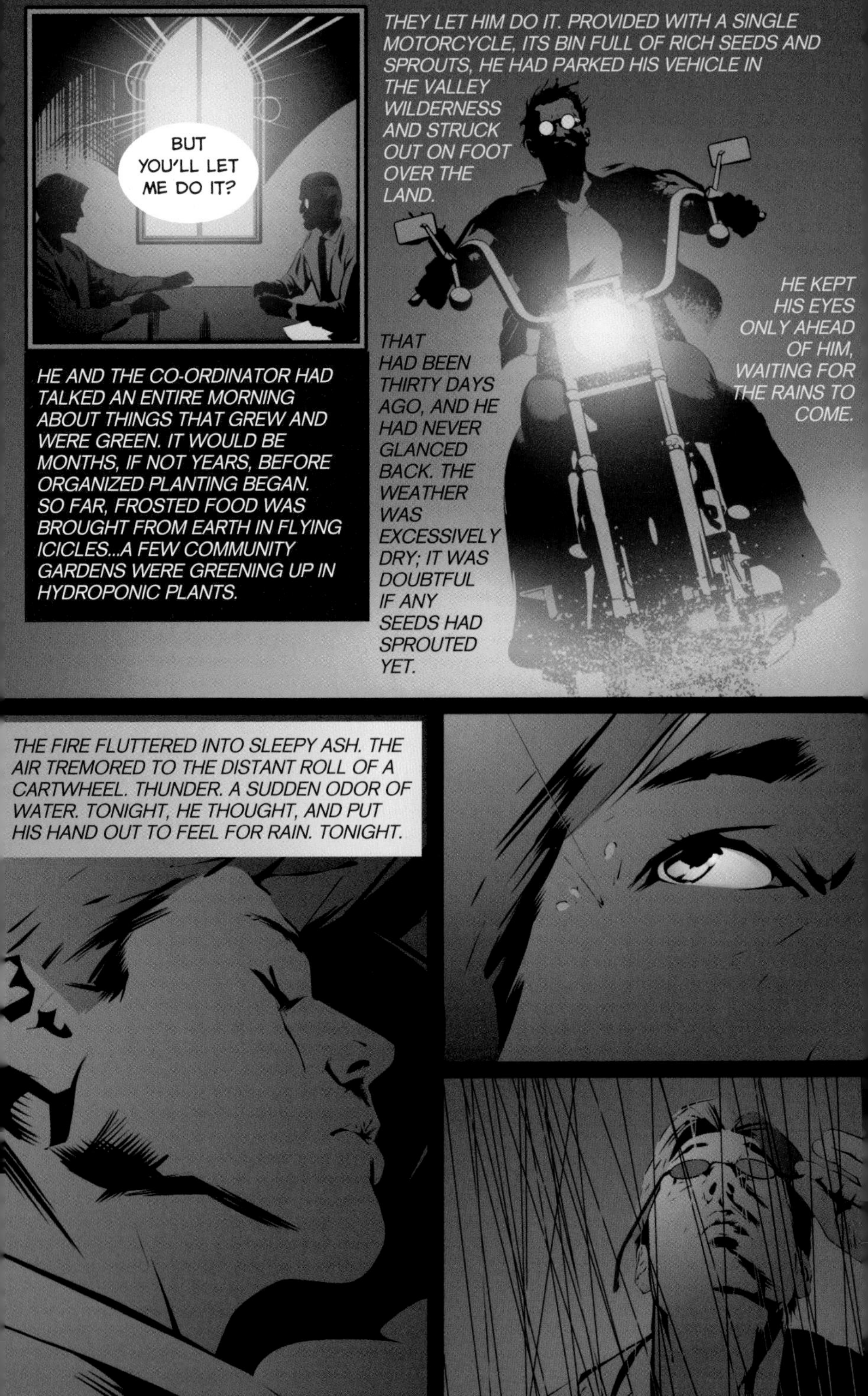
BUT YOU'LL LET ME DO IT?
HE AND THE CO-ORDINATOR HAD TALKED AN ENTIRE MORNING ABOUT THINGS THAT GREW AND WERE GREEN. IT WOULD BE MONTHS, IF NOT YEARS, BEFORE ORGANIZED PLANTING BEGAN. SO FAR, FROSTED FOOD WAS BROUGHT FROM EARTH IN FLYING ICICLES...A FEW COMMUNITY GARDENS WERE GREENING UP IN HYDROPONIC PLANTS.
THEY LET HIM DO IT. PROVIDED WITH A SINGLE MOTORCYCLE, ITS BIN FULL OF RICH SEEDS AND SPROUTS, HE HAD PARKED HIS VEHICLE IN THE VALLEY WILDERNESS AND STRUCK OUT ON FOOT OVER THE LAND.
THAT HAD BEEN THIRTY DAYS AGO, AND HE HAD NEVER GLANCED BACK. THE WEATHER WAS EXCESSIVELY DRY; IT WAS DOUBTFUL IF ANY SEEDS HAD SPROUTED YET.
HE KEPT HIS EYES ONLY AHEAD OF HIM, WAITING FOR THE RAINS TO COME.
THE FIRE FLUTTERED INTO SLEEPY ASH. THE AIR TREMORED TO THE DISTANT ROLL OF A CARTWHEEL. THUNDER. A SUDDEN ODOR OF WATER. TONIGHT, HE THOUGHT, AND PUT HIS HAND OUT TO FEEL FOR RAIN. TONIGHT.

IT RAINED STEADILY FOR TWO HOURS AND THEN STOPPED. THE STARS CAME OUT, FRESHLY WASHED AND CLEARER THAN EVER.

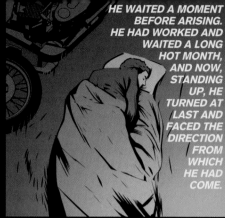

HE WAITED A MOMENT BEFORE ARISING. HE HAD WORKED AND WAITED A LONG HOT MONTH, AND NOW, STANDING UP, HE TURNED AT LAST AND FACED THE DIRECTION FROM WHICH HE HAD COME.

IT WAS A GREEN MORNING.

NOT ONE TREE, NOT TWO, NOT A DOZEN, BUT THE THOUSANDS HE HAD PLANTED IN SEED AND SPROUT.

AND NOT LITTLE TREES, NO, NOT SAPLINGS, NOT LITTLE TENDER SHOOTS, BUT GREAT TREES, HUGE TREES, TREES AS TALL AS TEN MEN, GREEN AND GREEN AND HUGE AND ROUND AND FULL, TREES SHIMMERING THEIR METALLIC LEAVES, TREES WHISPERING, TREES IN A LINE OVER HILLS.

IMPOSSIBLE!

LEMON TREES, LIME TREES, REDWOODS AND MIMOSAS AND OAKS AND ELMS AND ASPENS, CHERRY, MAPLE, ASH, APPLE, ORANGE, EUCALYPTUS, STUNG BY A TUMULTUOUS RAIN, NOURISHED BY ALIEN AND MAGICAL SOIL AND, EVEN AS HE WATCHED, THROWING OUT NEW BRANCHES, POPPING OPEN NEW BUDS.

THE VALLEY AND THE MORNING WERE GREEN. AND THE AIR!

ALL ABOUT, LIKE A MOVING CURRENT, A MOUNTAIN RIVER, CAME THE NEW AIR, THE OXYGEN BLOWING FROM THE GREEN TREES. YOU COULD SEE IT SHIMMER HIGH IN CRYSTAL BILLOWS. OXYGEN, FRESH, PURE, GREEN, COLD OXYGEN TURNING THE VALLEY INTO A RIVER DELTA.

MR. BENJAMIN DRISCOLL TOOK ONE LONG DEEP DRINK OF GREEN WATER AIR AND FAINTED.

BEFORE HE WOKE AGAIN FIVE THOUSAND NEW TREES HAD CLIMBED UP INTO THE YELLOW SUN.

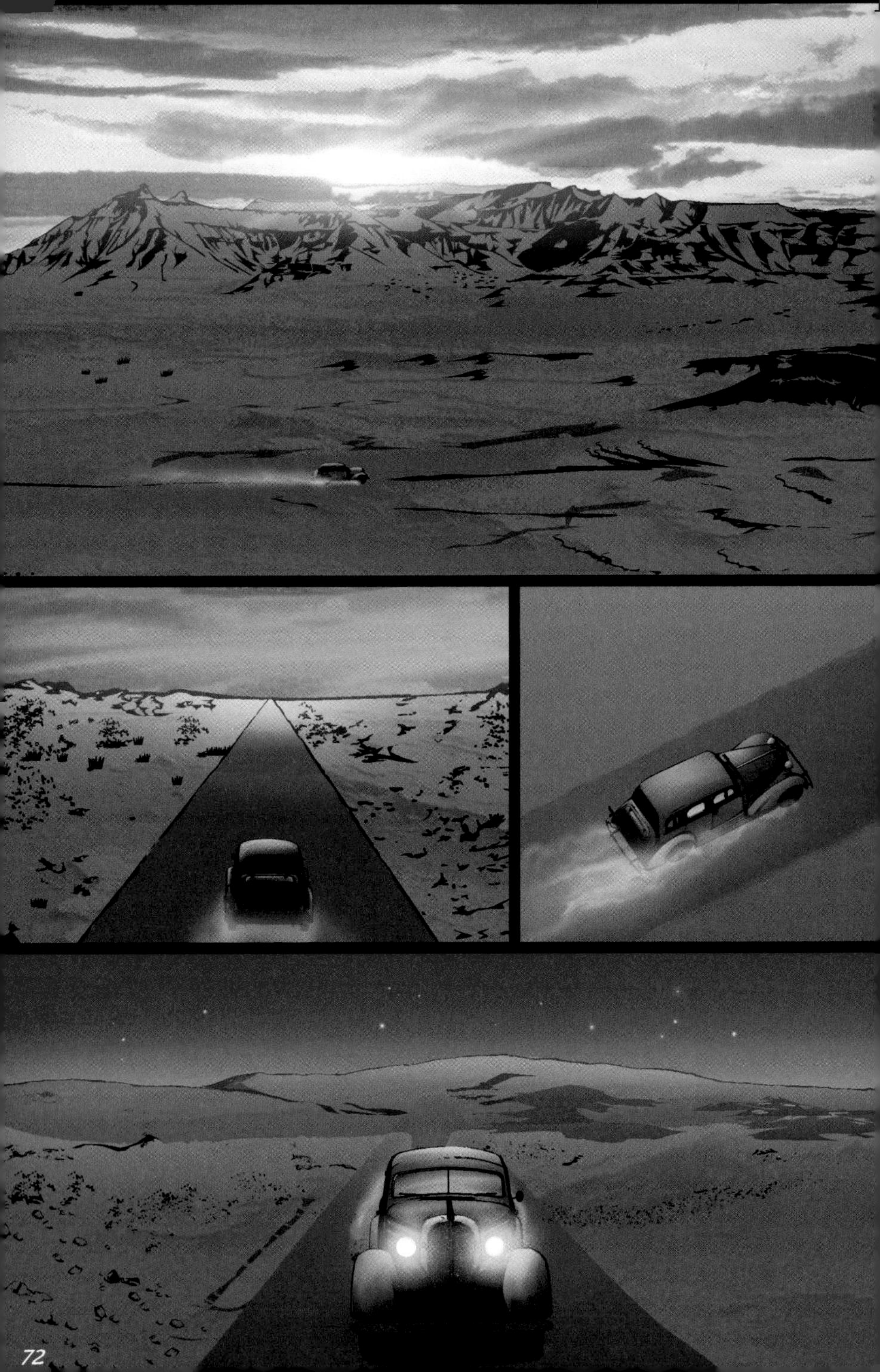

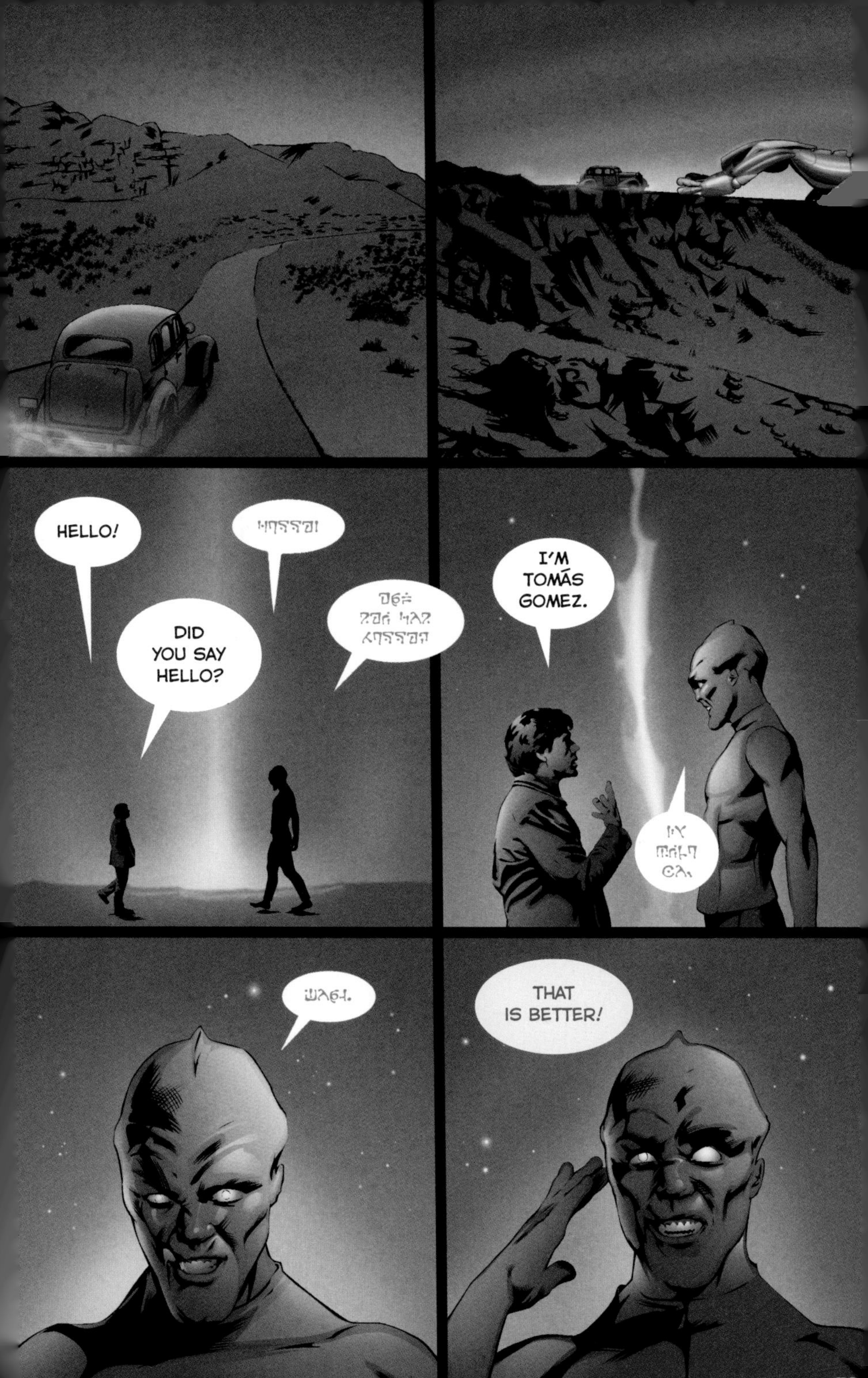
HELLO!
DID YOU SAY HELLO?
I'M TOMÁS GOMEZ.
THAT IS BETTER!

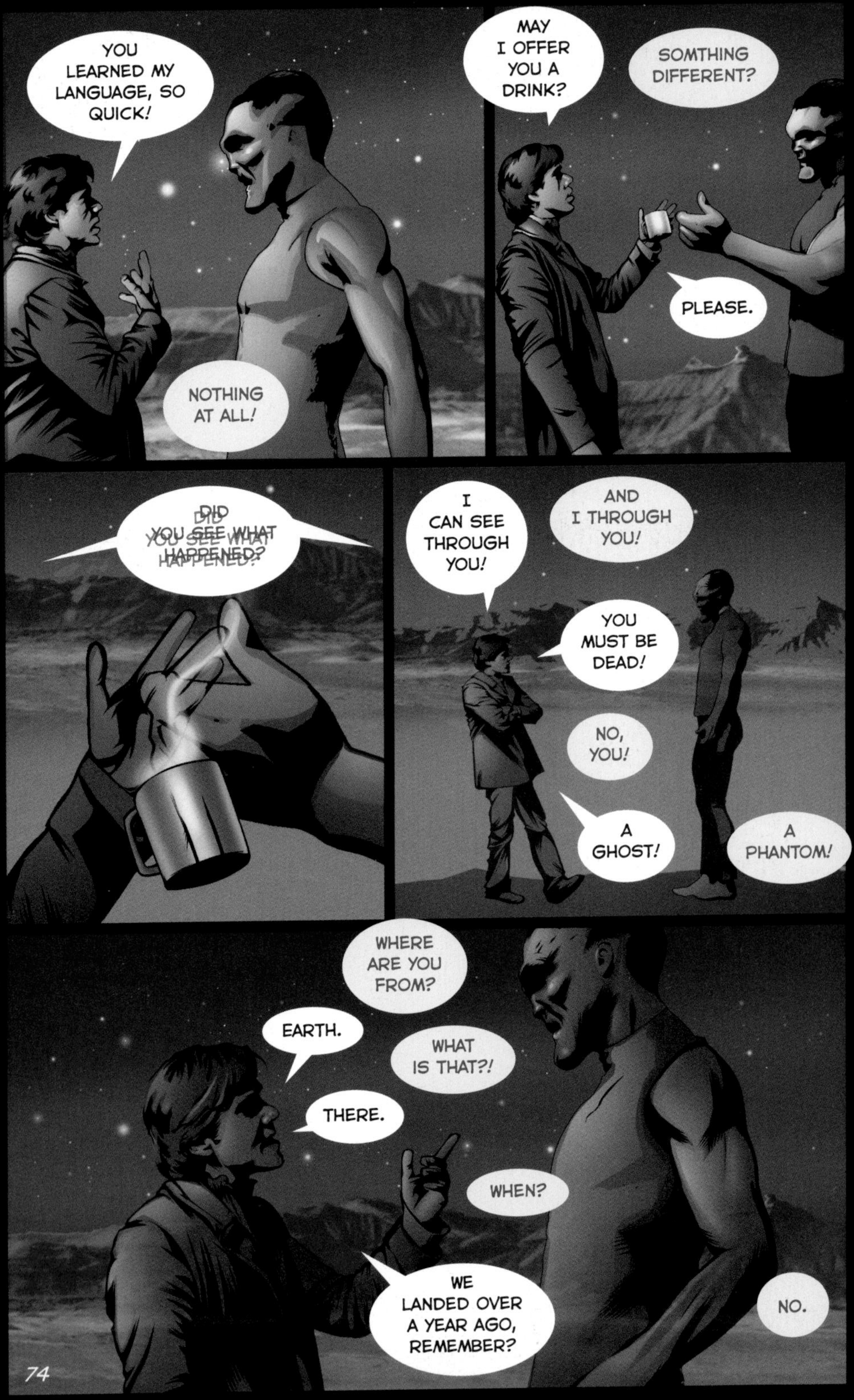

YOU LEARNED MY LANGUAGE, SO QUICK!
NOTHING AT ALL!
MAY I OFFER YOU A DRINK?
SOMTHING DIFFERENT?
PLEASE.
DID YOU SEE WHAT HAPPENED?
I CAN SEE THROUGH YOU!
AND I THROUGH YOU!
YOU MUST BE DEAD!
NO, YOU!
A GHOST!
A PHANTOM!
WHERE ARE YOU FROM?
EARTH.
WHAT IS THAT?!
THERE.
WHEN?
WE LANDED OVER A YEAR AGO, REMEMBER?
NO.

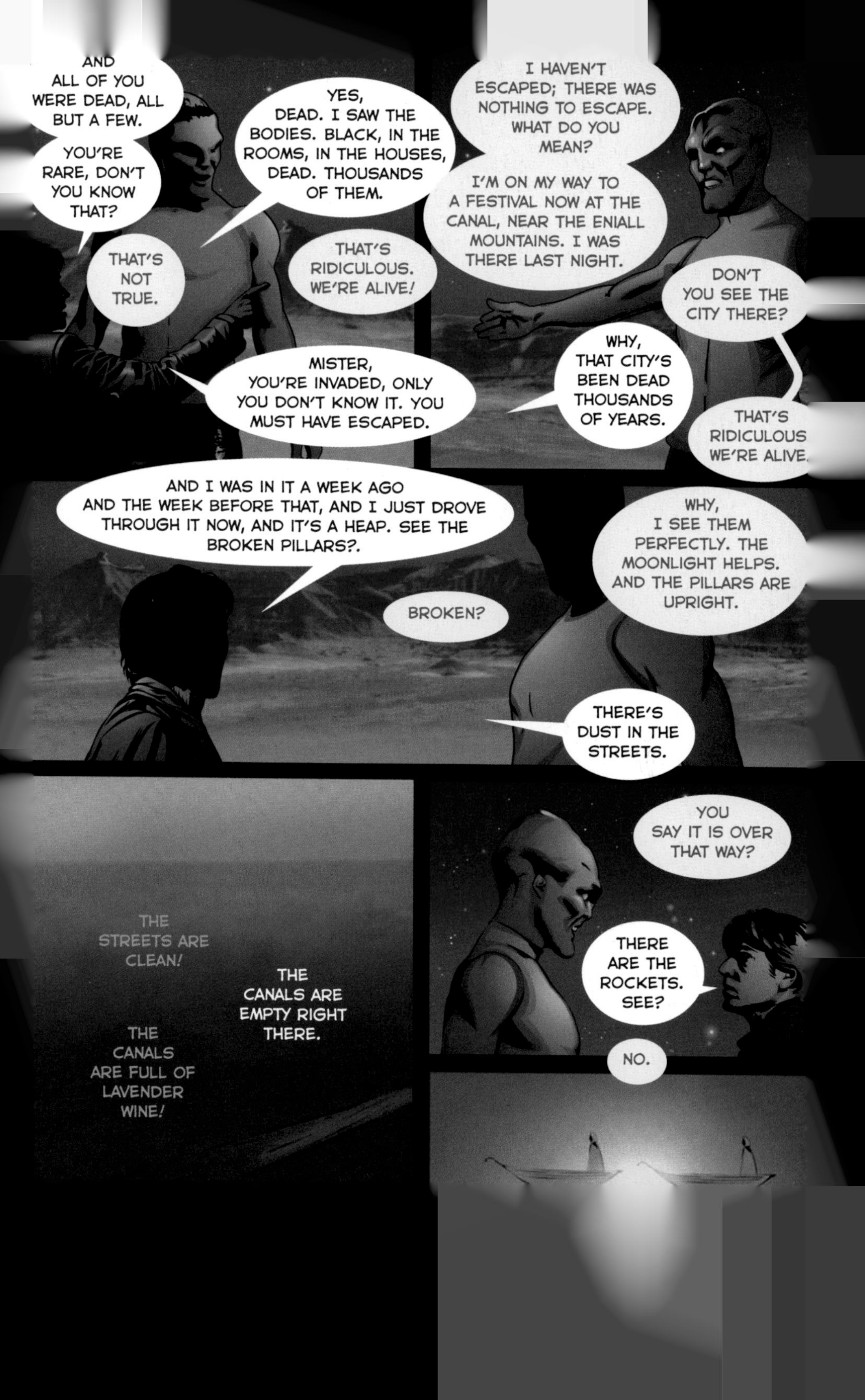
AND ALL OF YOU WERE DEAD, ALL BUT A FEW.
YOU'RE RARE, DON'T YOU KNOW THAT?
YES, DEAD. I SAW THE BODIES. BLACK, IN THE ROOMS, IN THE HOUSES, DEAD. THOUSANDS OF THEM.
THAT'S NOT TRUE.
THAT'S RIDICULOUS. WE'RE ALIVE!
MISTER, YOU'RE INVADED, ONLY YOU DON'T KNOW IT. YOU MUST HAVE ESCAPED.
I HAVEN'T ESCAPED; THERE WAS NOTHING TO ESCAPE. WHAT DO YOU MEAN?
I'M ON MY WAY TO A FESTIVAL NOW AT THE CANAL, NEAR THE ENIALL MOUNTAINS. I WAS THERE LAST NIGHT.
DON'T YOU SEE THE CITY THERE?
WHY, THAT CITY'S BEEN DEAD THOUSANDS OF YEARS.
THAT'S RIDICULOUS WE'RE ALIVE.
AND I WAS IN IT A WEEK AGO AND THE WEEK BEFORE THAT, AND I JUST DROVE THROUGH IT NOW, AND IT'S A HEAP. SEE THE BROKEN PILLARS?.
BROKEN?
WHY, I SEE THEM PERFECTLY. THE MOONLIGHT HELPS. AND THE PILLARS ARE UPRIGHT.
THERE'S DUST IN THE STREETS.
THE STREETS ARE CLEAN!
THE CANALS ARE EMPTY RIGHT THERE.
THE CANALS ARE FULL OF LAVENDER WINE!
YOU SAY IT IS OVER THAT WAY?
THERE ARE THE ROCKETS. SEE?
NO.

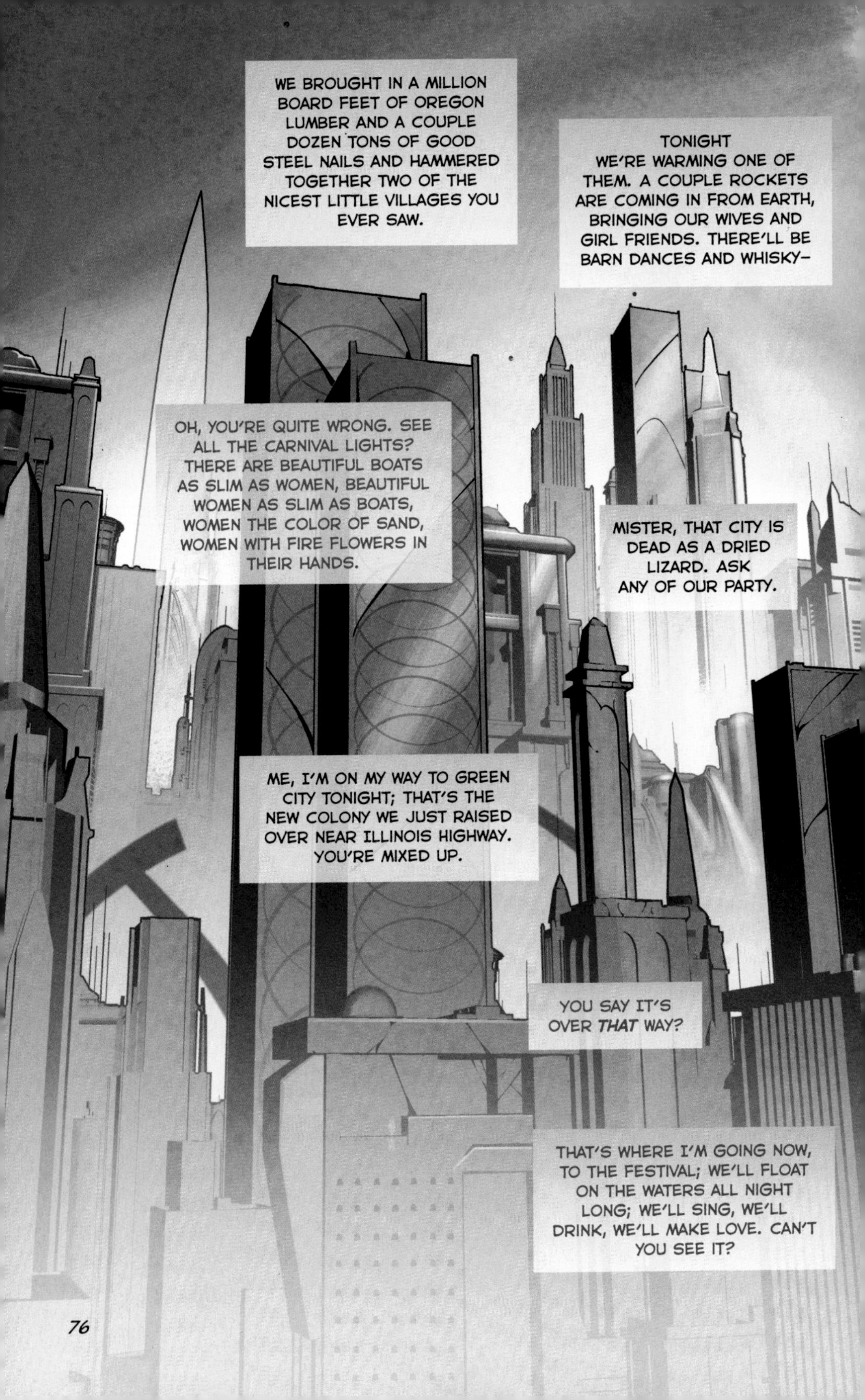

WE BROUGHT IN A MILLION BOARD FEET OF OREGON LUMBER AND A COUPLE DOZEN TONS OF GOOD STEEL NAILS AND HAMMERED TOGETHER TWO OF THE NICEST LITTLE VILLAGES YOU EVER SAW.
TONIGHT WE'RE WARMING ONE OF THEM. A COUPLE ROCKETS ARE COMING IN FROM EARTH, BRINGING OUR WIVES AND GIRL FRIENDS. THERE'LL BE BARN DANCES AND WHISKY–
OH, YOU'RE QUITE WRONG. SEE ALL THE CARNIVAL LIGHTS? THERE ARE BEAUTIFUL BOATS AS SLIM AS WOMEN, BEAUTIFUL WOMEN AS SLIM AS BOATS, WOMEN THE COLOR OF SAND, WOMEN WITH FIRE FLOWERS IN THEIR HANDS.
MISTER, THAT CITY IS DEAD AS A DRIED LIZARD. ASK ANY OF OUR PARTY.
ME, I'M ON MY WAY TO GREEN CITY TONIGHT; THAT'S THE NEW COLONY WE JUST RAISED OVER NEAR ILLINOIS HIGHWAY. YOU'RE MIXED UP.
YOU SAY IT'S OVER *THAT* WAY?
THAT'S WHERE I'M GOING NOW, TO THE FESTIVAL; WE'LL FLOAT ON THE WATERS ALL NIGHT LONG; WE'LL SING, WE'LL DRINK, WE'LL MAKE LOVE. CAN'T YOU SEE IT?

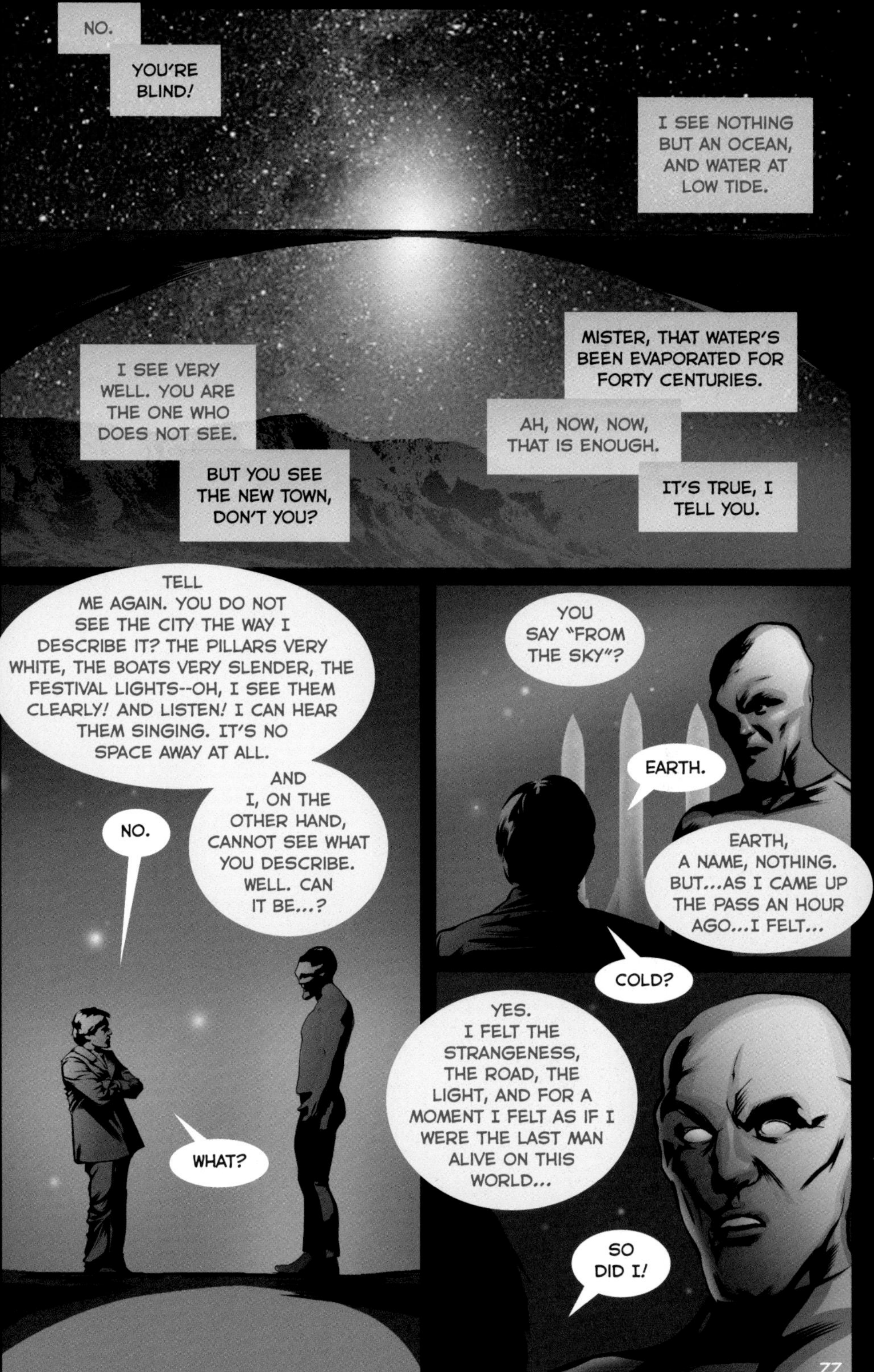
NO.
YOU'RE BLIND!
I SEE NOTHING BUT AN OCEAN, AND WATER AT LOW TIDE.
I SEE VERY WELL. YOU ARE THE ONE WHO DOES NOT SEE.
BUT YOU SEE THE NEW TOWN, DON'T YOU?
MISTER, THAT WATER'S BEEN EVAPORATED FOR FORTY CENTURIES.
AH, NOW, NOW, THAT IS ENOUGH.
IT'S TRUE, I TELL YOU.
TELL ME AGAIN. YOU DO NOT SEE THE CITY THE WAY I DESCRIBE IT? THE PILLARS VERY WHITE, THE BOATS VERY SLENDER, THE FESTIVAL LIGHTS--OH, I SEE THEM CLEARLY! AND LISTEN! I CAN HEAR THEM SINGING. IT'S NO SPACE AWAY AT ALL.
AND I, ON THE OTHER HAND, CANNOT SEE WHAT YOU DESCRIBE. WELL. CAN IT BE...?
NO.
WHAT?
YOU SAY "FROM THE SKY"?
EARTH.
EARTH, A NAME, NOTHING. BUT...AS I CAME UP THE PASS AN HOUR AGO...I FELT...
COLD?
YES. I FELT THE STRANGENESS, THE ROAD, THE LIGHT, AND FOR A MOMENT I FELT AS IF I WERE THE LAST MAN ALIVE ON THIS WORLD...
SO DID I!

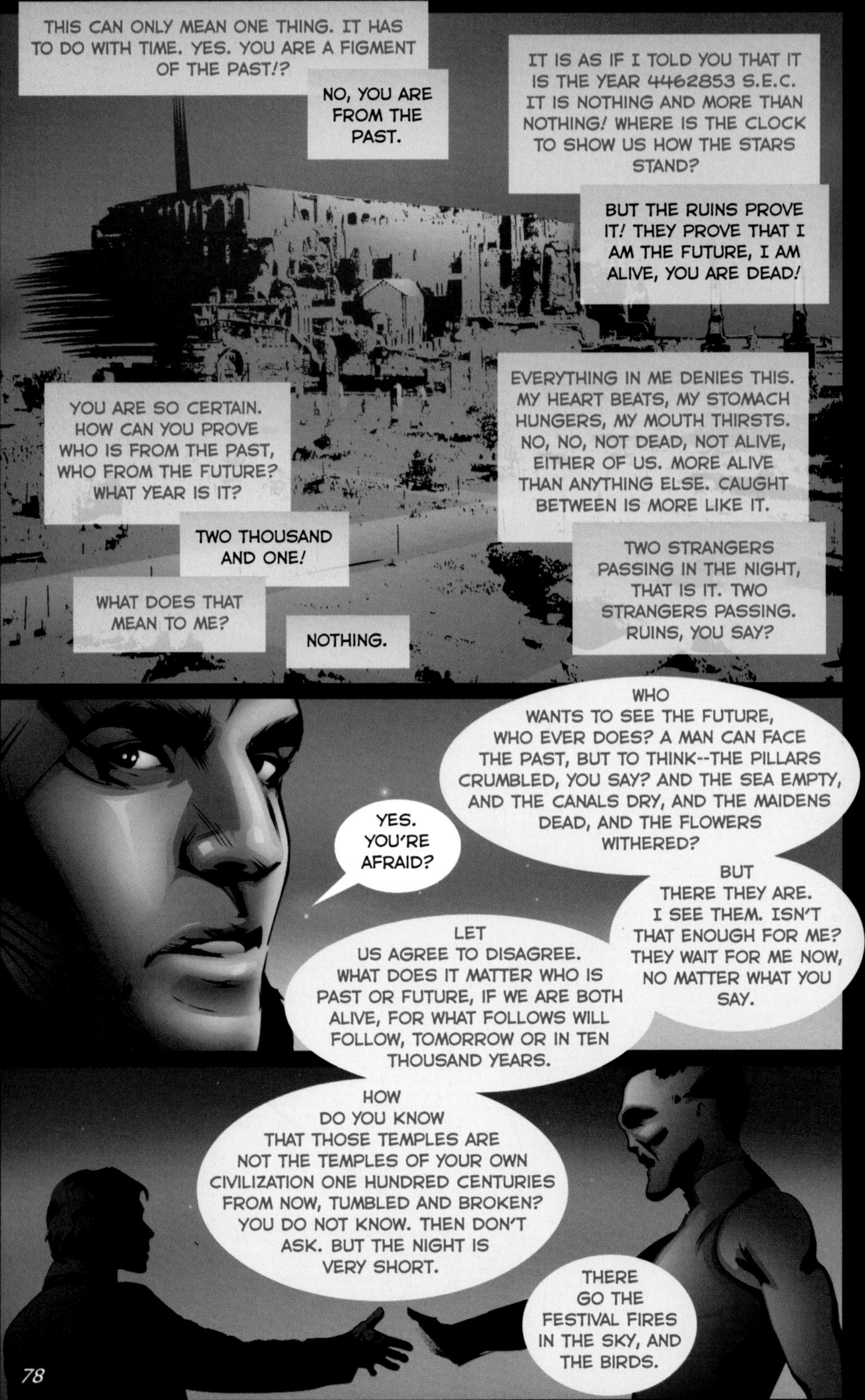
THIS CAN ONLY MEAN ONE THING. IT HAS TO DO WITH TIME. YES. YOU ARE A FIGMENT OF THE PAST!?
NO, YOU ARE FROM THE PAST.
IT IS AS IF I TOLD YOU THAT IT IS THE YEAR 4462853 S.E.C. IT IS NOTHING AND MORE THAN NOTHING! WHERE IS THE CLOCK TO SHOW US HOW THE STARS STAND?
BUT THE RUINS PROVE IT! THEY PROVE THAT I AM THE FUTURE, I AM ALIVE, YOU ARE DEAD!
YOU ARE SO CERTAIN. HOW CAN YOU PROVE WHO IS FROM THE PAST, WHO FROM THE FUTURE? WHAT YEAR IS IT?
TWO THOUSAND AND ONE!
WHAT DOES THAT MEAN TO ME?
NOTHING.
EVERYTHING IN ME DENIES THIS. MY HEART BEATS, MY STOMACH HUNGERS, MY MOUTH THIRSTS. NO, NO, NOT DEAD, NOT ALIVE, EITHER OF US. MORE ALIVE THAN ANYTHING ELSE. CAUGHT BETWEEN IS MORE LIKE IT.
TWO STRANGERS PASSING IN THE NIGHT, THAT IS IT. TWO STRANGERS PASSING. RUINS, YOU SAY?
WHO WANTS TO SEE THE FUTURE, WHO EVER DOES? A MAN CAN FACE THE PAST, BUT TO THINK--THE PILLARS CRUMBLED, YOU SAY? AND THE SEA EMPTY, AND THE CANALS DRY, AND THE MAIDENS DEAD, AND THE FLOWERS WITHERED?
YES. YOU'RE AFRAID?
BUT THERE THEY ARE. I SEE THEM. ISN'T THAT ENOUGH FOR ME? THEY WAIT FOR ME NOW, NO MATTER WHAT YOU SAY.
LET US AGREE TO DISAGREE. WHAT DOES IT MATTER WHO IS PAST OR FUTURE, IF WE ARE BOTH ALIVE, FOR WHAT FOLLOWS WILL FOLLOW, TOMORROW OR IN TEN THOUSAND YEARS.
HOW DO YOU KNOW THAT THOSE TEMPLES ARE NOT THE TEMPLES OF YOUR OWN CIVILIZATION ONE HUNDRED CENTURIES FROM NOW, TUMBLED AND BROKEN? YOU DO NOT KNOW. THEN DON'T ASK. BUT THE NIGHT IS VERY SHORT.
THERE GO THE FESTIVAL FIRES IN THE SKY, AND THE BIRDS.

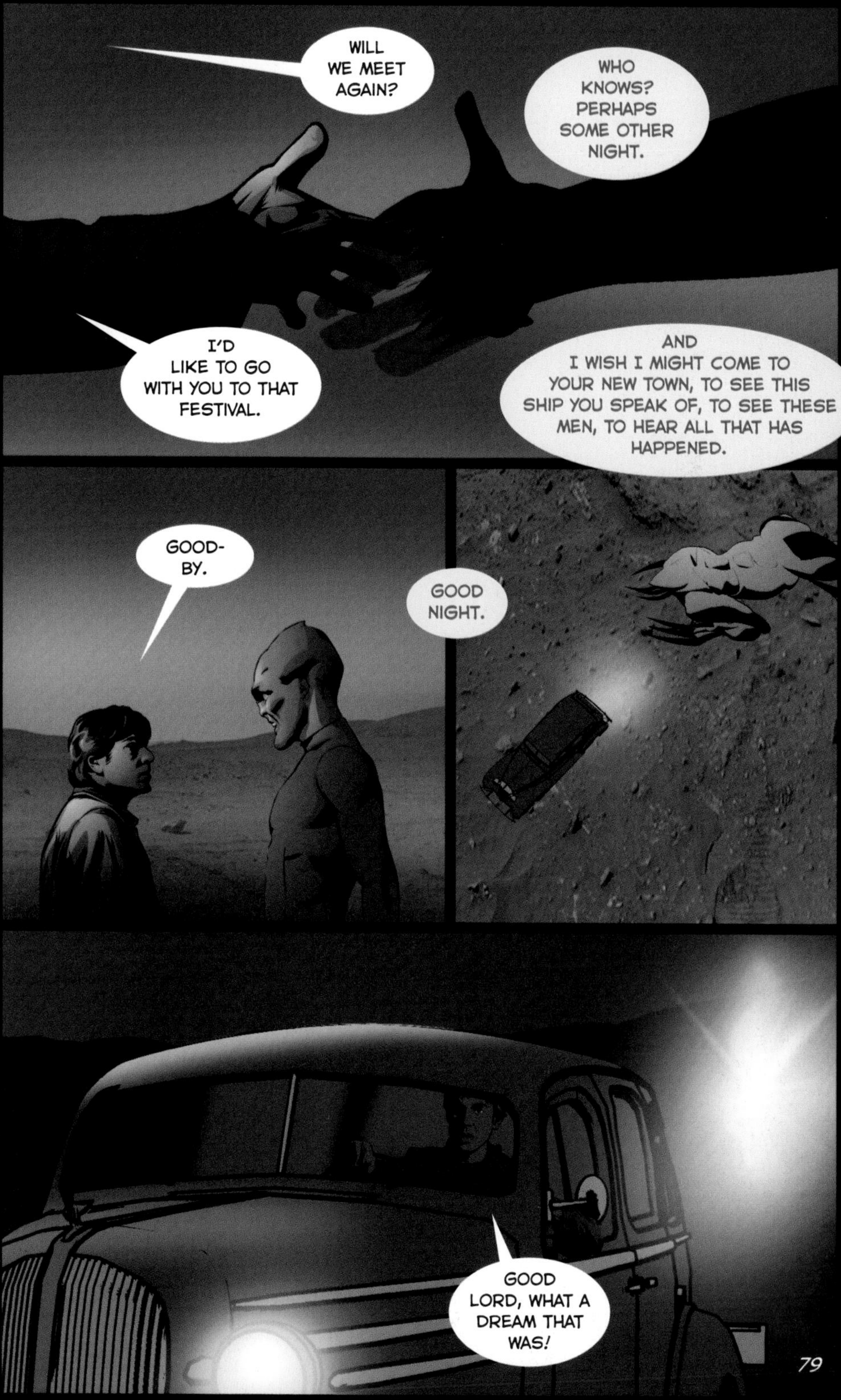
WILL WE MEET AGAIN?
WHO KNOWS? PERHAPS SOME OTHER NIGHT.
I'D LIKE TO GO WITH YOU TO THAT FESTIVAL.
AND I WISH I MIGHT COME TO YOUR NEW TOWN, TO SEE THIS SHIP YOU SPEAK OF, TO SEE THESE MEN, TO HEAR ALL THAT HAS HAPPENED.
GOOD-BY.
GOOD NIGHT.
GOOD LORD, WHAT A DREAM THAT WAS!

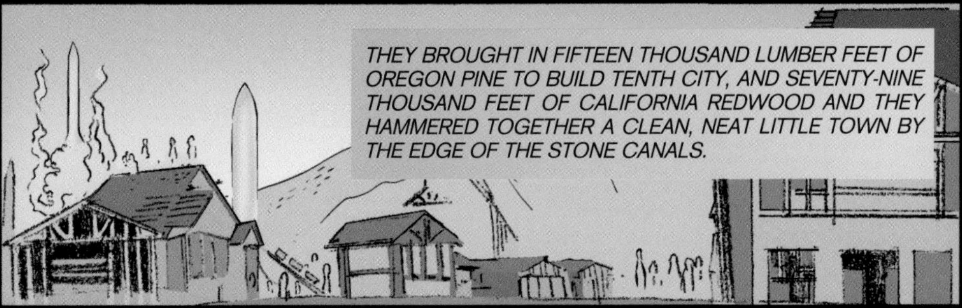
THEY BROUGHT IN FIFTEEN THOUSAND LUMBER FEET OF OREGON PINE TO BUILD TENTH CITY, AND SEVENTY-NINE THOUSAND FEET OF CALIFORNIA REDWOOD AND THEY HAMMERED TOGETHER A CLEAN, NEAT LITTLE TOWN BY THE EDGE OF THE STONE CANALS.

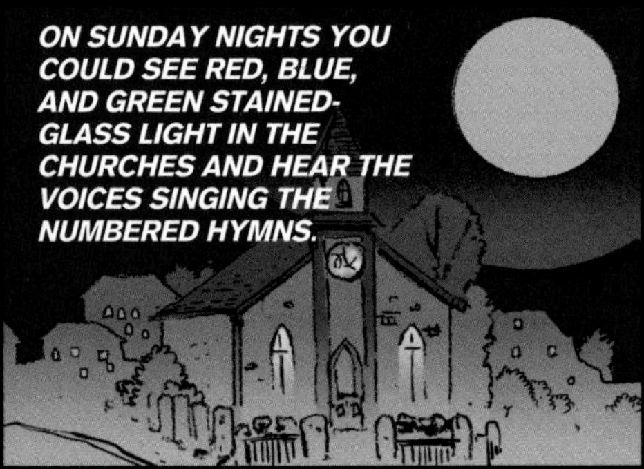
ON SUNDAY NIGHTS YOU COULD SEE RED, BLUE, AND GREEN STAINED-GLASS LIGHT IN THE CHURCHES AND HEAR THE VOICES SINGING THE NUMBERED HYMNS.

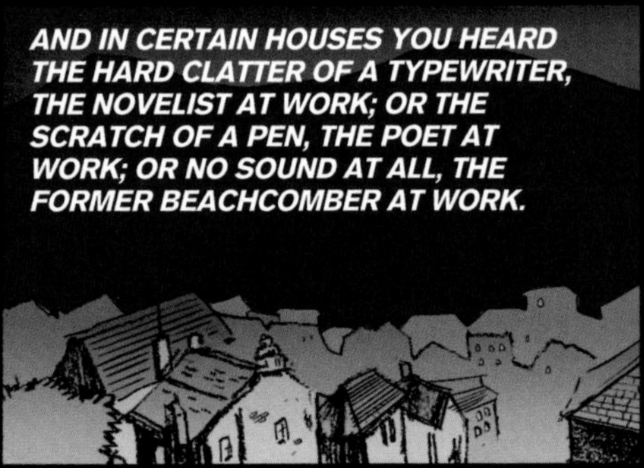
AND IN CERTAIN HOUSES YOU HEARD THE HARD CLATTER OF A TYPEWRITER, THE NOVELIST AT WORK; OR THE SCRATCH OF A PEN, THE POET AT WORK; OR NO SOUND AT ALL, THE FORMER BEACHCOMBER AT WORK.

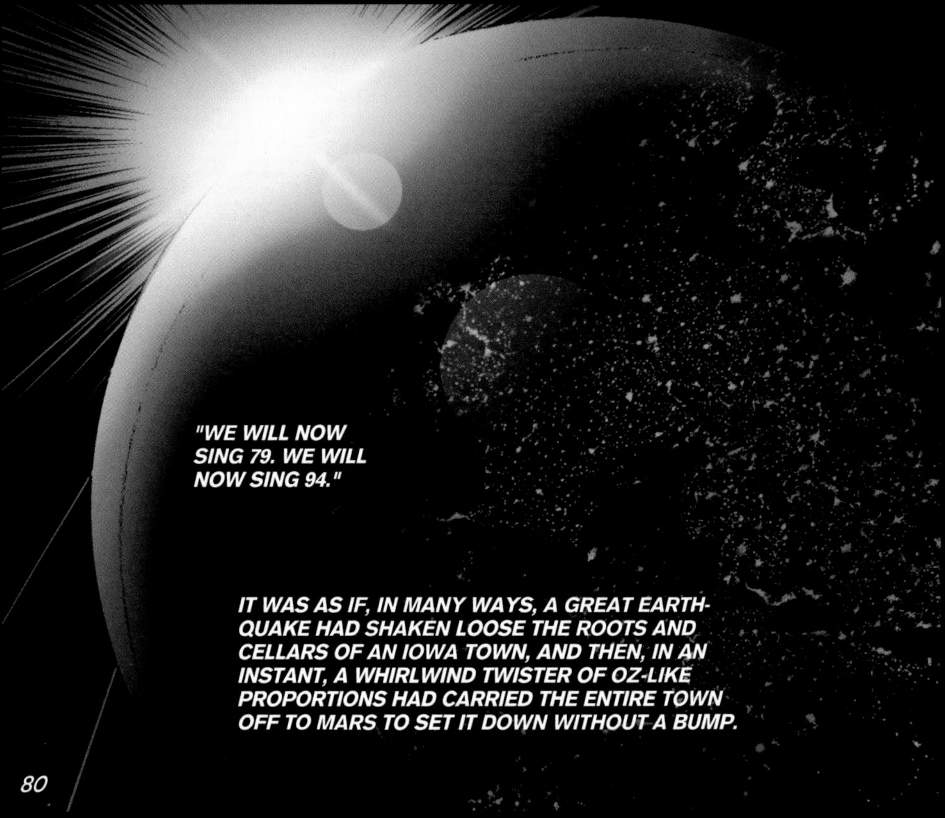
"WE WILL NOW SING 79. WE WILL NOW SING 94."
IT WAS AS IF, IN MANY WAYS, A GREAT EARTH-QUAKE HAD SHAKEN LOOSE THE ROOTS AND CELLARS OF AN IOWA TOWN, AND THEN, IN AN INSTANT, A WHIRLWIND TWISTER OF OZ-LIKE PROPORTIONS HAD CARRIED THE ENTIRE TOWN OFF TO MARS TO SET IT DOWN WITHOUT A BUMP.

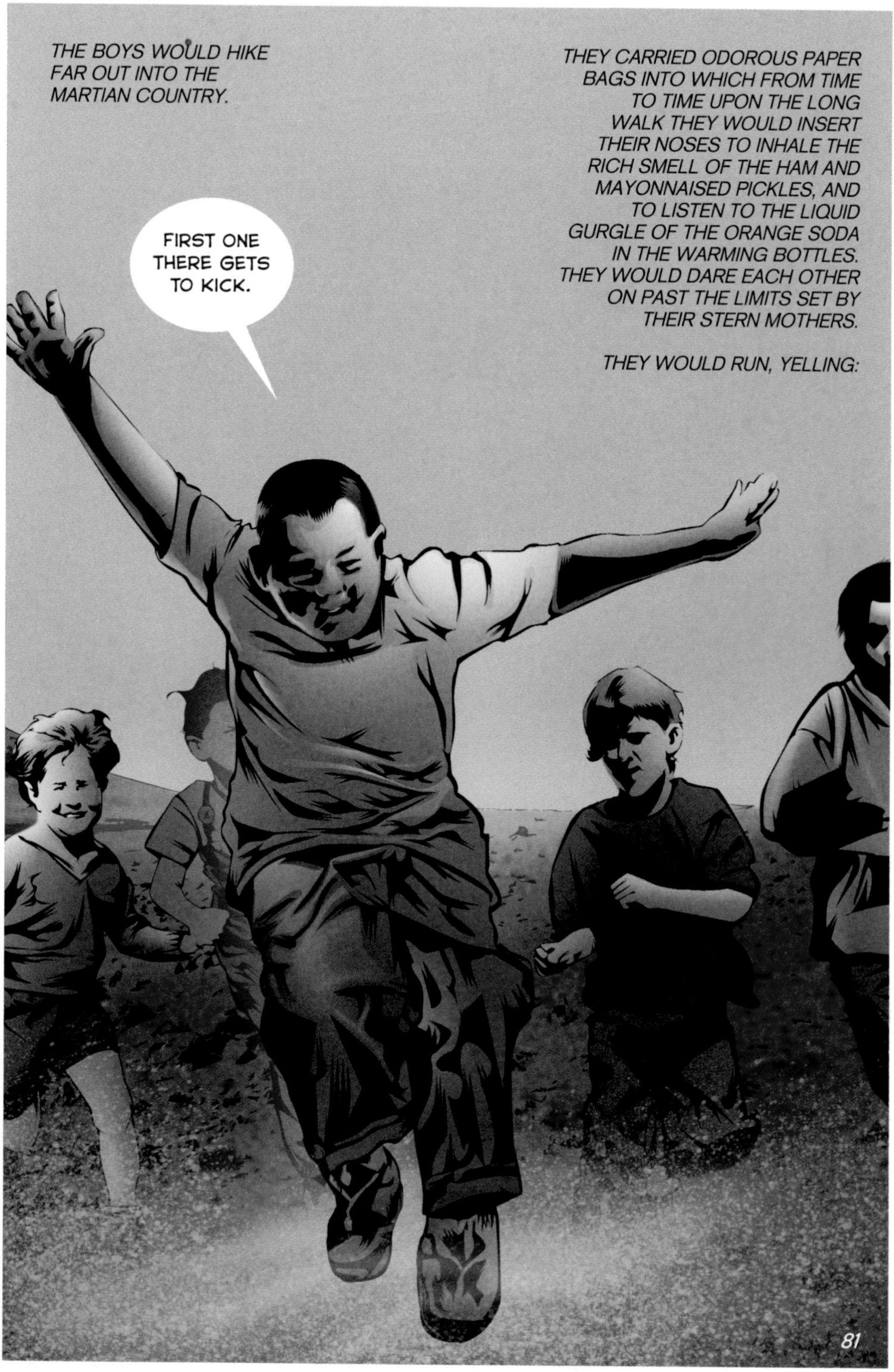
THE BOYS WOULD HIKE FAR OUT INTO THE MARTIAN COUNTRY.
THEY CARRIED ODOROUS PAPER BAGS INTO WHICH FROM TIME TO TIME UPON THE LONG WALK THEY WOULD INSERT THEIR NOSES TO INHALE THE RICH SMELL OF THE HAM AND MAYONNAISED PICKLES, AND TO LISTEN TO THE LIQUID GURGLE OF THE ORANGE SODA IN THE WARMING BOTTLES. THEY WOULD DARE EACH OTHER ON PAST THE LIMITS SET BY THEIR STERN MOTHERS.
THEY WOULD RUN, YELLING:
FIRST ONE THERE GETS TO KICK.

THEY HIKED IN SUMMER, AUTUMN, OR WINTER. AUTUMN WAS MOST FUN, BECAUSE THEN THEY IMAGINED, LIKE ON EARTH, THEY WERE SCUTTERING THROUGH AUTUMN LEAVES.

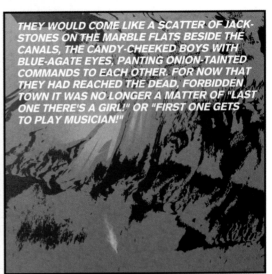

THEY WOULD COME LIKE A SCATTER OF JACK-STONES ON THE MARBLE FLATS BESIDE THE CANALS, THE CANDY-CHEEKED BOYS WITH BLUE-AGATE EYES, PANTING ONION-TAINTED COMMANDS TO EACH OTHER. FOR NOW THAT THEY HAD REACHED THE DEAD, FORBIDDEN TOWN IT WAS NO LONGER A MATTER OF "LAST ONE THERE'S A GIRL!" OR "FIRST ONE GETS TO PLAY MUSICIAN!"

NOW THE DEAD TOWN'S DOORS LAY WIDE AND THEY THOUGHT THEY COULD HEAR THE FAINTEST CRACKLE, LIKE AUTUMN LEAVES, FROM INSIDE. THEY WOULD HUSH THEMSELVES FORWARD, REMEMBERING THEIR PARENTS HAD TOLD THEM...

NOT THERE! NO, TO NONE OF THE OLD TOWNS! WATCH WHERE YOU HIKE. YOU'LL GET THE BEATING OF YOUR LIFE WHEN YOU COME HOME. WE'LL CHECK YOUR SHOES!!

HERE GOES NOTHING!

AND THERE THEY STOOD IN THE DEAD CITY, A HEAP OF BOYS, THEIR HIKING LUNCHES HALF DEVOURED, DARING EACH OTHER IN SHRIEKY WHISPERS.

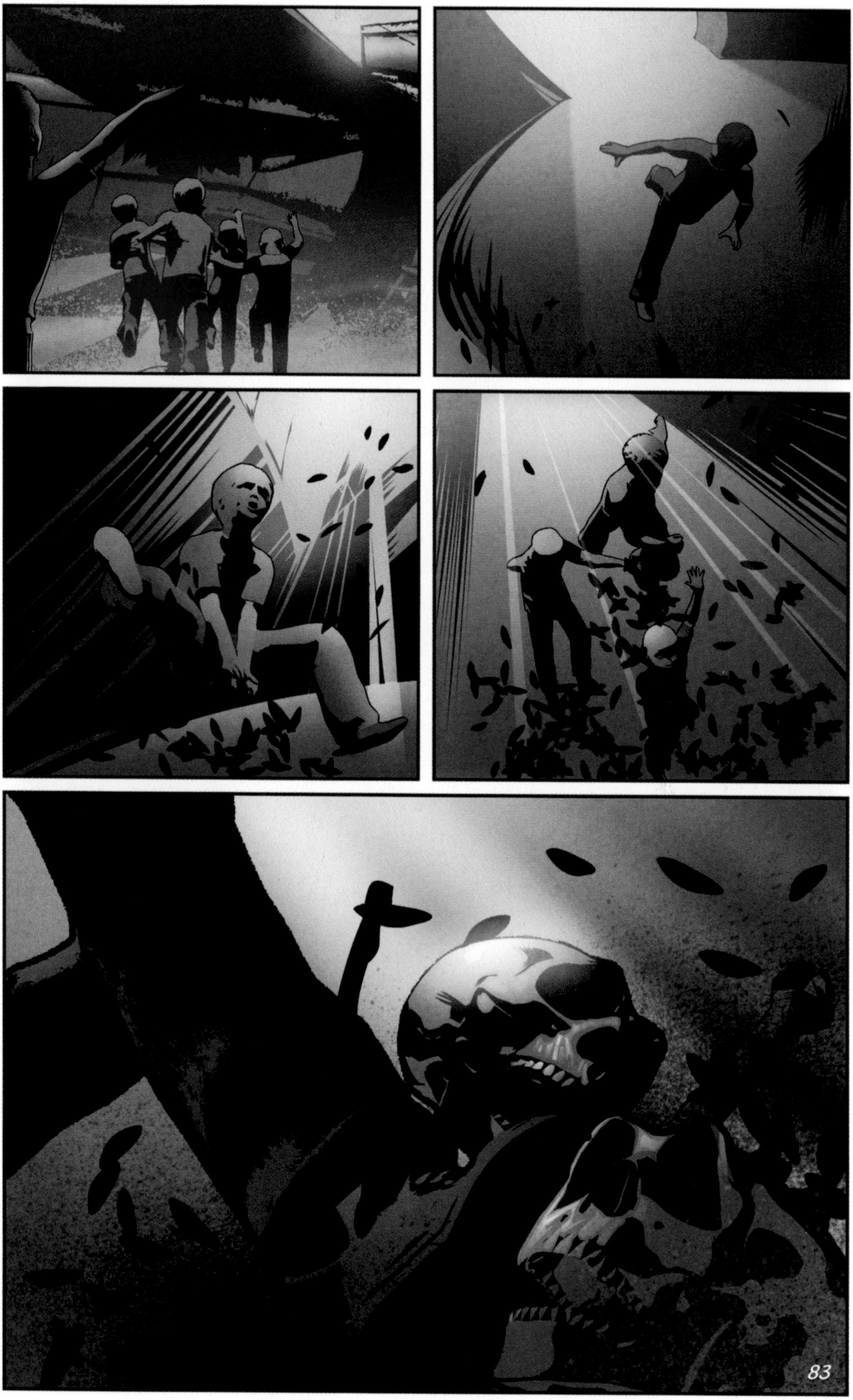

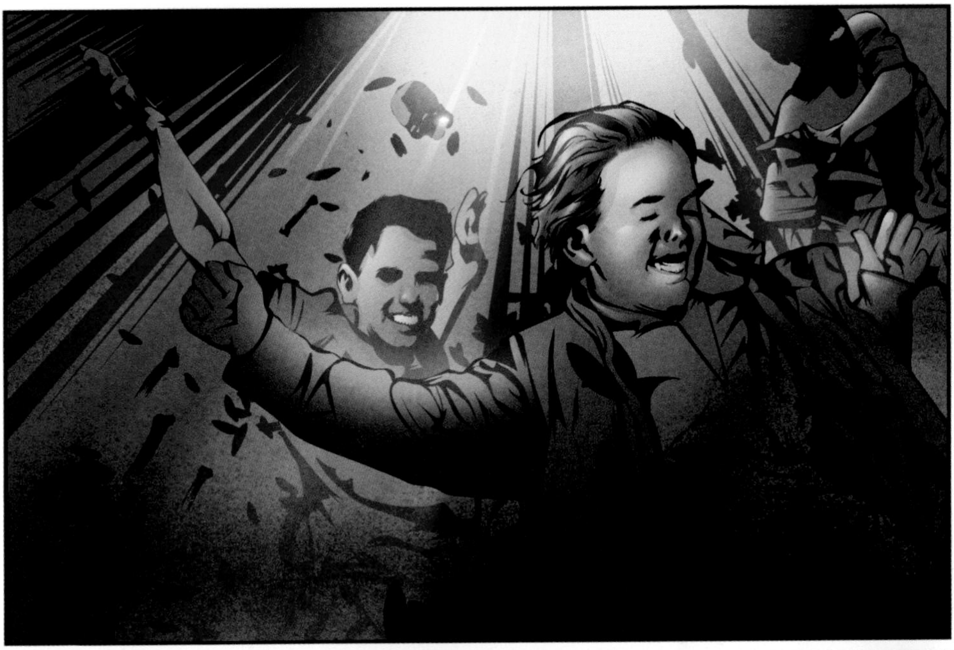

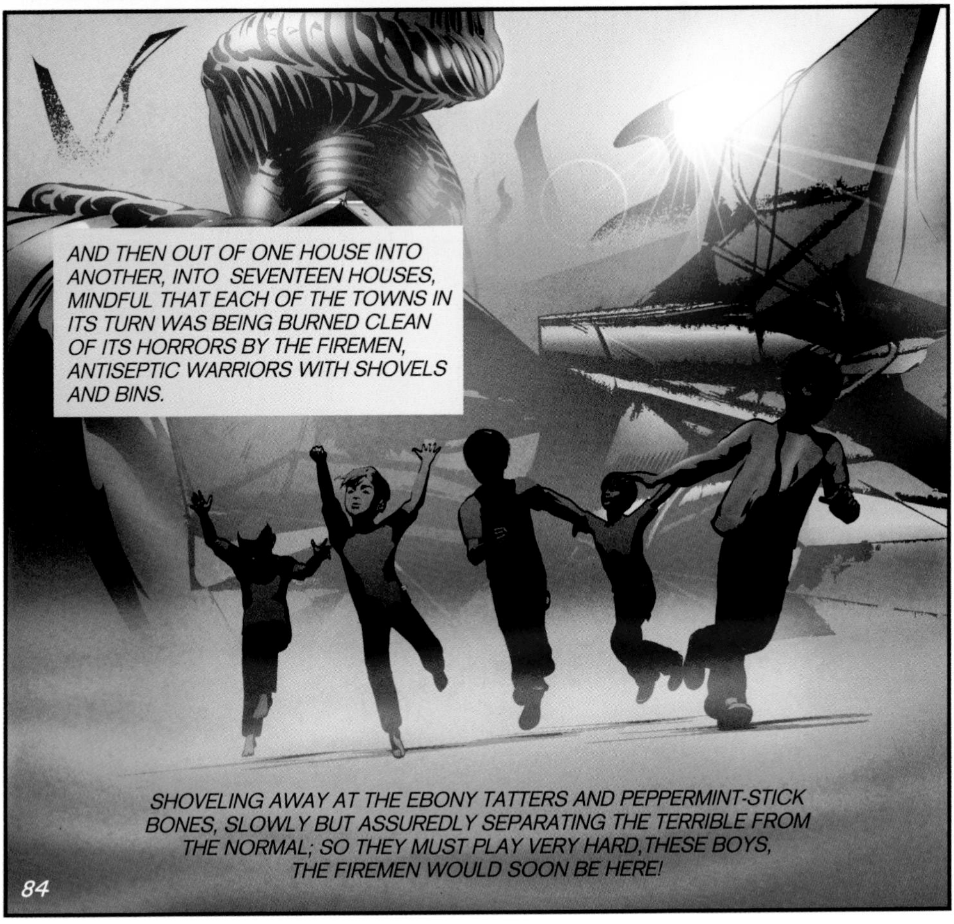
AND THEN OUT OF ONE HOUSE INTO ANOTHER, INTO SEVENTEEN HOUSES, MINDFUL THAT EACH OF THE TOWNS IN ITS TURN WAS BEING BURNED CLEAN OF ITS HORRORS BY THE FIREMEN, ANTISEPTIC WARRIORS WITH SHOVELS AND BINS.
SHOVELING AWAY AT THE EBONY TATTERS AND PEPPERMINT-STICK BONES, SLOWLY BUT ASSUREDLY SEPARATING THE TERRIBLE FROM THE NORMAL; SO THEY MUST PLAY VERY HARD,THESE BOYS, THE FIREMEN WOULD SOON BE HERE!

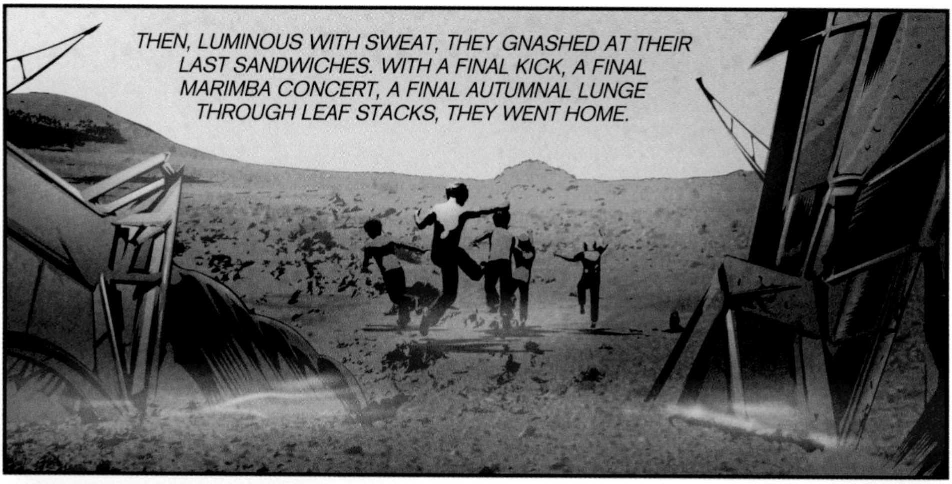
THEN, LUMINOUS WITH SWEAT, THEY GNASHED AT THEIR LAST SANDWICHES. WITH A FINAL KICK, A FINAL MARIMBA CONCERT, A FINAL AUTUMNAL LUNGE THROUGH LEAF STACKS, THEY WENT HOME.

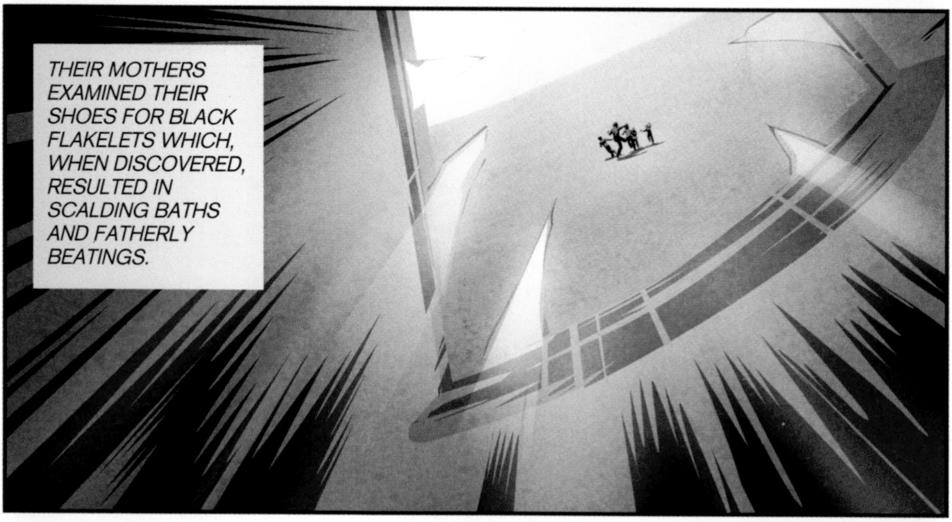
THEIR MOTHERS EXAMINED THEIR SHOES FOR BLACK FLAKELETS WHICH, WHEN DISCOVERED, RESULTED IN SCALDING BATHS AND FATHERLY BEATINGS.

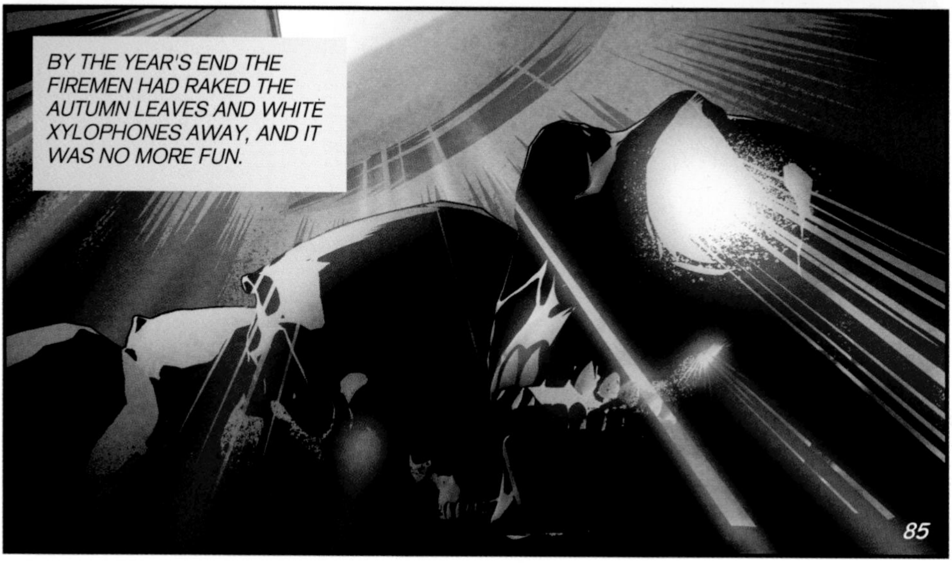
BY THE YEAR'S END THE FIREMEN HAD RAKED THE AUTUMN LEAVES AND WHITE XYLOPHONES AWAY, AND IT WAS NO MORE FUN.

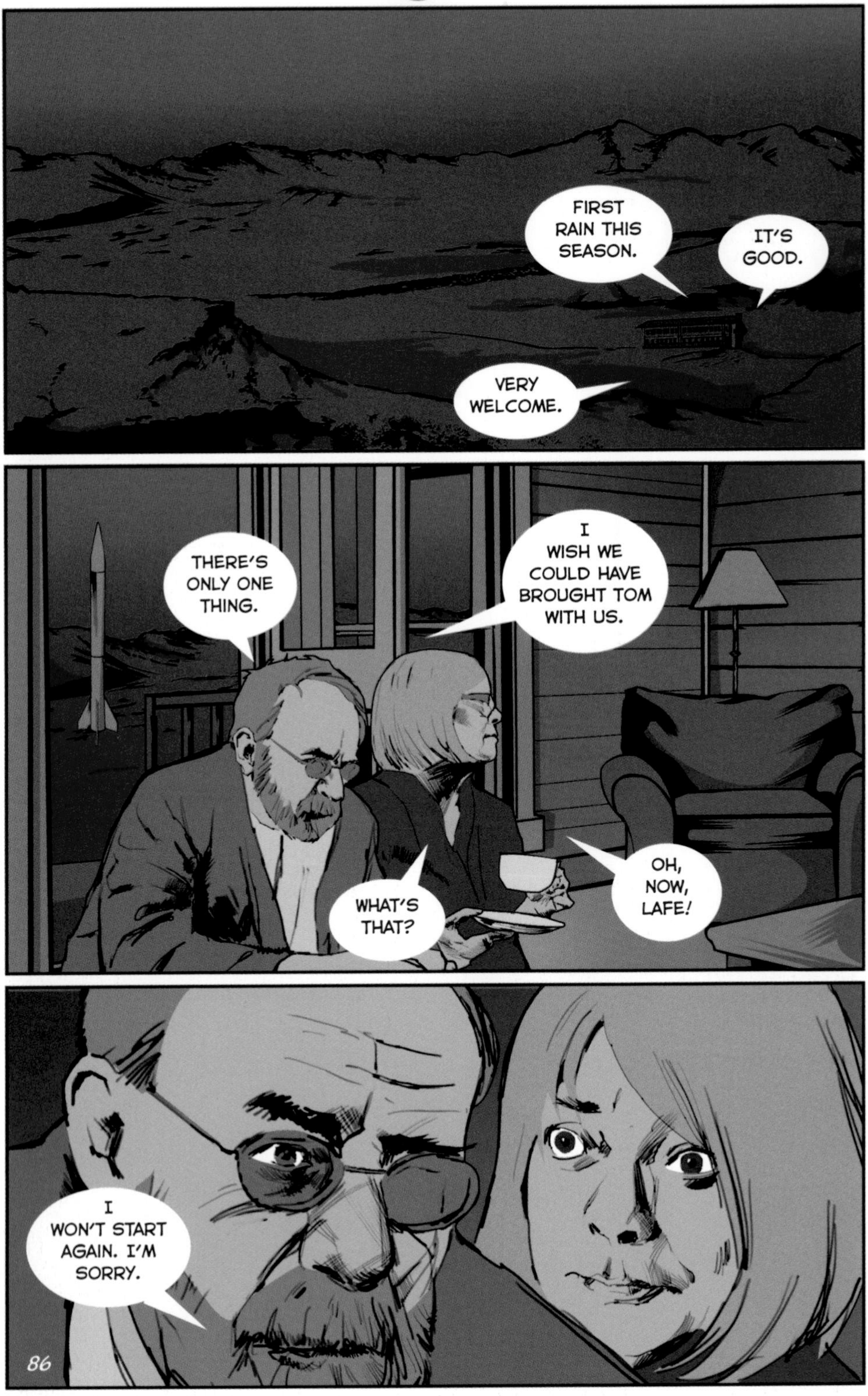
FIRST RAIN THIS SEASON.
IT'S GOOD.
VERY WELCOME.
THERE'S ONLY ONE THING.
I WISH WE COULD HAVE BROUGHT TOM WITH US.
WHAT'S THAT?
OH, NOW, LAFE!
I WON'T START AGAIN. I'M SORRY.

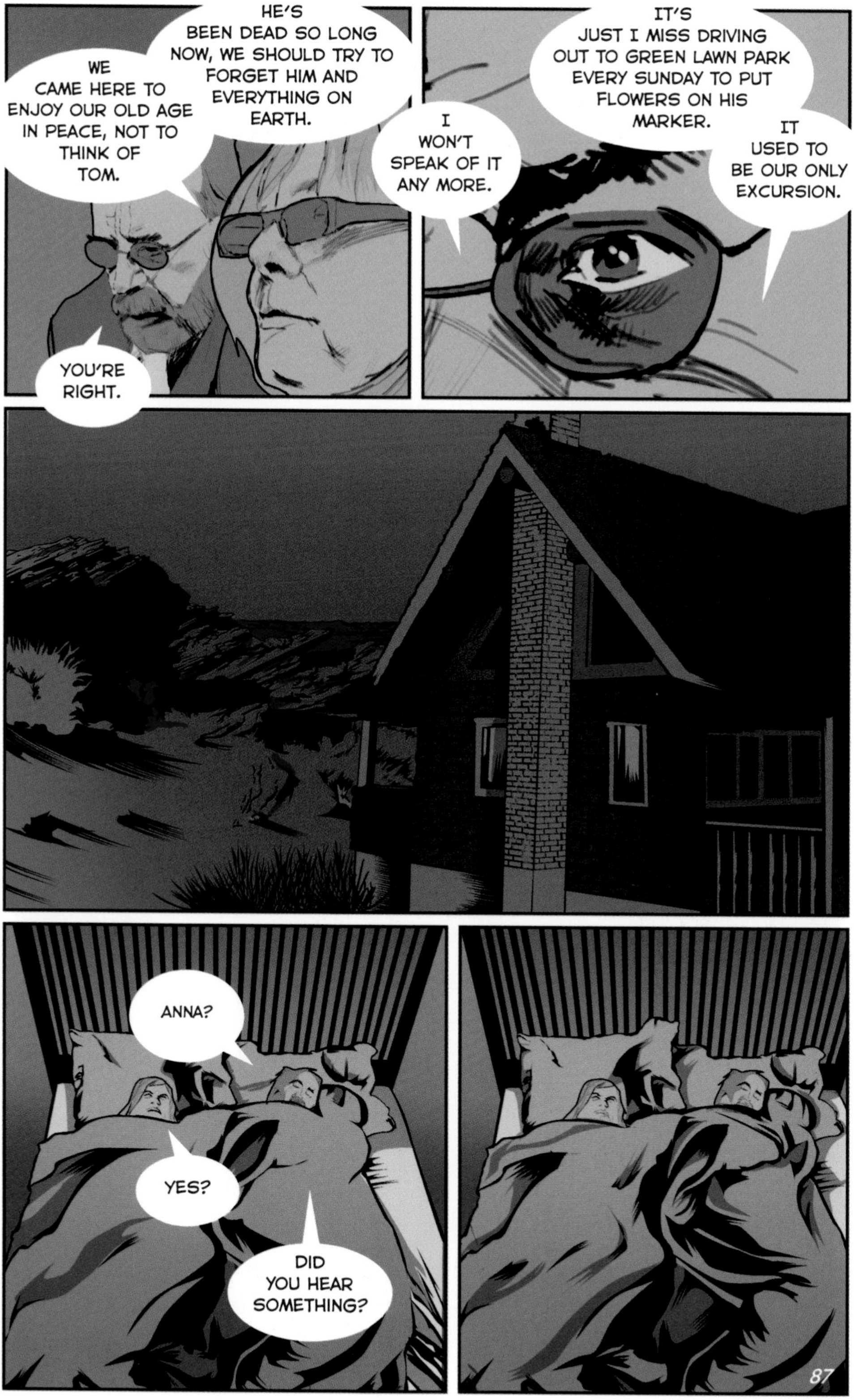
WE CAME HERE TO ENJOY OUR OLD AGE IN PEACE, NOT TO THINK OF TOM.
HE'S BEEN DEAD SO LONG NOW, WE SHOULD TRY TO FORGET HIM AND EVERYTHING ON EARTH.
YOU'RE RIGHT.
I WON'T SPEAK OF IT ANY MORE.
IT'S JUST I MISS DRIVING OUT TO GREEN LAWN PARK EVERY SUNDAY TO PUT FLOWERS ON HIS MARKER.
IT USED TO BE OUR ONLY EXCURSION.
ANNA?
YES?
DID YOU HEAR SOMETHING?

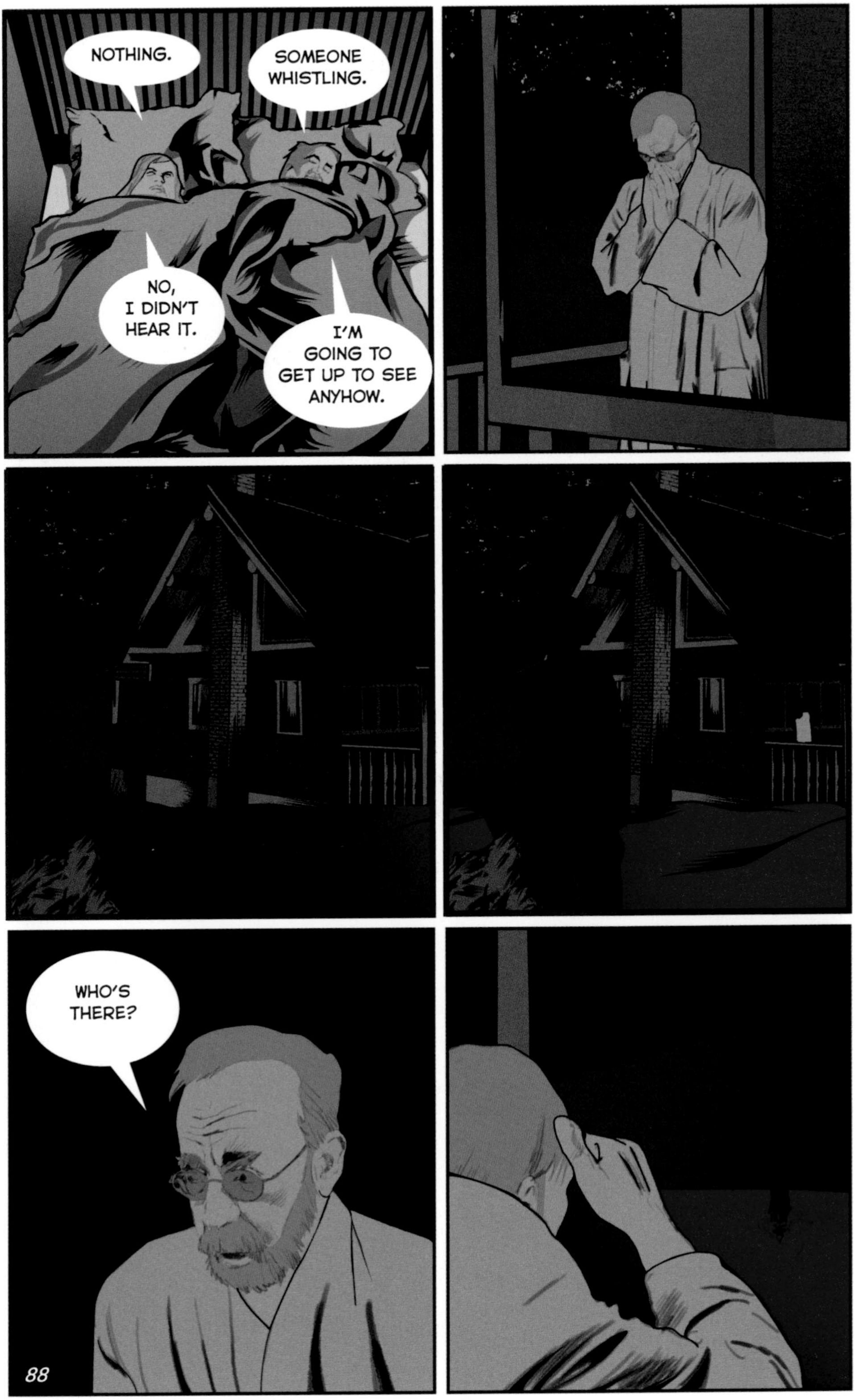
NOTHING.
SOMEONE WHISTLING.
NO, I DIDN'T HEAR IT.
I'M GOING TO GET UP TO SEE ANYHOW.
WHO'S THERE?

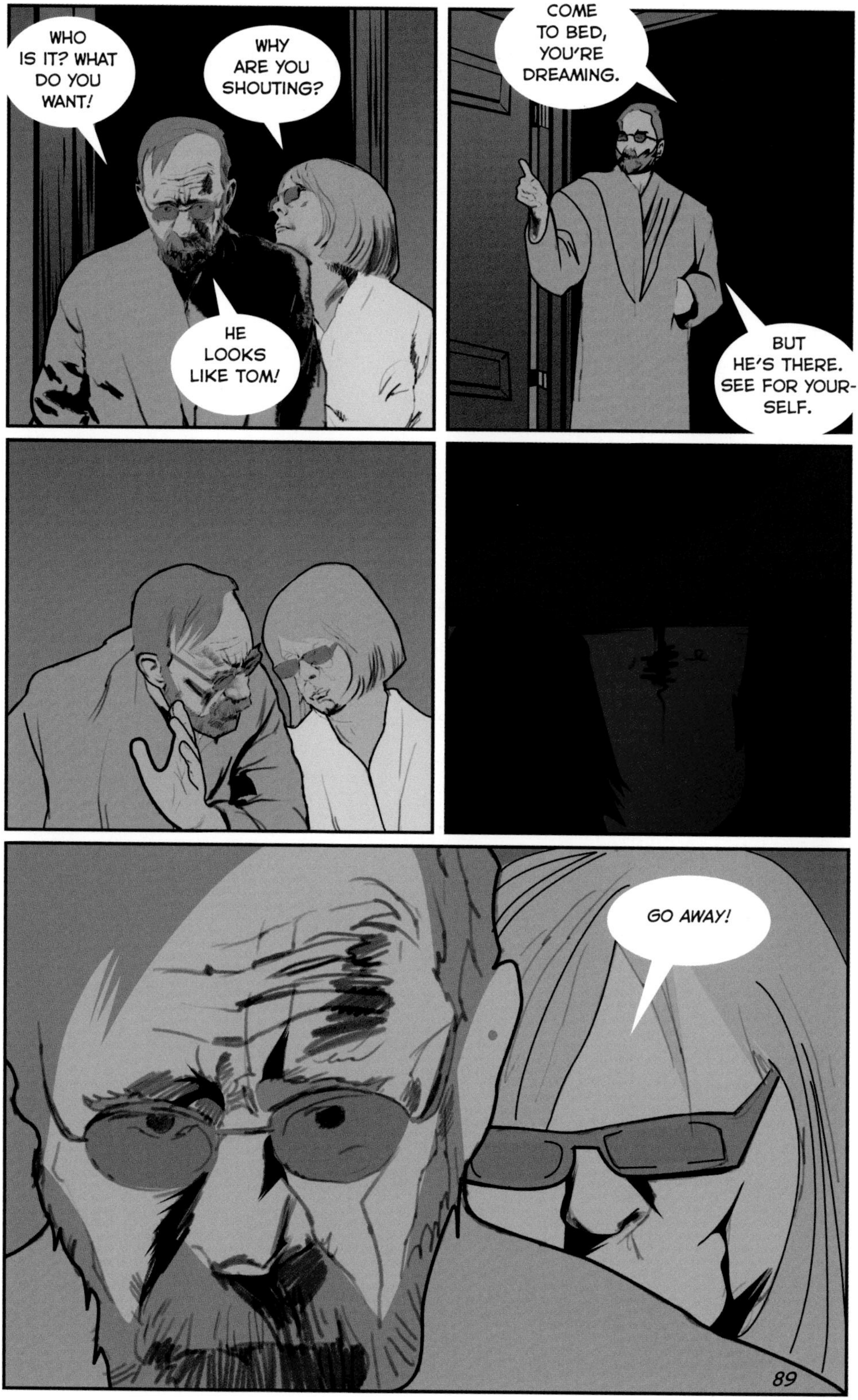
WHO IS IT? WHAT DO YOU WANT!
WHY ARE YOU SHOUTING?
HE LOOKS LIKE TOM!
COME TO BED, YOU'RE DREAMING.
BUT HE'S THERE. SEE FOR YOURSELF.
GO AWAY!

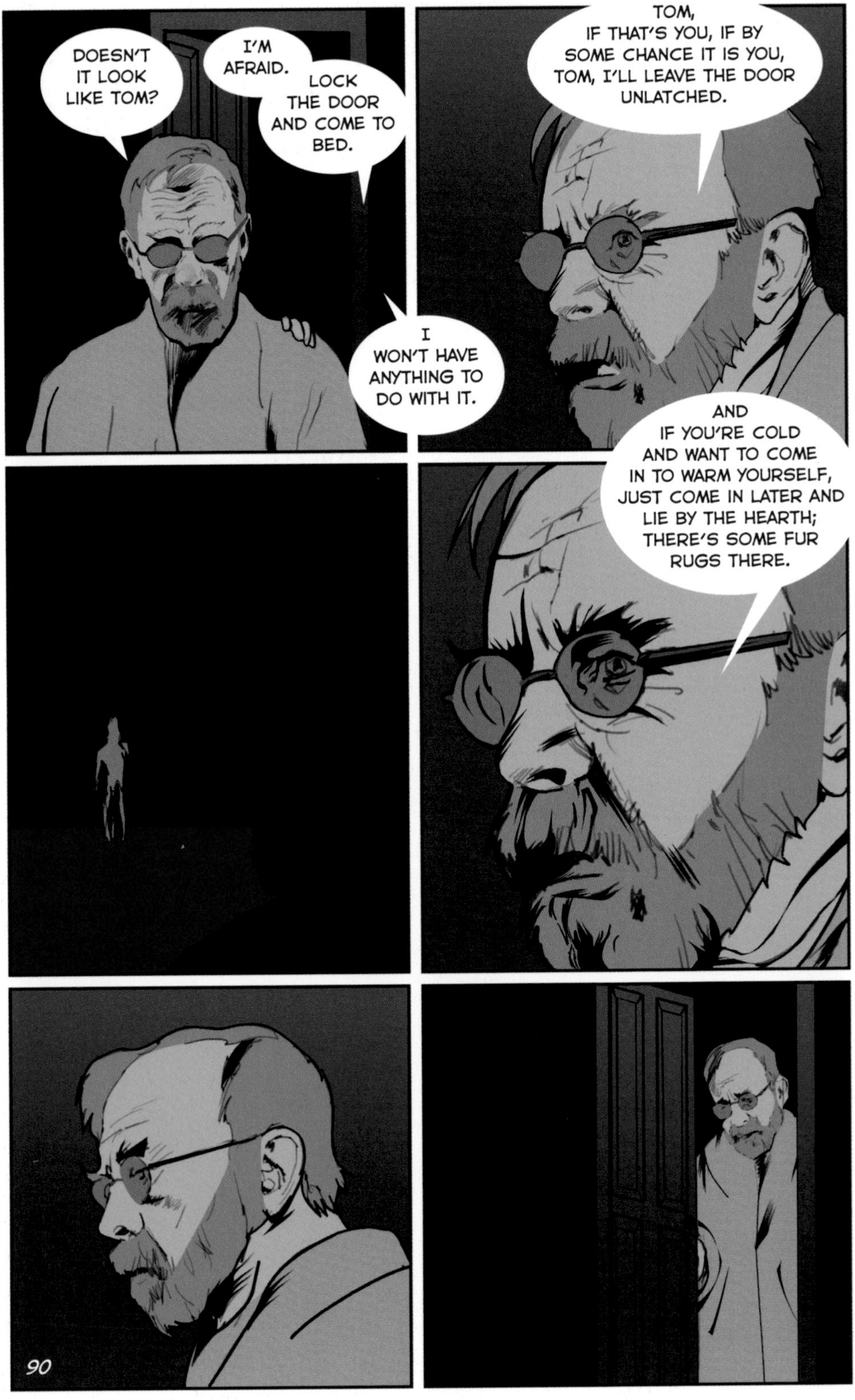
DOESN'T IT LOOK LIKE TOM?
I'M AFRAID.
LOCK THE DOOR AND COME TO BED.
I WON'T HAVE ANYTHING TO DO WITH IT.
TOM, IF THAT'S YOU, IF BY SOME CHANCE IT IS YOU, TOM, I'LL LEAVE THE DOOR UNLATCHED.
AND IF YOU'RE COLD AND WANT TO COME IN TO WARM YOURSELF, JUST COME IN LATER AND LIE BY THE HEARTH; THERE'S SOME FUR RUGS THERE.

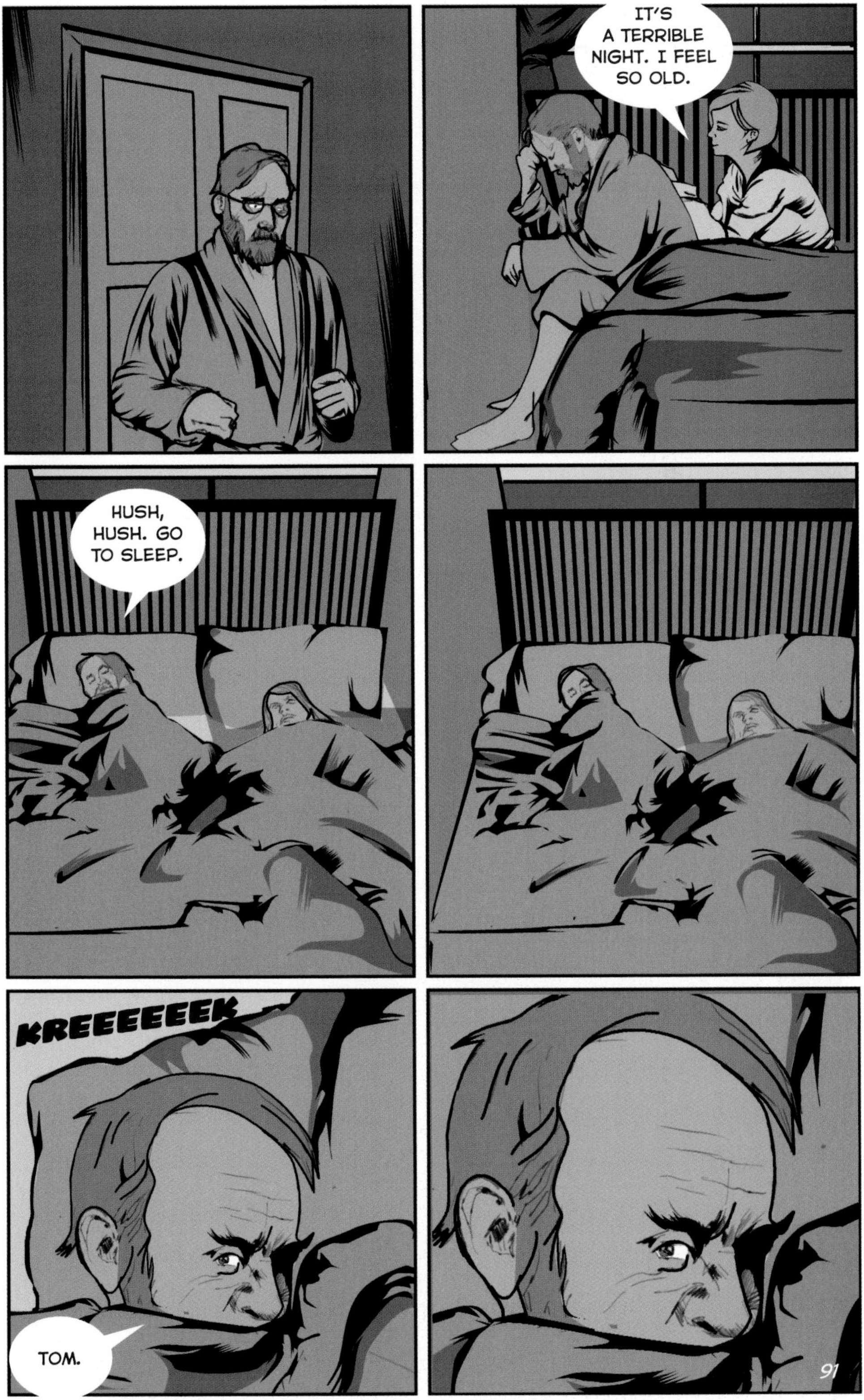
IT'S A TERRIBLE NIGHT. I FEEL SO OLD.
HUSH, HUSH. GO TO SLEEP.
KREEEEEEK
TOM.

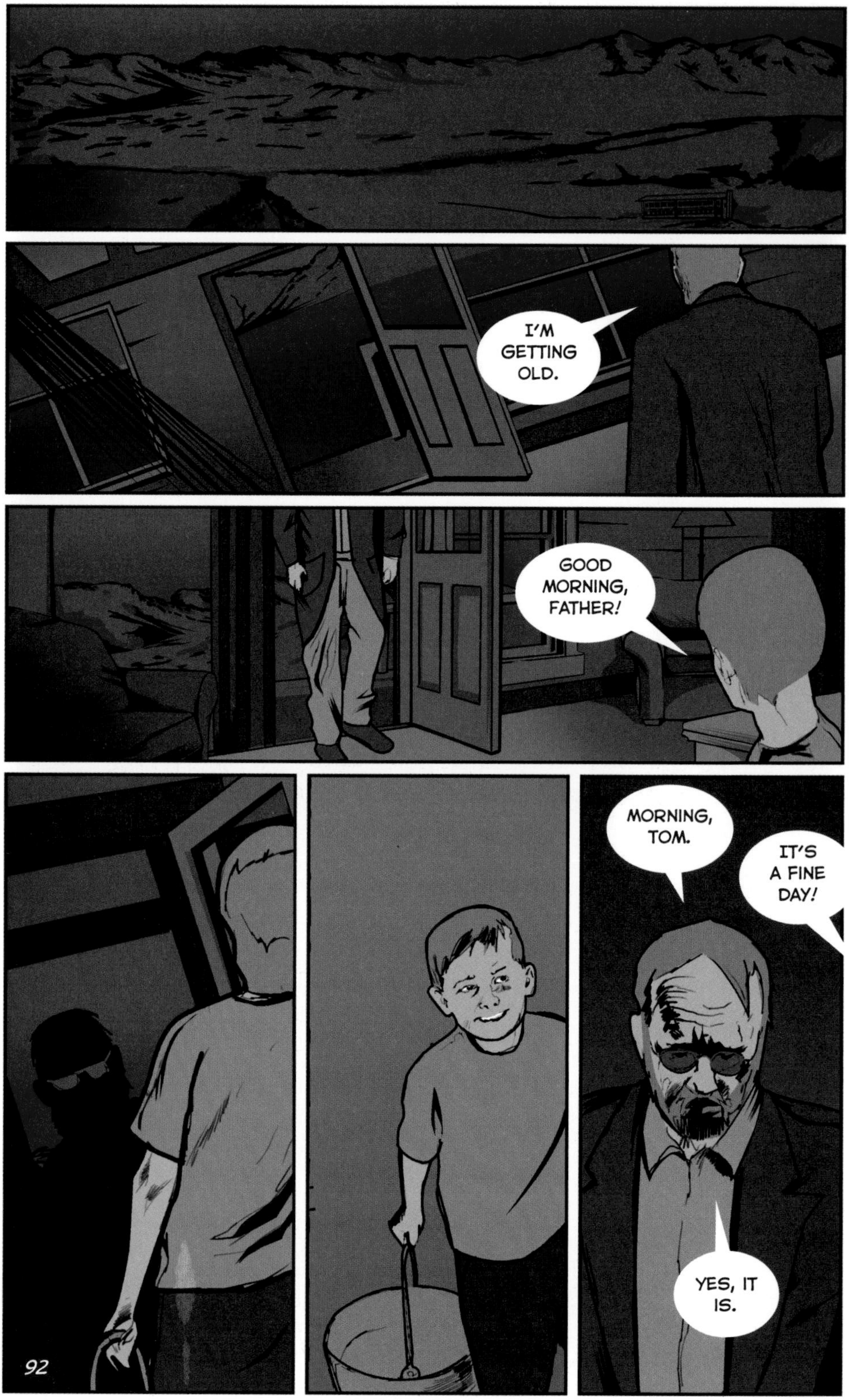
I'M GETTING OLD.
GOOD MORNING, FATHER!
MORNING, TOM.
IT'S A FINE DAY!
YES, IT IS.

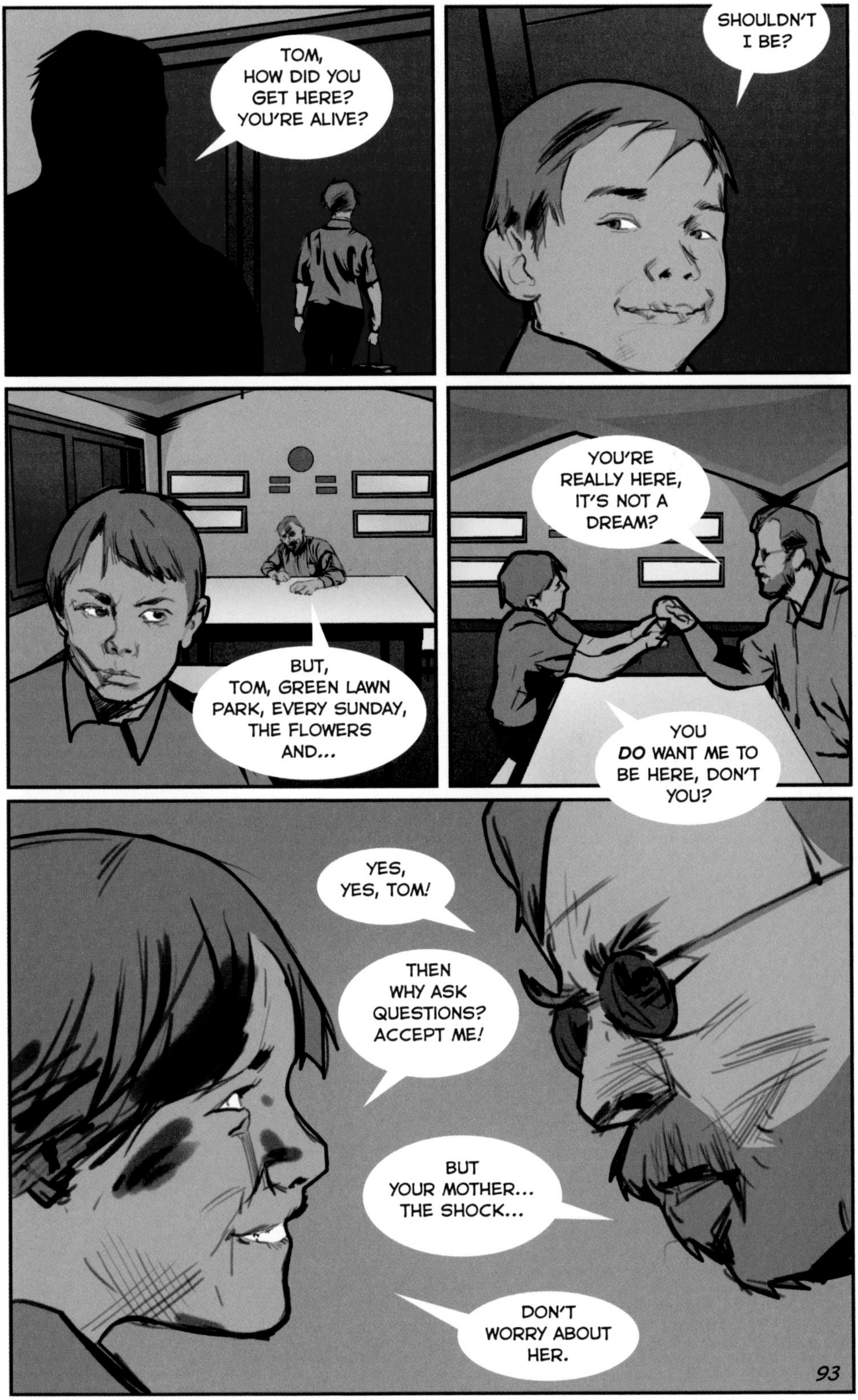
TOM, HOW DID YOU GET HERE? YOU'RE ALIVE?
SHOULDN'T I BE?
BUT, TOM, GREEN LAWN PARK, EVERY SUNDAY, THE FLOWERS AND...
YOU'RE REALLY HERE, IT'S NOT A DREAM?
YOU *DO* WANT ME TO BE HERE, DON'T YOU?
YES, YES, TOM!
THEN WHY ASK QUESTIONS? ACCEPT ME!
BUT YOUR MOTHER... THE SHOCK...
DON'T WORRY ABOUT HER.

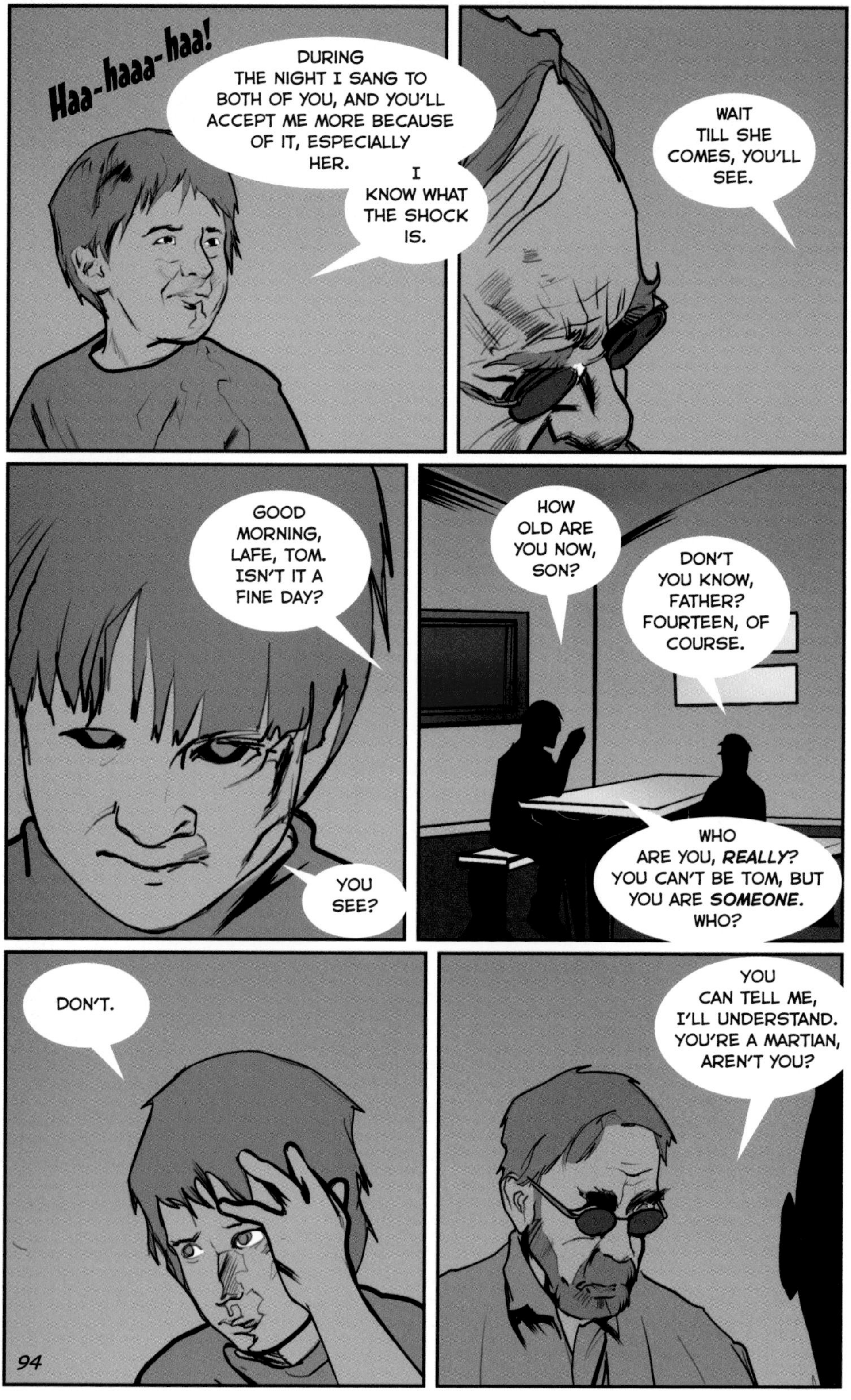
Haa-haaa-haa!
DURING THE NIGHT I SANG TO BOTH OF YOU, AND YOU'LL ACCEPT ME MORE BECAUSE OF IT, ESPECIALLY HER.
I KNOW WHAT THE SHOCK IS.
WAIT TILL SHE COMES, YOU'LL SEE.
GOOD MORNING, LAFE, TOM. ISN'T IT A FINE DAY?
YOU SEE?
HOW OLD ARE YOU NOW, SON?
DON'T YOU KNOW, FATHER? FOURTEEN, OF COURSE.
WHO ARE YOU, *REALLY*? YOU CAN'T BE TOM, BUT YOU ARE *SOMEONE*. WHO?
DON'T.
YOU CAN TELL ME, I'LL UNDERSTAND. YOU'RE A MARTIAN, AREN'T YOU?

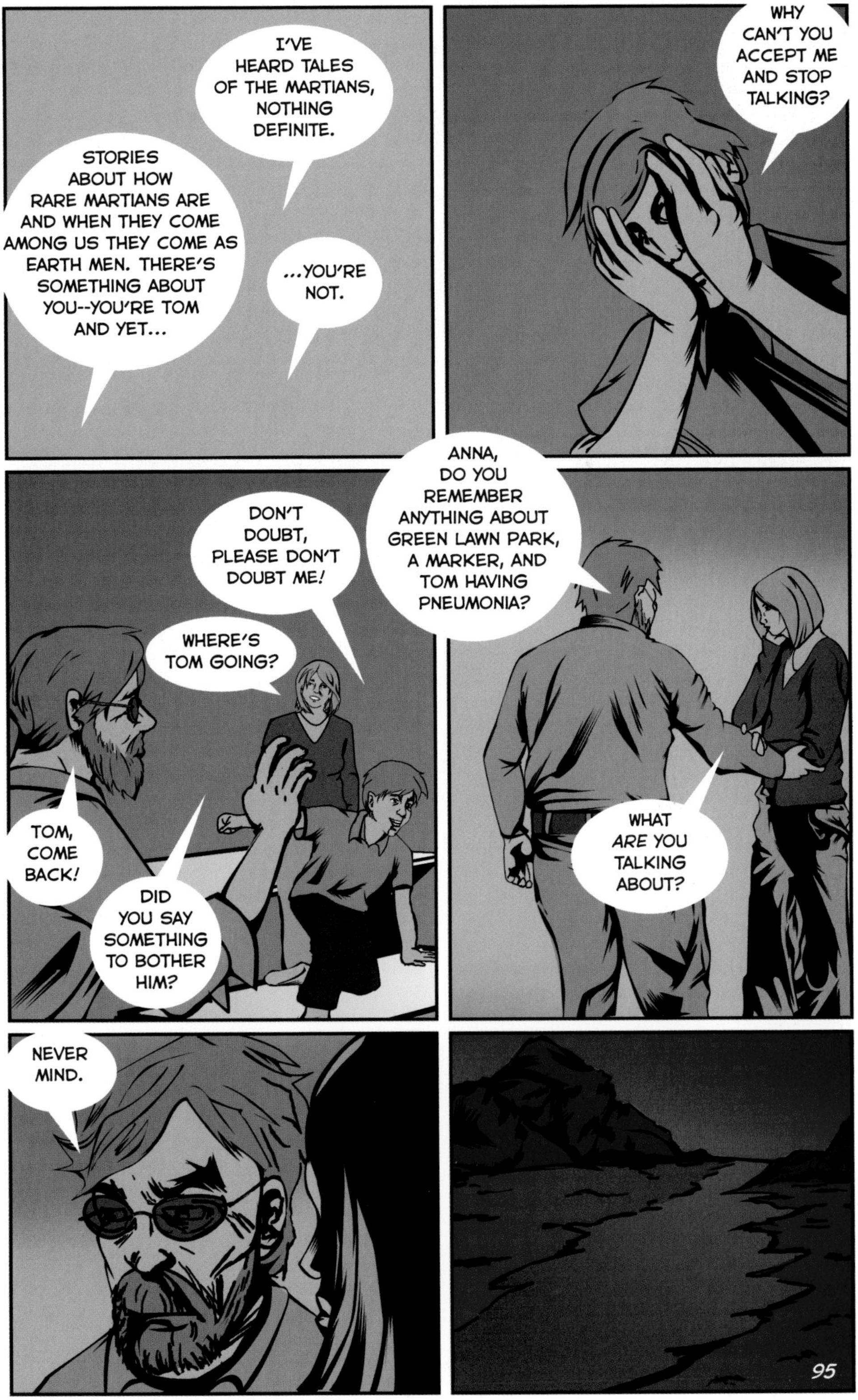
I'VE HEARD TALES OF THE MARTIANS, NOTHING DEFINITE.
STORIES ABOUT HOW RARE MARTIANS ARE AND WHEN THEY COME AMONG US THEY COME AS EARTH MEN. THERE'S SOMETHING ABOUT YOU--YOU'RE TOM AND YET...
...YOU'RE NOT.
WHY CAN'T YOU ACCEPT ME AND STOP TALKING?
DON'T DOUBT, PLEASE DON'T DOUBT ME!
WHERE'S TOM GOING?
TOM, COME BACK!
DID YOU SAY SOMETHING TO BOTHER HIM?
ANNA, DO YOU REMEMBER ANYTHING ABOUT GREEN LAWN PARK, A MARKER, AND TOM HAVING PNEUMONIA?
WHAT *ARE* YOU TALKING ABOUT?
NEVER MIND.

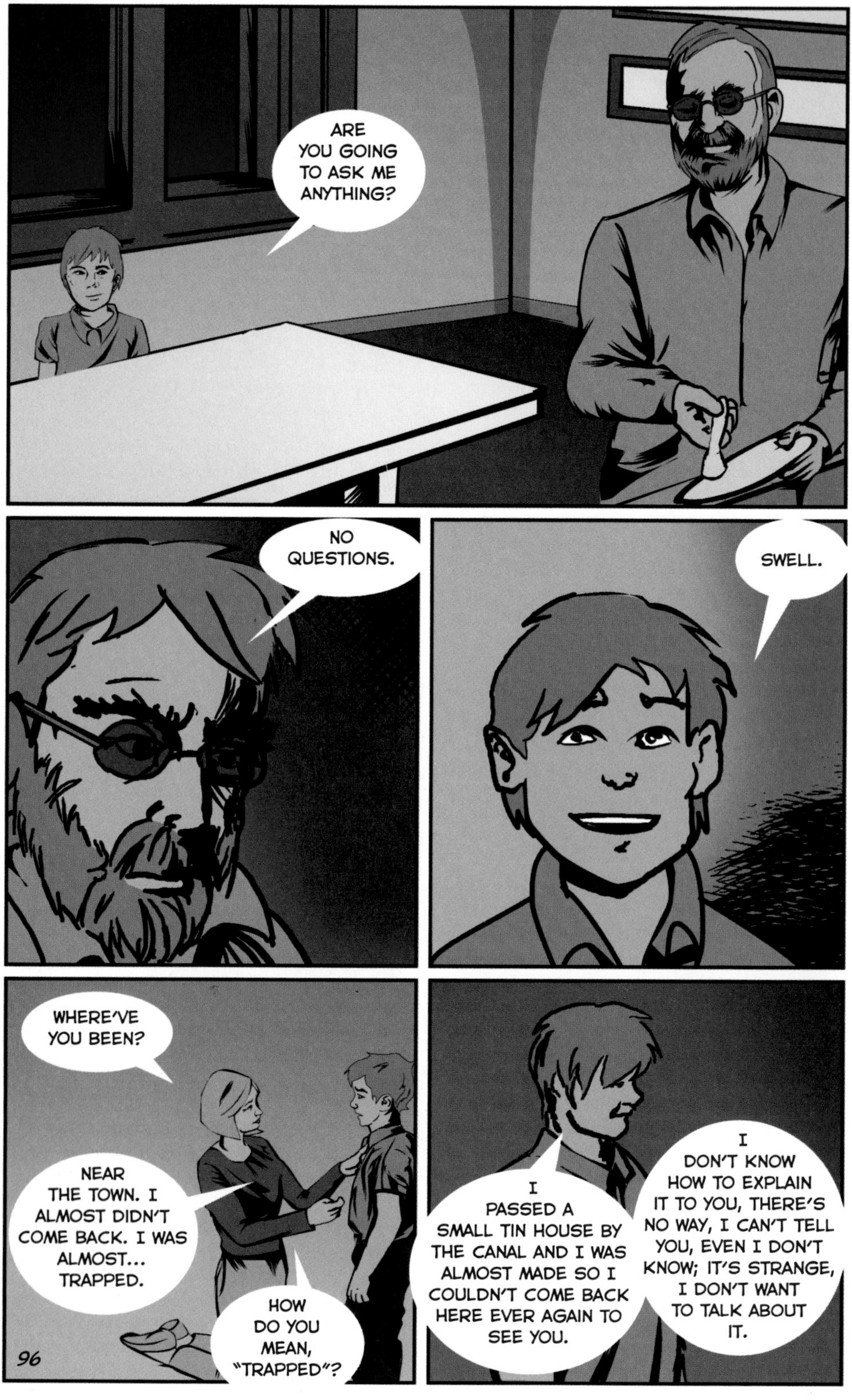
ARE YOU GOING TO ASK ME ANYTHING?
NO QUESTIONS.
SWELL.
WHERE'VE YOU BEEN?
NEAR THE TOWN. I ALMOST DIDN'T COME BACK. I WAS ALMOST... TRAPPED.
HOW DO YOU MEAN, "TRAPPED"?
I PASSED A SMALL TIN HOUSE BY THE CANAL AND I WAS ALMOST MADE SO I COULDN'T COME BACK HERE EVER AGAIN TO SEE YOU.
I DON'T KNOW HOW TO EXPLAIN IT TO YOU, THERE'S NO WAY, I CAN'T TELL YOU, EVEN I DON'T KNOW; IT'S STRANGE, I DON'T WANT TO TALK ABOUT IT.

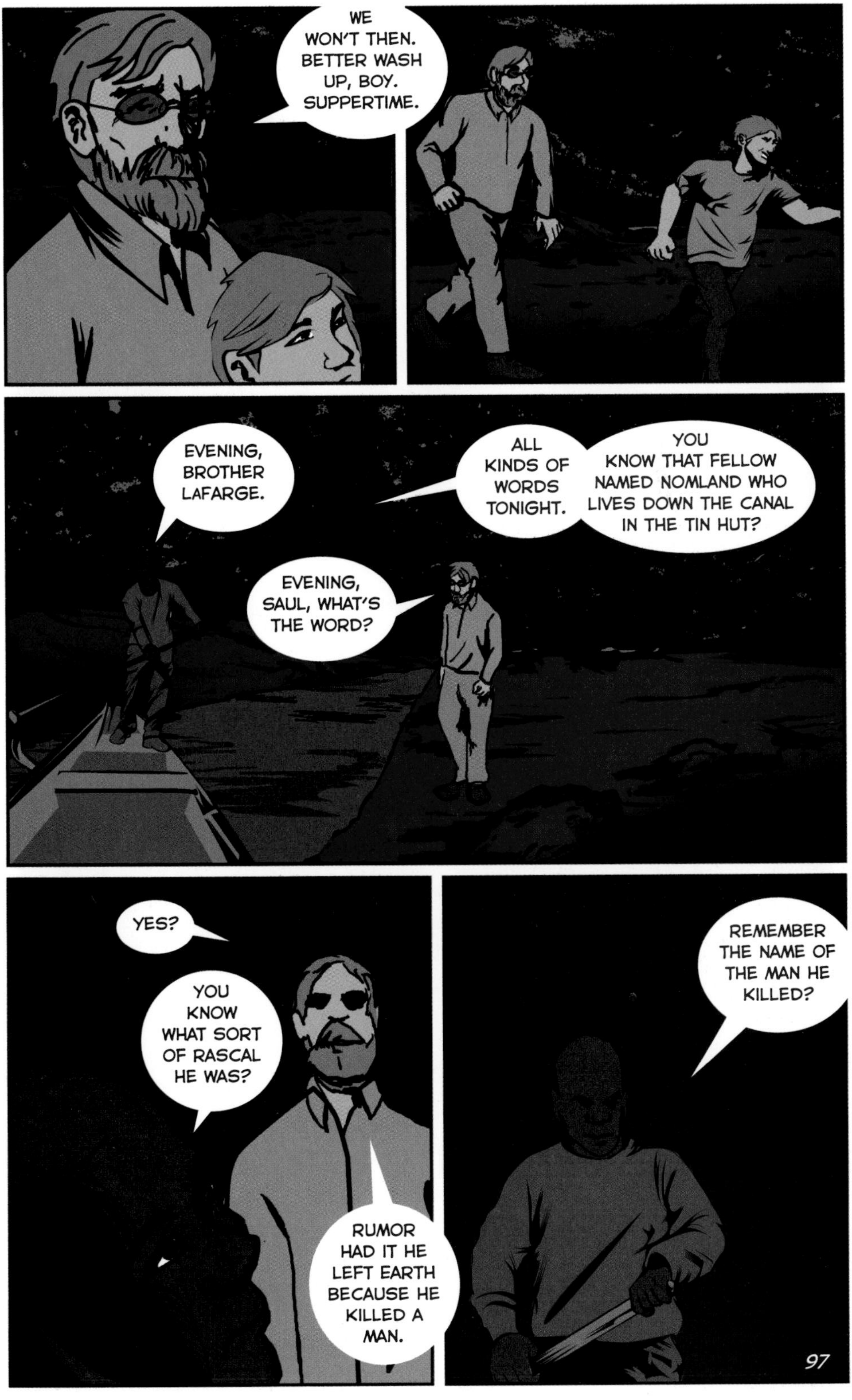
WE WON'T THEN. BETTER WASH UP, BOY. SUPPERTIME.
EVENING, BROTHER LAFARGE.
EVENING, SAUL, WHAT'S THE WORD?
ALL KINDS OF WORDS TONIGHT.
YOU KNOW THAT FELLOW NAMED NOMLAND WHO LIVES DOWN THE CANAL IN THE TIN HUT?
YES?
YOU KNOW WHAT SORT OF RASCAL HE WAS?
RUMOR HAD IT HE LEFT EARTH BECAUSE HE KILLED A MAN.
REMEMBER THE NAME OF THE MAN HE KILLED?

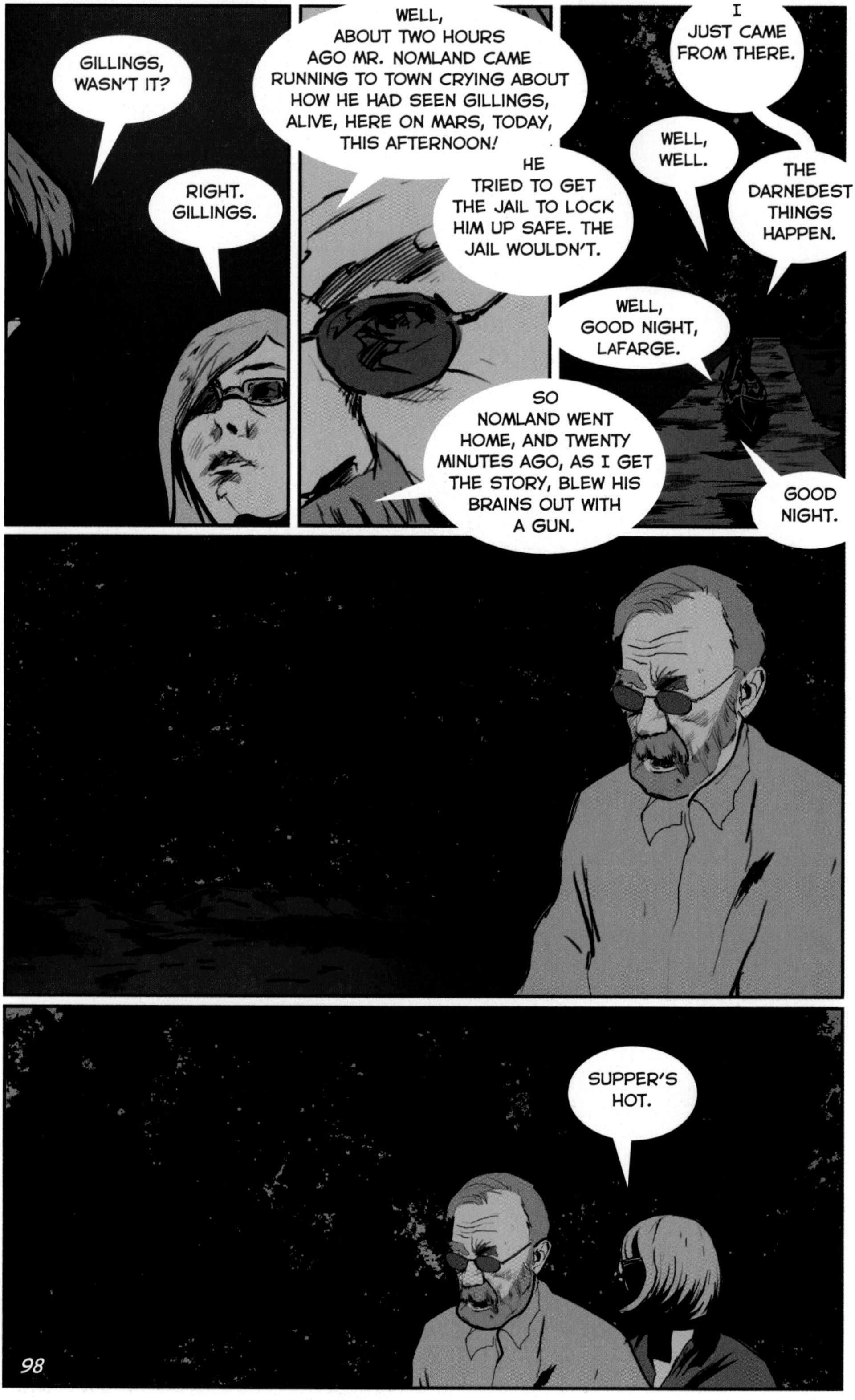
GILLINGS, WASN'T IT?
RIGHT. GILLINGS.
WELL, ABOUT TWO HOURS AGO MR. NOMLAND CAME RUNNING TO TOWN CRYING ABOUT HOW HE HAD SEEN GILLINGS, ALIVE, HERE ON MARS, TODAY, THIS AFTERNOON!
HE TRIED TO GET THE JAIL TO LOCK HIM UP SAFE. THE JAIL WOULDN'T.
SO NOMLAND WENT HOME, AND TWENTY MINUTES AGO, AS I GET THE STORY, BLEW HIS BRAINS OUT WITH A GUN.
I JUST CAME FROM THERE.
WELL, WELL.
THE DARNEDEST THINGS HAPPEN.
WELL, GOOD NIGHT, LAFARGE.
GOOD NIGHT.
SUPPER'S HOT.

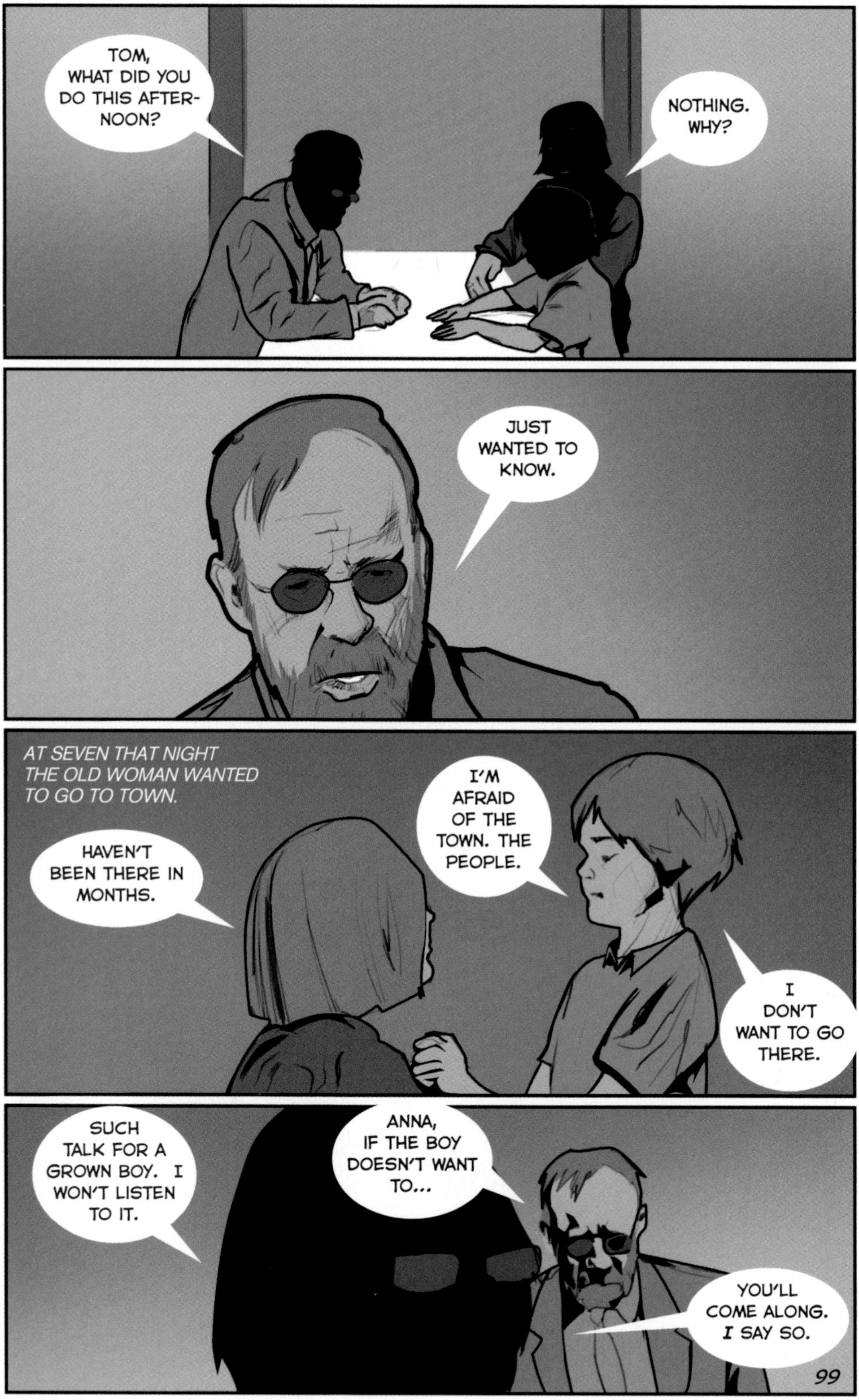
TOM, WHAT DID YOU DO THIS AFTER-NOON?
NOTHING. WHY?
JUST WANTED TO KNOW.
AT SEVEN THAT NIGHT THE OLD WOMAN WANTED TO GO TO TOWN.
HAVEN'T BEEN THERE IN MONTHS.
I'M AFRAID OF THE TOWN. THE PEOPLE.
I DON'T WANT TO GO THERE.
SUCH TALK FOR A GROWN BOY. I WON'T LISTEN TO IT.
ANNA, IF THE BOY DOESN'T WANT TO...
YOU'LL COME ALONG. I SAY SO.

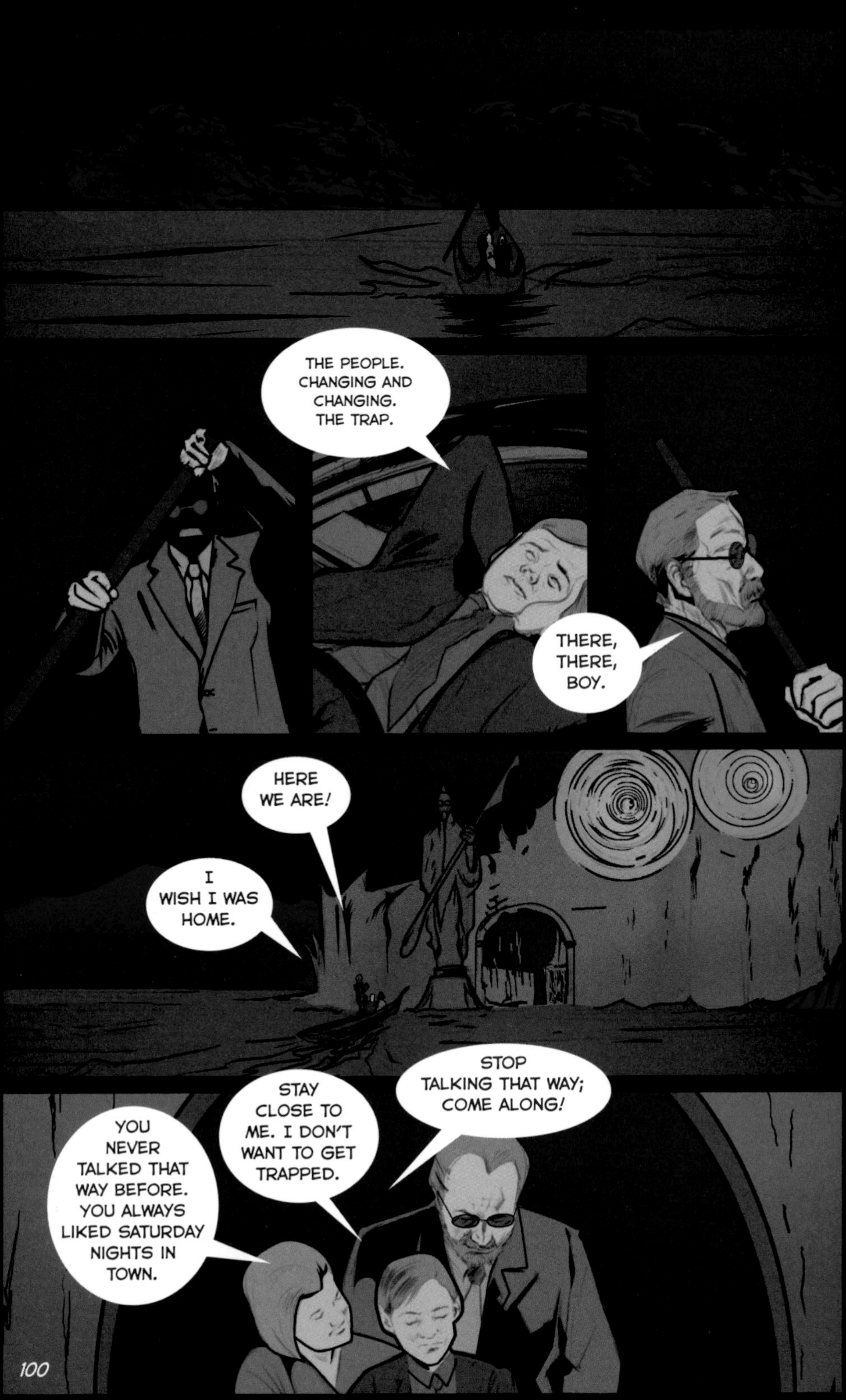
THE PEOPLE. CHANGING AND CHANGING. THE TRAP.
THERE, THERE, BOY.
HERE WE ARE!
I WISH I WAS HOME.
YOU NEVER TALKED THAT WAY BEFORE. YOU ALWAYS LIKED SATURDAY NIGHTS IN TOWN.
STAY CLOSE TO ME. I DON'T WANT TO GET TRAPPED.
STOP TALKING THAT WAY; COME ALONG!

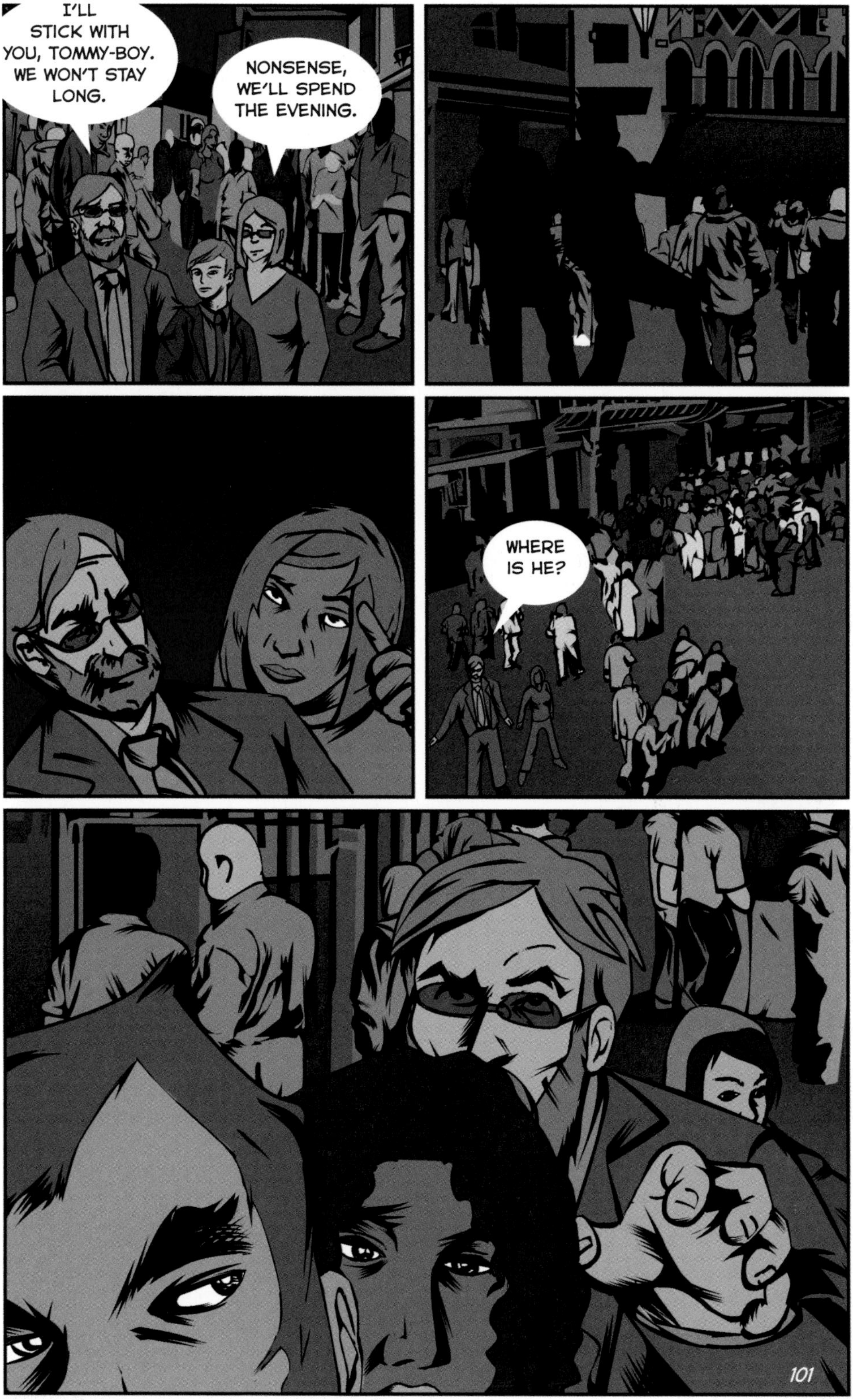
I'LL STICK WITH YOU, TOMMY-BOY. WE WON'T STAY LONG.
NONSENSE, WE'LL SPEND THE EVENING.
WHERE IS HE?

HE'LL COME BACK. HE'LL BE AT THE BOAT WHEN WE LEAVE.

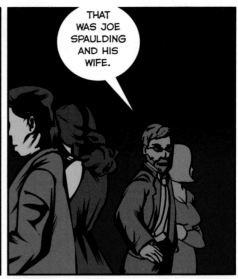

THAT WAS JOE SPAULDING AND HIS WIFE.

NOW, MOTHER, DON'T WORRY. I'LL FIND HIM. WAIT HERE.

HURRY BACK.

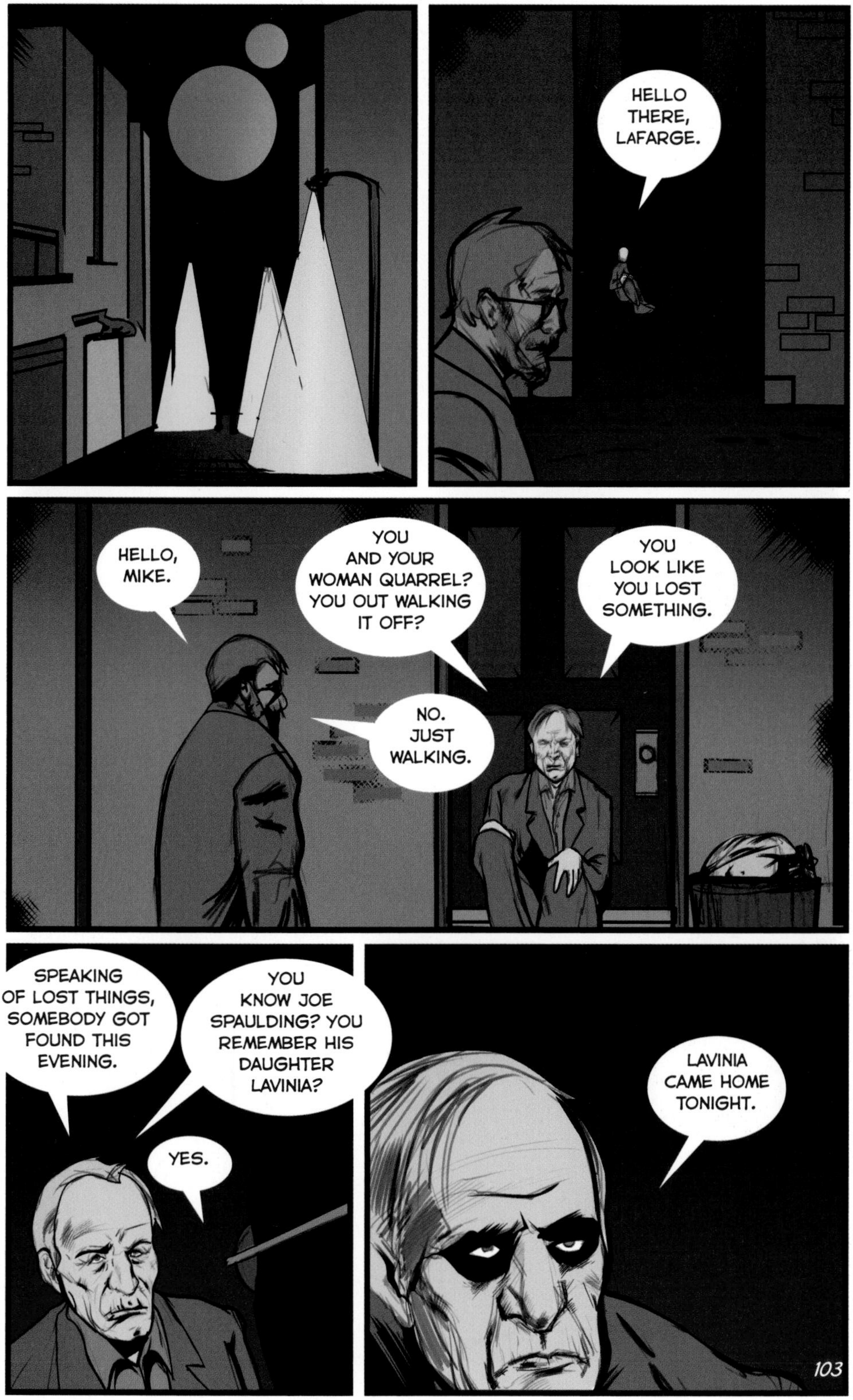
HELLO THERE, LAFARGE.
HELLO, MIKE.
YOU AND YOUR WOMAN QUARREL? YOU OUT WALKING IT OFF?
YOU LOOK LIKE YOU LOST SOMETHING.
NO. JUST WALKING.
SPEAKING OF LOST THINGS, SOMEBODY GOT FOUND THIS EVENING.
YOU KNOW JOE SPAULDING? YOU REMEMBER HIS DAUGHTER LAVINIA?
YES.
LAVINIA CAME HOME TONIGHT.

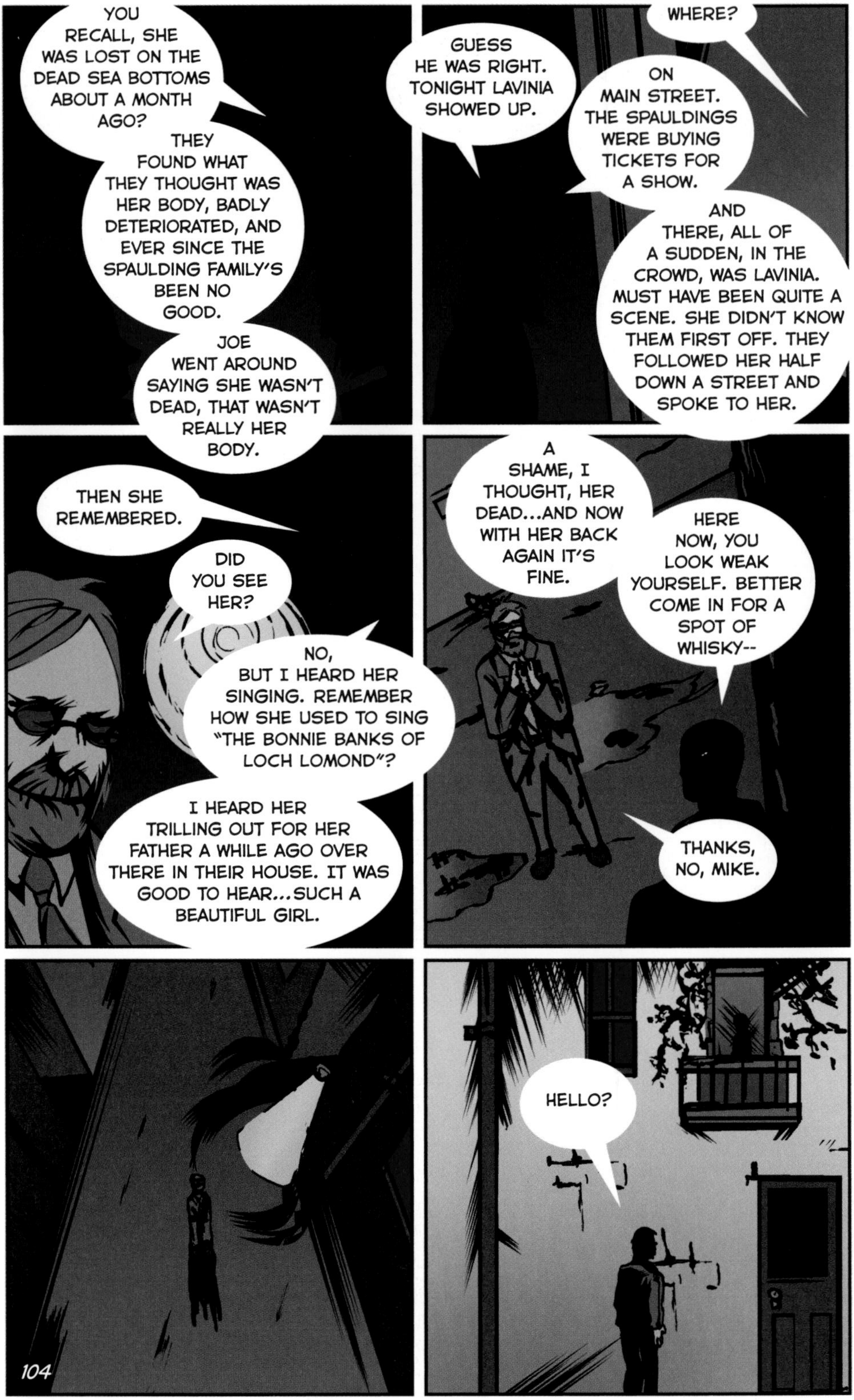
YOU RECALL, SHE WAS LOST ON THE DEAD SEA BOTTOMS ABOUT A MONTH AGO?
THEY FOUND WHAT THEY THOUGHT WAS HER BODY, BADLY DETERIORATED, AND EVER SINCE THE SPAULDING FAMILY'S BEEN NO GOOD.
JOE WENT AROUND SAYING SHE WASN'T DEAD, THAT WASN'T REALLY HER BODY.
GUESS HE WAS RIGHT. TONIGHT LAVINIA SHOWED UP.
WHERE?
ON MAIN STREET. THE SPAULDINGS WERE BUYING TICKETS FOR A SHOW.
AND THERE, ALL OF A SUDDEN, IN THE CROWD, WAS LAVINIA. MUST HAVE BEEN QUITE A SCENE. SHE DIDN'T KNOW THEM FIRST OFF. THEY FOLLOWED HER HALF DOWN A STREET AND SPOKE TO HER.
THEN SHE REMEMBERED.
DID YOU SEE HER?
NO, BUT I HEARD HER SINGING. REMEMBER HOW SHE USED TO SING "THE BONNIE BANKS OF LOCH LOMOND"?
I HEARD HER TRILLING OUT FOR HER FATHER A WHILE AGO OVER THERE IN THEIR HOUSE. IT WAS GOOD TO HEAR...SUCH A BEAUTIFUL GIRL.
A SHAME, I THOUGHT, HER DEAD...AND NOW WITH HER BACK AGAIN IT'S FINE.
HERE NOW, YOU LOOK WEAK YOURSELF. BETTER COME IN FOR A SPOT OF WHISKY--
THANKS, NO, MIKE.
HELLO?

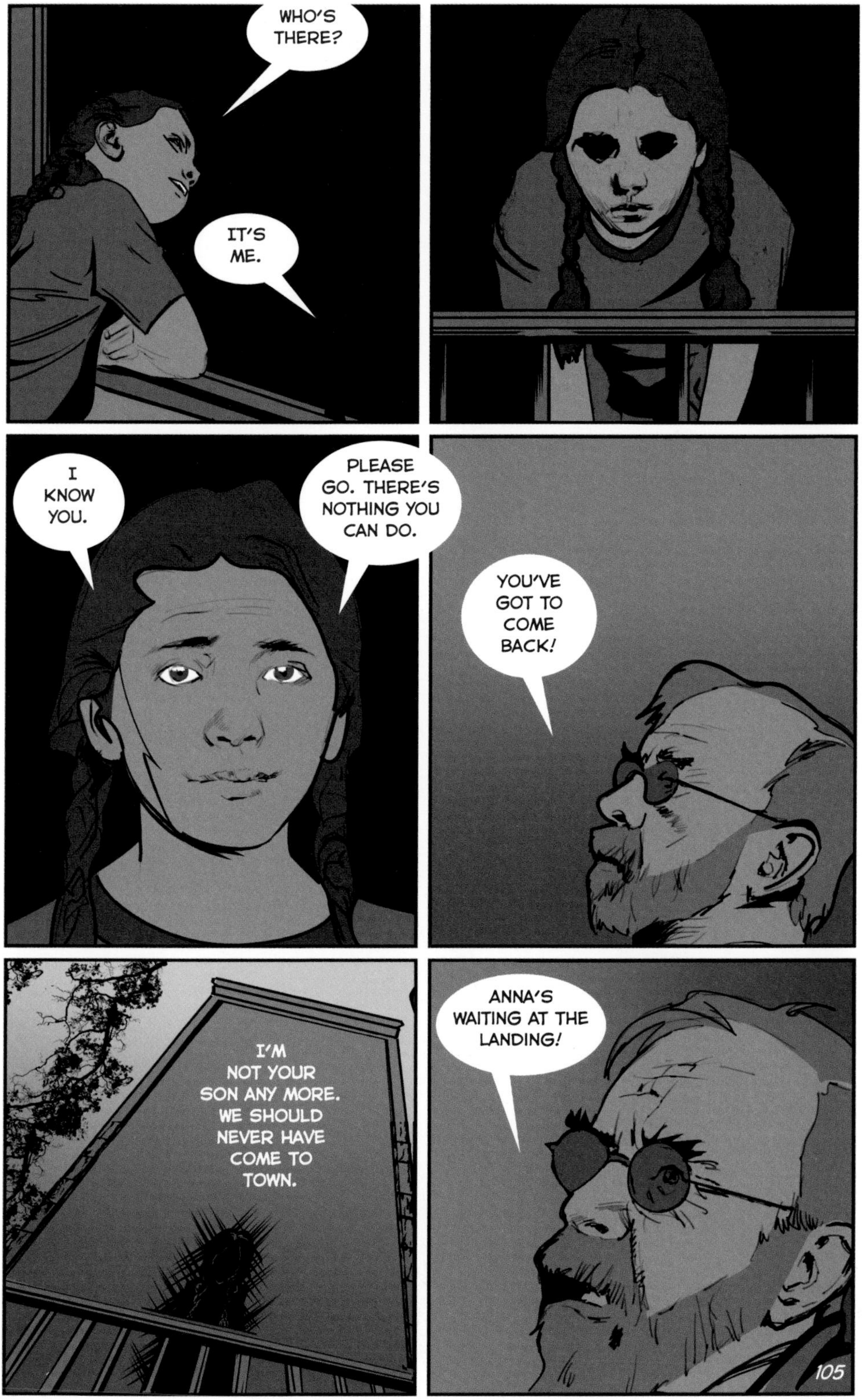
WHO'S THERE?
IT'S ME.
I KNOW YOU.
PLEASE GO. THERE'S NOTHING YOU CAN DO.
YOU'VE GOT TO COME BACK!
I'M NOT YOUR SON ANY MORE. WE SHOULD NEVER HAVE COME TO TOWN.
ANNA'S WAITING AT THE LANDING!

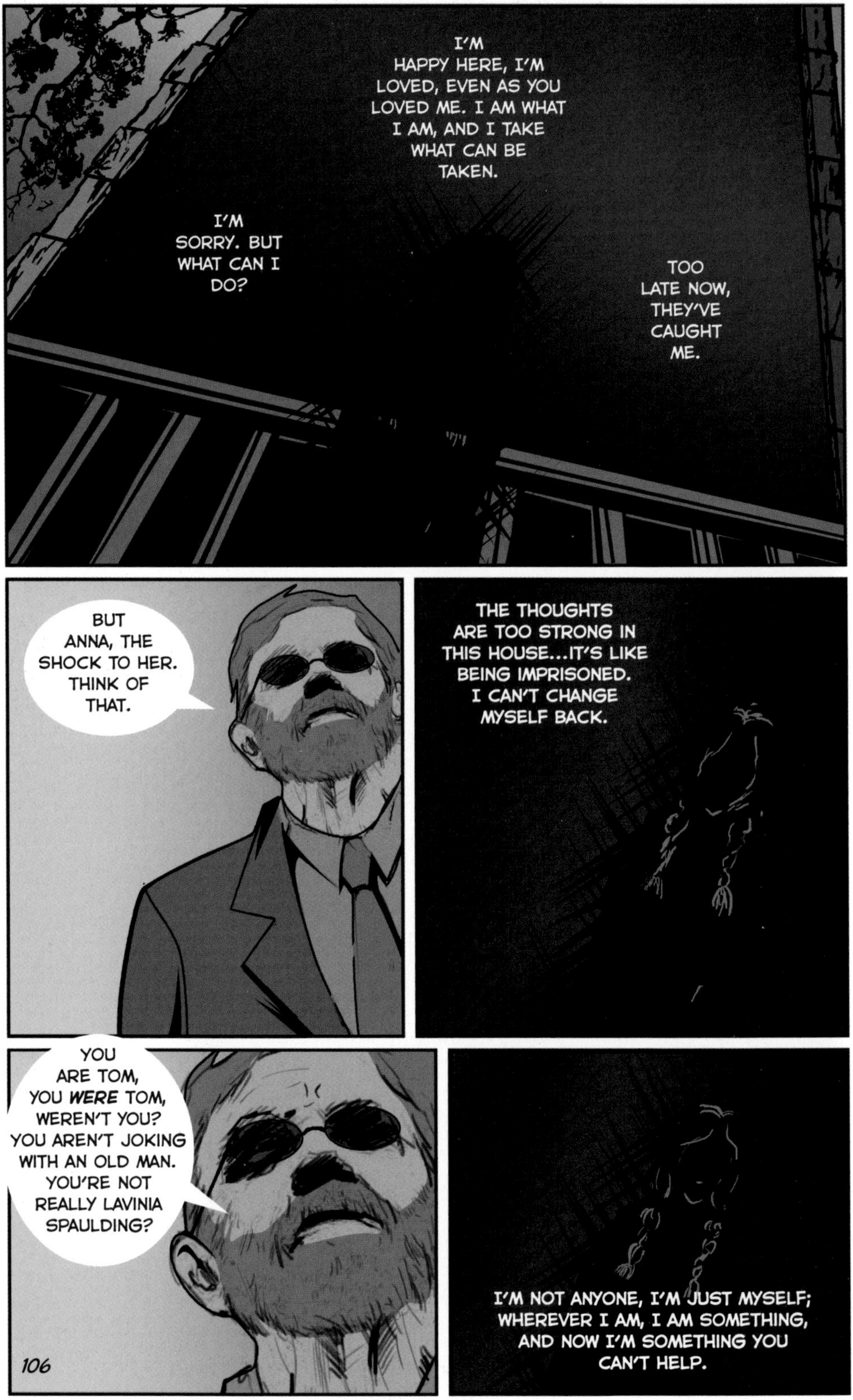
I'M HAPPY HERE, I'M LOVED, EVEN AS YOU LOVED ME. I AM WHAT I AM, AND I TAKE WHAT CAN BE TAKEN.
I'M SORRY. BUT WHAT CAN I DO?
TOO LATE NOW, THEY'VE CAUGHT ME.
BUT ANNA, THE SHOCK TO HER. THINK OF THAT.
THE THOUGHTS ARE TOO STRONG IN THIS HOUSE...IT'S LIKE BEING IMPRISONED. I CAN'T CHANGE MYSELF BACK.
YOU ARE TOM, YOU ***WERE*** TOM, WEREN'T YOU? YOU AREN'T JOKING WITH AN OLD MAN. YOU'RE NOT REALLY LAVINIA SPAULDING?
I'M NOT ANYONE, I'M JUST MYSELF; WHEREVER I AM, I AM SOMETHING, AND NOW I'M SOMETHING YOU CAN'T HELP.

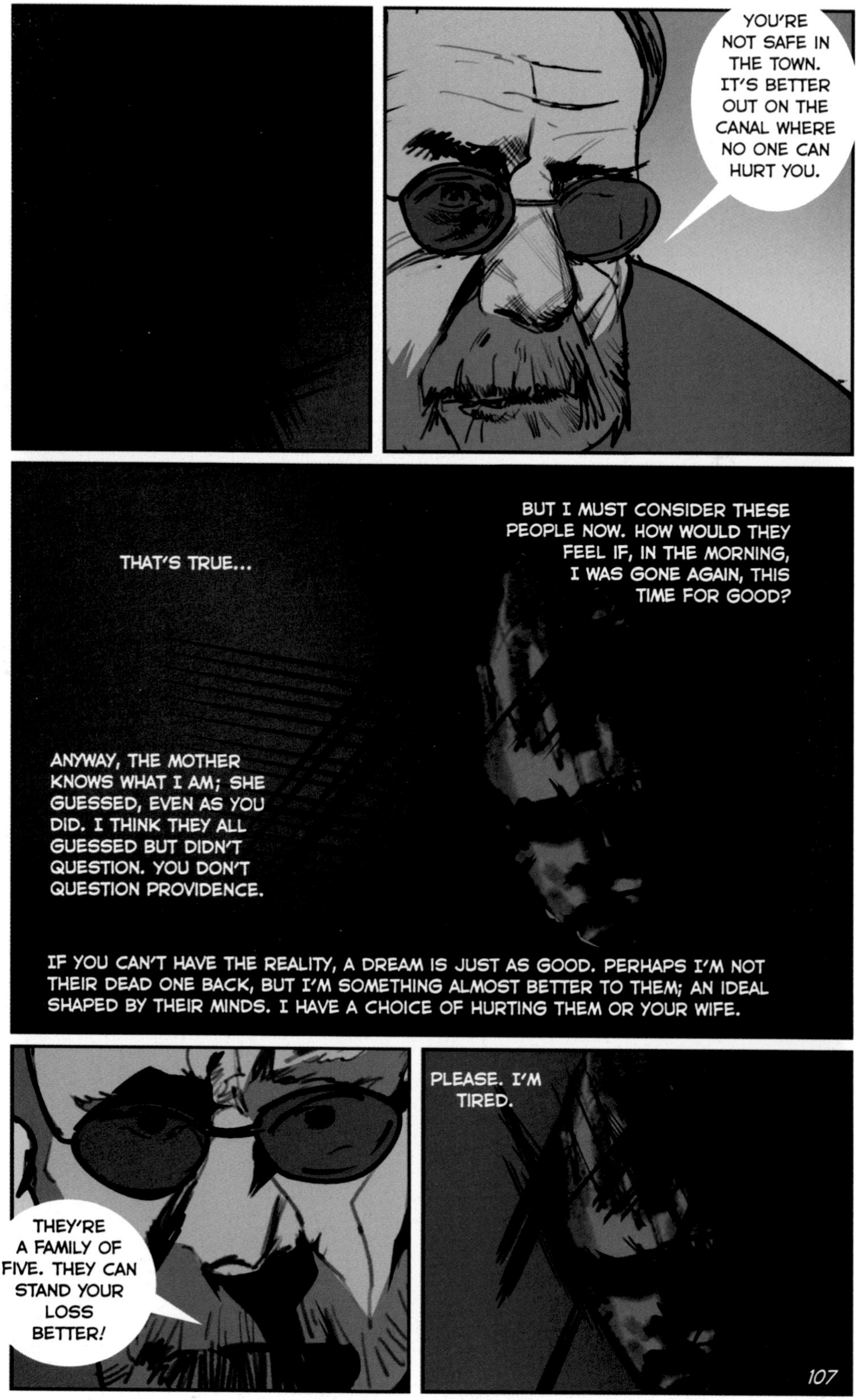
YOU'RE NOT SAFE IN THE TOWN. IT'S BETTER OUT ON THE CANAL WHERE NO ONE CAN HURT YOU.
THAT'S TRUE...
BUT I MUST CONSIDER THESE PEOPLE NOW. HOW WOULD THEY FEEL IF, IN THE MORNING, I WAS GONE AGAIN, THIS TIME FOR GOOD?
ANYWAY, THE MOTHER KNOWS WHAT I AM; SHE GUESSED, EVEN AS YOU DID. I THINK THEY ALL GUESSED BUT DIDN'T QUESTION. YOU DON'T QUESTION PROVIDENCE.
IF YOU CAN'T HAVE THE REALITY, A DREAM IS JUST AS GOOD. PERHAPS I'M NOT THEIR DEAD ONE BACK, BUT I'M SOMETHING ALMOST BETTER TO THEM; AN IDEAL SHAPED BY THEIR MINDS. I HAVE A CHOICE OF HURTING THEM OR YOUR WIFE.
THEY'RE A FAMILY OF FIVE. THEY CAN STAND YOUR LOSS BETTER!
PLEASE. I'M TIRED.

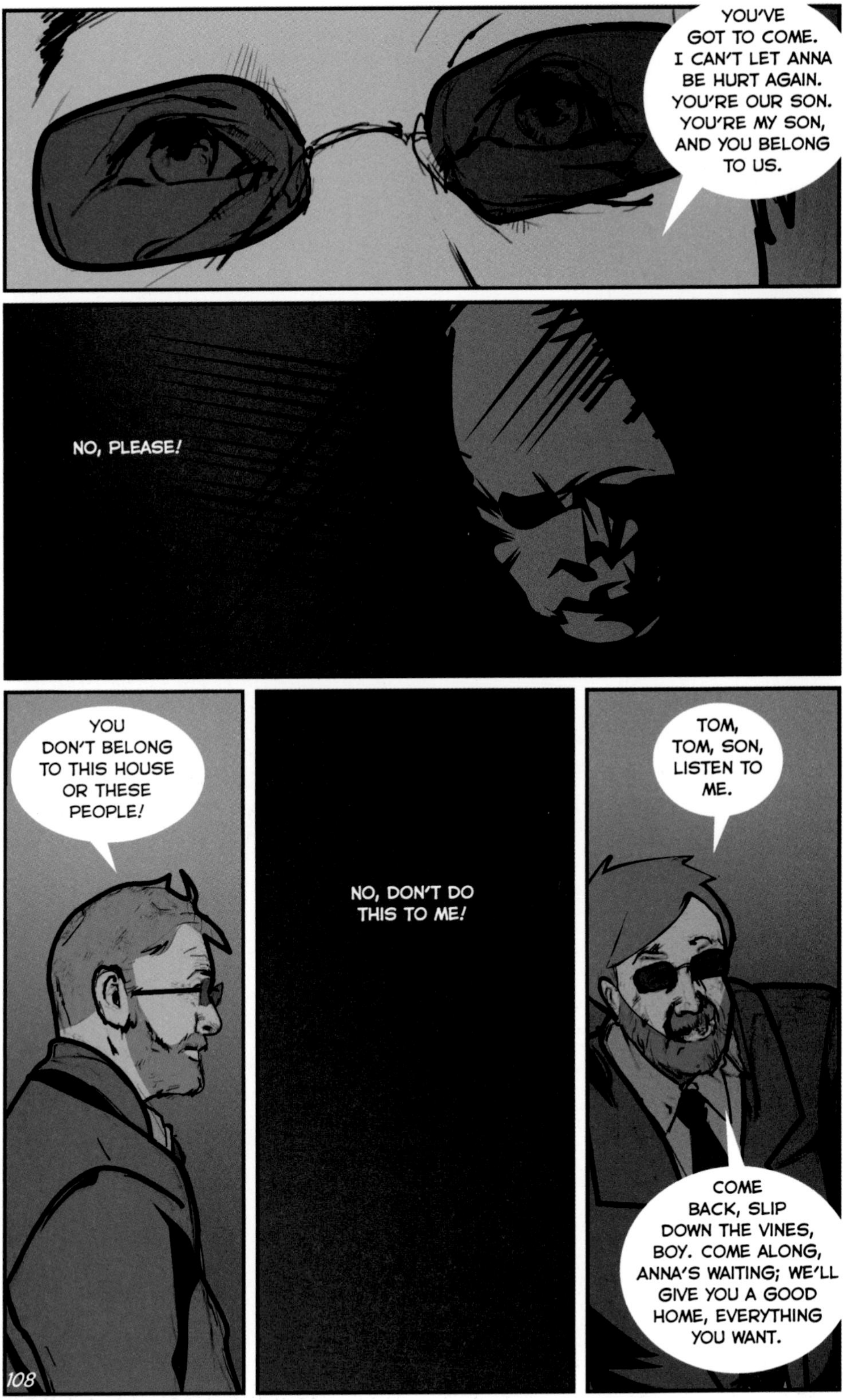
YOU'VE GOT TO COME. I CAN'T LET ANNA BE HURT AGAIN. YOU'RE OUR SON. YOU'RE MY SON, AND YOU BELONG TO US.
NO, PLEASE!
YOU DON'T BELONG TO THIS HOUSE OR THESE PEOPLE!
NO, DON'T DO THIS TO ME!
TOM, TOM, SON, LISTEN TO ME.
COME BACK, SLIP DOWN THE VINES, BOY. COME ALONG, ANNA'S WAITING; WE'LL GIVE YOU A GOOD HOME, EVERYTHING YOU WANT.

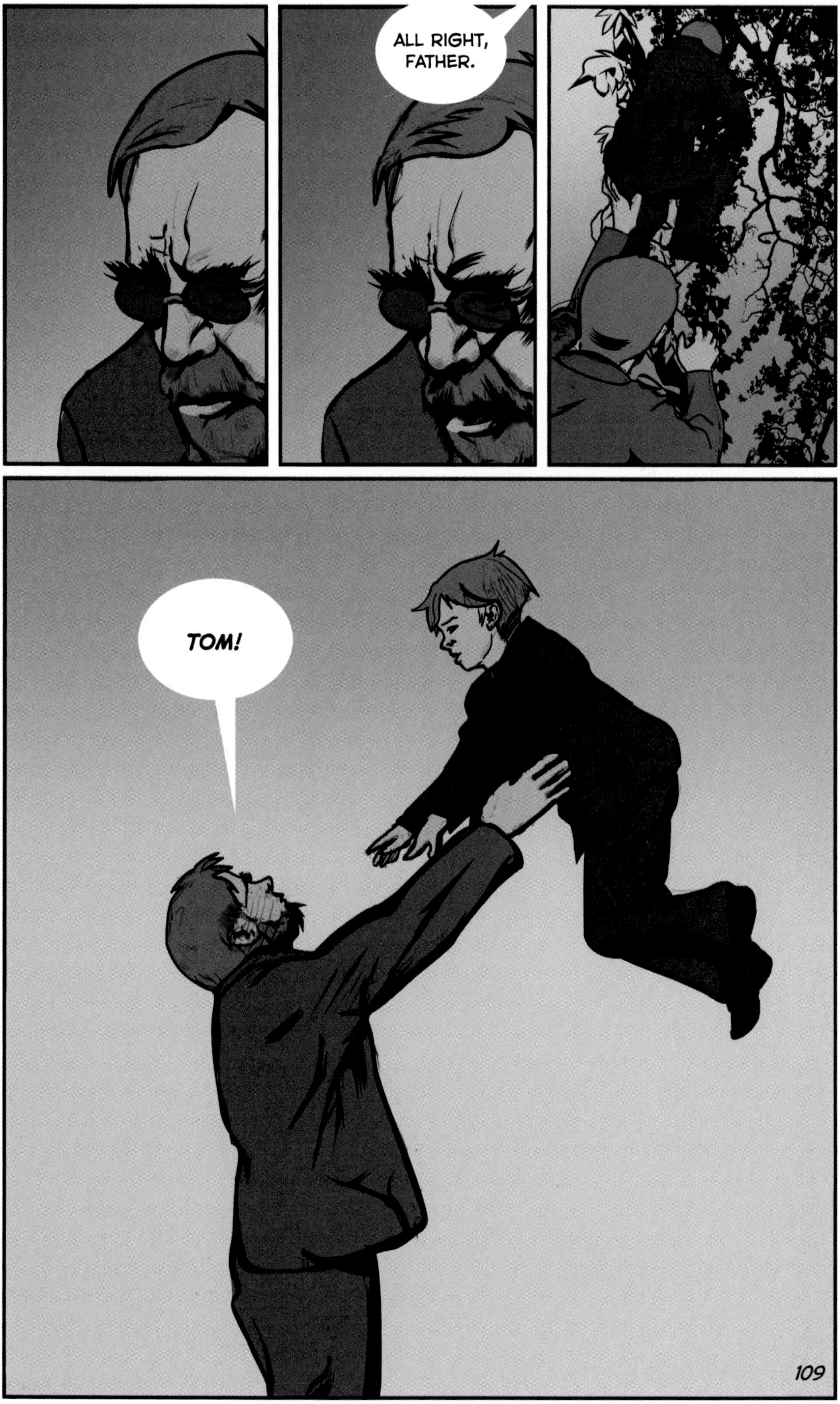
ALL RIGHT, FATHER.
TOM!

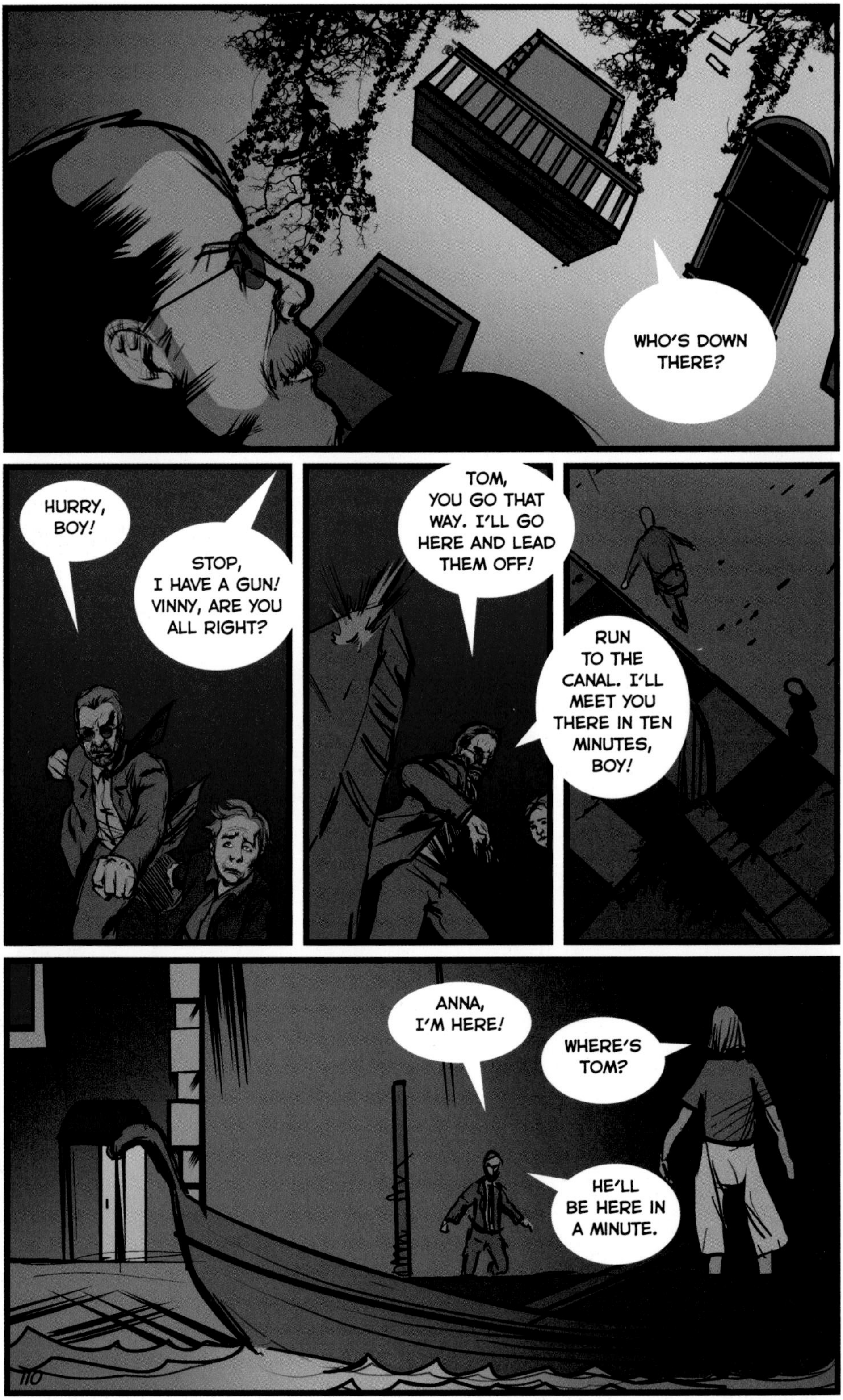
WHO'S DOWN THERE?
HURRY, BOY!
STOP, I HAVE A GUN! VINNY, ARE YOU ALL RIGHT?
TOM, YOU GO THAT WAY. I'LL GO HERE AND LEAD THEM OFF!
RUN TO THE CANAL. I'LL MEET YOU THERE IN TEN MINUTES, BOY!
ANNA, I'M HERE!
WHERE'S TOM?
HE'LL BE HERE IN A MINUTE.

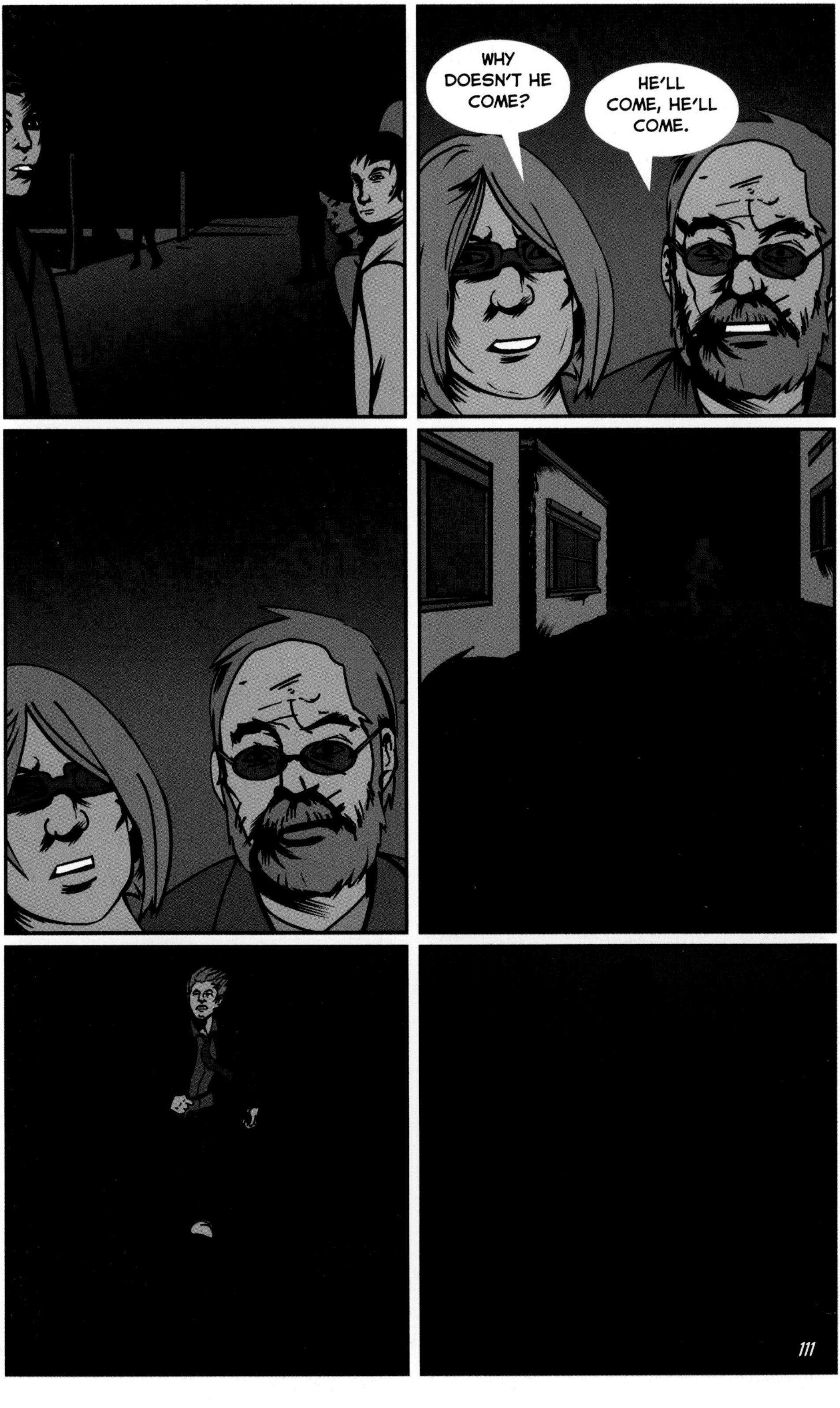
WHY DOESN'T HE COME?
HE'LL COME, HE'LL COME.

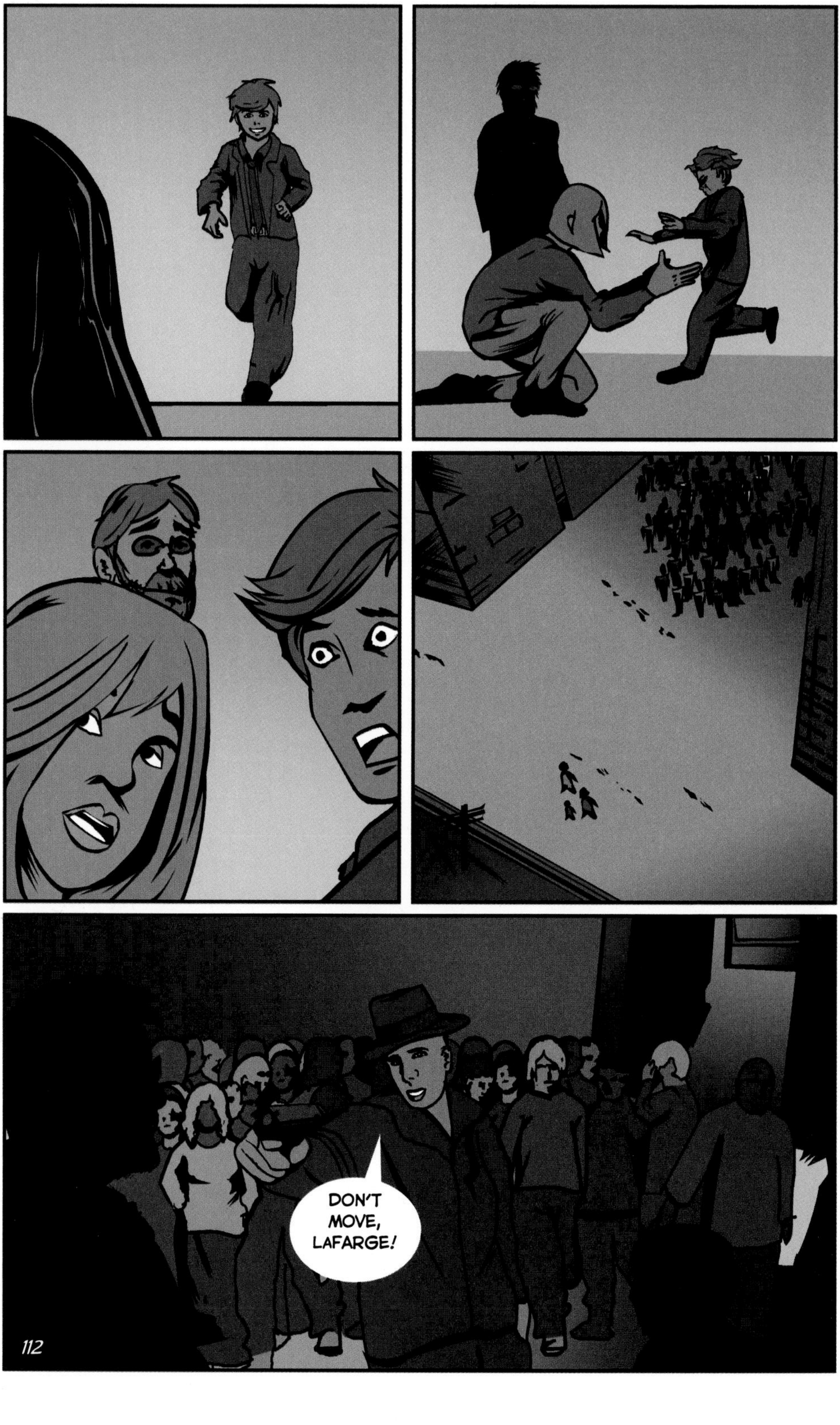
DON'T
MOVE,
LAFARGE!

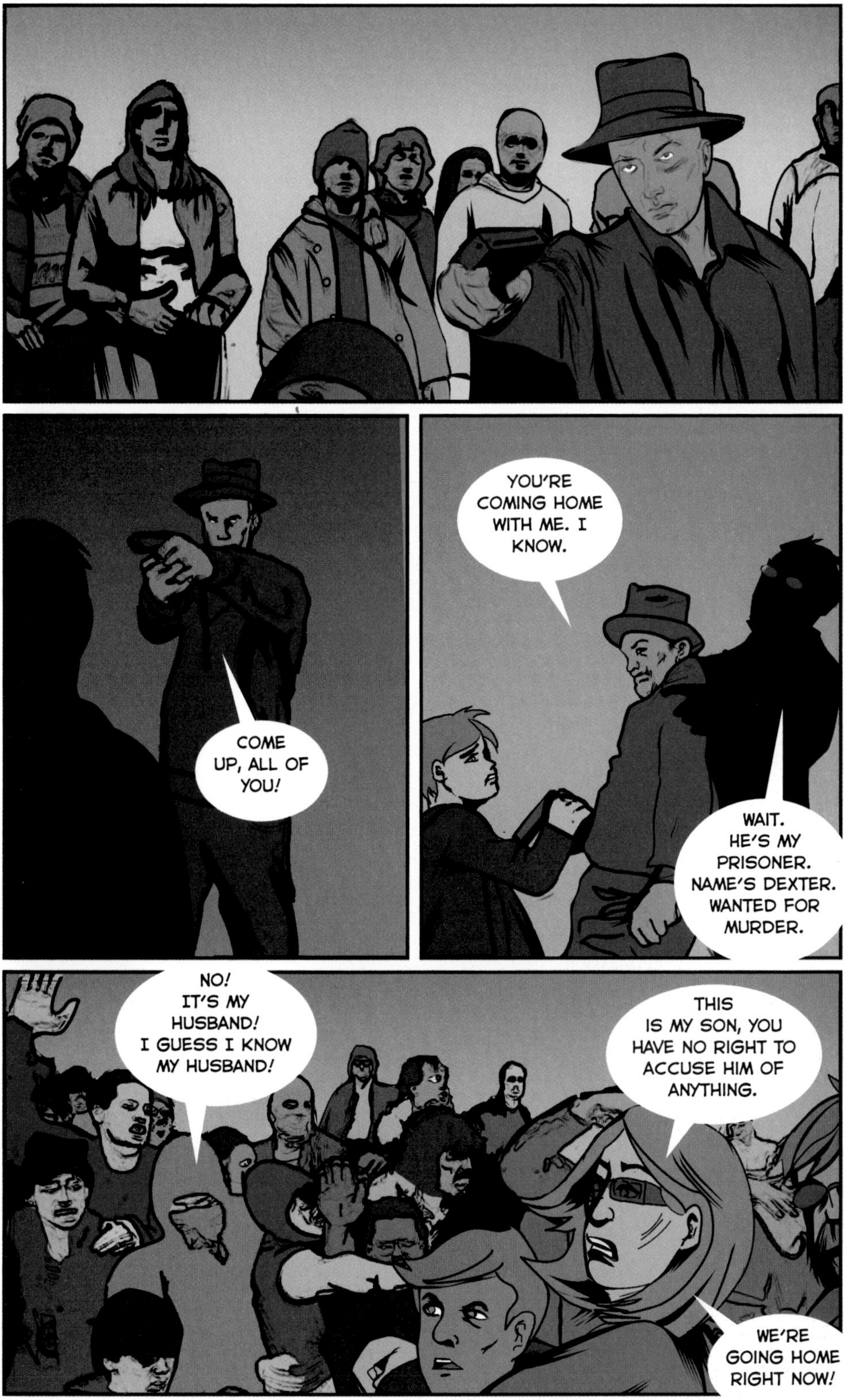
COME UP, ALL OF YOU!
YOU'RE COMING HOME WITH ME. I KNOW.
WAIT. HE'S MY PRISONER. NAME'S DEXTER. WANTED FOR MURDER.
NO! IT'S MY HUSBAND! I GUESS I KNOW MY HUSBAND!
THIS IS MY SON, YOU HAVE NO RIGHT TO ACCUSE HIM OF ANYTHING.
WE'RE GOING HOME RIGHT NOW!

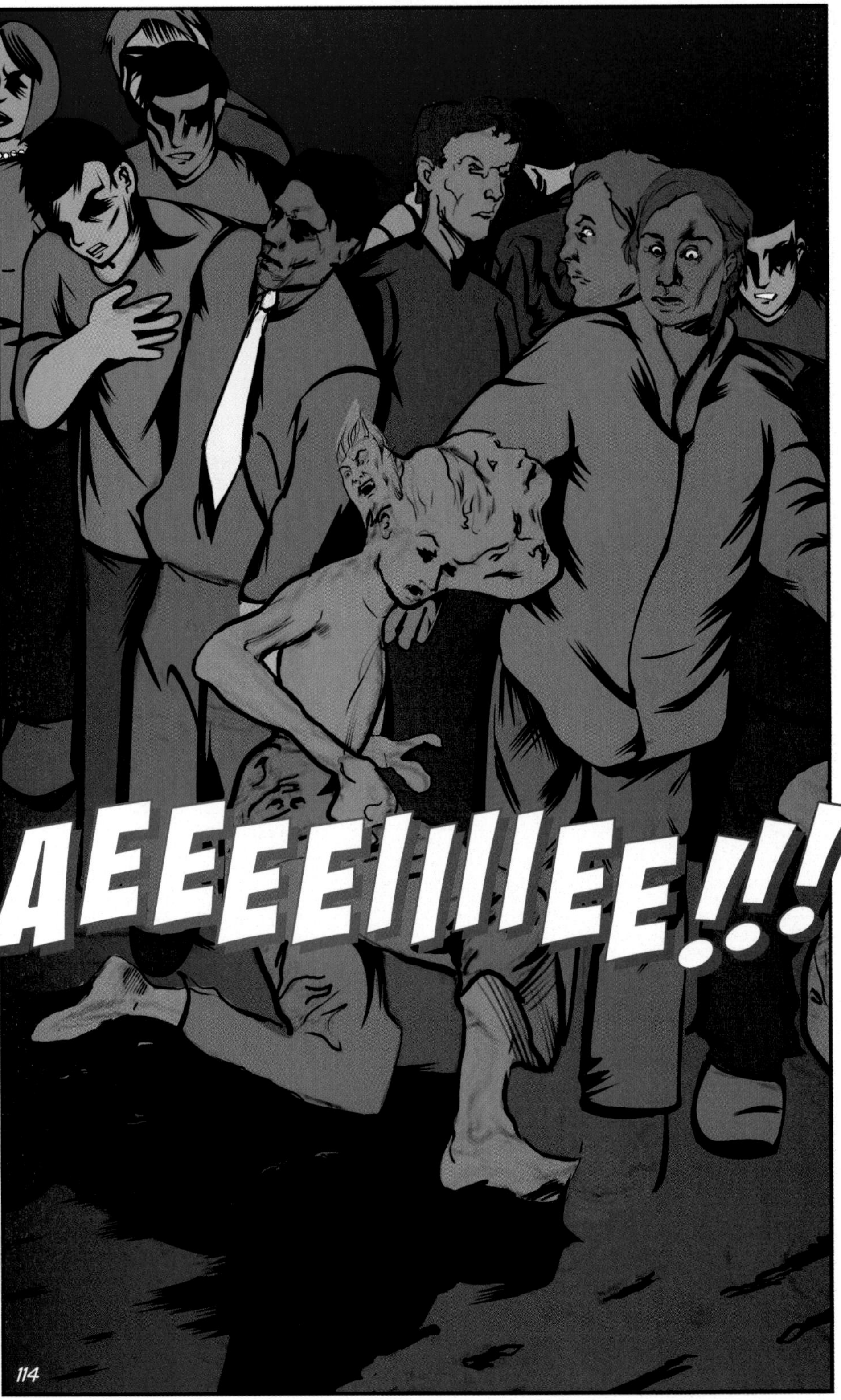
AEEEEIIIIEE!!!

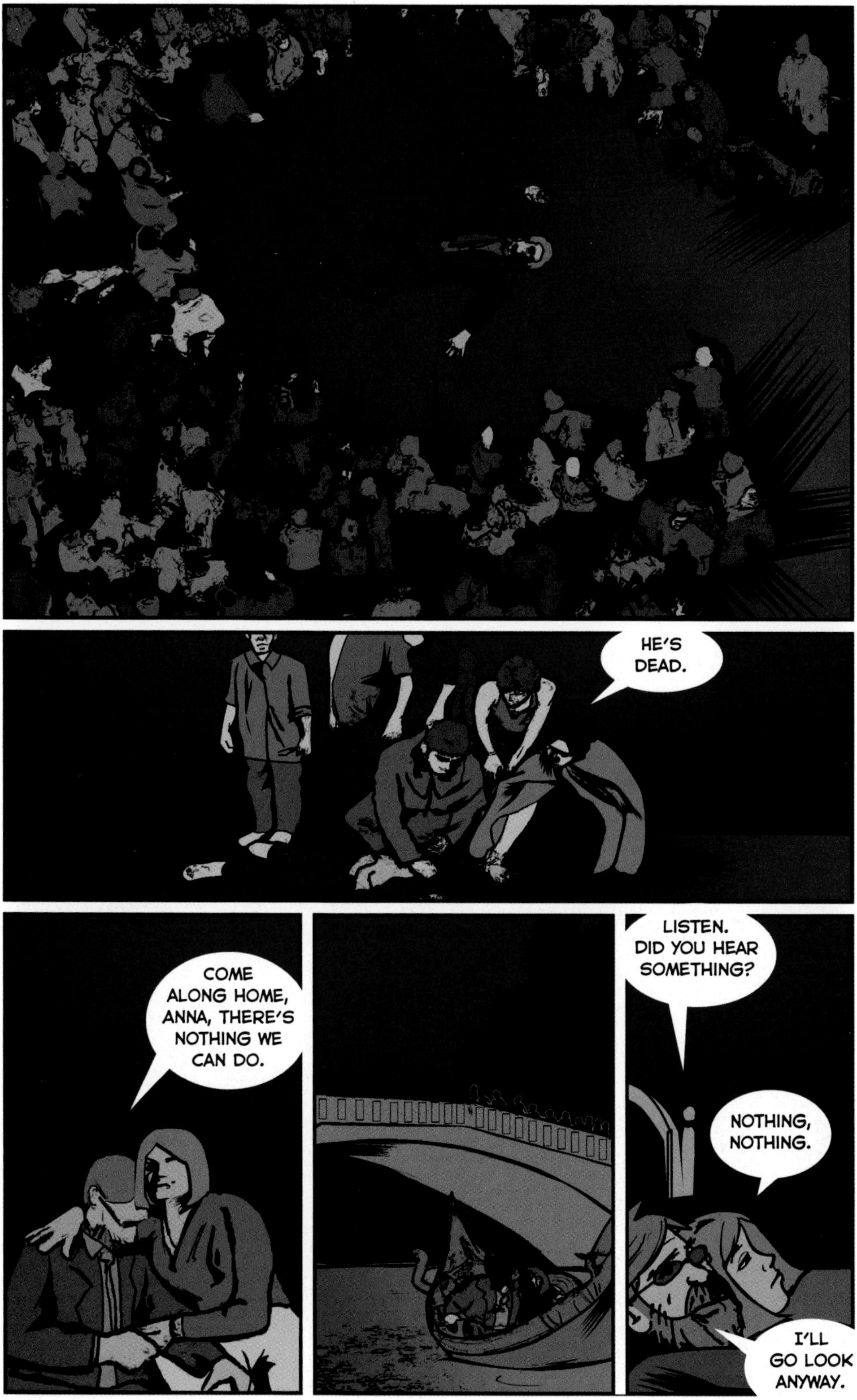
HE'S DEAD.
COME ALONG HOME, ANNA, THERE'S NOTHING WE CAN DO.
LISTEN. DID YOU HEAR SOMETHING?
NOTHING, NOTHING.
I'LL GO LOOK ANYWAY.

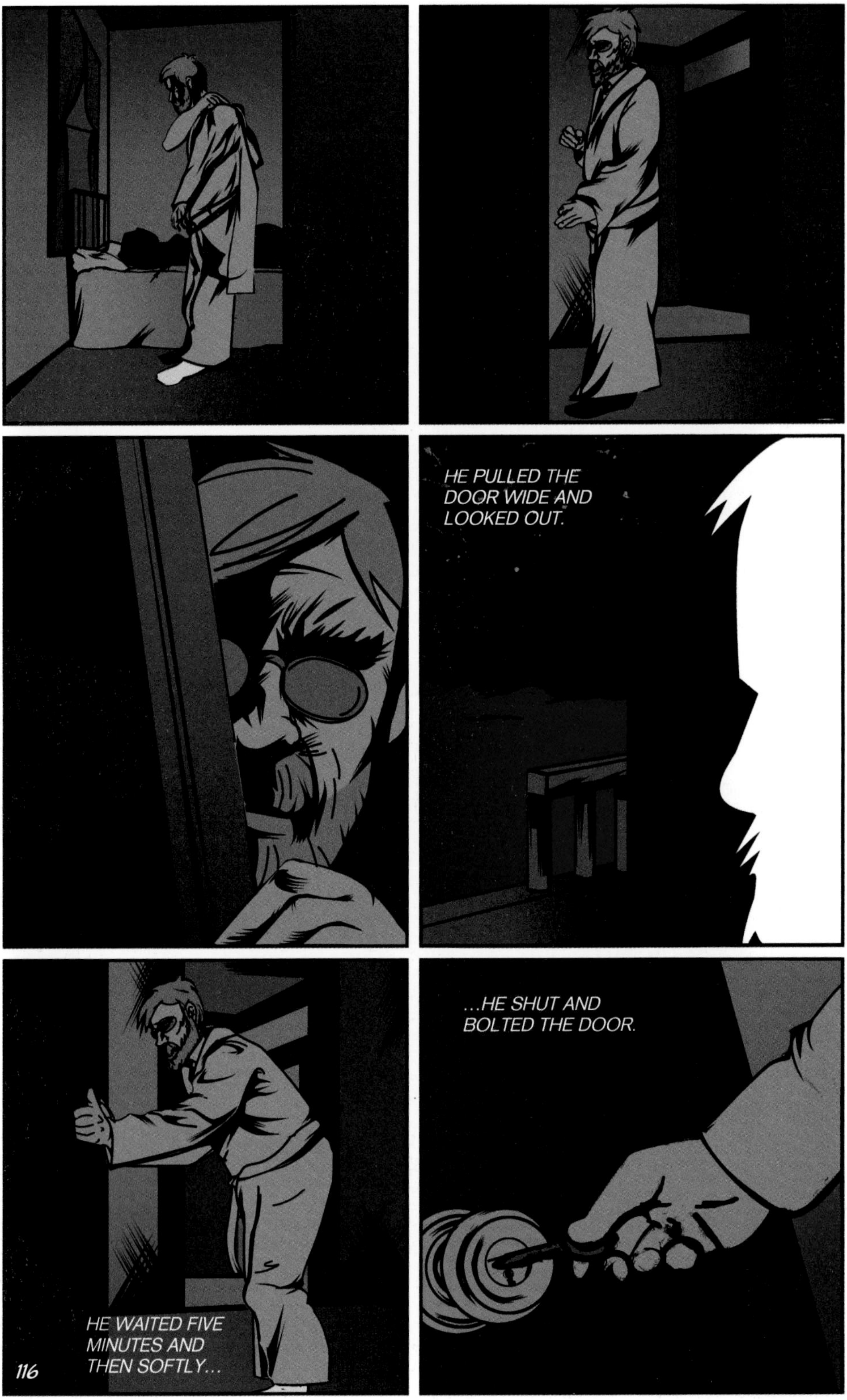
HE PULLED THE DOOR WIDE AND LOOKED OUT.
HE WAITED FIVE MINUTES AND THEN SOFTLY...
...HE SHUT AND BOLTED THE DOOR.

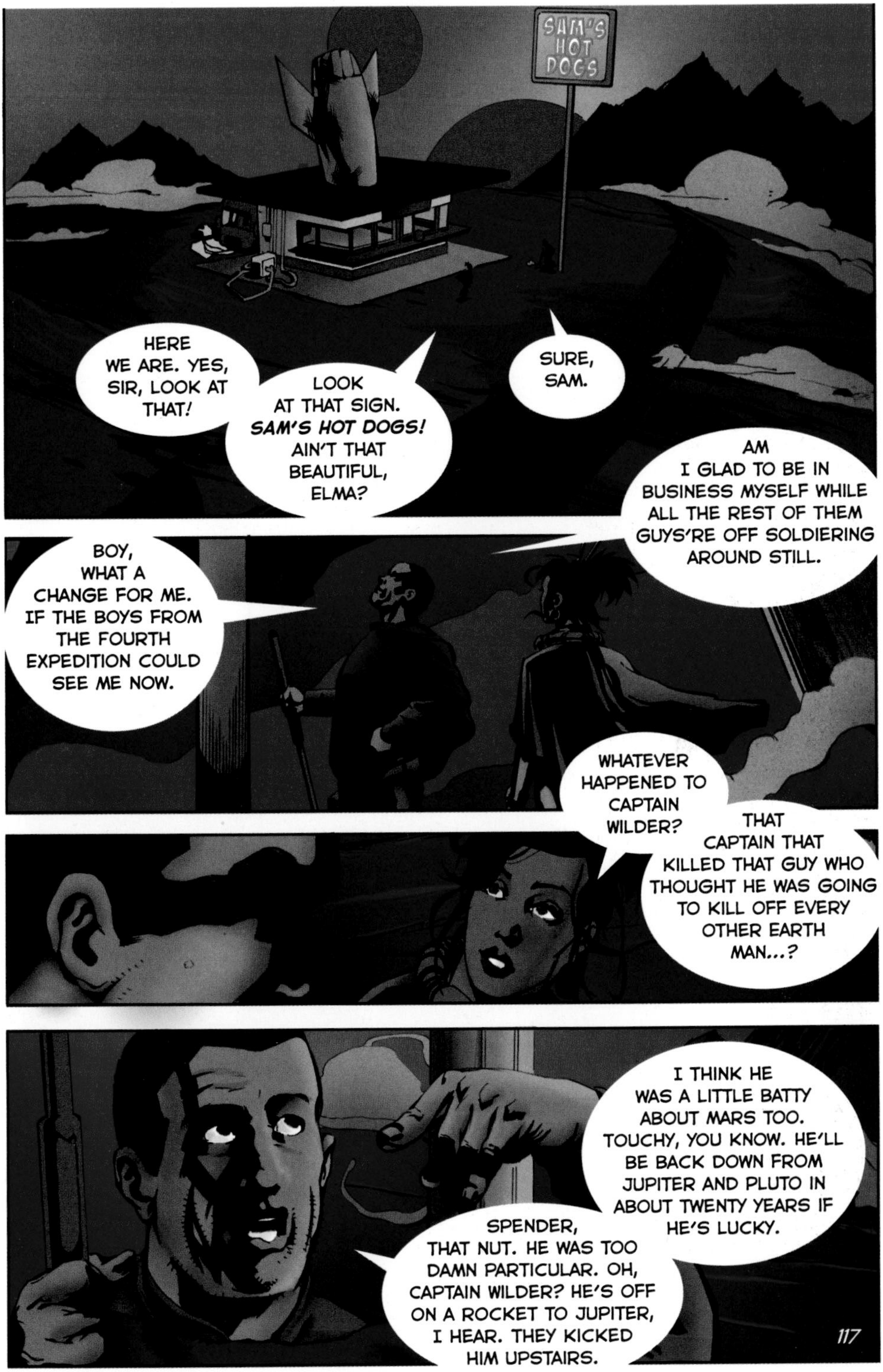
SAM'S HOT DOGS
HERE WE ARE. YES, SIR, LOOK AT THAT!
LOOK AT THAT SIGN. *SAM'S HOT DOGS!* AIN'T THAT BEAUTIFUL, ELMA?
SURE, SAM.
AM I GLAD TO BE IN BUSINESS MYSELF WHILE ALL THE REST OF THEM GUYS'RE OFF SOLDIERING AROUND STILL.
BOY, WHAT A CHANGE FOR ME. IF THE BOYS FROM THE FOURTH EXPEDITION COULD SEE ME NOW.
WHATEVER HAPPENED TO CAPTAIN WILDER?
THAT CAPTAIN THAT KILLED THAT GUY WHO THOUGHT HE WAS GOING TO KILL OFF EVERY OTHER EARTH MAN...?
SPENDER, THAT NUT. HE WAS TOO DAMN PARTICULAR. OH, CAPTAIN WILDER? HE'S OFF ON A ROCKET TO JUPITER, I HEAR. THEY KICKED HIM UPSTAIRS.
I THINK HE WAS A LITTLE BATTY ABOUT MARS TOO. TOUCHY, YOU KNOW. HE'LL BE BACK DOWN FROM JUPITER AND PLUTO IN ABOUT TWENTY YEARS IF HE'S LUCKY.

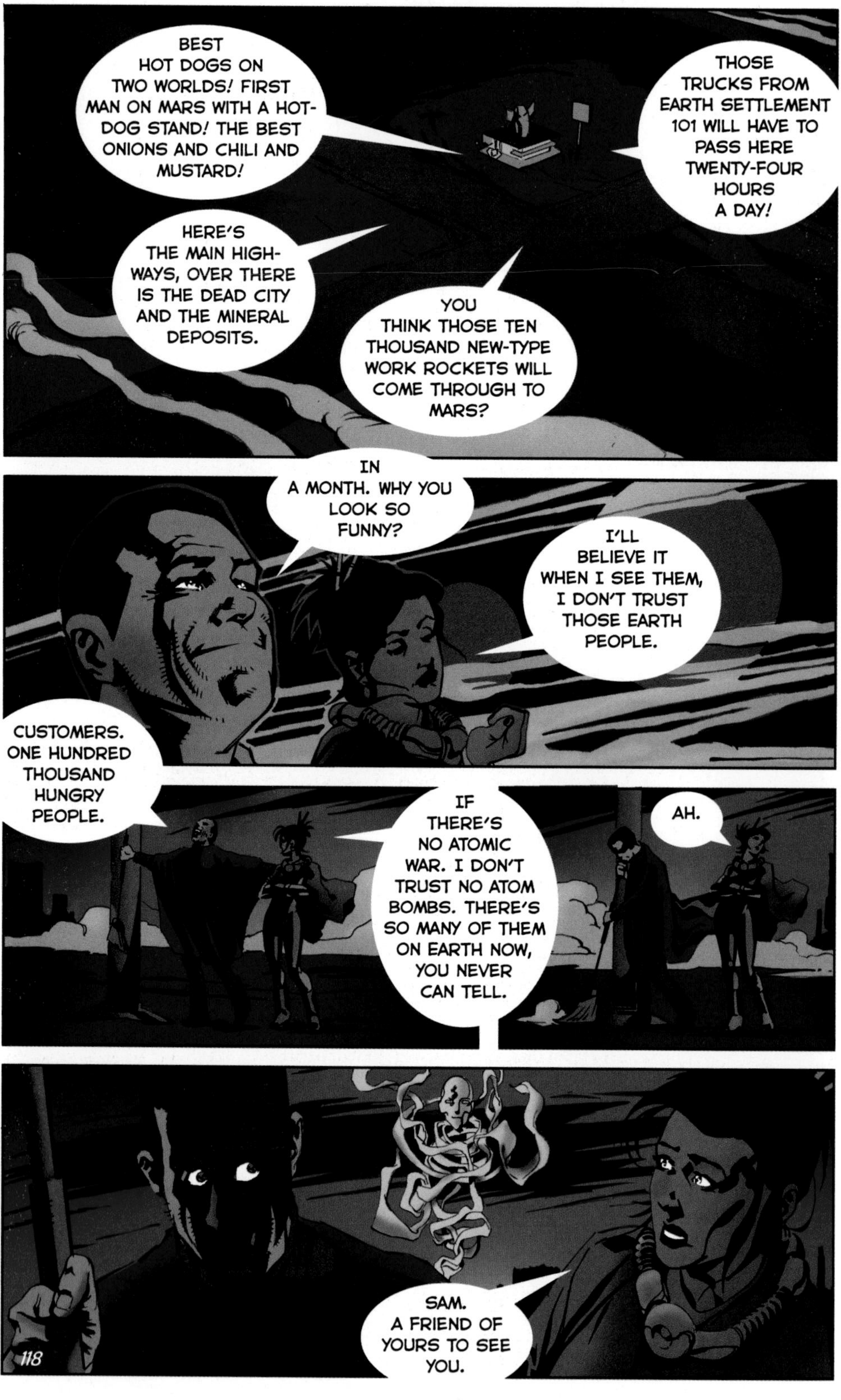
BEST HOT DOGS ON TWO WORLDS! FIRST MAN ON MARS WITH A HOT-DOG STAND! THE BEST ONIONS AND CHILI AND MUSTARD!
THOSE TRUCKS FROM EARTH SETTLEMENT 101 WILL HAVE TO PASS HERE TWENTY-FOUR HOURS A DAY!
HERE'S THE MAIN HIGH-WAYS, OVER THERE IS THE DEAD CITY AND THE MINERAL DEPOSITS.
YOU THINK THOSE TEN THOUSAND NEW-TYPE WORK ROCKETS WILL COME THROUGH TO MARS?
IN A MONTH. WHY YOU LOOK SO FUNNY?
I'LL BELIEVE IT WHEN I SEE THEM, I DON'T TRUST THOSE EARTH PEOPLE.
CUSTOMERS. ONE HUNDRED THOUSAND HUNGRY PEOPLE.
IF THERE'S NO ATOMIC WAR. I DON'T TRUST NO ATOM BOMBS. THERE'S SO MANY OF THEM ON EARTH NOW, YOU NEVER CAN TELL.
AH.
SAM. A FRIEND OF YOURS TO SEE YOU.

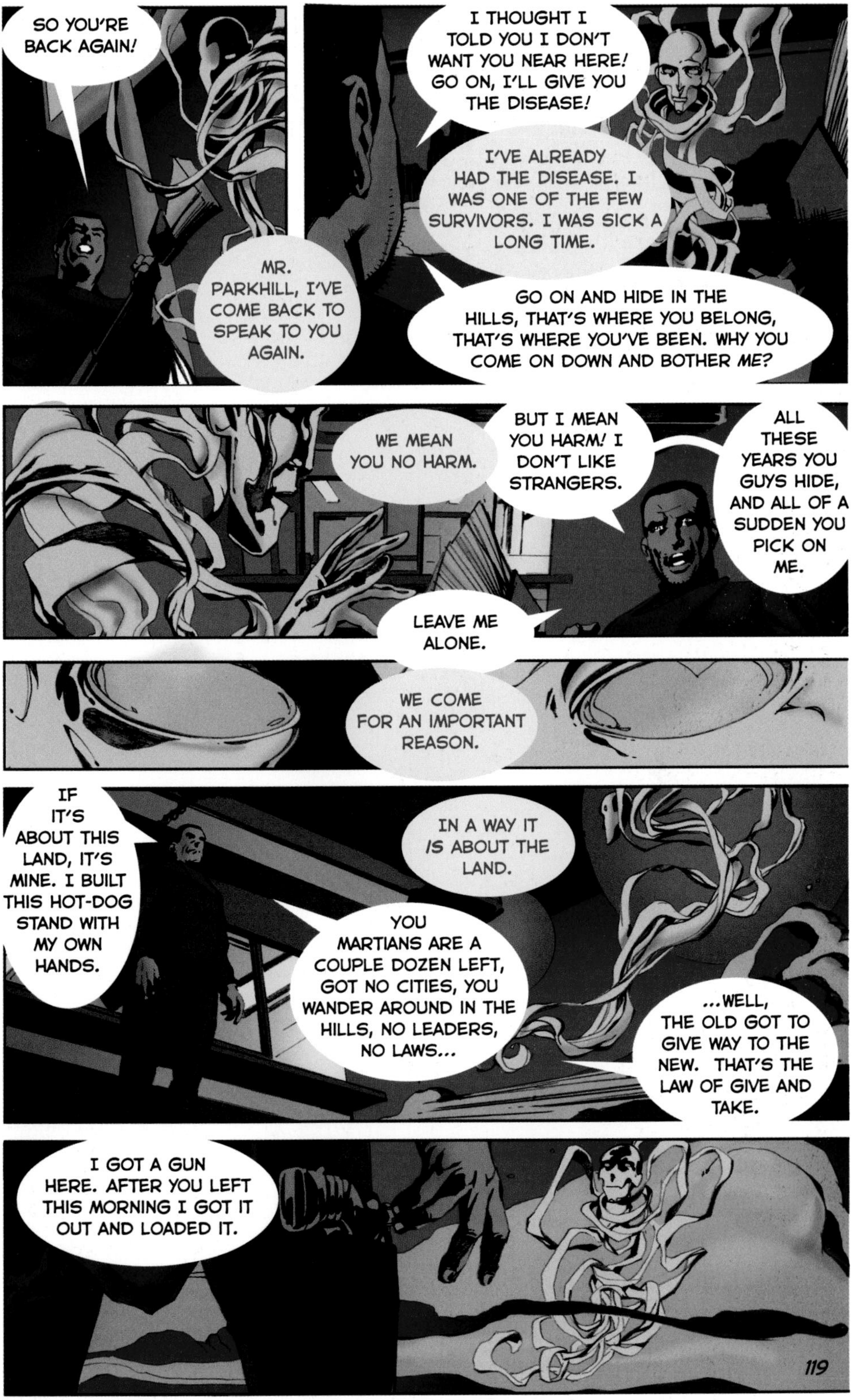

SO YOU'RE BACK AGAIN!
I THOUGHT I TOLD YOU I DON'T WANT YOU NEAR HERE! GO ON, I'LL GIVE YOU THE DISEASE!
I'VE ALREADY HAD THE DISEASE. I WAS ONE OF THE FEW SURVIVORS. I WAS SICK A LONG TIME.
MR. PARKHILL, I'VE COME BACK TO SPEAK TO YOU AGAIN.
GO ON AND HIDE IN THE HILLS, THAT'S WHERE YOU BELONG, THAT'S WHERE YOU'VE BEEN. WHY YOU COME ON DOWN AND BOTHER *ME*?
WE MEAN YOU NO HARM.
BUT I MEAN YOU HARM! I DON'T LIKE STRANGERS.
ALL THESE YEARS YOU GUYS HIDE, AND ALL OF A SUDDEN YOU PICK ON ME.
LEAVE ME ALONE.
WE COME FOR AN IMPORTANT REASON.
IF IT'S ABOUT THIS LAND, IT'S MINE. I BUILT THIS HOT-DOG STAND WITH MY OWN HANDS.
IN A WAY IT *IS* ABOUT THE LAND.
YOU MARTIANS ARE A COUPLE DOZEN LEFT, GOT NO CITIES, YOU WANDER AROUND IN THE HILLS, NO LEADERS, NO LAWS...
...WELL, THE OLD GOT TO GIVE WAY TO THE NEW. THAT'S THE LAW OF GIVE AND TAKE.
I GOT A GUN HERE. AFTER YOU LEFT THIS MORNING I GOT IT OUT AND LOADED IT.

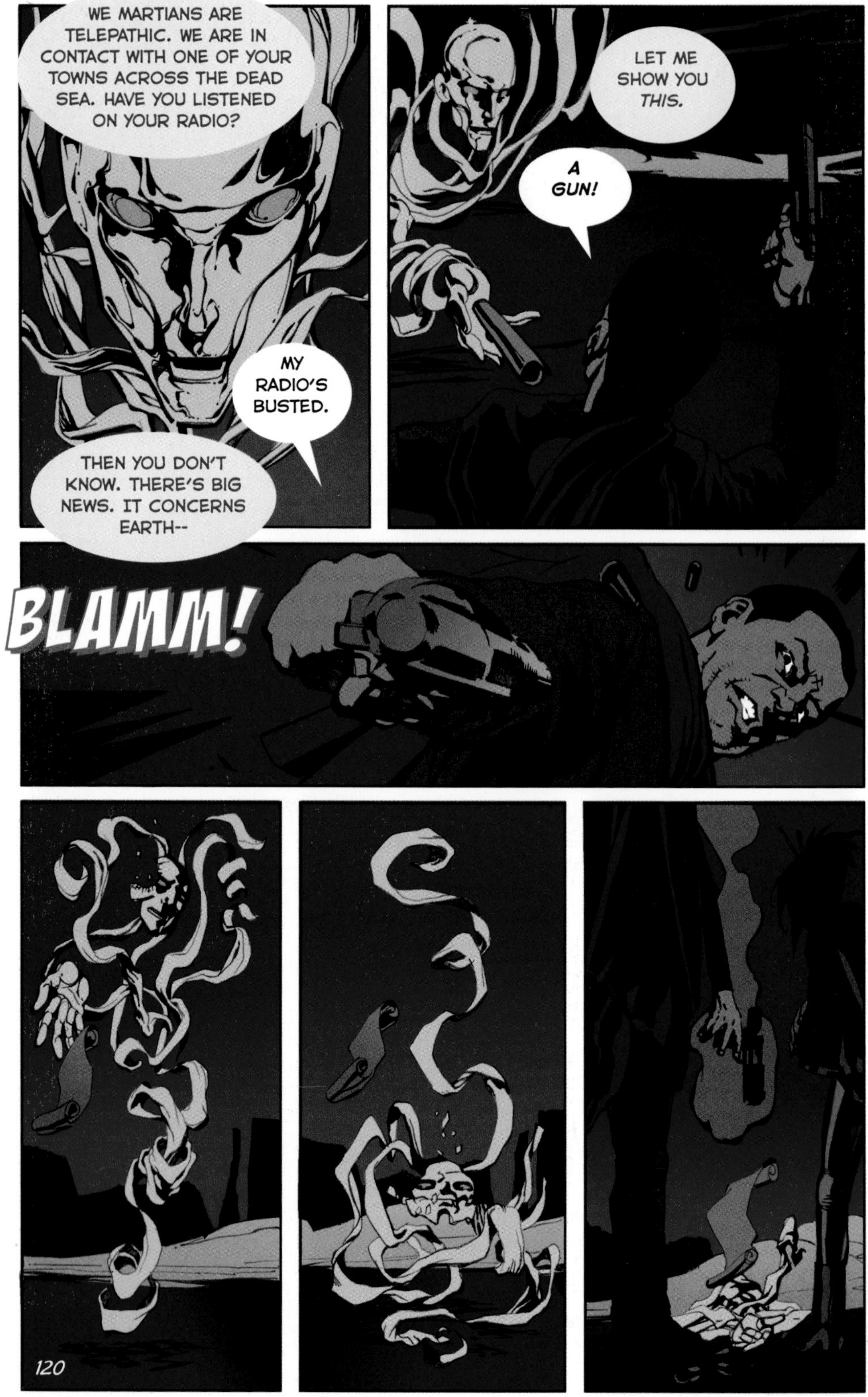
WE MARTIANS ARE TELEPATHIC. WE ARE IN CONTACT WITH ONE OF YOUR TOWNS ACROSS THE DEAD SEA. HAVE YOU LISTENED ON YOUR RADIO?
MY RADIO'S BUSTED.
THEN YOU DON'T KNOW. THERE'S BIG NEWS. IT CONCERNS EARTH--
LET ME SHOW YOU *THIS.*
A GUN!
BLAMM!

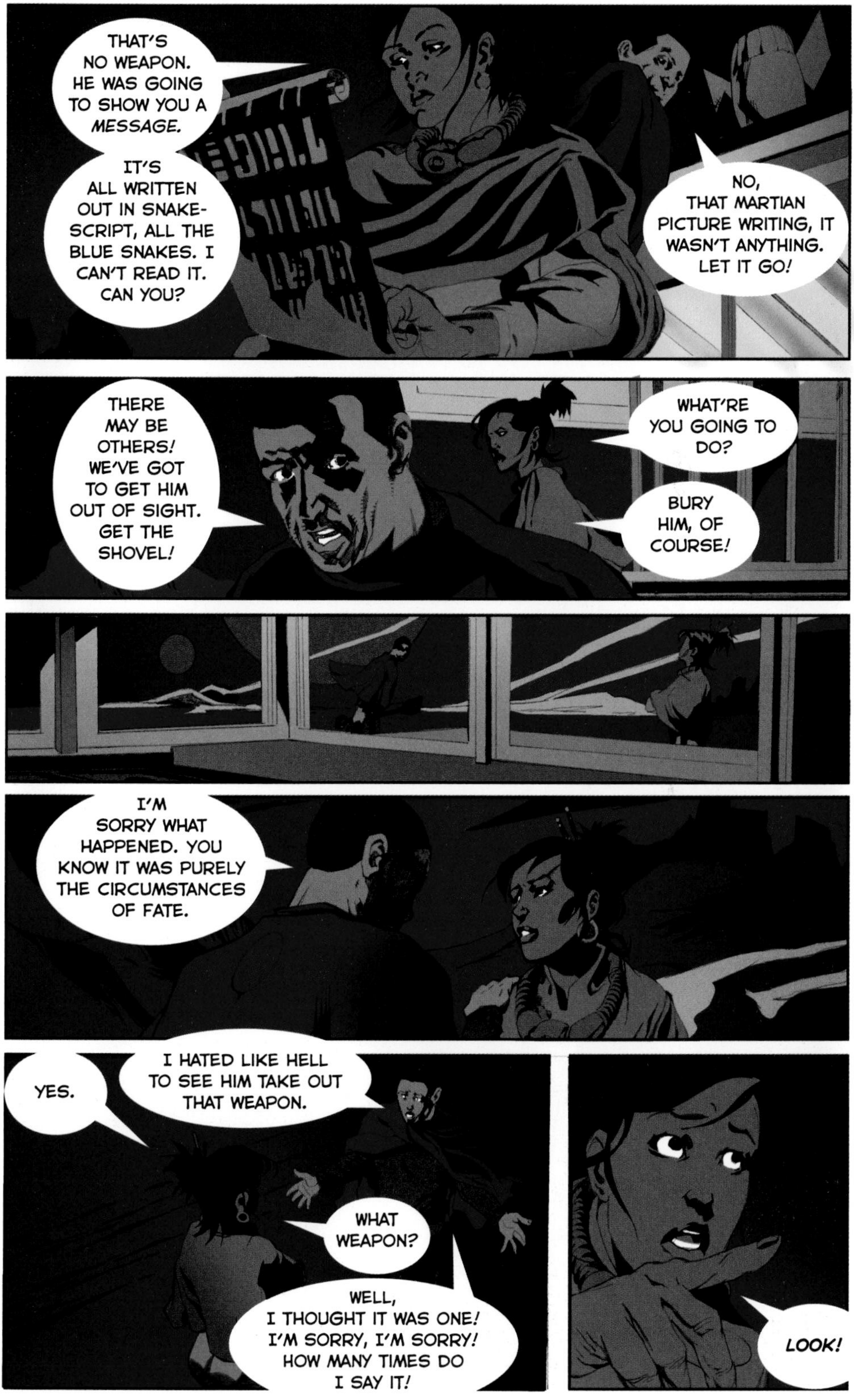
THAT'S NO WEAPON. HE WAS GOING TO SHOW YOU A *MESSAGE.*
IT'S ALL WRITTEN OUT IN SNAKE-SCRIPT, ALL THE BLUE SNAKES. I CAN'T READ IT. CAN YOU?
NO, THAT MARTIAN PICTURE WRITING, IT WASN'T ANYTHING. LET IT GO!
THERE MAY BE OTHERS! WE'VE GOT TO GET HIM OUT OF SIGHT. GET THE SHOVEL!
WHAT'RE YOU GOING TO DO?
BURY HIM, OF COURSE!
I'M SORRY WHAT HAPPENED. YOU KNOW IT WAS PURELY THE CIRCUMSTANCES OF FATE.
YES.
I HATED LIKE HELL TO SEE HIM TAKE OUT THAT WEAPON.
WHAT WEAPON?
WELL, I THOUGHT IT WAS ONE! I'M SORRY, I'M SORRY! HOW MANY TIMES DO I SAY IT!
LOOK!

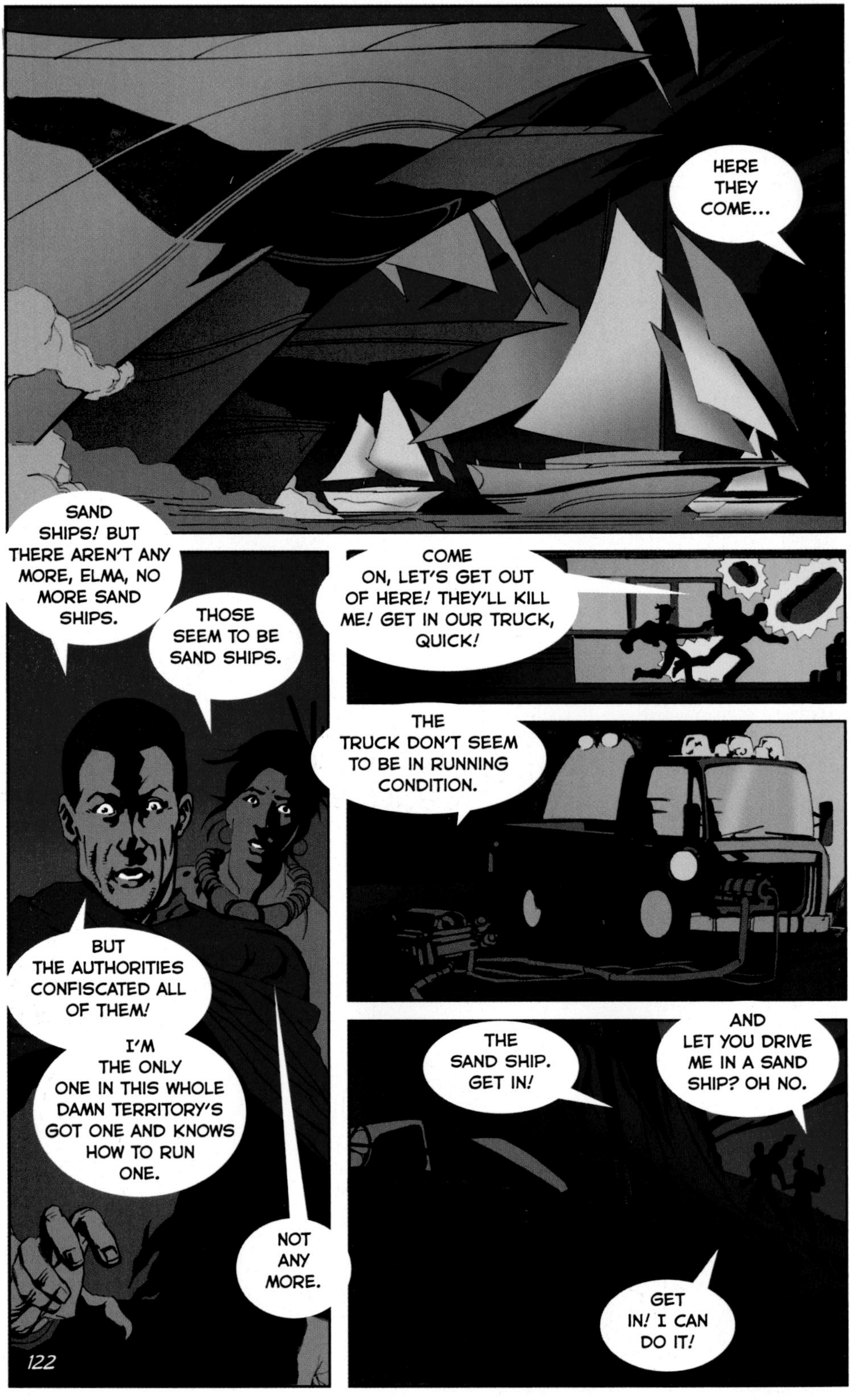
HERE THEY COME...
SAND SHIPS! BUT THERE AREN'T ANY MORE, ELMA, NO MORE SAND SHIPS.
THOSE SEEM TO BE SAND SHIPS.
BUT THE AUTHORITIES CONFISCATED ALL OF THEM!
I'M THE ONLY ONE IN THIS WHOLE DAMN TERRITORY'S GOT ONE AND KNOWS HOW TO RUN ONE.
NOT ANY MORE.
COME ON, LET'S GET OUT OF HERE! THEY'LL KILL ME! GET IN OUR TRUCK, QUICK!
THE TRUCK DON'T SEEM TO BE IN RUNNING CONDITION.
THE SAND SHIP. GET IN!
AND LET YOU DRIVE ME IN A SAND SHIP? OH NO.
GET IN! I CAN DO IT!

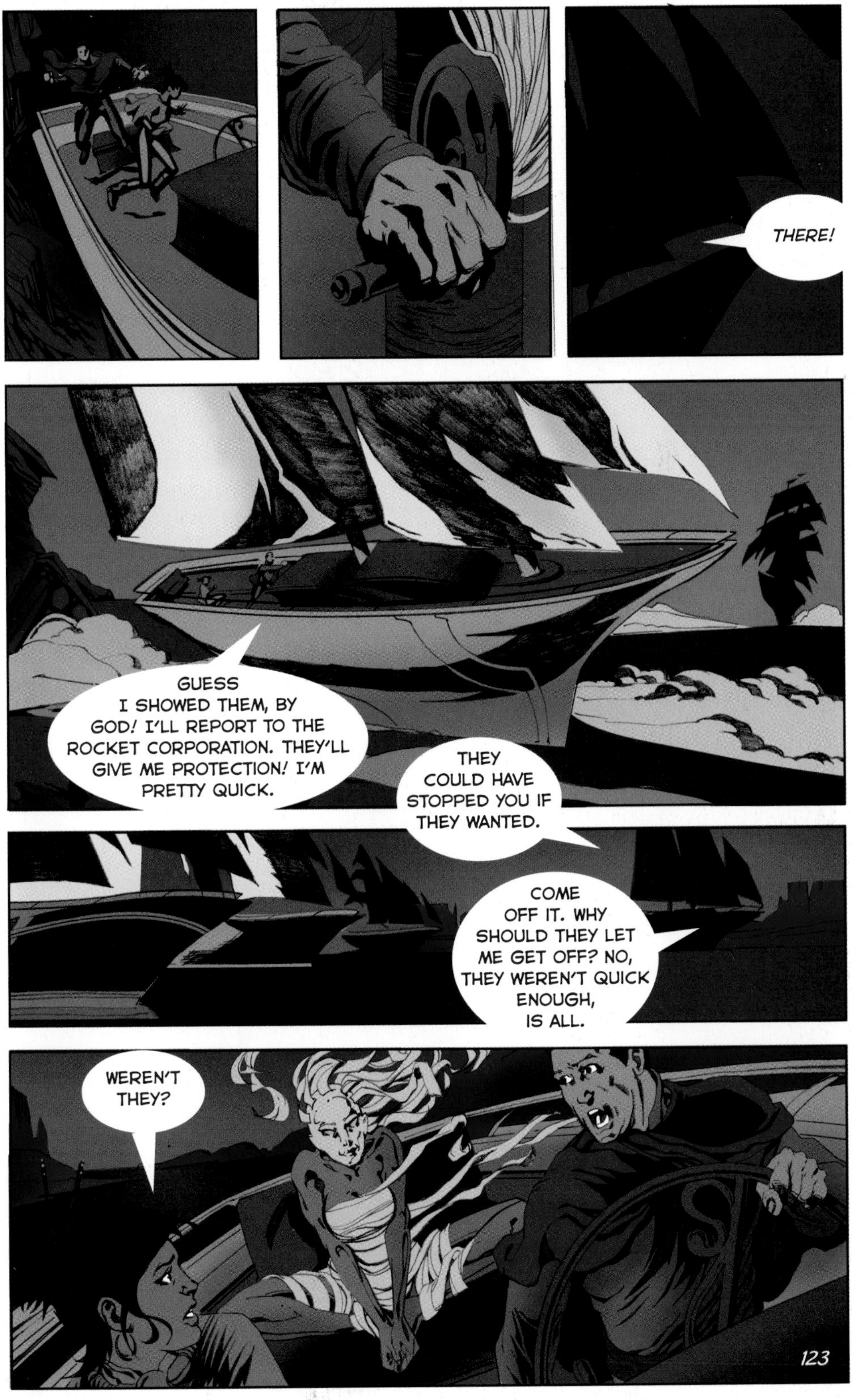
THERE!
GUESS I SHOWED THEM, BY GOD! I'LL REPORT TO THE ROCKET CORPORATION. THEY'LL GIVE ME PROTECTION! I'M PRETTY QUICK.
THEY COULD HAVE STOPPED YOU IF THEY WANTED.
COME OFF IT. WHY SHOULD THEY LET ME GET OFF? NO, THEY WEREN'T QUICK ENOUGH, IS ALL.
WEREN'T THEY?

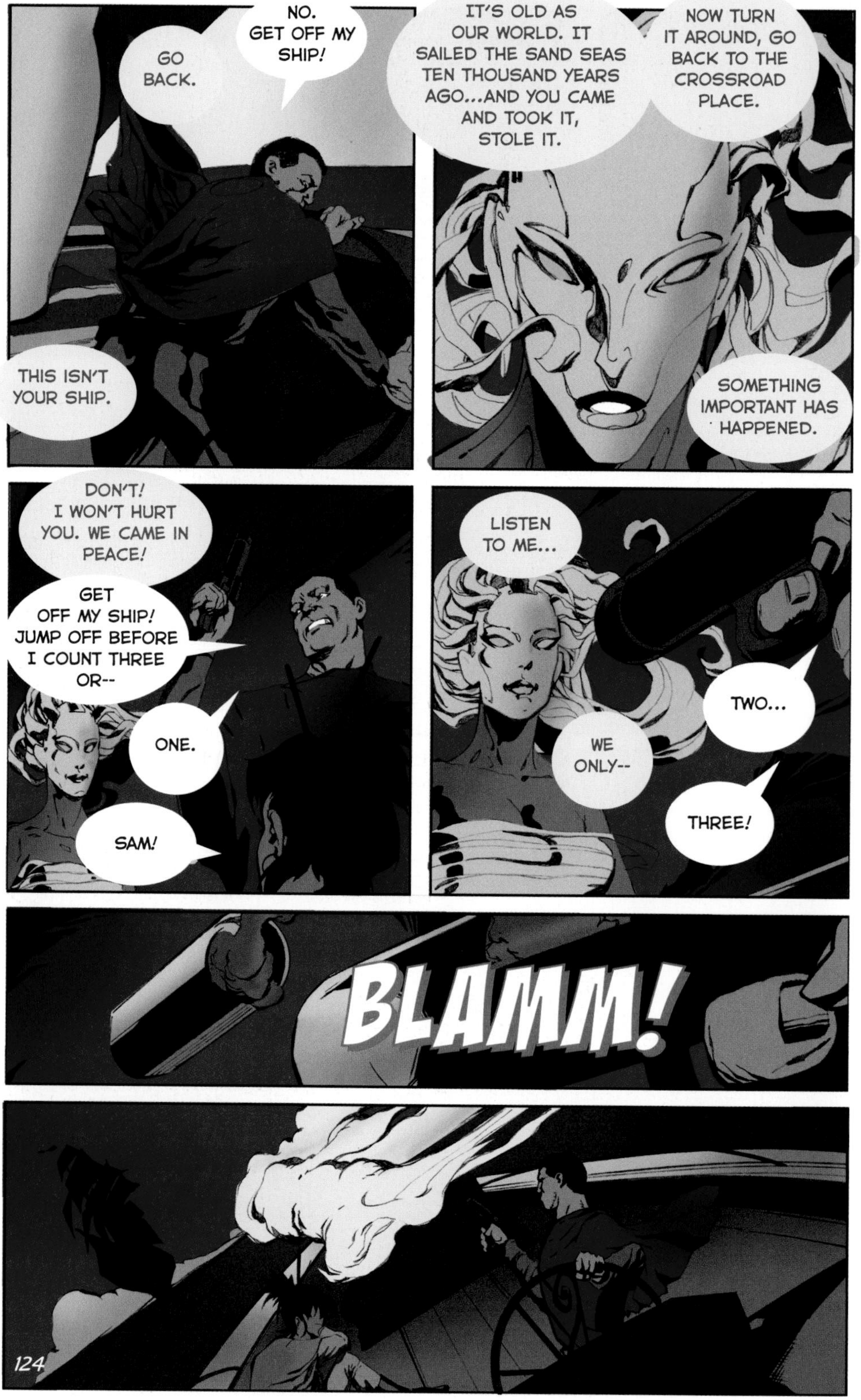
GO BACK.
NO. GET OFF MY SHIP!
THIS ISN'T YOUR SHIP.
IT'S OLD AS OUR WORLD. IT SAILED THE SAND SEAS TEN THOUSAND YEARS AGO...AND YOU CAME AND TOOK IT, STOLE IT.
NOW TURN IT AROUND, GO BACK TO THE CROSSROAD PLACE.
SOMETHING IMPORTANT HAS HAPPENED.
DON'T! I WON'T HURT YOU. WE CAME IN PEACE!
GET OFF MY SHIP! JUMP OFF BEFORE I COUNT THREE OR--
ONE.
SAM!
LISTEN TO ME...
TWO...
WE ONLY--
THREE!
BLAMM!

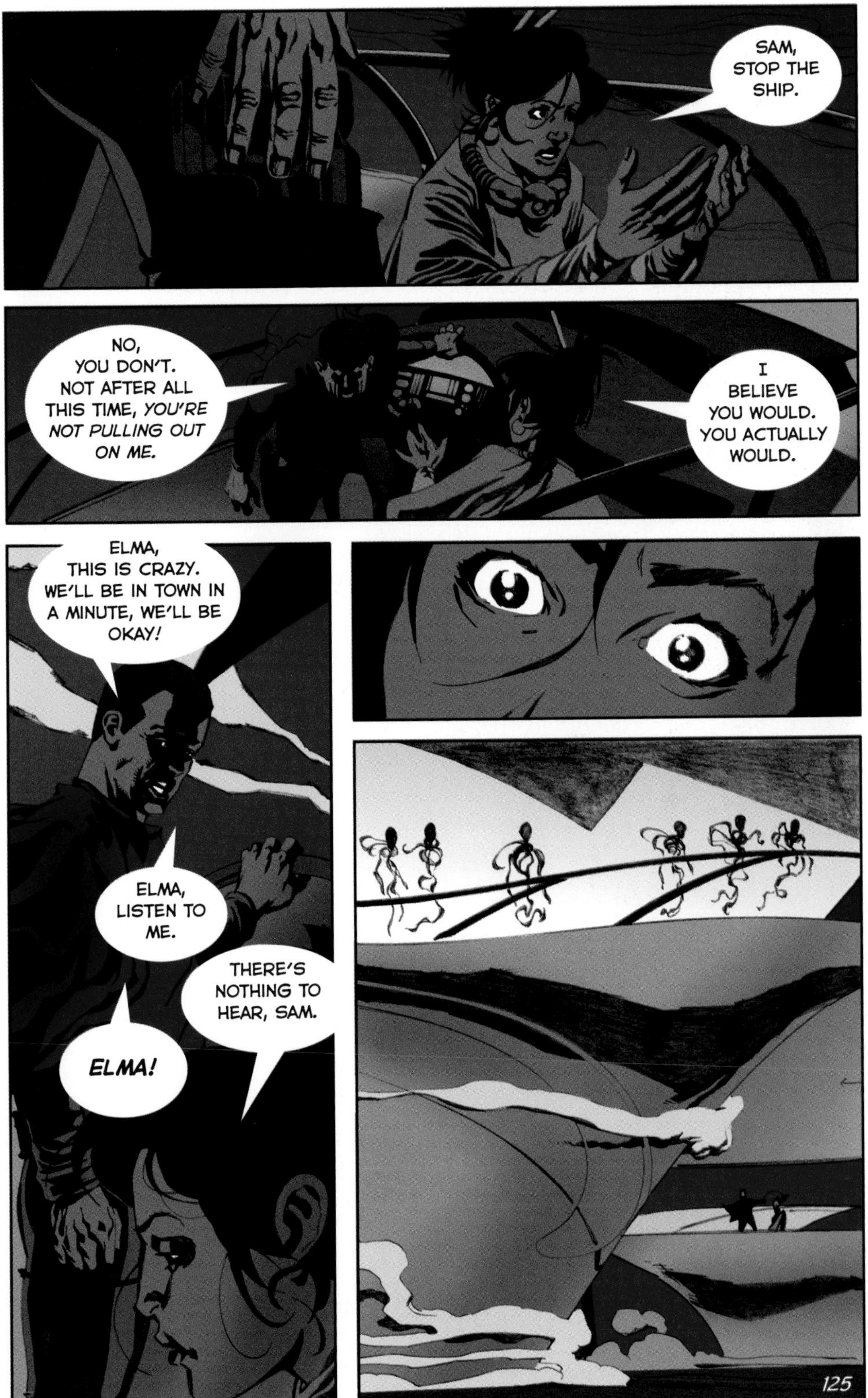
SAM, STOP THE SHIP.
NO, YOU DON'T. NOT AFTER ALL THIS TIME, *YOU'RE NOT PULLING OUT ON ME.*
I BELIEVE YOU WOULD. YOU ACTUALLY WOULD.
ELMA, THIS IS CRAZY. WE'LL BE IN TOWN IN A MINUTE, WE'LL BE OKAY!
ELMA, LISTEN TO ME.
THERE'S NOTHING TO HEAR, SAM.
ELMA!

BLAMM!
BLAMM!

ELMA, ELMA, I CAN'T HOLD THEM ALL OFF!

I'M OUT-NUMBERED, ELMA! THEY'LL KILL ME!

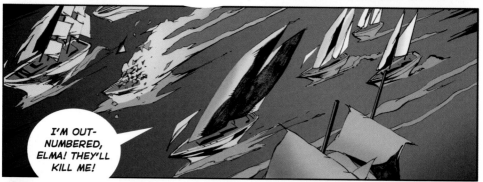

EARTH MAN.

I DIDN'T DO ANYTHING! IT WAS ALL A MISTAKE!

I CAME TO MARS LIKE ANY HONEST ENTERPRISING BUSINESSMAN.

I BUILT ME THE FINEST LITTLE STAND YOU EVER SAW RIGHT THERE ON THAT LAND BY THE CROSSROADS-- YOU KNOW WHERE IT IS.

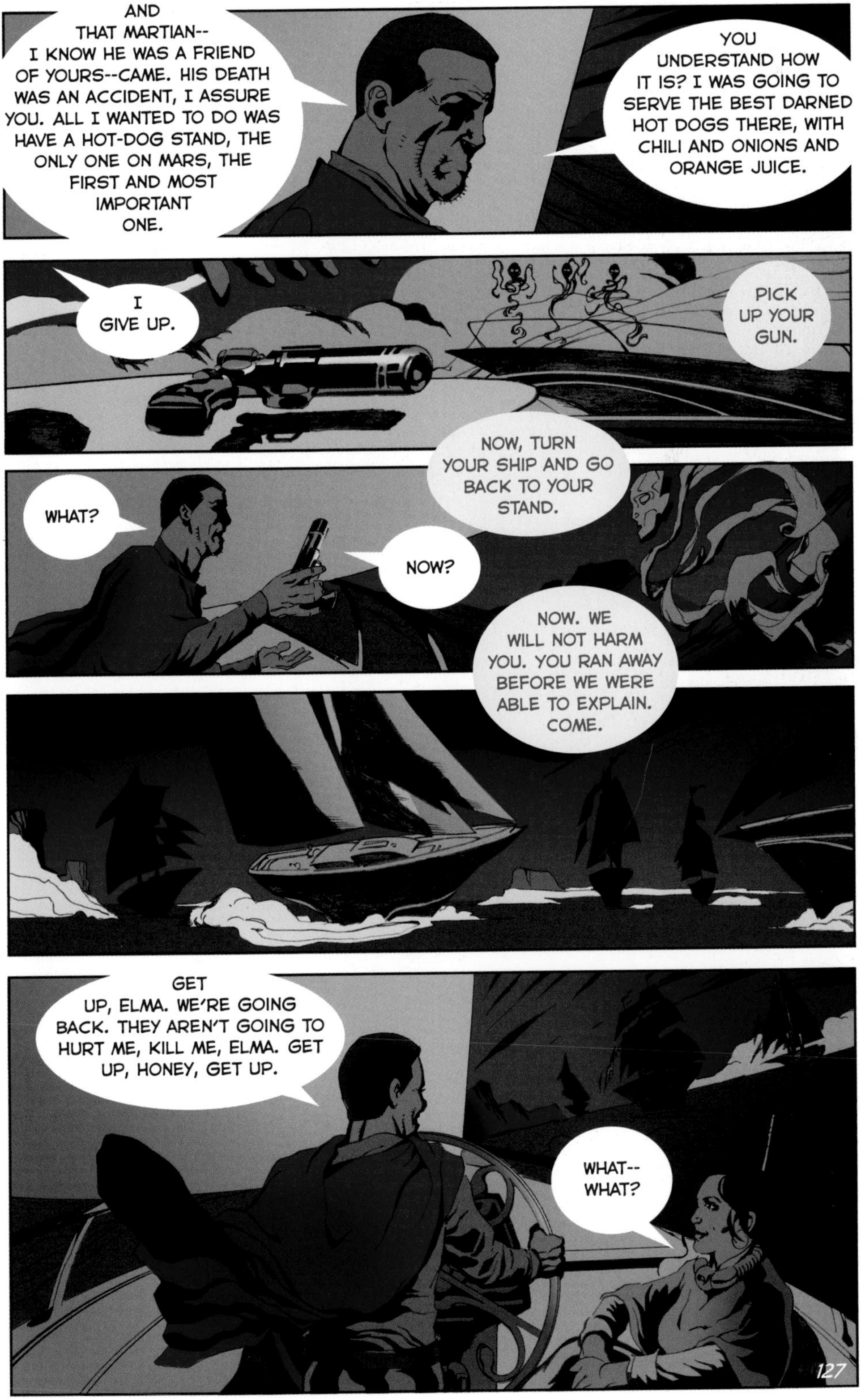
AND THAT MARTIAN-- I KNOW HE WAS A FRIEND OF YOURS--CAME. HIS DEATH WAS AN ACCIDENT, I ASSURE YOU. ALL I WANTED TO DO WAS HAVE A HOT-DOG STAND, THE ONLY ONE ON MARS, THE FIRST AND MOST IMPORTANT ONE.
YOU UNDERSTAND HOW IT IS? I WAS GOING TO SERVE THE BEST DARNED HOT DOGS THERE, WITH CHILI AND ONIONS AND ORANGE JUICE.
I GIVE UP.
PICK UP YOUR GUN.
WHAT?
NOW, TURN YOUR SHIP AND GO BACK TO YOUR STAND.
NOW?
NOW. WE WILL NOT HARM YOU. YOU RAN AWAY BEFORE WE WERE ABLE TO EXPLAIN. COME.
GET UP, ELMA. WE'RE GOING BACK. THEY AREN'T GOING TO HURT ME, KILL ME, ELMA. GET UP, HONEY, GET UP.
WHAT-- WHAT?

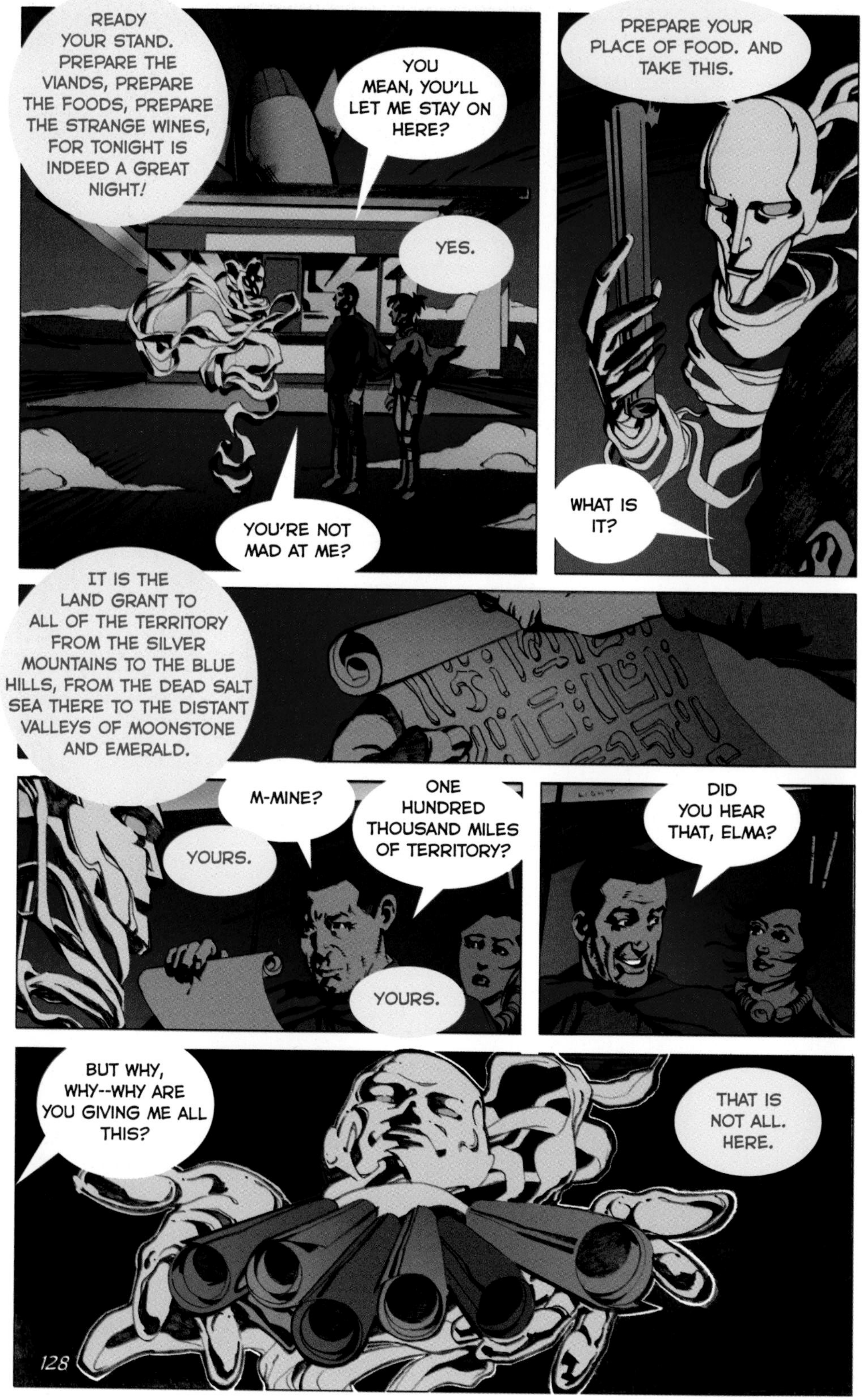
READY YOUR STAND. PREPARE THE VIANDS, PREPARE THE FOODS, PREPARE THE STRANGE WINES, FOR TONIGHT IS INDEED A GREAT NIGHT!
YOU MEAN, YOU'LL LET ME STAY ON HERE?
YES.
YOU'RE NOT MAD AT ME?
PREPARE YOUR PLACE OF FOOD. AND TAKE THIS.
WHAT IS IT?
IT IS THE LAND GRANT TO ALL OF THE TERRITORY FROM THE SILVER MOUNTAINS TO THE BLUE HILLS, FROM THE DEAD SALT SEA THERE TO THE DISTANT VALLEYS OF MOONSTONE AND EMERALD.
M-MINE?
YOURS.
ONE HUNDRED THOUSAND MILES OF TERRITORY?
YOURS.
DID YOU HEAR THAT, ELMA?
BUT WHY, WHY--WHY ARE YOU GIVING ME ALL THIS?
THAT IS NOT ALL. HERE.

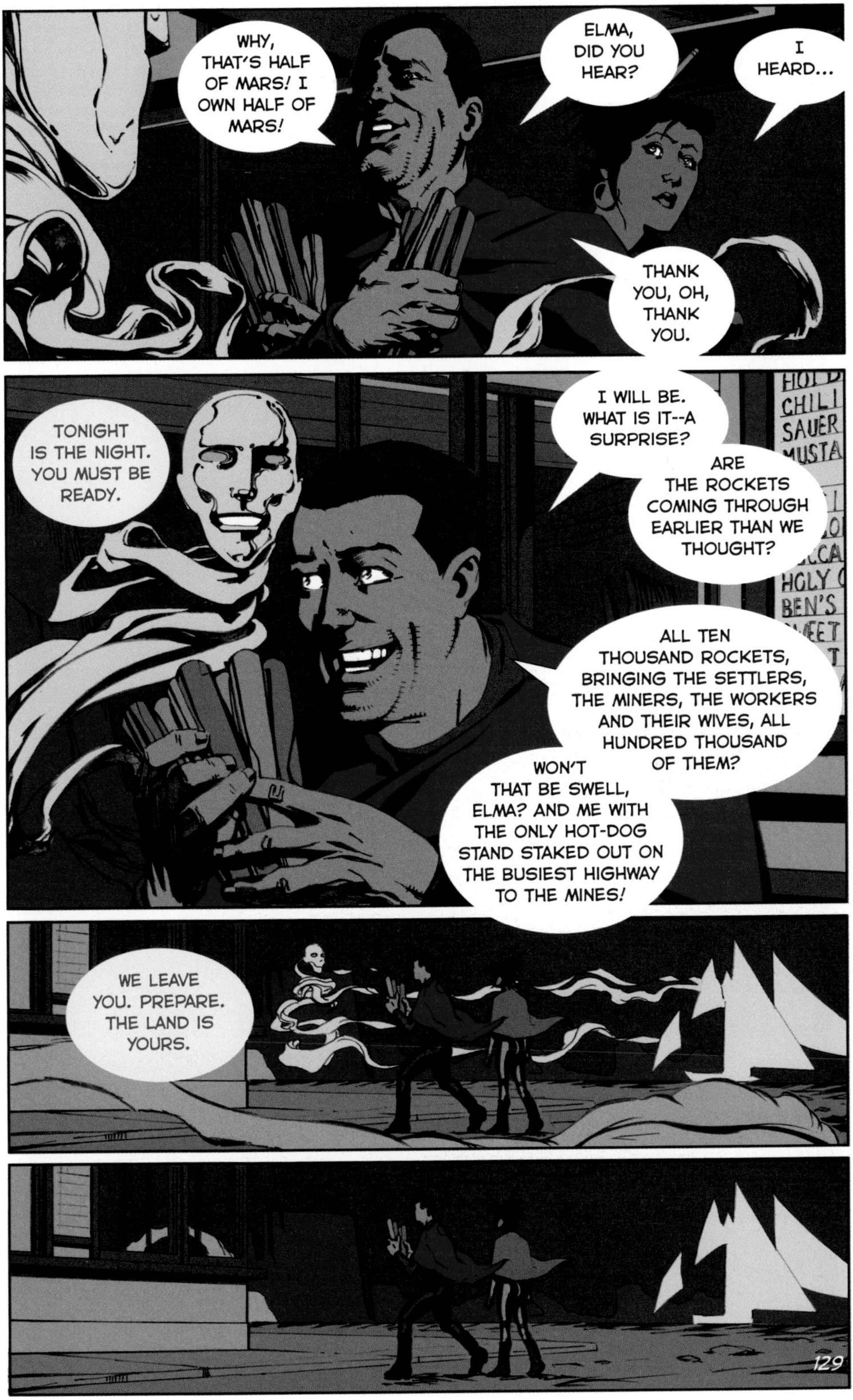
WHY, THAT'S HALF OF MARS! I OWN HALF OF MARS!
ELMA, DID YOU HEAR?
I HEARD...
THANK YOU, OH, THANK YOU.
TONIGHT IS THE NIGHT. YOU MUST BE READY.
I WILL BE. WHAT IS IT--A SURPRISE?
ARE THE ROCKETS COMING THROUGH EARLIER THAN WE THOUGHT?
ALL TEN THOUSAND ROCKETS, BRINGING THE SETTLERS, THE MINERS, THE WORKERS AND THEIR WIVES, ALL HUNDRED THOUSAND OF THEM?
WON'T THAT BE SWELL, ELMA? AND ME WITH THE ONLY HOT-DOG STAND STAKED OUT ON THE BUSIEST HIGHWAY TO THE MINES!
WE LEAVE YOU. PREPARE. THE LAND IS YOURS.

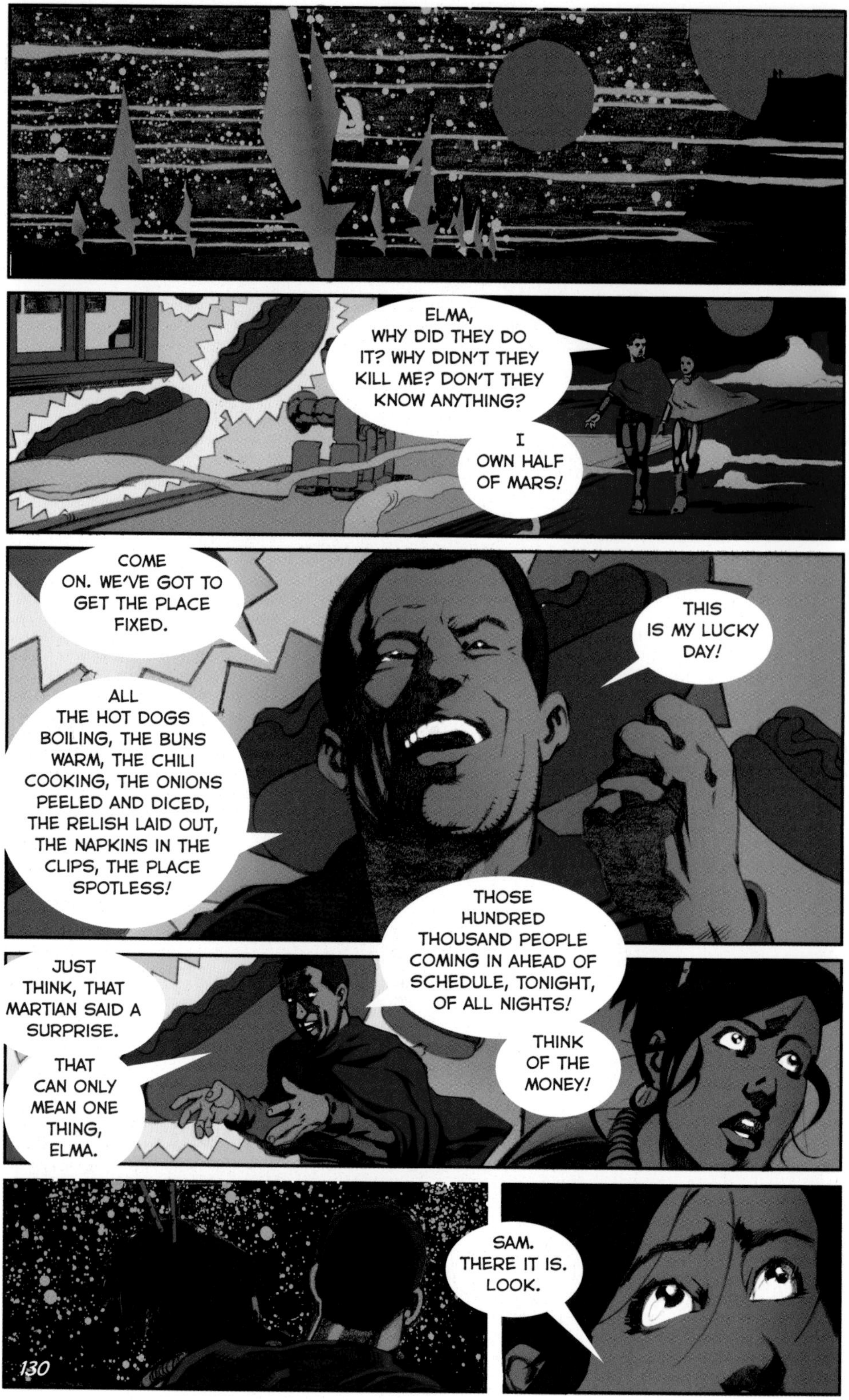
ELMA, WHY DID THEY DO IT? WHY DIDN'T THEY KILL ME? DON'T THEY KNOW ANYTHING?
I OWN HALF OF MARS!
COME ON. WE'VE GOT TO GET THE PLACE FIXED.
ALL THE HOT DOGS BOILING, THE BUNS WARM, THE CHILI COOKING, THE ONIONS PEELED AND DICED, THE RELISH LAID OUT, THE NAPKINS IN THE CLIPS, THE PLACE SPOTLESS!
THIS IS MY LUCKY DAY!
THOSE HUNDRED THOUSAND PEOPLE COMING IN AHEAD OF SCHEDULE, TONIGHT, OF ALL NIGHTS!
THINK OF THE MONEY!
JUST THINK, THAT MARTIAN SAID A SURPRISE.
THAT CAN ONLY MEAN ONE THING, ELMA.
SAM. THERE IT IS. LOOK.

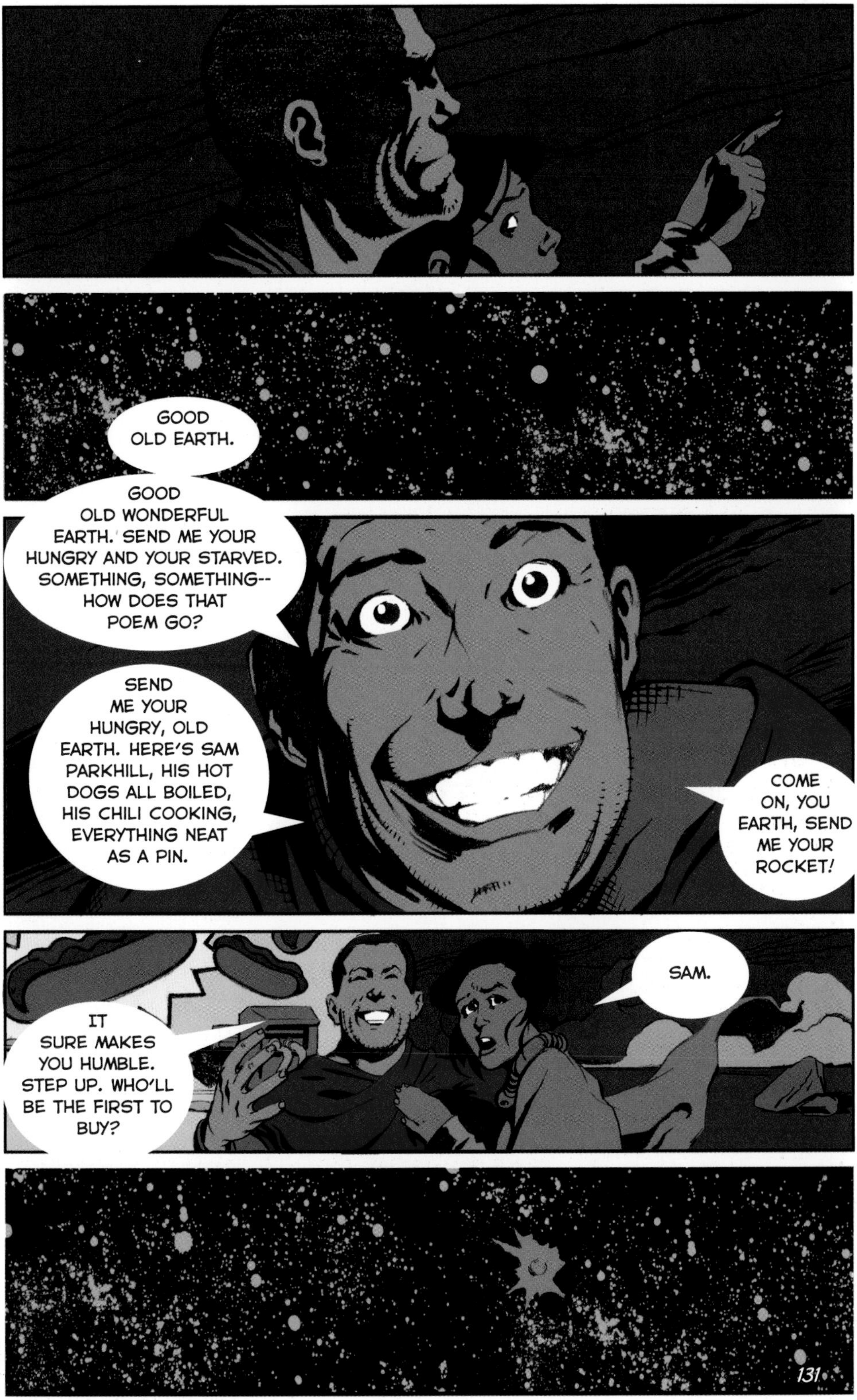
GOOD OLD EARTH.
GOOD OLD WONDERFUL EARTH. SEND ME YOUR HUNGRY AND YOUR STARVED. SOMETHING, SOMETHING-- HOW DOES THAT POEM GO?
SEND ME YOUR HUNGRY, OLD EARTH. HERE'S SAM PARKHILL, HIS HOT DOGS ALL BOILED, HIS CHILI COOKING, EVERYTHING NEAT AS A PIN.
COME ON, YOU EARTH, SEND ME YOUR ROCKET!
IT SURE MAKES YOU HUMBLE. STEP UP. WHO'LL BE THE FIRST TO BUY?
SAM.

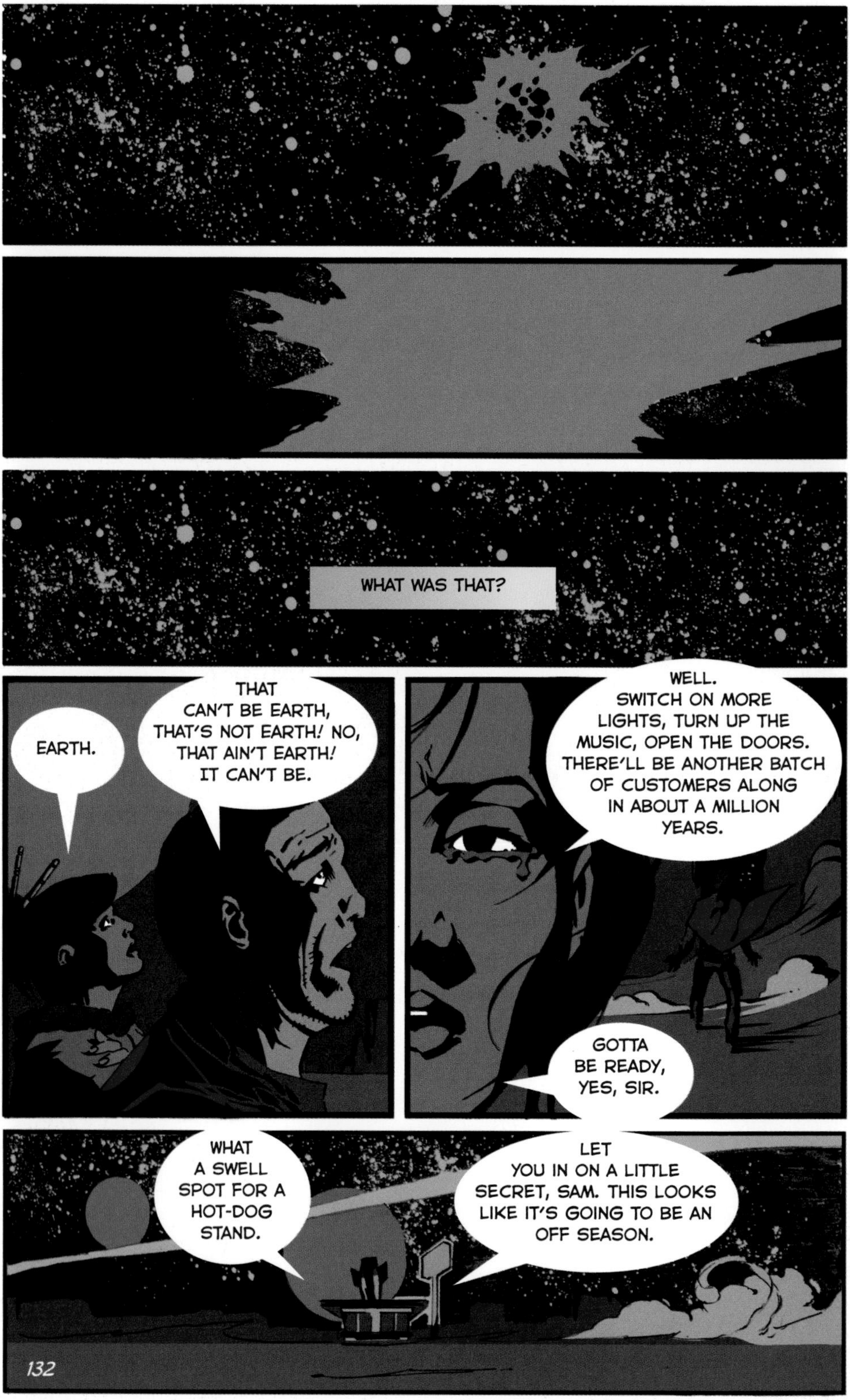
WHAT WAS THAT?
EARTH.
THAT CAN'T BE EARTH, THAT'S NOT EARTH! NO, THAT AIN'T EARTH! IT CAN'T BE.
WELL. SWITCH ON MORE LIGHTS, TURN UP THE MUSIC, OPEN THE DOORS. THERE'LL BE ANOTHER BATCH OF CUSTOMERS ALONG IN ABOUT A MILLION YEARS.
GOTTA BE READY, YES, SIR.
WHAT A SWELL SPOT FOR A HOT-DOG STAND.
LET YOU IN ON A LITTLE SECRET, SAM. THIS LOOKS LIKE IT'S GOING TO BE AN OFF SEASON.

THEY ALL CAME OUT AND LOOKED AT THE SKY THAT NIGHT.

THEY LEFT THEIR SUPPERS OR THEIR WASHING UP OR THEIR DRESSING FOR THE SHOW AND THEY CAME OUT UPON THEIR NOW-NOT-QUITE-AS-NEW PORCHES AND WATCHED THE GREEN STAR OF EARTH THERE.

IT WAS A MOVE WITHOUT CONSCIOUS EFFORT; THEY ALL DID IT, TO HELP THEM UNDERSTAND THE NEWS THEY HAD HEARD ON THE RADIO A MOMENT BEFORE.

HERE WAS EARTH AND THERE THE COMING WAR, AND THERE HUNDREDS OF THOUSANDS OF MOTHERS OR GRANDMOTHERS OR FATHERS OR BROTHERS OR AUNTS OR UNCLES OR COUSINS. THEY STOOD ON THE PORCHES AND TRIED TO BELIEVE IN THE EXISTENCE OF EARTH, MUCH AS THEY HAD ONCE TRIED TO BELIEVE IN THE EXISTENCE OF MARS; IT WAS A PROBLEM REVERSED.

TO ALL INTENTS AND PURPOSES, EARTH NOW WAS DEAD.

AT NINE O'CLOCK EARTH SEEMED TO EXPLODE, CATCH FIRE, AND BURN.

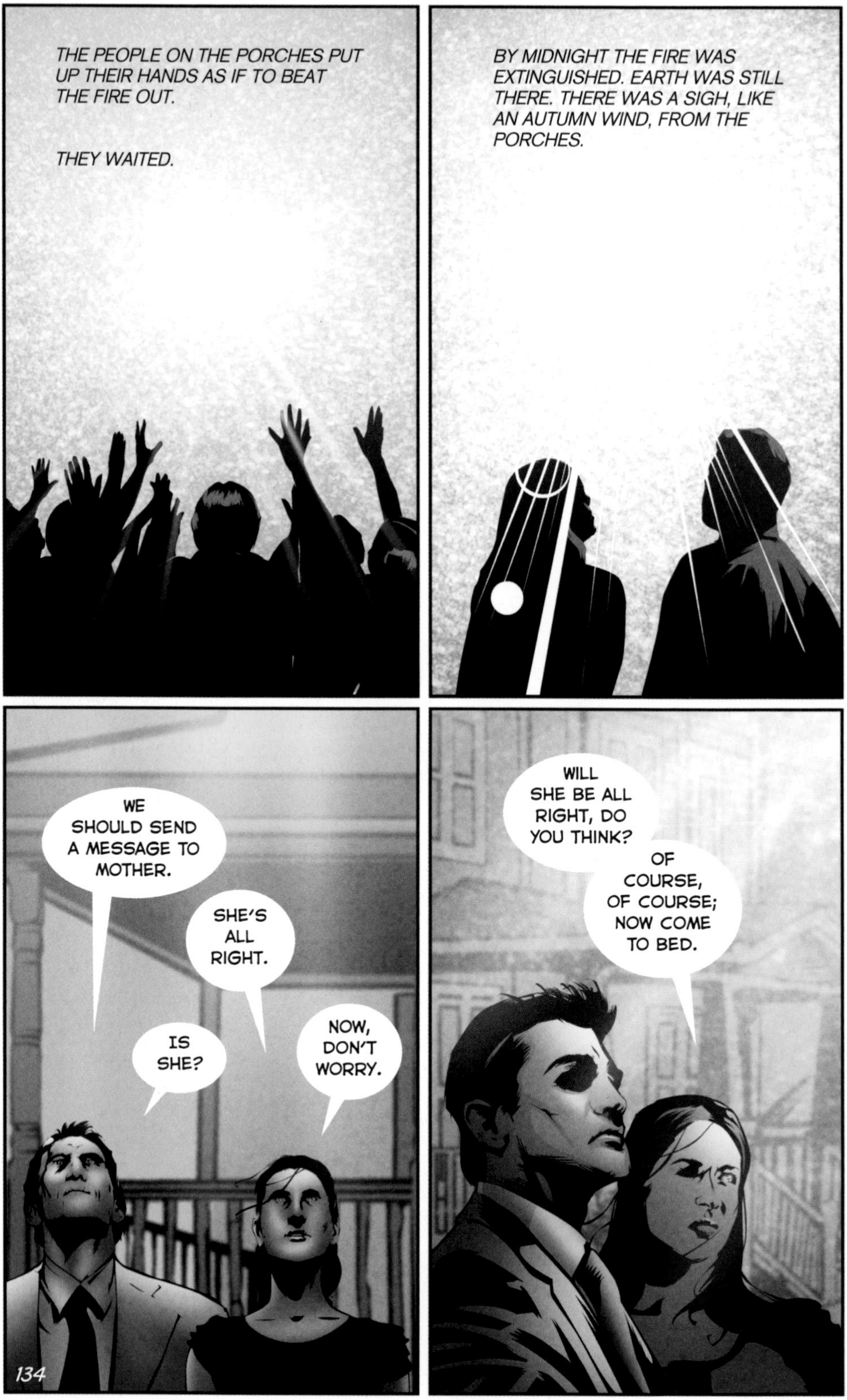
THE PEOPLE ON THE PORCHES PUT UP THEIR HANDS AS IF TO BEAT THE FIRE OUT.
THEY WAITED.
BY MIDNIGHT THE FIRE WAS EXTINGUISHED. EARTH WAS STILL THERE. THERE WAS A SIGH, LIKE AN AUTUMN WIND, FROM THE PORCHES.
WE SHOULD SEND A MESSAGE TO MOTHER.
SHE'S ALL RIGHT.
IS SHE?
NOW, DON'T WORRY.
WILL SHE BE ALL RIGHT, DO YOU THINK?
OF COURSE, OF COURSE; NOW COME TO BED.

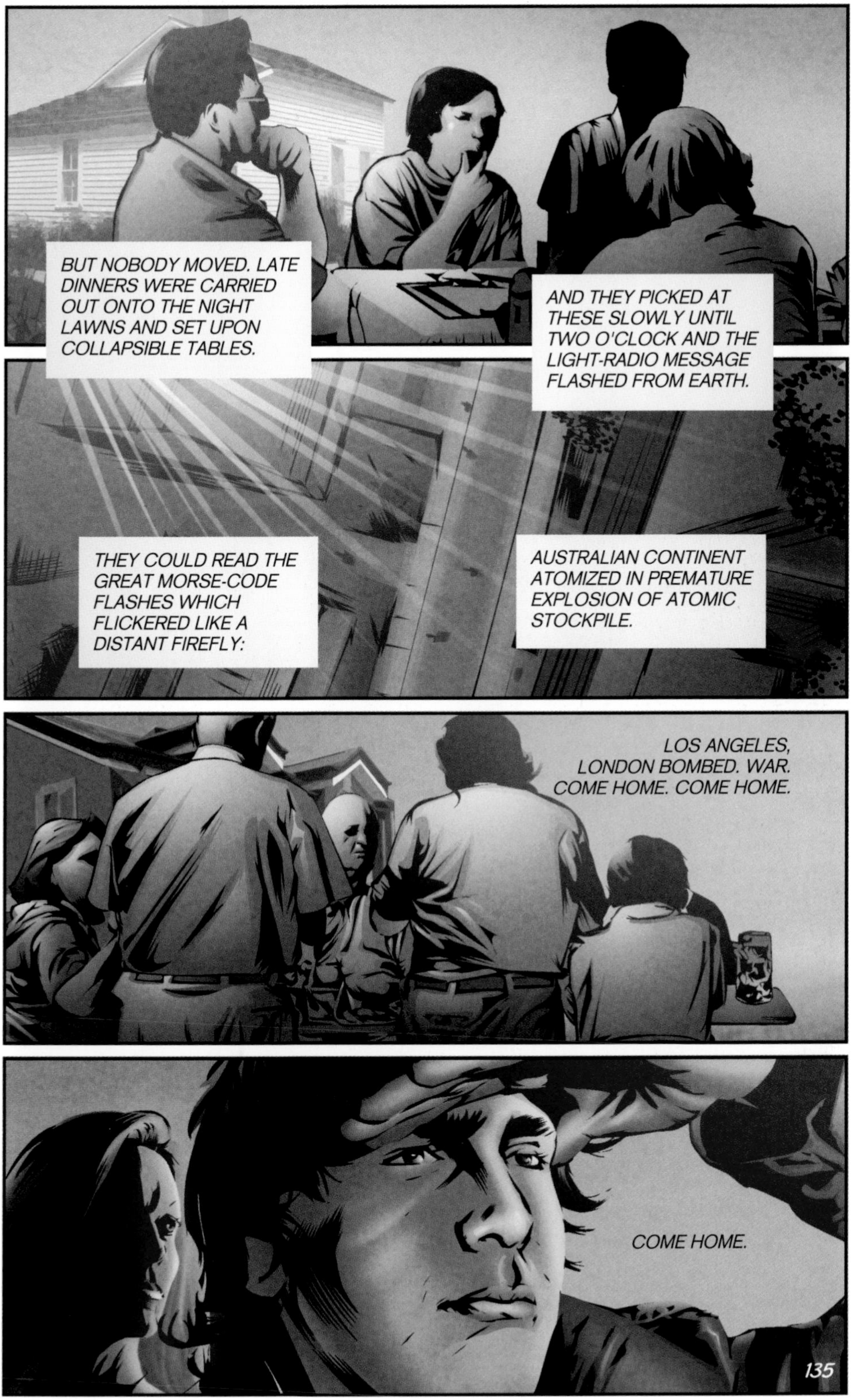
BUT NOBODY MOVED. LATE DINNERS WERE CARRIED OUT ONTO THE NIGHT LAWNS AND SET UPON COLLAPSIBLE TABLES.
AND THEY PICKED AT THESE SLOWLY UNTIL TWO O'CLOCK AND THE LIGHT-RADIO MESSAGE FLASHED FROM EARTH.
THEY COULD READ THE GREAT MORSE-CODE FLASHES WHICH FLICKERED LIKE A DISTANT FIREFLY:
AUSTRALIAN CONTINENT ATOMIZED IN PREMATURE EXPLOSION OF ATOMIC STOCKPILE.
LOS ANGELES, LONDON BOMBED. WAR. COME HOME. COME HOME.
COME HOME.

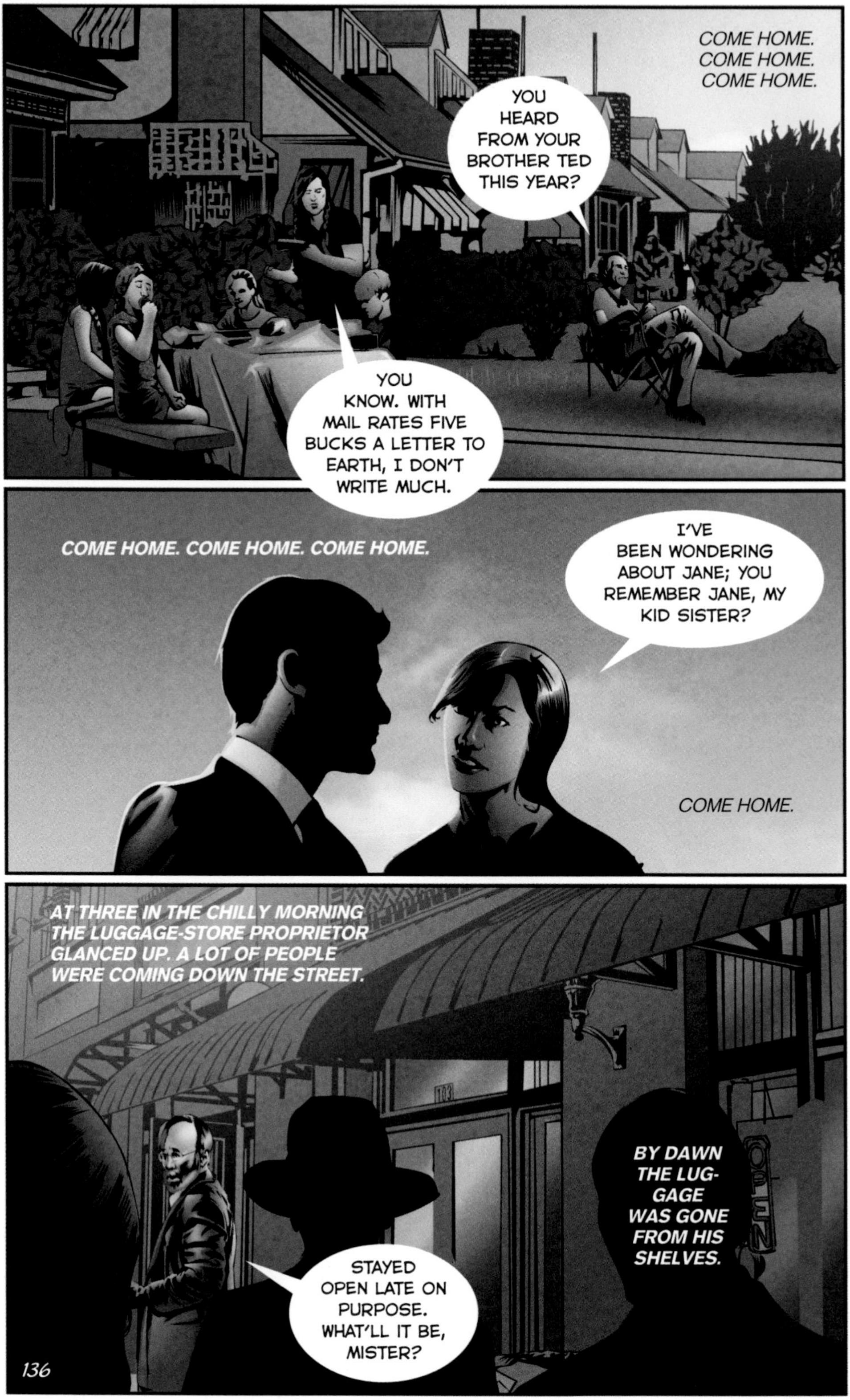
COME HOME. COME HOME. COME HOME.
YOU HEARD FROM YOUR BROTHER TED THIS YEAR?
YOU KNOW. WITH MAIL RATES FIVE BUCKS A LETTER TO EARTH, I DON'T WRITE MUCH.
COME HOME. COME HOME. COME HOME.
I'VE BEEN WONDERING ABOUT JANE; YOU REMEMBER JANE, MY KID SISTER?
COME HOME.
AT THREE IN THE CHILLY MORNING THE LUGGAGE-STORE PROPRIETOR GLANCED UP. A LOT OF PEOPLE WERE COMING DOWN THE STREET.
103
STAYED OPEN LATE ON PURPOSE. WHAT'LL IT BE, MISTER?
BY DAWN THE LUG-GAGE WAS GONE FROM HIS SHELVES.
OPEN

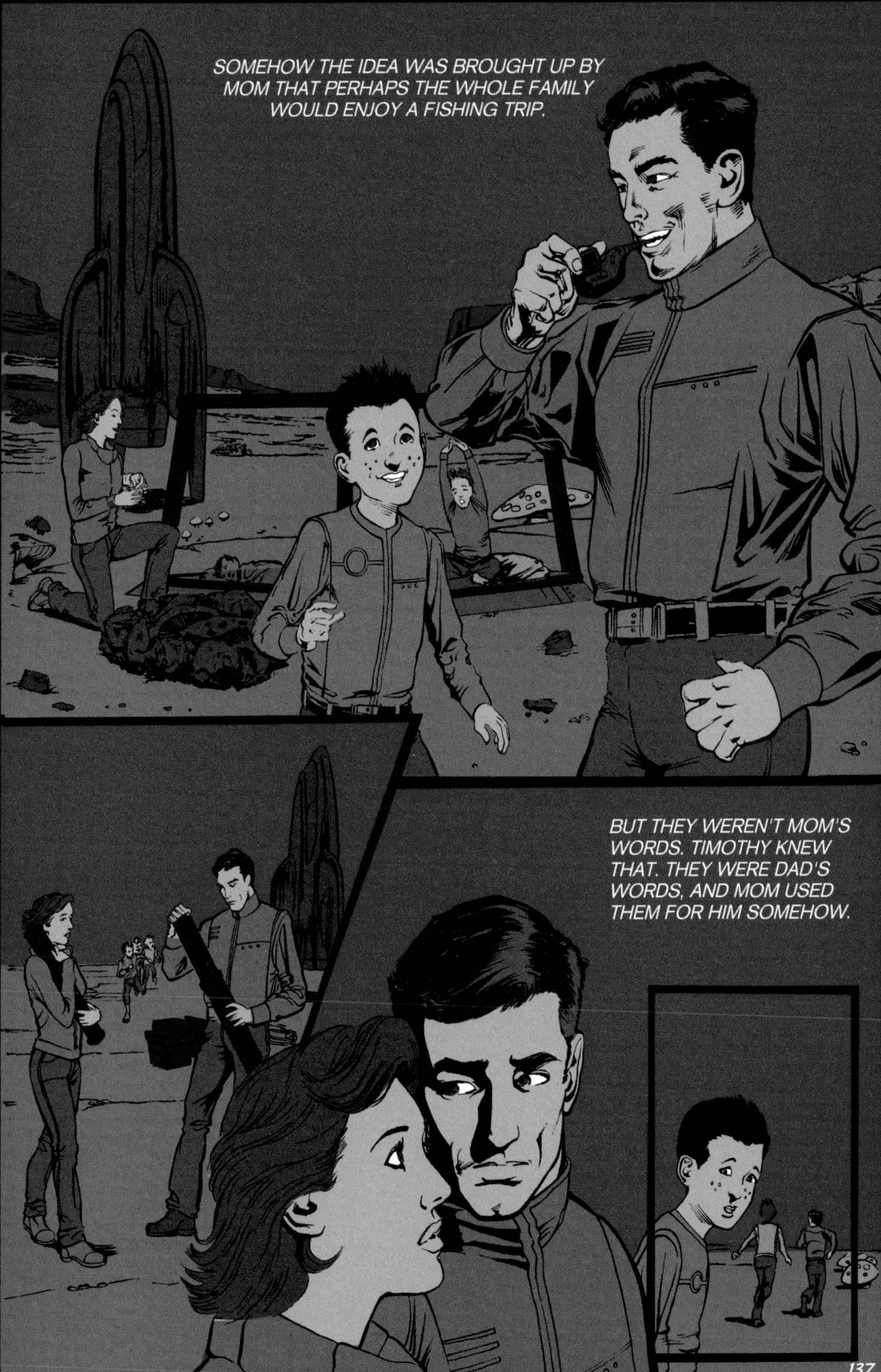
SOMEHOW THE IDEA WAS BROUGHT UP BY MOM THAT PERHAPS THE WHOLE FAMILY WOULD ENJOY A FISHING TRIP.
BUT THEY WEREN'T MOM'S WORDS. TIMOTHY KNEW THAT. THEY WERE DAD'S WORDS, AND MOM USED THEM FOR HIM SOMEHOW.

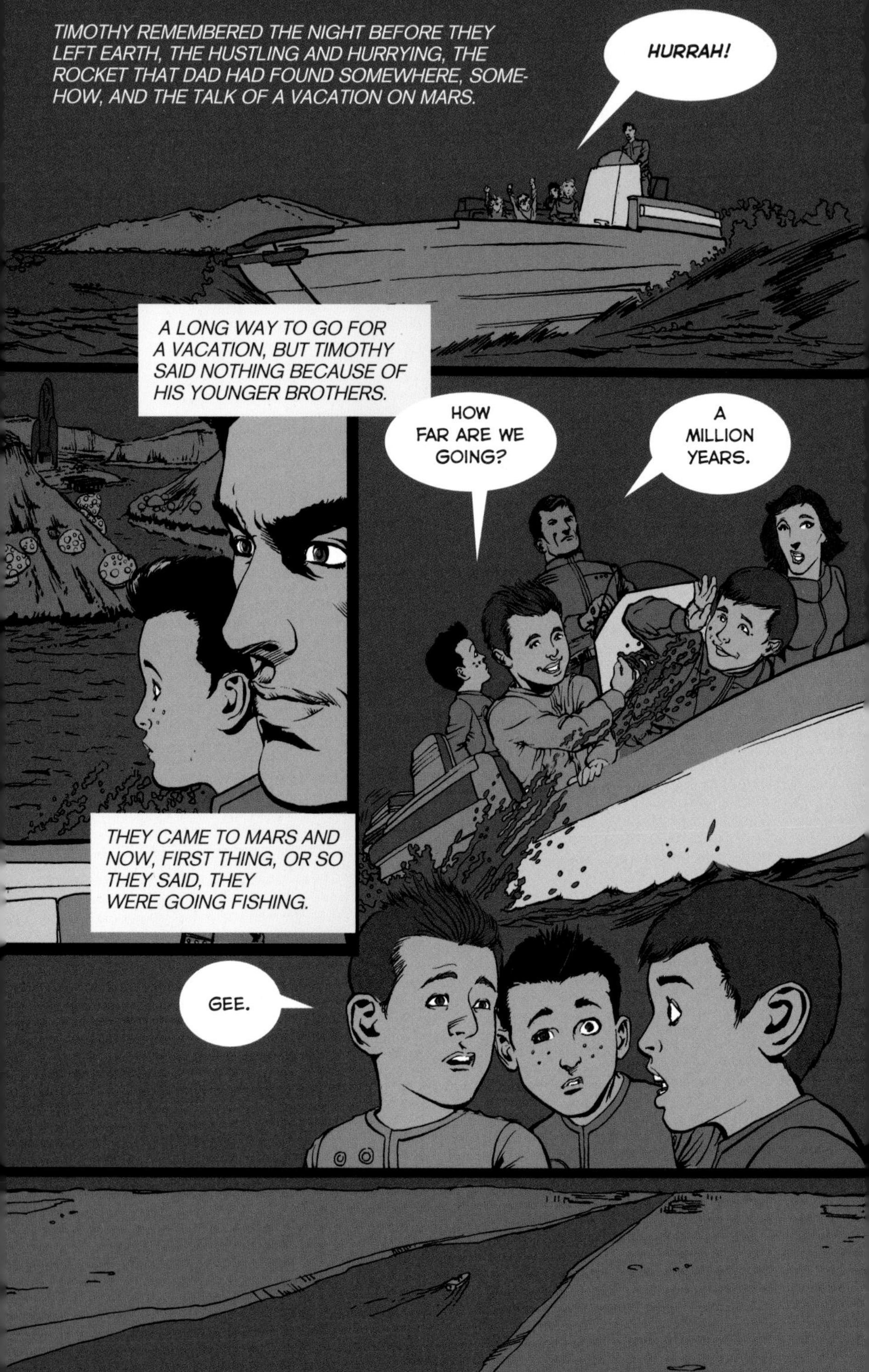

TIMOTHY REMEMBERED THE NIGHT BEFORE THEY LEFT EARTH, THE HUSTLING AND HURRYING, THE ROCKET THAT DAD HAD FOUND SOMEWHERE, SOMEHOW, AND THE TALK OF A VACATION ON MARS.
HURRAH!
A LONG WAY TO GO FOR A VACATION, BUT TIMOTHY SAID NOTHING BECAUSE OF HIS YOUNGER BROTHERS.
HOW FAR ARE WE GOING?
A MILLION YEARS.
THEY CAME TO MARS AND NOW, FIRST THING, OR SO THEY SAID, THEY WERE GOING FISHING.
GEE.

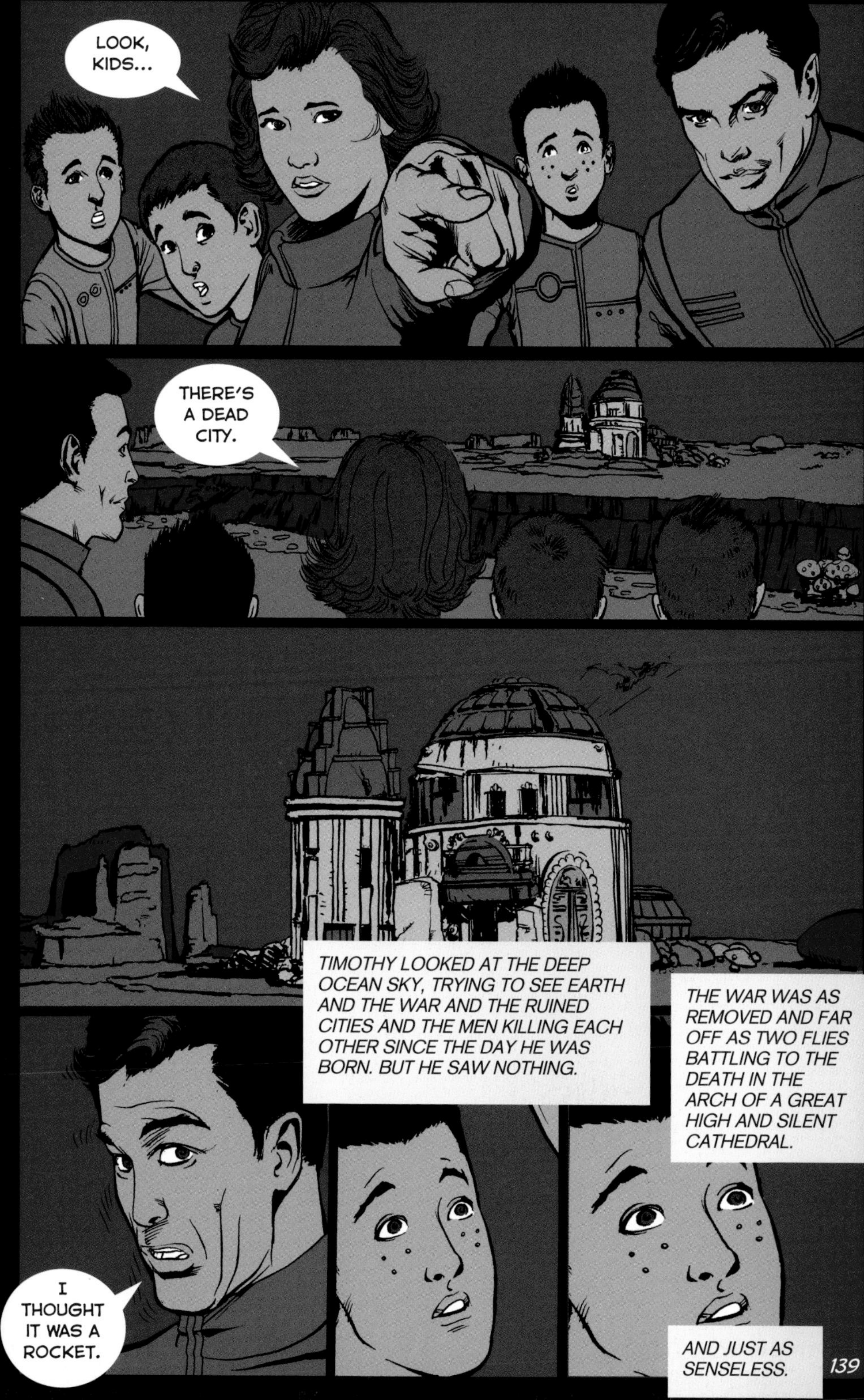
LOOK, KIDS...
THERE'S A DEAD CITY.
TIMOTHY LOOKED AT THE DEEP OCEAN SKY, TRYING TO SEE EARTH AND THE WAR AND THE RUINED CITIES AND THE MEN KILLING EACH OTHER SINCE THE DAY HE WAS BORN. BUT HE SAW NOTHING.
THE WAR WAS AS REMOVED AND FAR OFF AS TWO FLIES BATTLING TO THE DEATH IN THE ARCH OF A GREAT HIGH AND SILENT CATHEDRAL.
I THOUGHT IT WAS A ROCKET.
AND JUST AS SENSELESS.

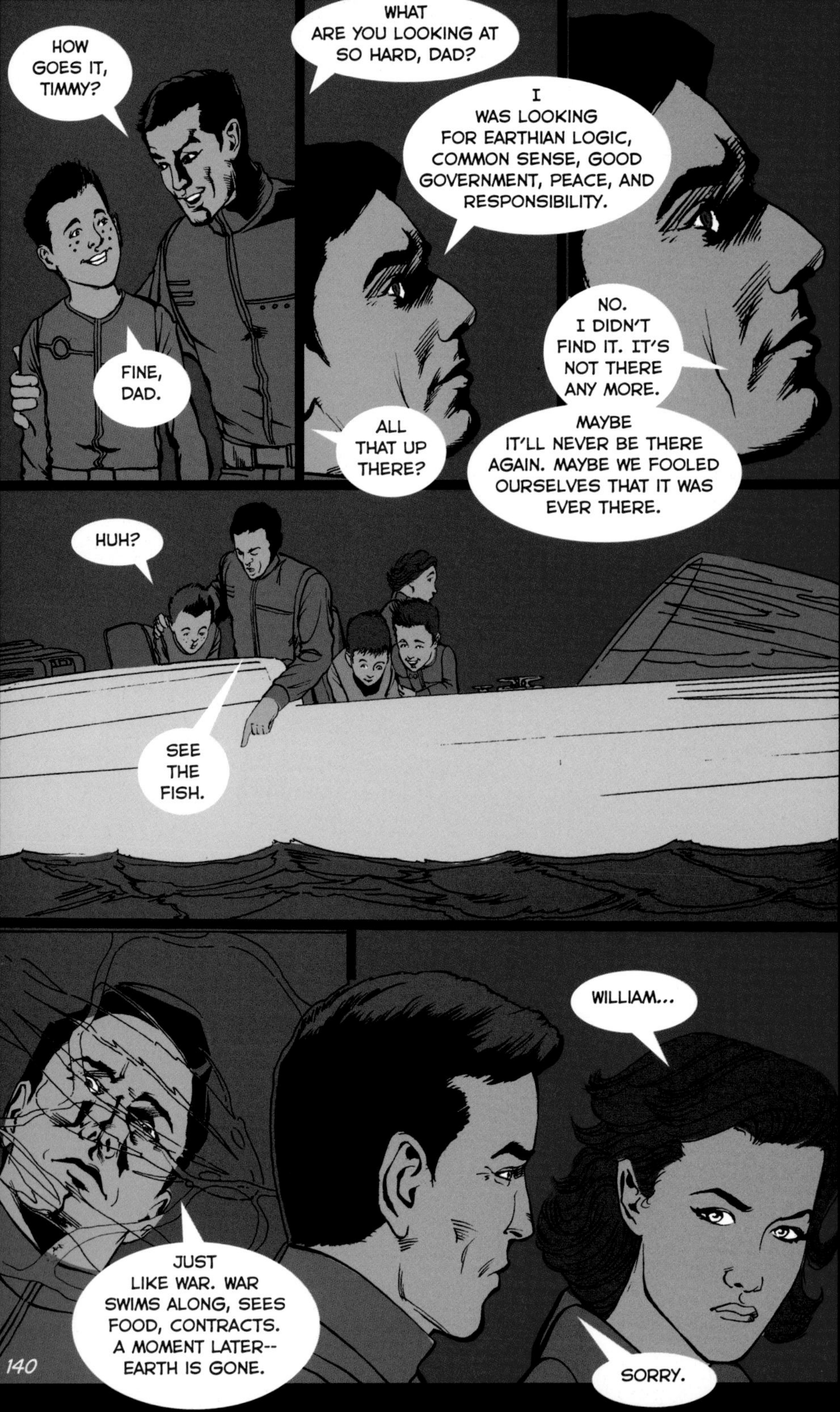

HOW GOES IT, TIMMY?
FINE, DAD.
WHAT ARE YOU LOOKING AT SO HARD, DAD?
I WAS LOOKING FOR EARTHIAN LOGIC, COMMON SENSE, GOOD GOVERNMENT, PEACE, AND RESPONSIBILITY.
ALL THAT UP THERE?
NO. I DIDN'T FIND IT. IT'S NOT THERE ANY MORE.
MAYBE IT'LL NEVER BE THERE AGAIN. MAYBE WE FOOLED OURSELVES THAT IT WAS EVER THERE.
HUH?
SEE THE FISH.
JUST LIKE WAR. WAR SWIMS ALONG, SEES FOOD, CONTRACTS. A MOMENT LATER-- EARTH IS GONE.
WILLIAM...
SORRY.

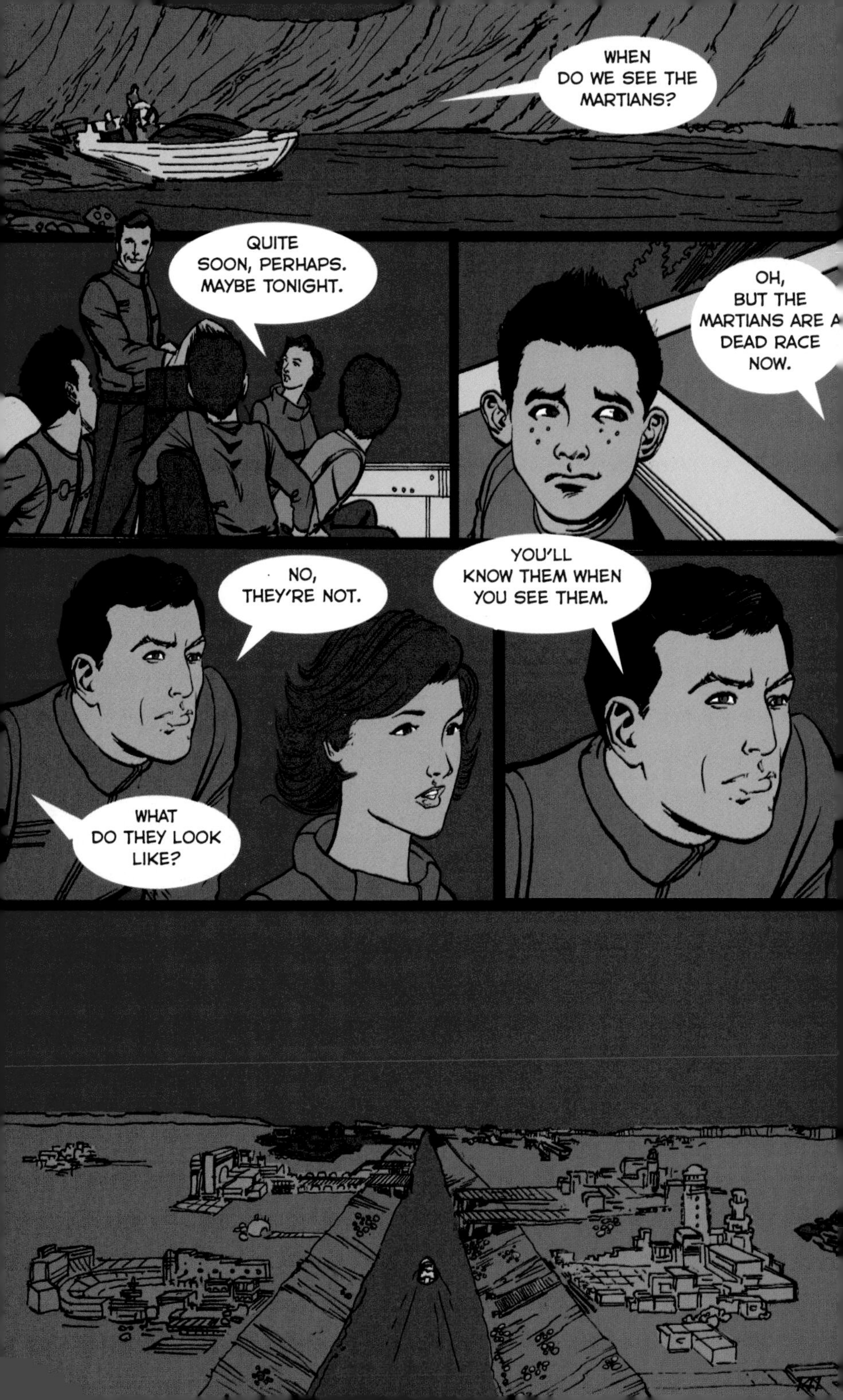
WHEN DO WE SEE THE MARTIANS?
QUITE SOON, PERHAPS. MAYBE TONIGHT.
OH, BUT THE MARTIANS ARE A DEAD RACE NOW.
NO, THEY'RE NOT.
WHAT DO THEY LOOK LIKE?
YOU'LL KNOW THEM WHEN YOU SEE THEM.

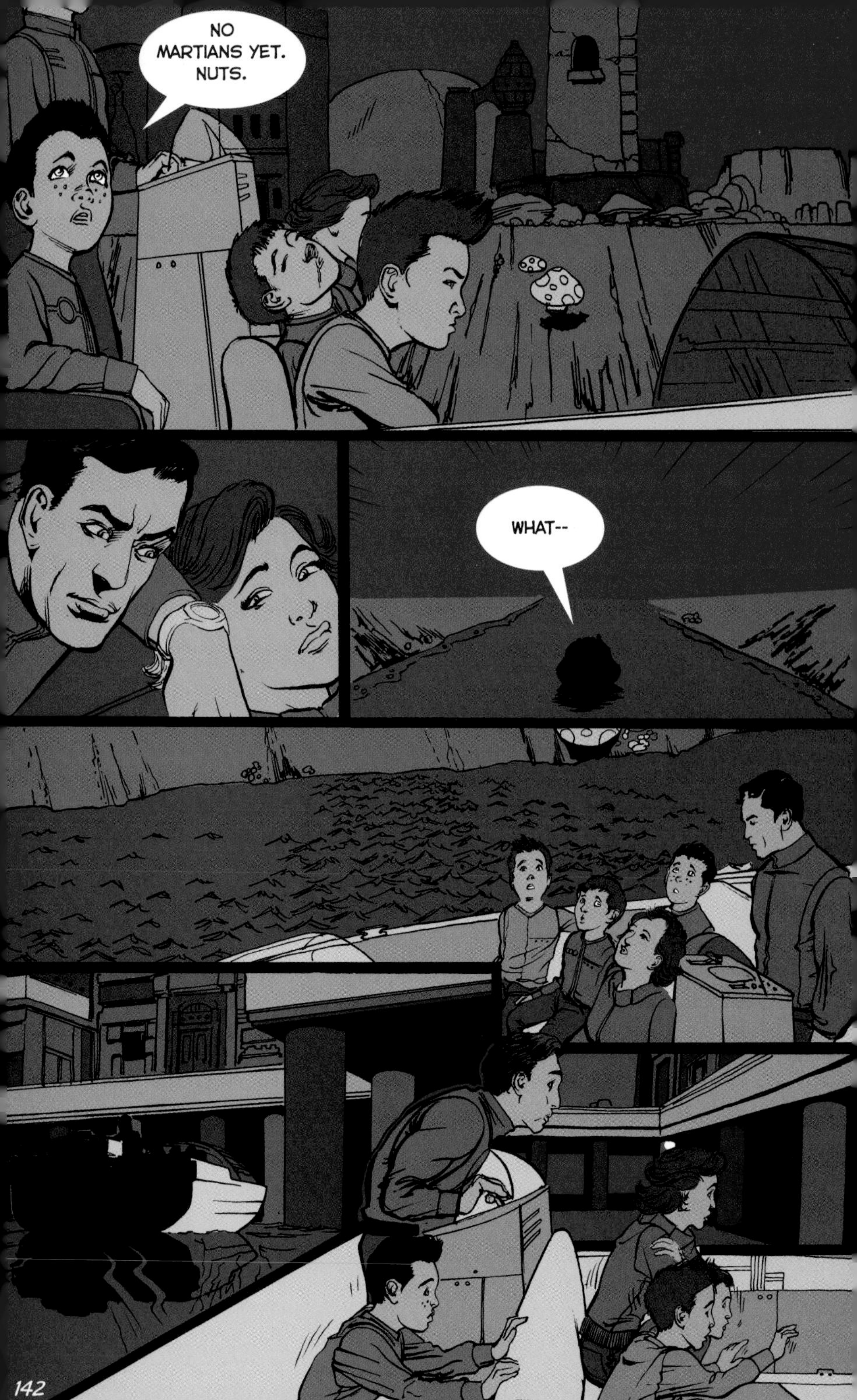
NO MARTIANS YET. NUTS.
WHAT--

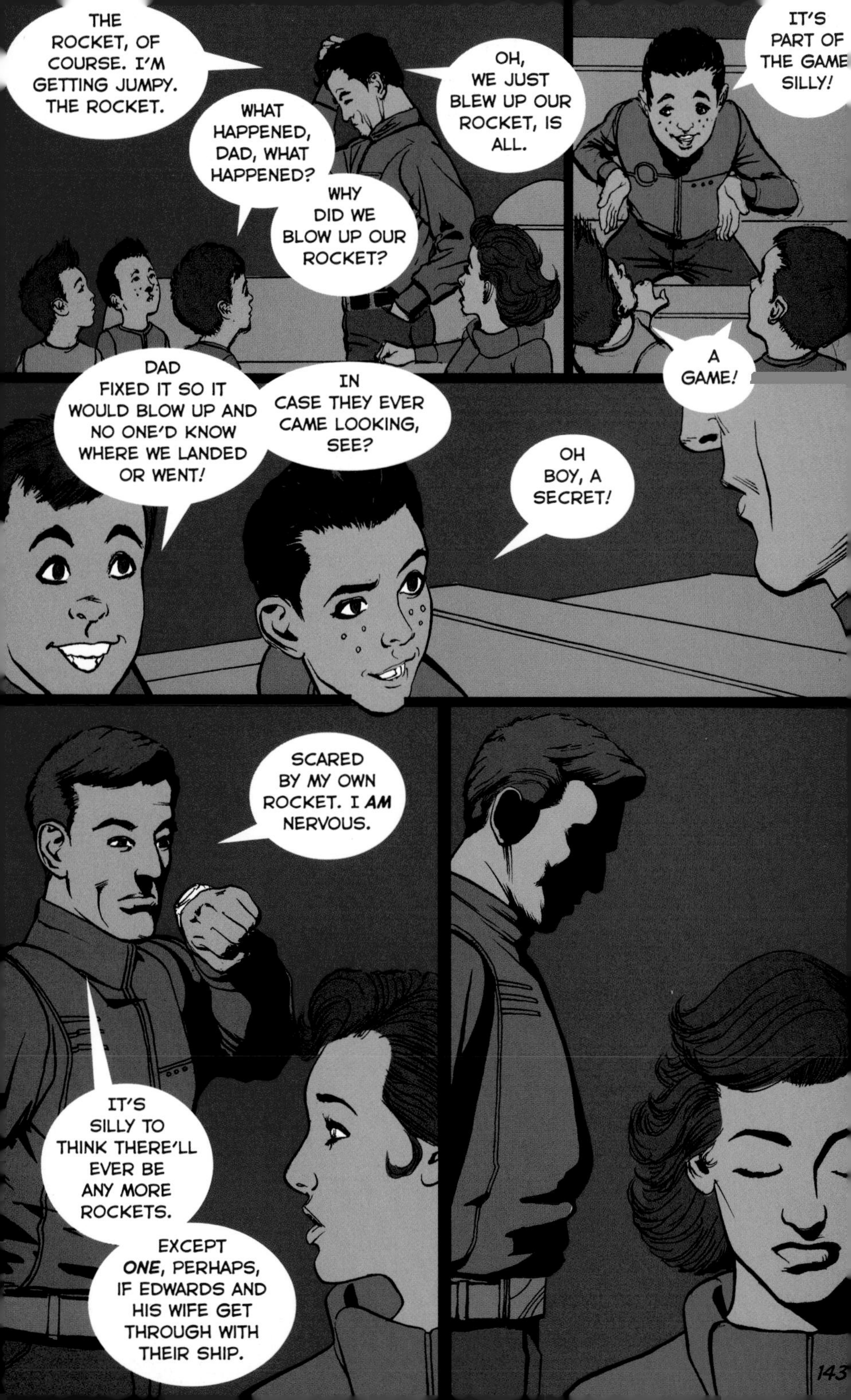
THE ROCKET, OF COURSE. I'M GETTING JUMPY. THE ROCKET.
WHAT HAPPENED, DAD, WHAT HAPPENED?
WHY DID WE BLOW UP OUR ROCKET?
OH, WE JUST BLEW UP OUR ROCKET, IS ALL.
IT'S PART OF THE GAME SILLY!
A GAME!
DAD FIXED IT SO IT WOULD BLOW UP AND NO ONE'D KNOW WHERE WE LANDED OR WENT!
IN CASE THEY EVER CAME LOOKING, SEE?
OH BOY, A SECRET!
SCARED BY MY OWN ROCKET. I *AM* NERVOUS.
IT'S SILLY TO THINK THERE'LL EVER BE ANY MORE ROCKETS.
EXCEPT *ONE*, PERHAPS, IF EDWARDS AND HIS WIFE GET THROUGH WITH THEIR SHIP.

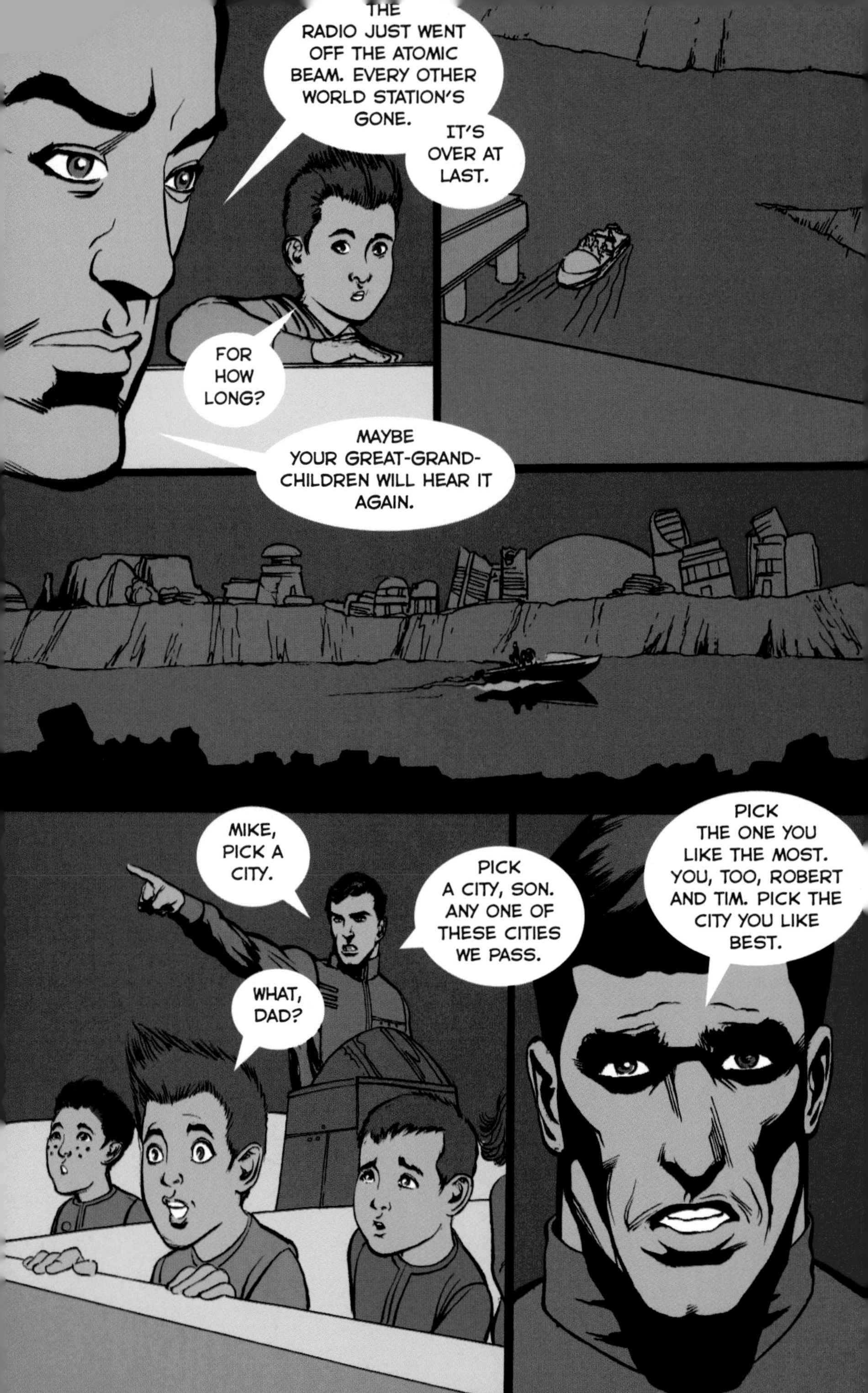
THE RADIO JUST WENT OFF THE ATOMIC BEAM. EVERY OTHER WORLD STATION'S GONE.
IT'S OVER AT LAST.
FOR HOW LONG?
MAYBE YOUR GREAT-GRAND-CHILDREN WILL HEAR IT AGAIN.
MIKE, PICK A CITY.
WHAT, DAD?
PICK A CITY, SON. ANY ONE OF THESE CITIES WE PASS.
PICK THE ONE YOU LIKE THE MOST. YOU, TOO, ROBERT AND TIM. PICK THE CITY YOU LIKE BEST.

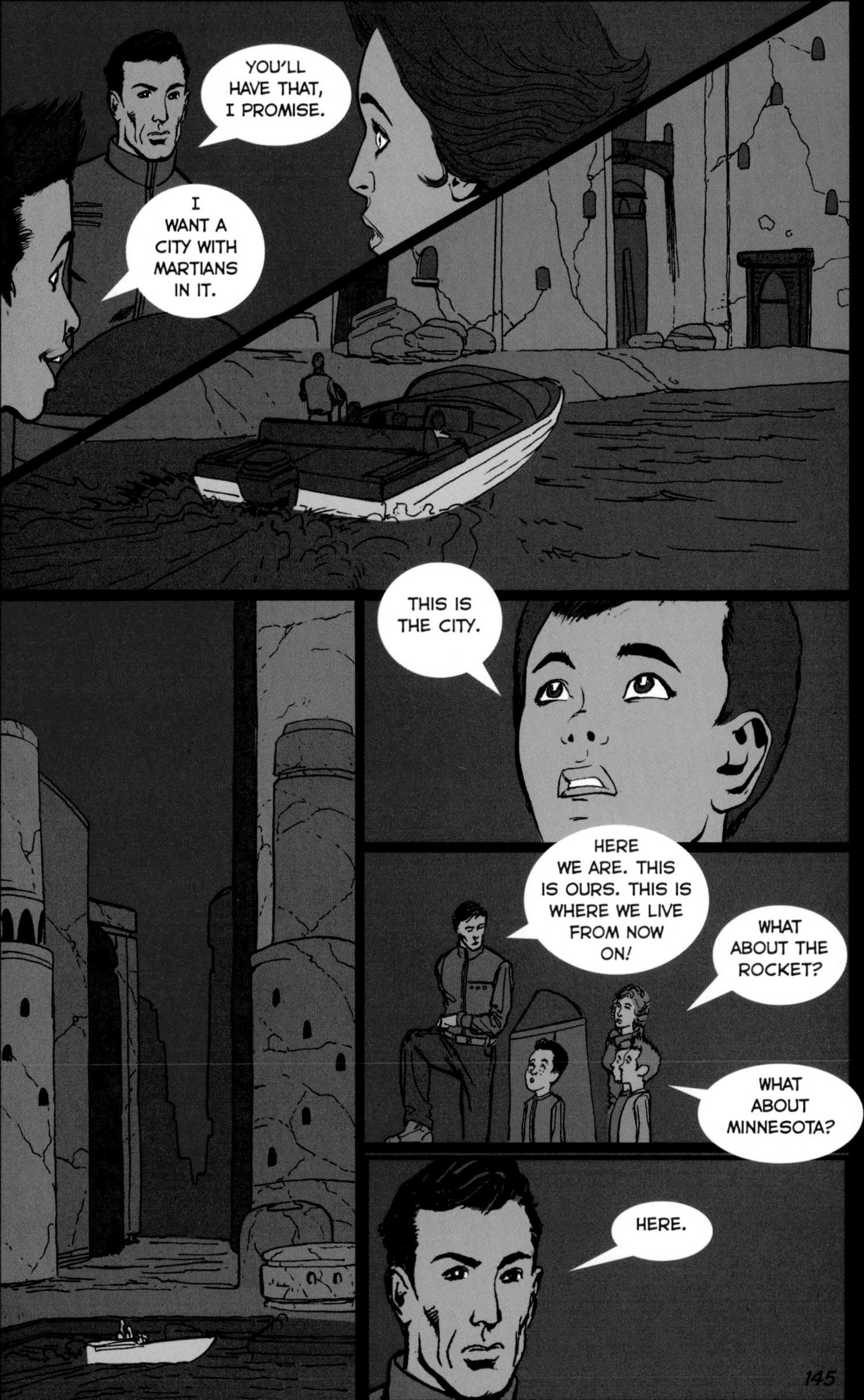
YOU'LL HAVE THAT, I PROMISE.
I WANT A CITY WITH MARTIANS IN IT.
THIS IS THE CITY.
HERE WE ARE. THIS IS OURS. THIS IS WHERE WE LIVE FROM NOW ON!
WHAT ABOUT THE ROCKET?
WHAT ABOUT MINNESOTA?
HERE.

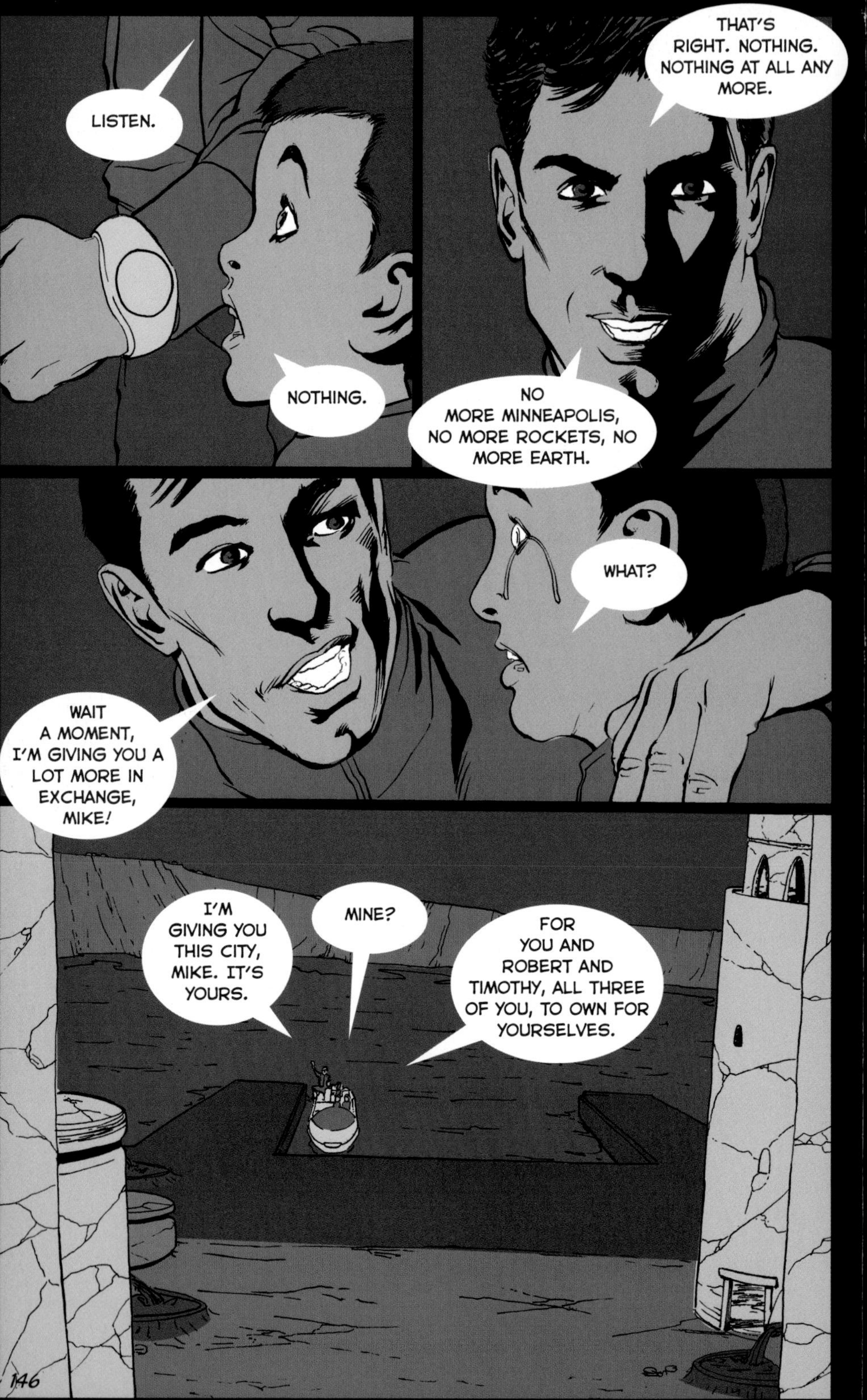
LISTEN.
NOTHING.
THAT'S RIGHT. NOTHING. NOTHING AT ALL ANY MORE.
NO MORE MINNEAPOLIS, NO MORE ROCKETS, NO MORE EARTH.
WHAT?
WAIT A MOMENT, I'M GIVING YOU A LOT MORE IN EXCHANGE, MIKE!
I'M GIVING YOU THIS CITY, MIKE. IT'S YOURS.
MINE?
FOR YOU AND ROBERT AND TIMOTHY, ALL THREE OF YOU, TO OWN FOR YOURSELVES.

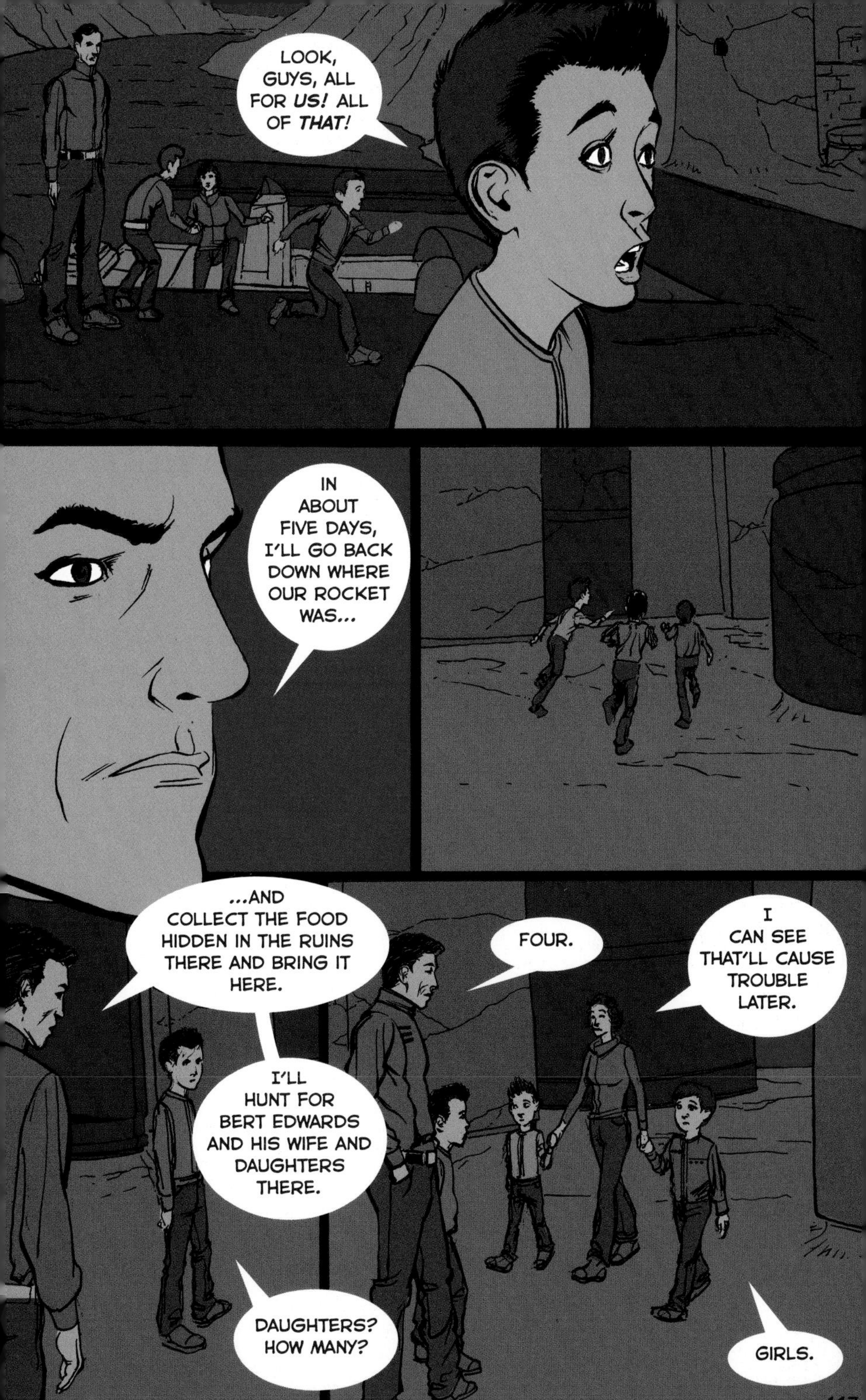
LOOK, GUYS, ALL FOR US! ALL OF THAT!
IN ABOUT FIVE DAYS, I'LL GO BACK DOWN WHERE OUR ROCKET WAS...
...AND COLLECT THE FOOD HIDDEN IN THE RUINS THERE AND BRING IT HERE.
I'LL HUNT FOR BERT EDWARDS AND HIS WIFE AND DAUGHTERS THERE.
DAUGHTERS? HOW MANY?
FOUR.
I CAN SEE THAT'LL CAUSE TROUBLE LATER.
GIRLS.

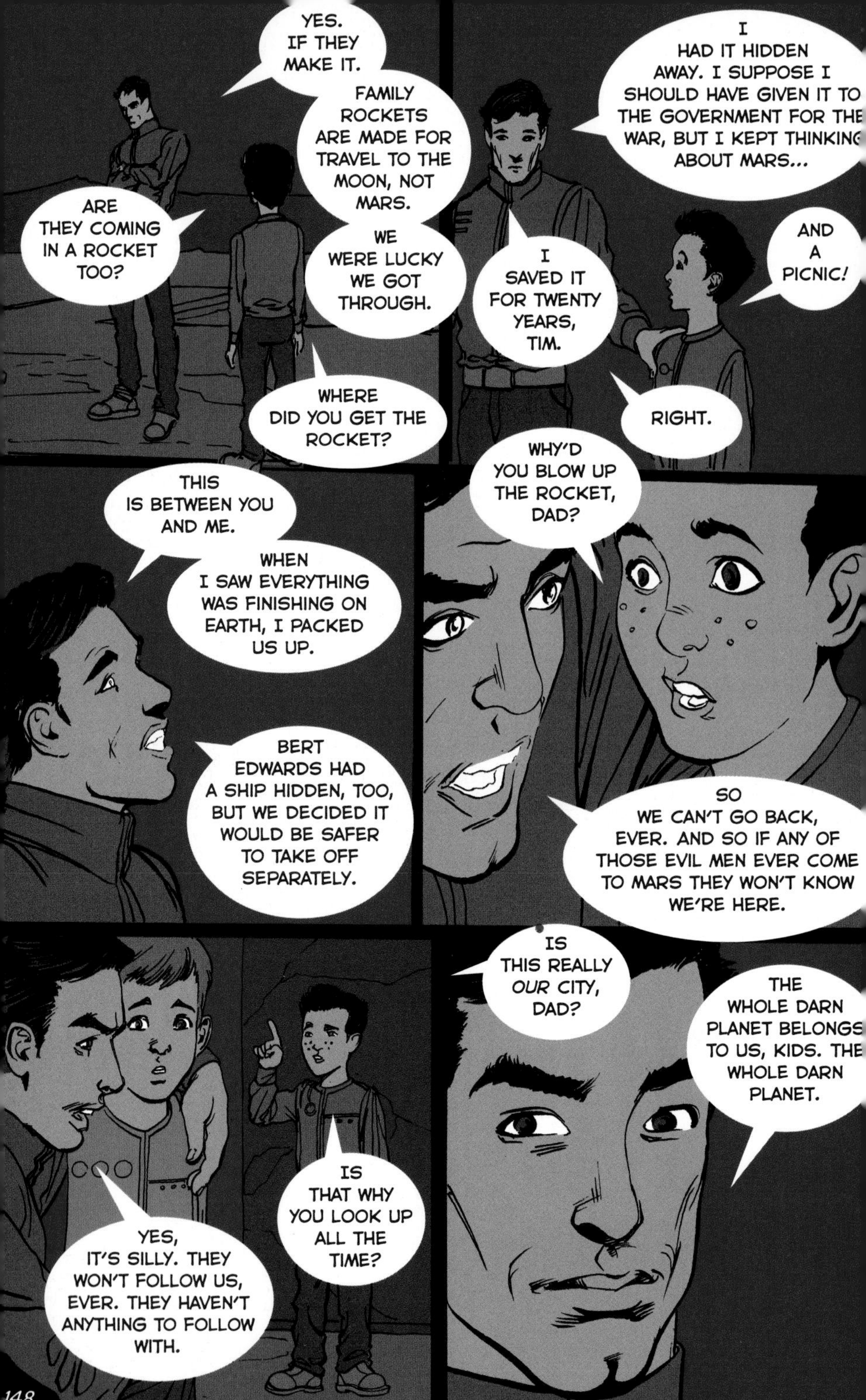
ARE THEY COMING IN A ROCKET TOO?
YES. IF THEY MAKE IT.
FAMILY ROCKETS ARE MADE FOR TRAVEL TO THE MOON, NOT MARS.
WE WERE LUCKY WE GOT THROUGH.
WHERE DID YOU GET THE ROCKET?
I HAD IT HIDDEN AWAY. I SUPPOSE I SHOULD HAVE GIVEN IT TO THE GOVERNMENT FOR THE WAR, BUT I KEPT THINKING ABOUT MARS...
I SAVED IT FOR TWENTY YEARS, TIM.
AND A PICNIC!
RIGHT.
THIS IS BETWEEN YOU AND ME.
WHEN I SAW EVERYTHING WAS FINISHING ON EARTH, I PACKED US UP.
BERT EDWARDS HAD A SHIP HIDDEN, TOO, BUT WE DECIDED IT WOULD BE SAFER TO TAKE OFF SEPARATELY.
WHY'D YOU BLOW UP THE ROCKET, DAD?
SO WE CAN'T GO BACK, EVER. AND SO IF ANY OF THOSE EVIL MEN EVER COME TO MARS THEY WON'T KNOW WE'RE HERE.
IS THAT WHY YOU LOOK UP ALL THE TIME?
YES, IT'S SILLY. THEY WON'T FOLLOW US, EVER. THEY HAVEN'T ANYTHING TO FOLLOW WITH.
IS THIS REALLY *OUR* CITY, DAD?
THE WHOLE DARN PLANET BELONGS TO US, KIDS. THE WHOLE DARN PLANET.

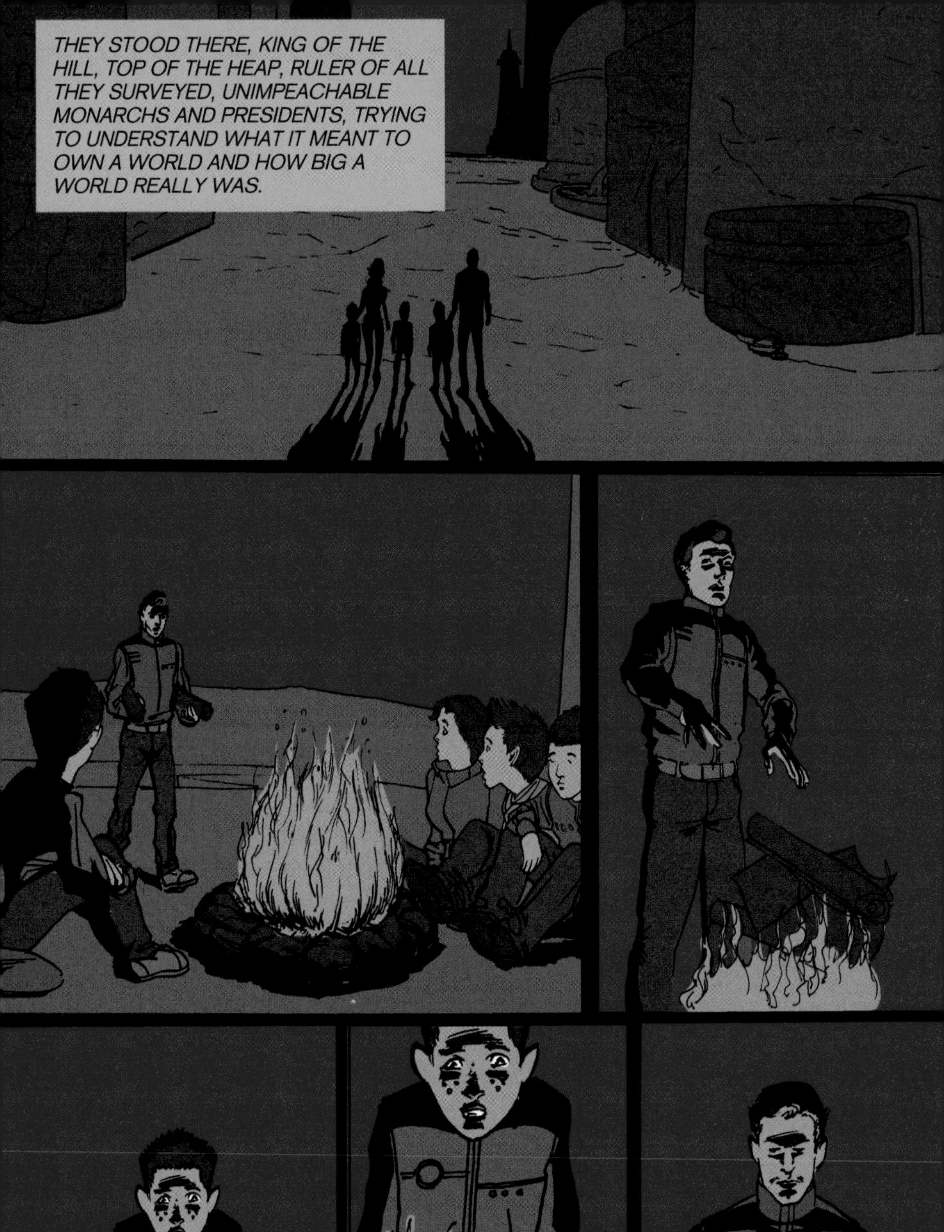
THEY STOOD THERE, KING OF THE HILL, TOP OF THE HEAP, RULER OF ALL THEY SURVEYED, UNIMPEACHABLE MONARCHS AND PRESIDENTS, TRYING TO UNDERSTAND WHAT IT MEANT TO OWN A WORLD AND HOW BIG A WORLD REALLY WAS.
GOVERNMENT BONDS
BUSINESS GRAPH, 1999:
IT'S TIME I TOLD YOU A FEW THINGS.

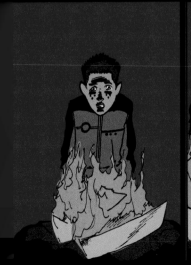

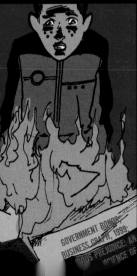

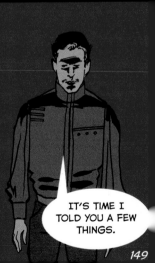

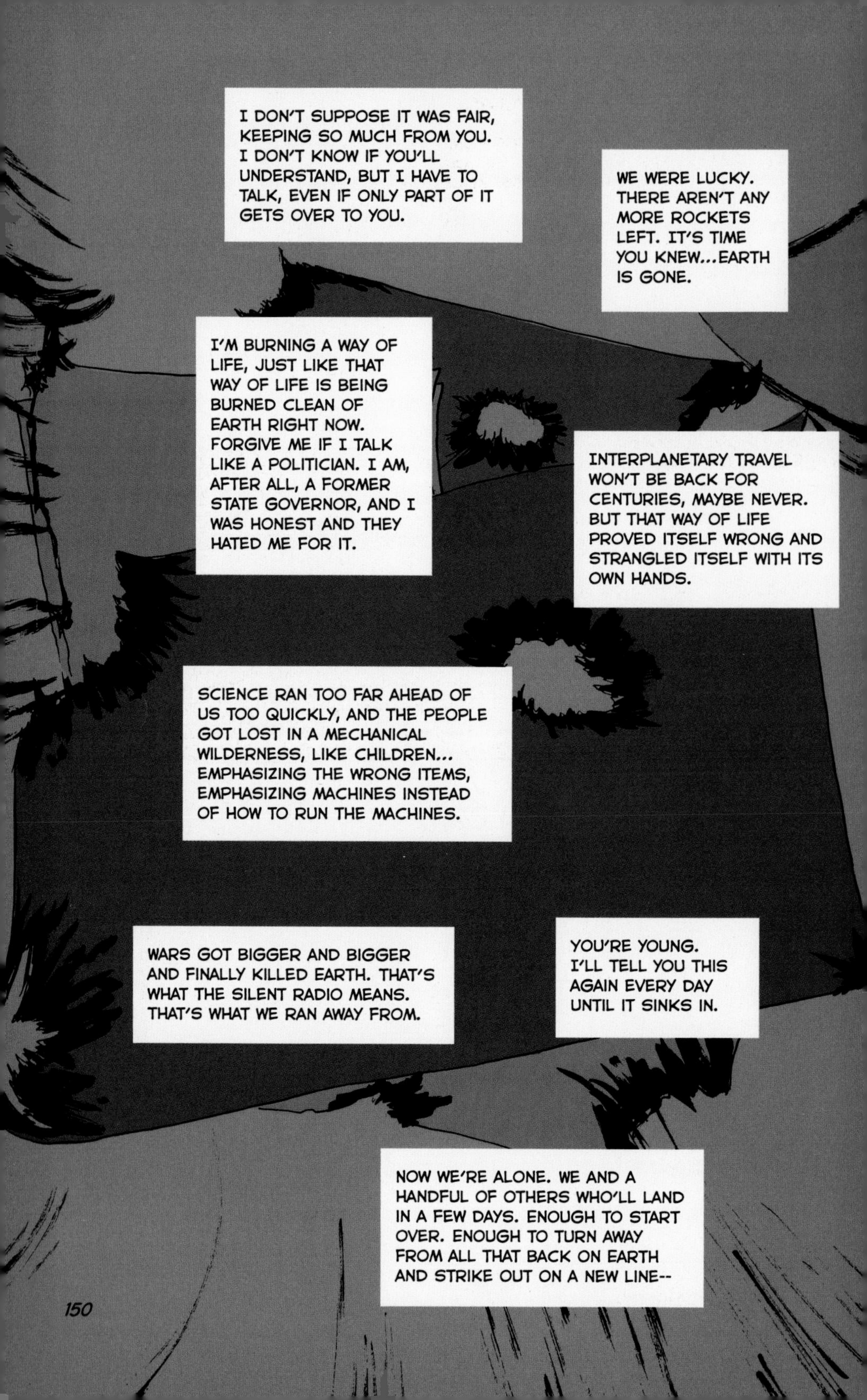
I DON'T SUPPOSE IT WAS FAIR, KEEPING SO MUCH FROM YOU. I DON'T KNOW IF YOU'LL UNDERSTAND, BUT I HAVE TO TALK, EVEN IF ONLY PART OF IT GETS OVER TO YOU.
WE WERE LUCKY. THERE AREN'T ANY MORE ROCKETS LEFT. IT'S TIME YOU KNEW...EARTH IS GONE.
I'M BURNING A WAY OF LIFE, JUST LIKE THAT WAY OF LIFE IS BEING BURNED CLEAN OF EARTH RIGHT NOW. FORGIVE ME IF I TALK LIKE A POLITICIAN. I AM, AFTER ALL, A FORMER STATE GOVERNOR, AND I WAS HONEST AND THEY HATED ME FOR IT.
INTERPLANETARY TRAVEL WON'T BE BACK FOR CENTURIES, MAYBE NEVER. BUT THAT WAY OF LIFE PROVED ITSELF WRONG AND STRANGLED ITSELF WITH ITS OWN HANDS.
SCIENCE RAN TOO FAR AHEAD OF US TOO QUICKLY, AND THE PEOPLE GOT LOST IN A MECHANICAL WILDERNESS, LIKE CHILDREN... EMPHASIZING THE WRONG ITEMS, EMPHASIZING MACHINES INSTEAD OF HOW TO RUN THE MACHINES.
WARS GOT BIGGER AND BIGGER AND FINALLY KILLED EARTH. THAT'S WHAT THE SILENT RADIO MEANS. THAT'S WHAT WE RAN AWAY FROM.
YOU'RE YOUNG. I'LL TELL YOU THIS AGAIN EVERY DAY UNTIL IT SINKS IN.
NOW WE'RE ALONE. WE AND A HANDFUL OF OTHERS WHO'LL LAND IN A FEW DAYS. ENOUGH TO START OVER. ENOUGH TO TURN AWAY FROM ALL THAT BACK ON EARTH AND STRIKE OUT ON A NEW LINE--

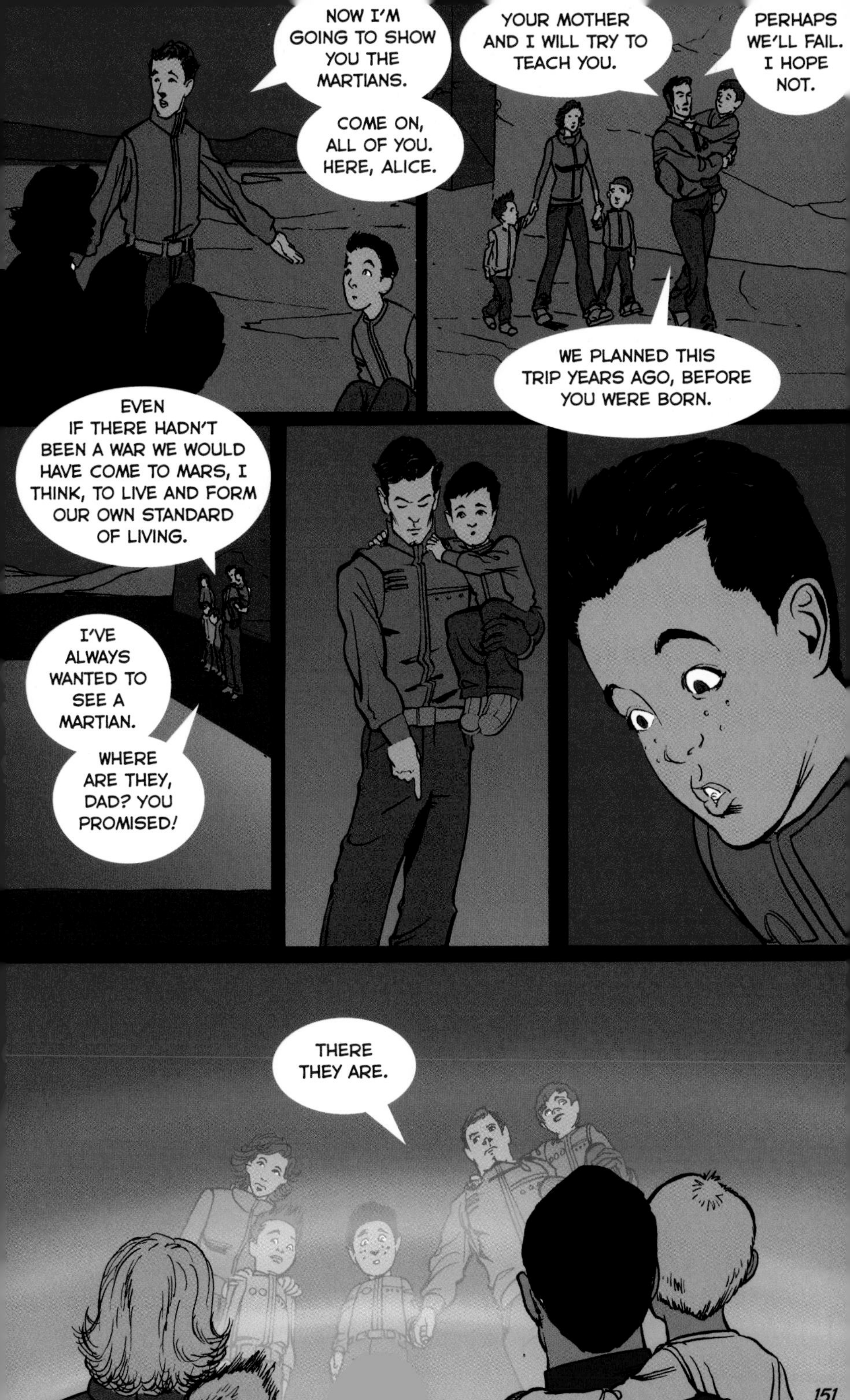
NOW I'M GOING TO SHOW YOU THE MARTIANS.
COME ON, ALL OF YOU. HERE, ALICE.
YOUR MOTHER AND I WILL TRY TO TEACH YOU.
PERHAPS WE'LL FAIL. I HOPE NOT.
WE PLANNED THIS TRIP YEARS AGO, BEFORE YOU WERE BORN.
EVEN IF THERE HADN'T BEEN A WAR WE WOULD HAVE COME TO MARS, I THINK, TO LIVE AND FORM OUR OWN STANDARD OF LIVING.
I'VE ALWAYS WANTED TO SEE A MARTIAN.
WHERE ARE THEY, DAD? YOU PROMISED!
THERE THEY ARE.

A NOTE ABOUT THE AUTHOR

RAY BRADBURY IS A WRITER OF MYSTERIES, SCIENCE FICTION, HORROR, FANTASY, AND MAINSTREAM FICTION, AND IS WIDELY CONSIDERED ONE OF THE GREATEST AND MOST POPULAR AMERICAN WRITERS OF THE TWENTIETH CENTURY. HE HAS WRITTEN NOVELS, SHORT STORIES, PLAYS, POETRY, SCREENPLAYS, AND TELEPLAYS. MANY OF HIS WORKS HAVE BEEN ADAPTED FOR TELEVISION AND FILM.

HIS MOST POPULAR BOOKS ARE THE NOVELS *FAHRENHEIT 451* AND *SOMETHING WICKED THIS WAY COMES*, AND THE STORY COLLECTION *THE MARTIAN CHRONICLES*. SINCE HIS WORK WAS FIRST PUBLISHED IN THE 1940s, BRADBURY HAS RECEIVED MANY AWARDS. AMONG THESE ARE A SPECIAL CITATION FROM THE PULITZER PRIZE BOARD IN 2007 FOR HIS "DISTINGUISHED, PROLIFIC, AND DEEPLY INFLUENTIAL CAREER AS AN UNMATCHED AUTHOR OF SCIENCE FICTION AND FANTASY." HE HAS ALSO RECEIVED THE NATIONAL MEDAL OF ARTS, A WORLD FANTASY AWARD, THE SCIENCE FICTION AND FANTASY WRITERS OF AMERICA GRAND MASTER AWARD, AND AN EMMY AWARD, AMONG OTHERS.

MORE INFORMATION ABOUT THE AUTHOR, HIS CAREER, AND HIS CURRENT PROJECTS CAN BE FOUND AT WWW.RAYBRADBURY.COM.

A NOTE ABOUT THE ARTIST

DENNIS CALERO ATTENDED THE NEW WORLD SCHOOL OF THE ARTS IN MIAMI, THEN STUDIED ARCHITECTURE AT THE PRATT INSTITUTE IN BROOKLYN, BEFORE SWITCHING TO ITS ILLUSTRATION PROGRAM AND STUDYING COMIC BOOK ILLUSTRATION AND CONTINUITY. ALONG WITH KRISTIN SORRA IN 1995, CALERO CREATED ATOMIC PAINTBRUSH TO PROVIDE COMPUTER COLORING FOR MARVEL AND DC COMICS, AND ACCLAIM ENTERTAINMENT. THIS CREATED AN OPPORTUNITY FOR COMMISSIONED POSTERS FOR MARVEL COMICS AND VARIOUS PROJECTS FOR AOL TIME WARNER AND SONY.

AFTER A NUMBER OF YEARS PAINTING BOOK COVERS, HE RETURNED TO COMICS ON MARVEL'S HARVEY AWARD-NOMINATED *X-FACTOR* (2006). HE ILLUSTRATED A RUN OF *LEGION OF SUPERHEROES* FOR DC COMICS, AND HIS GRAPHIC ADAPTATION OF *FRANKENSTEIN* FOR STONE ARCH BOOKS WAS A JUNIOR LIBRARY GUILD SELECTION. HE RETURNED TO MARVEL FOR THE ACCLAIMED X-MEN NOIR SERIES, DOING INTERIOR ART AND A WELL-RECEIVED SERIES OF COVERS.